Overview

The Bureau of Justice Assistance (BJA) is a leader in developing and implementing evidence-based criminal justice policy and practice. BJA's mission is to provide leadership in services, grant administration, and criminal justice policy development to support local, state, and tribal justice strategies in achieving safer communities. This is accomplished in many criminal justice topic areas, including adjudication, corrections, counter-terrorism, crime prevention, justice information sharing, law enforcement, justice and mental health, substance abuse, and tribal justice.

Under each topic area, BJA funds numerous programs and initiatives at the tribal, local, and state level. In collaboration with the National Institute of Justice (NIJ) and other federal and research partners, many of these programs have been evaluated.

The Evaluation and Research Literature report has several goals:

- To assess the state of knowledge on BJA-funded programs as determined by data collection, research, and evaluation;
- To be a resource on evaluation and research literature related to BJA programs;
- To identify U.S. Department of Justice-funded innovative programs and sound practices;
- To highlight programs and practices that have a solid foundation of evidence; and
- To identify programs that may benefit from further research and evaluation.

In FY 2014, this report's compilers conducted a systemic literature review to find appropriate process evaluations. The FY 2016 version builds upon the earlier version. Program evaluation is a systematic, objective process for determining the success of a policy or program. Evaluations assess whether and to what extent the program is achieving its goals and objectives. Strong data collection practices are critical for understanding the scope and nature of an issue. Consequently, where appropriate, the report compilers identified certain descriptive reports that are not evaluative in nature when there was limited evaluation literature on a program.

The report's compilers used the following methods to evaluate the 34 BJA programs detailed here.

- Using keyword searches, they idenfied and summarized program and process evaluations from the National Criminal Justice Reference Services, federal websites (e.g., NIJ, BJS), Google Scholar, state websites, national associations, research institutions, and training and technical assistance provider websites.
- They searched the Crimesolutions.gov website by topic area to include programs and practices that have already been evaluated.
- When no evaluations on a certain program/initiative were identified, they widened the search criteria to include scholarly research (i.e., research published in scholarly journals).
- They identified and referenced recent federal audits.

This report includes a summary table highlighting the number of evaluations, Crimesolutions.gov ratings of programs and practices, and other related research. The summary table quantifies the number of reports, reviews, or articles in each topic area. It also includes a key that defines the terms used in the summary table and program sections.

Although this report is as comprehensive as possible, it is not intended to be a complete accounting of all research and evaluations on a certain program or initiative. BJA will continue to update this report reguarly as new information is published.

Table of Contents

Evaluation Initiative Tracking Key

Crime Solutions: The data in these columns indicate the number of ratings of the reviewed program on the CrimeSolutions.gov website. Each program with a rating has been provided by type for review, where available.

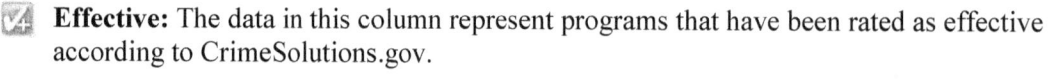 **Effective:** The data in this column represent programs that have been rated as effective according to CrimeSolutions.gov.

Promising: The data in this column represent programs that have been rated as promising according to CrimeSolutions.gov.

No Effects: The data in this column represent programs that have been rated as having no effect according to CrimeSolutions.gov.

Insufficient Evidence: The data in this column represent the total number of evaluations of the program that are found on the insufficient evidence list on the CrimeSolutions.gov website. These evaluations were found to not meet the minimum rating criteria and as a result were not used to determine a rating for the program.

Highlighted Reports: These articles represent evaluations of BJA's national initiative, and/or the study is nationwide in scope.

NIJ Evaluations: The data in this column represent the total number of NIJ-sponsored evaluations of the reviewed program.

Other Office of Justice Program (OJP) Evaluations: The data in this column represent all other OJP-sponsored evaluations. These evaluations can be sponsored by BJA, Bureau for Justice Statistics (BJS), Office for Victims of Crime (OVC), Office of Juvenile Justice and Delinquency Prevention (OJJDP), or the Office of Sex Offender Sentencing, Monitoring, Apprehending, Registering, and Tracking (SMART).

Total Evaluations: The data in this column represent the total number of evaluations of the reviewed program, including OJP and non-OJP funded evaluations.

Other Academic Articles: These articles represent peer reviewed and non-peer reviewed literature that is relevant to the reviewed program. These are included to provide background and to help further understand the need for future evaluations.

Other Reports: These reports represent a variety of types and lengths, such as program overviews, technical information, and policy briefs related to the reviewed program. These are included to provide background and to help further understand the need for future evaluations.

Bureau of Justice Assistance Evaluation Scan Initiative Tracking

	Program Name	Crime Solutions				Research and Evaluation				
		Effective	Promising	No Effect	Insufficient Evidence	NIJ Evaluations	Other OJP Evaluations	Total Evaluations	Other Academic Articles	Other Reports
1	Body-Worn Camera Program	0	0	0	0	1	2	3	3	6
2	Border Prosecution Initiatives	0	0	0	0	0	3	3	2	3
3	Bulletproof Vest Partnership	0	0	0	0	1	0	1	7	4
4	Byrne Criminal Justice Innovation	4	0	1	0	1	1	2	9	10
5	Capital Case Litigation Initiative Program	0	0	0	0	0	0	0	2	2
6	Coordinated Tribal Assistance Solicitation Programs/Tribal Initiatives	0	0	0	0	12	4	19	4	11
7	Drug Court Programs: Including Specialized and Problem-Solving Courts	7	15	2	11	5	7	47	58	0
8	Economic High-Tech and Cyber Crime Prevention	0	0	0	0	1	0	1	7	7
9	Harold Rogers Prescription Drug Monitoring Program	0	0	0	0	0	3	3	18	7
10	Human Trafficking Reporting System; Anti-Human Trafficking Task Force Initiative	0	0	0	0	3	9	12	9	11
11	Intellectual Property Enforcement Program	0	0	0	0	0	0	0	2	6
12	Edward Byrne Memorial Justice Assistance Grant Program	0	0	0	0	1	1	2	0	7
13	Justice and Mental Health Collaboration Program	3	7	0	0	1	13	24	26	1
14	Justice Reinvestment Initiative	0	0	0	0	0	1	1	22	30
15	Missing Alzheimer's Disease Patient Alert Program	0	0	0	0	0	0	0	5	5
16	National Center for Campus Public Safety	2	0	0	0	0	0	0	12	5
17	Pay for Success Program	0	0	0	0	0	0	0	9	21
18	Prison Rape Elimination Act Program	0	0	0	0	0	2	6	10	7
19	Project HOPE/Swift and Certain Sanctions	0	2	0	1	2	0	2	3	8
20	Project Safe Neighborhood	3	7	2	2	20	4	24	23	5
21	Public Safety Officers' Benefits Program	0	0	0	0	0	0	0	1	5
22	Reentry Courts	0	0	0	0	4	1	5	12	10
23	Regional Information Sharing System	0	0	0	0	1	0	1	4	10
24	Residential Substance Abuse Treatment	0	4	0	1	28	0	33	16	4
25	Sexual Assault Kit Initiative	0	0	0	0	15	0	15	1	2

	Program Name	Crime Solutions				Research and Evaluation				
		Effective	Promising	No Effect	Insufficient Evidence	NIJ Evaluations	Other OJP Evaluations	Total Evaluations	Other Academic Articles	Other Reports
26	Second Chance Act	0	14	2	0	20	2	38	23	8
	Grants for Family-Based Substance Abuse Treatment (SCA Family)	0	0	0	0	2	0	2	0	1
	Grants to Nonprofit Organizations for Mentoring and Transitional Services (SCA Mentoring)	0	12	0	0	5	1	18	0	3
	Offender Reentry Substance Abuse and Criminal Justice Collaboration (SCA Reentry)	0	2	0	0	2	0	4	2	1
	Technology Careers Training Demonstration Grants (SCA Tech Careers)	0	2	0	0	0	0	2	5	1
27	Smart Policing Initiative	1	2	0	0	0	13	14	11	5
28	Smart Prosecution Program	0	1	0	0	0	0	0	3	9
29	Smart Supervision Program	1	0	0	0	3	2	6	9	4
30	State and Local Anti-Terrorism Training	0	0	0	0	0	0	0	0	2
31	Statewide Automated Victim Information and Notification	0	0	0	0	1	0	1	7	6
32	VALOR	0	0	0	0	0	0	0	8	7
33	Veterans Treatment Courts	1	0	0	0	0	1	2	11	17
34	Wrongful Prosecution Review Program	0	0	0	0	0	0	0	10	0

Body-Worn Camera Pilot Implementation Program

Project Description

The Body-Worn Camera (BWC) program, funded in 2015 under a statutory set-aside for technology purposes under 42 U.S.C. 3756(a) (1) and funded in 2016 in the Department of Justice Appropriations Act, 2016 (P.L. 114-113), provides law enforcement personnel a promising tool to assist in building transparency within their communities. These cameras could be an integral part of a jurisdiction's holistic problem-solving and community-engagement strategy, helping to increase both trust and transparency between the police officers and the communities they serve. BWCs can provide an inalterable audio and visual record that captures empirical evidence in the event of a crime, police-citizen interactions, or use-of-force incidents. Preliminary research indicates that departments that effectively implemented BWC programs have received fewer public complaints, file fewer use-of-force reports, and show a reduction in adjudicated complaints.

Implementing BWCs requires an agency-wide process because their technological impact will be felt at every level of a police department. Successful programs require a collaborative effort because they impact external stakeholders including prosecutors, defense attorneys, the courts, victims, and the community.

CrimeSolutions.gov Ratings:
No ratings at this time

OJP-Sponsored Evaluations

U.S. Department of Justice, Office of Justice Programs, National Institute of Justice. *Research on Body-Worn Cameras and Law Enforcement*. Washington, DC: Author.
http://www.nij.gov/topics/law-enforcement/technology/Pages/body-worn-cameras.aspx
This report, funded by the Office of Community Oriented Policing Services and conducted by the Police Executive Research Forum, identifies several perceived benefits of using BWCs, including better evidence documentation and increased accountability and transparency. But the report also notes many other factors that law enforcement executives must consider, such as privacy issues, officer and community concerns, data retention and public disclosure policies, and financial considerations. The costs of implementing BWCs include not only the cost of the cameras but also of any ancillary equipment (e.g., tablets that let officers tag data in the field), data storage and management, training, administration, and disclosure.

Katz, C. M., Choate, D. E., Ready, J. R., & Nuño, L. (2014). *Evaluating the Impact of Officer Worn Body Cameras in the Phoenix Police Department*. Phoenix, AZ: Center for Violence Prevention & Community Safety, Arizona State University.
https://www.bja.gov/bwc/pdfs/Evaluating-the-Impact-of-Officer-Worn-Body-Cameras.pdf
This evaluation was conducted to examine the effect of implementing police worn body cameras on complaints against the police and domestic violence case processing and outcomes.
Analysis of the camera metadata indicated that only 13.2 to 42.2 % of incidents were recorded by the body cameras. Domestic violence incidents were the most likely to be recorded (47.5%), followed by violent offenses (38.7), back-up (37%), status offenses (32.9%), and subject/vehicle stops (30.9%). Other offense types were recorded less often. Although in general, the technology was found to be comfortable and easy to use, officers were dissatisfied with long download times, increased amount of time that it took to complete reports, and the possibility that video recordings might be used against them by the department. We also found that video submitted to the court was difficult to process because of logistical problems associated with chain of custody and the length of time that it took prosecutors to review video files.

Katz, C. M., Kurtenbach, M., Choate, D. E., & Ready, J. R. (2014). *Evaluating the Impact of Officer Worn Body Cameras in the Phoenix Police Department.* **The project was supported by Grant No. 2013-DP-BX-K006 awarded by the BJA.**
http://www.smartpolicinginitiative.com/sites/all/files/SPI%20Body%20Worn%20Cameras%20Phoenix%20Webinar%20Slides%20FINAL.pdf

This webinar was presented to achieve the following goals: (1) Understand the basic facets of body-worn camera technology; (2) discuss the benefits of body-worn cameras; (3) discuss common concerns about body-worn cameras; and (4) review the evaluation of body-worn cameras. Findings from this evaluation include: increased acceptance of body-worn cameras by officers after program implementation; mixed officer response to the ease of downloading data from the cameras; call for the program to be expanded to other police agencies; decrease in complaints; increase in unfounded incidents; increase in arrests; and prosecution of domestic violence cases.

OJP-Sponsored Research

White, M. D. (2014). *Police Officer Body-Worn Cameras: Assessing the Evidence.* **Washington, DC: Office of Community Oriented Policing Services.**
https://www.ojpdiagnosticcenter.org/sites/default/files/spotlight/download/Police%20Officer%20Body-Worn%20Cameras.pdf

This report examines five empirical studies geared toward the police body-worn camera program. Several of the empirical studies have documented substantial decreases in citizen complaints (Rialto, Mesa, Plymouth, and Renfrewshire/Aberdeen studies) as well as in use of force by police (Rialto) and assaults on officers (Aberdeen). There is also anecdotal support for a civilizing effect reported elsewhere (Phoenix, for example). However, the behavior dynamics that explain these complaints and use-of-force trends are by no means clear. The decline in complaints and use of force may be tied to improved citizen behavior, improved police officer behavior, or a combination of the two. It may also be due to changes in citizen complaint reporting patterns (rather than a civilizing effect), as there is evidence that citizens are less likely to file frivolous complaints against officers wearing cameras (Goodall, 2007; Stross, 2013). Available research cannot disentangle these effects; thus, more research is needed.

Miller, L., Toliver, J., & Police Executive Research Forum. (2014). *Implementing a Body-Worn Camera Program: Recommendations and Lessons Learned.* **Washington, DC: Office of Community Oriented Policing Services.**
http://www.justice.gov/iso/opa/resources/472014912134715246869.pdf

Even as police departments are increasingly adopting body-worn cameras, many questions about this technology have yet to be answered. In an effort to address these questions and produce policy guidance to law enforcement agencies, the Police Executive Research Forum, with support from the U.S. Department of Justice's Office of Community Oriented Policing Services, conducted research in 2013 on the use of body-worn cameras. This research project consisted of three major components: an informal survey of 500 law enforcement agencies nationwide; interviews with police executives; and a conference in which police chiefs and other experts from across the country gathered to discuss the use of body-worn cameras. Police leaders who have deployed body-worn cameras say there are many benefits associated with the devices. They note that body-worn cameras are useful for documenting evidence; officer training; preventing and resolving complaints brought by members of the public; and strengthening police transparency, performance, and accountability. In addition, given that police now operate in a world in which anyone with a cell phone camera can record video footage of a police encounter, body-worn cameras help police departments ensure events are also captured from an officer's perspective.

National Institute of Justice. (2014). *Body-Worn Cameras for Criminal Justice: Market Survey.* **Report prepared by ManTech Corporation under Grant No. 2010-IJ-CX-K024.**
https://www.justnet.org/pdf/Body-Worn-Camera-Market-Survey-508.pdf

This market survey report aggregates and summarizes information on commercial BWCs to aid criminal justice practitioners considering planning, acquisition, and implementation of the technology in their agency. In 2011, a brief market survey reference was published by the National Institute of Justice

Sensor, Surveillance and Biometric Technologies Center of Excellence , *Body Worn Camera Information Sheet* (http://goo.gl/rSWrcV).[1] The following year, a report was published that highlighted topics for agencies to consider while pursuing BWC implementation, *A Primer on Body-Worn Cameras for Law Enforcement* (https://www.justnet.org/pdf/00-Body-Worn-Cameras-508.pdf). This report updates product information in those earlier offerings.

Other Reports

Ramirez, E. P. (2014). A *Report on Body Worn Cameras.*
https://www.bja.gov/bwc/pdfs/14-005_Report_BODY_WORN_CAMERAS.pdf
This article discusses the emergence of the police body-worn camera. It also discusses an experimental study on the use of body-worn cameras conducted by Tony Farrar of the Rialto, CA, Police Department, an analysis of body-worn cameras by the American Civil Liberties Union, and a survey of police departments on the use of body-worn cameras by the Police Executive Research Forum.

Harvard Law Review. (2015). "Considering Police Body Cameras." *Harvard Law Review, 128* (6): 1–42
http://harvardlawreview.org/2015/04/considering-police-body-cameras/
This article explores the contours of the body-camera debate. It lays out the purported benefits of body cameras, particularly their potential for increasing public trust and police accountability. It also catalogs several downsides of the cameras, all of which should be critically explored prior to their widespread adoption. It then discusses recommendations for other legal reforms necessary to ensure that body cameras do in fact increase transparency and improve relations between police and the communities they are supposed to serve.

The White House. (2015). *Fact Sheet: Enhancing the Fairness and Effectiveness of the Criminal Justice System.* **Washington, DC: Author.**
https://www.whitehouse.gov/the-press-office/2015/07/14/fact-sheet-enhancing-fairness-and-effectiveness-criminal-justice-system
The Department of Justice announced in early 2015 a $263 million initiative to expand funding and training to law enforcement agencies to advance community policing initiatives. The proposal includes a $75 million investment over 3 years that could help purchase 50,000 body-worn cameras. In May 2015, the Office of Justice Programs announced a $20 million solicitation to help law enforcement agencies purchase body-worn cameras, and its Bureau of Justice Assistance released an online toolkit to help communities implement body-worn camera programs.

The White House. (2015). *Fact Sheet: Creating Opportunity for All Through Stronger, Safer Communities.* **Washington, DC: Author.**
https://www.whitehouse.gov/the-press-office/2015/05/18/fact-sheet-creating-opportunity-all-through-stronger-safer-communities
This fact sheet discusses the National Body-Worn Camera Toolkit, an online clearinghouse of resources designed to assist law enforcement professionals and the communities they serve plan and implement BWC programs. The toolkit consolidates and translates research, promising practices, templates, and tools that have been developed by subject matter experts. Areas of focus include procurement; training; implementation; retention; and policies along with interests of prosecutors, defense attorneys, victim and privacy advocates, and community members.

City of Wichita, Kansas. (2015). *Police Body Worn Cameras (BWCs): Background, Issues, and Funding Options.* **Wichita, KS: Author.**
http://www.wichita.gov/Government/Departments/WPD/PoliceDocuments/Police%20BWC%20Report%2026%20Nov%202014.pdf
This report reviews recent law enforcement trends regarding BWCs. Issues are examined, specifically from three cities that have piloted and evaluated BWC programs (Rialto, CA; Mesa, AZ; and Phoenix, AZ). Expected outcomes from a BWC strategy (as related to the City of Wichita) are discussed, as are the

costs and potential financing options for BWC implementation by the Wichita Police Department (WPD). Finally, the report concludes with potential implementation issues for the WPD as well as funding recommendations for an expanded BWC program.

Harris, D. A. (2010). "Picture This: Body Worn Video Devices ('Head Cams') as Tools for Ensuring Fourth Amendment Compliance by Police. " *Texas Tech Law Review*, *43*: 357–372. **U. of Pittsburgh Legal Studies Research Paper No. 2010-13.**
http://ssrn.com/abstract=1596901

This article explores the good that BWV can do for both the police and members of the public, particularly how these recordings might play a role in assuring that officers comply with Fourth Amendment search and seizure rules. Field tests of BWV in Britain have shown that police used the devices to keep records and record evidence, and that the devices were a uniquely effective bulwark against false complaints. Coupled with a requirement that every citizen encounter involving a search or seizure be recorded, and a presumption that without a recording the factfinder must draw inferences in favor of the defendant, BWV can help resolve disputes over search and seizure activities, and give the public a heretofore unattainable degree of assurance that police officers enforcing the law obey it as they do so. Although BWV is certainly no panacea and presents significant issues of tampering and reliability, it can help bring accountability and rule following to an aspect of police behavior that has largely proven resistant to it.

Website

Bureau of Justice Assistance Body-Worn Camera Toolkit
https://www.bja.gov/bwc/

Border Prosecution Initiatives

Project Description

The Border Prosecution Initiatives refer to the Southwest Border Prosecution Initiative Reimbursement Program and the Northern Border Prosecution Initiative Program. These initiatives help local communities pay for judicial, penal, and enforcement expenses that result from federal border-related crime, such as captured international fugitives or international drug trafficking. When the U.S. Department of Justice declines to prosecute these federal border-related crimes, the burden often falls on border communities to prosecute them under state law. These initiatives help to alleviate the resulting financial burdens.[1]

CrimeSolutions.gov Ratings:
No ratings at this time

Partners and Professional Organizations:
✓ **National District Attorneys Association**

OJP-Sponsored and Non-OJP-Sponsored Evaluations

Audit of the Office of Justice Programs Southwest Border Prosecution Initiative Funding Received by Doña Ana County, New Mexico. (2012). OJP Sponsored.
https://oig.justice.gov/reports/2012/g6012018.pdf
The Office of the Inspector General, Audit Division, completed an audit of the Southwest Border Prosecution Initiative (SWBPI) funding awarded by the Office of Justice Programs to Doña Ana County, New Mexico. For the third and fourth quarter of fiscal year 2008, Doña Ana County received funding totaling $651,386. We found that Doña Ana County claimed and was reimbursed for cases that were ineligible under the SWBPI guidelines.

OJP-Sponsored Research[2]

Salant, T. J., Hoover, A. L., et al. (2001). *Illegal Immigrants in U.S.–Mexico Border Counties: The Costs of Law Enforcement Criminal Justice and Emergency Medical Services—Executive Summary.* Tucson, AZ: University of Arizona, Eller College of Management, School of Public Administration and Policy, Institute for Local Government. NIJ sponsored.
https://www.ncjrs.gov/pdffiles1/nij/grants/201491.pdf
This report explores the financial burden placed on border states when their criminal justice and medical systems are overwhelmed with illegal immigrants. The authors find that although the federal government recognizes its responsibility for the spillover effects of illegal immigration on local communities, it has yet to take on fiscal responsibility for these effects.

Salant, T. J., Weeks, J. R., et al., & U.S./Mexico Border Counties Coalition. (2008). *Undocumented Immigrants in U.S.–Mexico Border Counties: The Costs of Law Enforcement and Criminal Justice Services.* Tucson, AZ: University of Arizona, Eller College of Management, School of Public Administration and Policy. NIJ sponsored.
https://www.ncjrs.gov/pdffiles1/nij/grants/223285.pdf
The report gives a detailed discussion of the financial challenges created by border states when they are enforcing Federal statutes. The authors suggest reimbursing border counties for these costs to lighten the burden on these local law enforcement agencies.

---

[1] More in-depth information about these programs can be found at these websites:
https://www.bja.gov/ProgramDetails.aspx?Program_ID=81
https://www.bja.gov/ProgramDetails.aspx?Program_ID=71
[2] For each article, a link has been provided to either the full-length document or the website where it can be accessed.

Other Reports

Burns, S. (2009). *Federal Officials, Agencies and Law Enforcement Have Suggestions to Address the Drug Problem in the United States.* **Alexandria, VA: National Alliance for Model State Drug Laws.**
https://www.ncjrs.gov/pdffiles1/Archive/229092NCJRS.pdf
This report assesses the current status of illicit drug use in the United States and predicts trends and challenges for 2009 and 2010. Findings show that the then-existing drug problems that officials, agencies, and Congressional members or staff sought to address presented a wide range of concerns. On the supply side, these included all issues related to the southwest border of the United States, such as smuggling, violence, firearms, gangs, and prosecution guidelines; and on the demand side, expanding treatment, such as early intervention, diversion, drug court emphasis, and prison reform.

Clearinghouse, D. P. I. (2010). *National Southwest Border Counternarcotics Strategy Implementation Update.* **Washington, DC: Office of National Drug Control Policy.**
https://www.ncjrs.gov/pdffiles1/ondcp/swb_implementation10.pdf
This report presents an update on the progress of implementation of the National Southwest Border Counternarcotics Strategy since its release in 2009. The report briefly describes the Southwest Border Prosecution Initiative, which accounts for a small portion of this program's funding.

Finklea, K. M., Lake, J. E., Franco, C., Haddal, C. C., Krouse, W. J., & Randol, M. A. (2010). *Southwest Border Violence: Issues in Identifying and Measuring Spillover Violence.* **Washington, DC: Congressional Research Service.**
http://digitalcommons.ilr.cornell.edu/key_workplace/767
The Congressional Research Service (CRS) analyzed violent crime data from the Federal Bureau of Investigation's Uniform Crime Report program to analyze whether violence at the border can be attributed to spillover violence. The data, however, do not allow analysts to determine what proportion of the violent crime rate is related to drug trafficking or, even more specifically, what proportion of drug trafficking-related violent crimes can be attributed to spillover violence. CRS is unable to draw definitive claims about trends in drug trafficking-related violence spilling over from Mexico into the United States.

Academic Articles

Gathmann, C. (2008). "Effects of Enforcement on Illegal Markets: Evidence from Migrant Smuggling Along the Southwestern Border." *Journal of Public Economics* **92(10–11): 1926–1941.**
http://repec.iza.org/dp1004.pdf
The paper analyzes the effects of tighter border control on the illegal crossing market between Mexico and the United States. Enforcement has shifted illegal migrants to remote crossing places. Illegal border crossing is now more time intensive, with higher prices for coyotes and greater risk of death.

Hartley, R., & Armendariz, L. (2011). "Border Justice? Sentencing Federal Narcotics Offenders in Southwest Border Districts: A Focus on Citizenship Status." *Criminology and Penology,* **27(1): 43–62.**
http://ccj.sagepub.com/content/27/1/43.abstract
This study examined judicial sentencing practices for federal narcotics offenders in five southwestern border districts to explore the effect of citizenship status on sentence length. The researchers partitioned their analysis by district to enable assessment of variation in sentencing practices across the five federal border districts.

Websites

Southwest Border Prosecution Initiative Reimbursement Program
http://www.ojp.usdoj.gov/swbpi/

Northern Border Prosecution Initiative
http://www.ojp.usdoj.gov/nbpi/

Bulletproof Vest Partnership

Project Description

Created by the Bulletproof Vest Partnership Grant Act of 1998, the Bulletproof Vest Partnership (BVP) Program, administered by BJA, is a U.S. Department of Justice initiative designed to provide a critical resource to state and local law enforcement.

Since 1999, more than 13,000 jurisdictions have participated in the BVP program, using $412 million in federal funds for the purchase of more than 1 million vests (1,235,593 as of January 2016). BVP is a critical resource for state and local jurisdictions that saves lives. In FY 2012, at least 33 law enforcement and correctional officers were saved by protective vests. At least 14 of those vests were purchased, in part, with BVP funds.

CrimeSolutions.gov Ratings:
No ratings at this time

Partners and Professional Organizations:
✓ **National Institute of Justice**
✓ **National Law Enforcement and Corrections Technology Center**

Note: The articles that follow include not only BVP evaluations but also research on the effectiveness and use of protective vests in general. The following articles and evaluations have been selected from CrimeSolutions.gov, publicly available reports, and academic journals.[3]

NIJ-Sponsored Evaluations[4]

Taylor, B., Grant, H., et al. (2012). *A Practitioner's Guide to the 2011 National Body Armor Survey of Law Enforcement Officers.* Washington, DC: U.S. Department of Justice, Office of Justice Programs, National Institute of Justice.[5]
https://www.ncjrs.gov/pdffiles1/nij/grants/240225.pdf
This report is a summary of a national survey of more than 1,000 sworn officers about body armor usage. One key finding is that most departments (78%) have written mandatory wear policies, and almost all officers report following these policies. This is up from 45% in 2009. This increase is at least partially attributable to the requirement, implemented by BJA in FY2011, that a police department must have a written mandatory wear policy to receive BVP funding.

Other Academic Articles

No other evaluations were found during the review. The articles in this section serve as evidence of the successful elements of BVP. These references are not direct BVP evaluations but may be an important resource as background regarding BVP's success. These articles are examples of the importance of bulletproof vest in helping protect law enforcement officers' lives.

James, N. (2015). *Body Armor for Law Enforcement Officers: In Brief.* Washington, DC: Congressional Research Service.
http://fas.org/sgp/crs/misc/R43544.pdf
This policy paper provides background for policymakers as they consider reauthorizing the BVP program. It is proposed that Congress consider the following matters when deciding whether to reauthorize the legislation: (1) what role the federal government should play, if any, in providing armor vests for state and local law enforcement; (2) whether Congress should rescind deobligated balances from the BPV

---

[3] CrimeSolutions.gov program and practice areas are discussed through the articles and reports cited for each program or practice. In some cases, one article may have multiple ratings, or multiple articles may be used to determine a single rating. Therefore, the number of reports or articles given a CrimeSolutions.gov rating in this report may not match what is found by searching CrimeSolutions.gov.
[4] For each article, a link has been provided to either the full-length document or the website where it can be accessed.
[5] Although this report is not an evaluation of BVP, its findings do relate to BVP process outcomes.

program; (3) whether Congress should invest in developing new technology for armor vests; and (4) whether Congress should require law enforcement agencies to provide training on the care and maintenance of body armor as a condition of receiving funding under the BPV program.

LaTourrette, T. (2010). The Life-Saving Effectiveness of Body Armor for Police Officers. *Journal of Occupational & Environmental Hygiene, 7*(10): 557–562.
http://www.ncbi.nlm.nih.gov/pubmed/20635298
The objective of this study was to determine the effect of protective body armor on a police officer's risk of being killed and estimate the benefits and costs of outfitting police with body armor. The results show that outfitting all officers with vests would save at least 8.5 lives per year, resulting in a cost savings that is nearly twice the cost of the vests.

McMullen, M. J., & Williams, C. J. (2008). Injuries to Law Enforcement Officers Shot Wearing Personal Body Armor: A 30-Year Review. *The Police Chief, 75*(8): 20–22, 24.
http://www.policechiefmagazine.org/magazine/index.cfm?fuseaction=display_arch&article_id=1571&issue_id=82008
This article discusses the frequency, nature, and severity of nonfatal ballistic injuries sustained by police officers while wearing personal body armor. Data used in the study focused on events in the United States and involving sworn police officers between 1972 and 2002. The results show that even with a vest, penetrating and backface trauma occurs about 10 to 15 percent of the time.

National Institute of Justice. (2008). *Ballistic Resistance of Body Armor NIJ Standard-0101.06.* **Gaithersburg, MD: Office of Law Enforcement Standards, National Institute of Standards and Technology. OJP Sponsored.**
https://www.ncjrs.gov/pdffiles1/nij/223054.pdf
This document is a testing and performance standard from the Office of Science and Technology through the Standards and Testing Program. It outlines precise and detailed test methods for the ballistic resistance of personal body armor intended to protect against gunfire. The detailed documentation includes topics such as NIJ body armor classification, different types of armor models and a requirements list, hard armor conditioning protocol, and ballistic test methods. These standards are established to ensure that individual items of equipment are suitable for use by criminal justice agencies and serve as performance benchmarks against which commercial equipment is measured.

National Institute of Justice. (2014). *Supplement I: Status Report to the Attorney General on Body Armor Safety Initiative Testing and Activities.* **Washington, DC: Author. OJP Sponsored.**
https://www.ncjrs.gov/pdffiles1/nij/207605.pdf
This article outlines NIJ's test on new and used Zylon-based bullet-resistant armor performance, evaluation of the upgrade kits from manufacturers to retrofit Zylon-based bullet-resistant armors, and assessment of the existing body armor standard and compliance testing process. From its assessment, NIJ concluded that ballistic-resistant materials can degrade, which may reduce the ballistic-resistance safety margin.

Wethal, T. (2009). "Beefing up Ballistic Resistance." *Law Enforcement Technology, 36*(9): 36–40, 42–43.
http://www.officer.com/article/10233289/beefing-up-ballistic-resistance
This article presents modifications to the new NIJ standard on police body armor to increase the ballistic resistance. The new standard, "Ballistic Resistance of Body Armor NIJ Standard-0101.06," was released in July 2008. The standard increases the ballistic resistance of certified armor and examines and confirms durable bullet-resistant materials that withstand various challenges. It carries harsher testing and advanced environmental conditioning to better protect officers. Ballistic vests that perform under the new NIJ standard are tested to be stronger, more resistant, and hold up better against atmospheric conditions and wear. The intent of the new standard is to prevent future injuries or deaths due to failing body armor and

to beef up ballistic resistance and endurance. There are several companies with body armor products that have been NIJ tested and certified to the new 0101.06 standard.

Wilhelm, M., & Bir, C. (2008.) "Injuries to Law Enforcement Officers: The Backface Signature Injury." *Forensic Science International, 174*(1): 6–11.
http://www.fsijournal.org/article/S0379-0738(07)00130-2/abstract
This study suggest that in addition to armor testing, analyzing data on law enforcement personnel who have been shot while wearing soft body armor is also a valuable tool for determining the effectiveness of certification standards. It concludes that it is important for medical personnel to recognize the backface signature injury (an injury occurring from the deformation of the backface of the vest after a bullet strike) and document this as a type of injury separate from blunt trauma or penetrating trauma behind armor injuries.

Other Reports

Husted, J. & Hammond-Deckard, L. (2014, May). *Bulletproof Vest Partnership Initiative* **[NCJ 246402]. Washington, DC: Bureau of Justice Assistance.**
https://www.bja.gov/Publications/BVP_FS.pdf
This fact sheet presents information about activities associated with the Bulletproof Vest Partnership (BVP) Initiative. Since 1999, the BVP has awarded more than $375 million to assist in the purchase of more than 1 million protective vests.

Government Accountability Office (GAO). (2012). *Law Enforcement Body Armor: DOJ Could Enhance Grant Management Controls and Better Ensure Consistency in Grant Program Requirements.* **Washington, DC: Author.**
http://www.gao.gov/assets/590/588573.pdf
This GAO report reviews the Bulletproof Vest Partnership program and makes several recommendations for improvements. GAO was asked to examine the following: (1) the Department of Justice's (DOJ's) efforts to support the use of body armor, (2) the extent to which DOJ has designed controls to manage and coordinate these efforts, and (3) the factors affecting body armor's use and effectiveness and steps DOJ has taken to address them.

Government Accountability Office (GAO). (2014). Law Enforcement Body Armor: Status of DOJ's Efforts to Address GAO Recommendations. Washington, DC: Author.
http://www.gao.gov/assets/670/663176.pdf
This report is a follow-up to the 2012 report on the Bulletproof Vest Partnership (BVP) program. The report covers progress made in responding to the original recommendations. Steps taken include the following: (1) deobligated undisbursed funds from grants whose terms have ended, (2) expanded information available to grantees on documentation retention requirements, (3) ensured consistency in the body armor requirements for the Edward Byrne Memorial Justice Assistance program and the BVP program, (4) documented pertinent monitoring procedures, and (5) tracked Justice Assistance Grant grantee purchases of stab-resistant body armor.

Taylor, B., Kubu, B., et al. (2009). *The BJA/PERF Body Armor National Survey: Protecting the Nation's Law Enforcement Officers.* **Washington, DC: PERF. BJA sponsored.**
http://www.policeforum.org/assets/docs/Free_Online_Documents/Police_Equipment/the%20bja-perf%20body%20armor%20national%20survey%202009.pdf
This report details a 2007 survey of 782 law enforcement agencies about their use of body armor. The survey found that 99% of agencies provided armor to their officers but that only 59% had a mandatory wear policy. The report concludes with a call for further research on how mandatory wear policies affect officer safety.

Websites

OJP Resource for Bulletproof Vest Partnership
http://ojp.gov/bvpbasi/bvpprogramresources.htm

National Institute of Justice Ballistic and Stab Resistance Testing and Resources
http://www.nij.gov/topics/technology/body-armor/pages/compliant-ballistic-armor.aspx

National Law Enforcement and Corrections Technology Center
https://www.justnet.org/

Police Armor Website
https://policearmor.org/

Byrne Criminal Justice Innovation

Project Description

Launched in 2012, the Byrne Criminal Justice Innovation (BCJI) program is a central component of larger place-based programming efforts, which include the Promise Zones and neighborhood revitalization initiatives. These initiatives help transform distressed places in local and tribal communities into neighborhoods of opportunity. Through coordinated federal support, these interagency efforts align programs of the Departments of Education, Justice, Health and Human Services, Housing and Urban Development, Agriculture, Interior, and Treasury.[6]

The BCJI program focuses on chronic crime hot spots—areas with proportionally more crime and disorder than other areas of the jurisdiction—that typically have deeply imbedded, long-term social issues. Through a broad cross-sector partnership team, the program works to reduce crime, build collective efficacy, and revitalize the hot spot and surrounding neighborhood through strong community engagment in identification of both problems and solutions.

Note: Process and outcome evaluations of the BCJI program and its grantees have not yet been completed and are not included in this report. Instead, the articles listed below provide evaluations and information on the four core aspects of BCJI: the use of data and research, community engagement, linking crime reduction to revitalization strategies, and building partnerships.[7] Evaluations fitting these criteria have been selected from CrimeSolutions.gov, publicly available reports, and academic journals.[8]

In FY 2016, NIJ, in partnership with BJA, will fund a cooperative agreement to conduct an initial assessment of the overall BCJI program and select BCJI sites.

The objectives of the assessment include:

1. Studying the overall BCJI program goals, objectives, design, operation, and history.
2. Observing the program in action to assess operations and model fidelity.
3. Determining the program's current efforts and capacity for data collection, data management, and analysis.
4. Identifying key indicators of outcomes that go beyond crime reduction and community safety.
5. Assessing the likelihood that BCJI sites are achieving stated goals and objectives.

CrimeSolutions.gov Ratings:
Effective (4)
Promising (0)
No Effect (1)
Insufficient Evidence (0)

Partners and Professional Organizations:
✓ **Neighborhood Revitalization Initiative**
✓ **Community Safety Initiative**
✓ **Local Initiatives Support Corporation**

---

[6] For more information, go to:
- Promise Neighborhoods: www2.ed.gov/programs/promiseneighborhoods/index.html
- Choice Neighborhoods: portal.hud.gov/hudportal/HUD?src=/program_offices/public_indian_housing/programs/ph/cn
- Promise Zones: https://www.hudexchange.info/promise-zones/
- Building Neighborhood Capacity Program: http://www.buildingcommunitycapacity.org/

[7] For an example of a specific practice that falls under BCJI, see the literature review of Project Safe Neighborhood. For more information on police strategies, see the literature review of the Smart Policing Initiative.

[8] CrimeSolutions.gov program and practice areas are discussed through the articles and reports cited for each program or practice. In some cases, one article may have multiple ratings, or multiple articles may be used to determine a single rating. Therefore, the number of reports or articles given a CrimeSolutions.gov rating in this report may not match what is found by searching CrimeSolutions.gov.

OJP-Sponsored Research[9]

NIJ-Sponsored Evaluation

McEwan, T. (2003). *Evaluation of the Locally Initiated Research Partnership Program.* **Alexandria, VA: Institute for Law and Justice.**
http://www.ilj.org/publications/docs/Evaluation_Locally_Initiated_Research_Partnership.pdf
This report evaluates the Locally Initiated Research Partnerships program, which sought to promote the research and evaluation of community policing through police-researcher partnerships. The report found that the majority of police-researcher partnerships were successful and that the most important factors for success were an effective working relationship and an understanding of the role of police culture and research.

Other OJP-Sponsored Evaluations

Roman, C. G., Cahill, M., et al. (2005). *The Weed and Seed Initiative and Crime Displacement in South Florida: An Examination of Spatial Displacement Associated with Crime Control Initiatives and the Redevelopment of Public Housing.* **Washington, DC: Urban Institute Justice Policy Center. Community Capacity Development Office Sponsored.**
http://www.jrsa.org/ws-eval/studies_other/displacement-final-report.pdf

This program was rated on CrimeSolutions.gov as having no effect.
This report details the Weed and Seed program in Miami, FL. This program seeks to "weed" out the criminals and "seed" the community by revitalizing the neighborhood. It combines a hot spots approach with community involvement to solve chronic problems. The results show no significant decrease in violence and an increase in drug offenses in the target areas.

Other OJP-Sponsored Research

International Association of Chiefs of Police. (2004). *Unresolved Problems and Powerful Potentials: Improving Partnerships Between Law Enforcement Leaders and University Based Researchers.* **Washington, DC: Author. NIJ sponsored.**
http://www.theiacp.org/portals/0/pdfs/LawEnforcement-UniversityPartnership.pdf
This report details a roundtable held to make recommendations about the partnering of police and researchers. The attendees suggested 49 recommendations in 6 areas: (1) selecting skilled researchers, (2) training law enforcement leasers in evaluation, (3) formalizing the research agenda, (4) developing and sustaining relationships, (5) responding to research results, and (6) managing funding.

Justice Research and Statistics Association. (2005). *Use of Data in Police Departments: A Survey of Police Chiefs and Data Analysts.* **Washington, DC: Author. NIJ sponsored.**
http://www.jrsa.org/pubs/reports/improving-crime-data/improving-crime-data_full.pdf
This study surveyed more than 1,300 police agencies to determine how they were using data. In general, agencies serving larger populations (more than 100,000 residents) were more likely than smaller agencies to use data to improve performance and planning. It was also common for agencies to share data with outside groups such as community leaders and the media.

Plant, J. B., & Scott, M. S. (2009). *Effective Policing and Crime Prevention.* **Washington, DC: Center for Problem Oriented Policing. Office of Community Oriented Policing Services Sponsored.**
http://www.popcenter.org/library/reading/pdfs/mayorsguide.pdf
This report details several tips for enhancing the quality of policing and crime prevention. Related to this literature review, it calls for the use of collaboration, evidence-based practices, and the reliance on data to inform decisions.

---

[9] For each article, a link has been provided to either the full-length document or the website where it can be accessed.

Rojek, J., Smith, H., et al. (2012). "The Prevalence and Characteristics of Police Practitioner–Research Partnerships." *Police Quarterly, 15*(3): 241–261. NIJ sponsored.
http://pqx.sagepub.com/content/15/3/241.short
This report looked at police-research partnerships in various police agencies across the country. The report found that larger agencies were more likely to have a partnership and that most of these were short term and low commitment. The number one reason for not having a partnership was a lack of funding. Funding usually came from the agency (39%), the researcher (31%), or an external grant (27%).

Sampson, R. J., Raudenbush, S. W., & Earls, F. (1998). *Neighborhood Collective Efficacy–Does It Help Reduce Violence?* **Washington, DC: U.S. Department of Justice.**
https://www.ncjrs.gov/pdffiles1/nij/184377NCJRS.pdf
This report looked at the link between collective efficacy and crime in 343 neighborhood clusters in Chicago, IL. Collective efficacy was measured via survey, and violence was measured via police reports, citizen perceptions, and citizen victimization. Results showed that neighborhoods with high collective efficacy had crime rates 40 % below neighborhoods with low collective efficacy.

Academic Articles[10]

Braga, A. A., & Bond, B. J. (2008). "Policing Crime and Disorder Hot Spots: A Randomized Controlled Trial." *Criminology, 46* (3): 577–607.
http://www.smartpolicinginitiative.com/sites/all/files/Braga%20%20Bond%202008.pdf

This program was rated on CrimeSolutions.gov as effective.
This article evaluated the hot spots policing program in Lowell, MA, aimed at restoring social order to crime hot spots. The program sought to increase arrests while providing social services to the treatment areas. The results showed a significant decrease (19.8%) in calls for service in treatment areas and a decrease in social disorder in 14 of the 17 treatment areas.

Braga, A. A., Papachristos, A. V., et al. (2014). "The Effects of Hot Spots Policing on Crime: An Updated Systematic Review and Meta-Analysis." *Justice Quarterly, 31*(4): 633–663.
http://www.tandfonline.com/doi/abs/10.1080/07418825.2012.673632#.U9-ypfldX6I

This practice was rated on CrimeSolutions.gov as effective.
This meta-analysis examined the practice of hot spots policing from 10 randomized controlled trials. The results showed a significant but small reduction in crime due to the practice. The results also showed that using problem-oriented policing strategies in crime hot spots led to a larger reduction in crime compared with using traditional policing techniques.

Brisson, D., & Roll, S. (2012). "The Effect of Neighborhood on Crime and Safety: A Review of the Evidence." *Journal of Evidence-Based Social Work, 9*(4): 333–350.
http://www.ncbi.nlm.nih.gov/pubmed/22830936
In this article, the authors present findings from a systematic, integrative review of neighborhood effects, specifically for crime and safety. Thirty-seven research studies using random samples from urban U.S. areas between 2002 and 2008 are reviewed. Findings suggest sociodemographic characteristics of neighborhoods and neighborhood processes are both predictive of crime and safety. Some neighborhood conditions may also affect crime and safety in unexpected ways.

---

[10] Links to abstracts are provided when full articles are not available.

Collins, C. R., Neal, J. W., & Neal, Z. P. (2014). "Transforming Individual Civic Engagement into Community Collective Efficacy: The Role of Bonding Social Capital." *American Journal of Community Psychology, 54*(3–4): 328–336.

http://link.springer.com/article/10.1007/s10464-014-9675-x#

This research found that civic engagement gave residents the opportunity to build relationships with the community that translated into collective efficacy. It also found that bonding social capital, or the links between like-minded people, could give residents unity and increase collective efficacy. The authors conclude that community organizing initiatives that promote relationships among residents are an effective way to increase collective efficacy.

Galster, G., Tatrian, P., et al. (2006). "Targeting Investments for Neighborhood Revitalization." *Journal of the American Planning Association, 72* 4): 457–474.

http://www.tandfonline.com/doi/abs/10.1080/01944360608976766?journalCode=rjpa20

This study examines a neighborhood revitalization project in Richmond, VA. This project, which is partially funded by Federal Community Development Block Grants, selected target areas and smaller impact areas based on the best available data. The study showed success in revitalizing the neighborhoods through a significant increase in the value of homes in target areas. Although this project was not aimed at crime reduction, it mirrored BCJI goals and core elements .

Sampson, R. J., Raudenbush, S. W., & Earls, F. (1997). "Neighborhoods and Violent Crime: A Multilevel Study of Collective Efficacy." *Science, 277,* 918–924.

http://www.sciencemag.org/content/277/5328/918.short

This study looked at collective efficacy, defined as social cohesion among residents combined with the shared expectation of social control over public space. Though a survey and in-depth analysis, the authors found that colletive efficacy is an important factor in violence and is explained mainly by concentrated disadvantage, immigration concentration, and residential stablility within communities.

Sherman, L. W., & Weisburd, D. A. (1995). General Deterrent Effects of Police Patrol in Crime "Hot Spots": A Randomized, Controlled Trial. *Justice Quarterly, 12*(4): 625–648.

http://cebcp.org/wp-content/onepagers/ShermanWeisburd1995.pdf

This program was rated on CrimeSolutions.gov as effective.
This article was the first evaluation of a hot spots program. It sought to determine the decrease in crime that could be achieved from increasing police patrols in crime hot spots. The results showed that calls for service were about 75% greater for the control group than the experimental group and observed disorder was about 25% greater.

Taylor, B., Koper, C. S., et al. (2011). "A Randomized Controlled Trial of Different Policing Strategies at Hot Spots of Violent Crime in Jacksonville." *Journal of Experimental Criminology, 7*(2): 149–181.

http://cebcp.org/wp-content/onepagers/RCTofDiffStrategiesAtHotSpots_TaylorEtAl.pdf

This program was rated on CrimeSolutions.gov as effective.
This article is an evaluation of the hot spots policing program in Jacksonville, FL, designed to reduce violent crime. Hot spots received either saturated patrol or a problem-oriented policing focus. Although the results were mixed, they did indicate greater crime reduction when using a problem-oriented focus.

Other Reports

Braga, A. A., Papachristos, A., et al. (2012). *Hot Spots Policing Effects on Crime.* **Oslo, Norway: Campbell Collaboration.**[11]
http://campbellcollaboration.org/lib/download/2350/
This review seeks to determine the effects of focusing crime prevention efforts at crime hot spots. Nineteen studies containing 25 tests of hot spots policing were evaluated. The results indicate that 20 of the 25 tests showed a significant decrease in crime and disorder. The authors conclude that hot spots policing is an effective strategy.

Kingsley, G. T., Coulton, C. J., & Pettit, K. L. S. (2014). *Strengthening Communities with Neighborhood Data.* **Washington, DC: Urban Institute.**
http://www.urban.org/strengtheningcommunities
This e-book shows how modern data can be used to help solve decades-old problems in distressed urban neighborhoods. It provides sections on using local data to improve communities, using data to form city-wide and regional strategies for improvement, and using spatial analytics for place-based programs.

Local Initiatives Support Corporation. (2015). *BCJI Spring 2015 Update.* **Washington, DC: BJA.**
https://www.bja.gov/Publications/BCJI_Spring-2015-Update.pdf
This document provides an update to the Byrne Criminal Justice Innovation program including some early results from project sites. Results from the Detroit, Milwaukee, and Buffalo sites all show a decrease in violent crime of around 20%. In Charleston, WV, Milwaukee, and San Bernardino, the abatement of problem properties resulted in nuisances and crime hubs being turned into community assets.

Lum, C. (2009). *Translating Police Research into Practice.* **Washington, DC: Police Foundation.**
http://www.policefoundation.org/wp-content/uploads/2015/06/Ideas_Lum_0.pdf
This article calls for the use of evidence-based policies in policing. Specifically, it states that the research on policing will not stand on its own and that it needs to be promoted until it becomes widely used. It also suggests that funding agencies need to make a strategic effort to push the use of evidence-based practices.

Sherman, L.W. (1998). *Evidence-Based Policing.* **Washington, DC: Police Foundation.**
http://www.policefoundation.org/content/evidence-based-policing
This article argues that police practices should be based on what has been shown to work through rigorous scientific evaluation. It also argues that the use of evidence in guiding practices should be pushed nationally. The Byrne Criminal Justice Innovation program does just this by advocating for the use of evidence-based practices.

Worden, R. E., & McLean, S. J. (2009). *DDACTS in Theory and Practice.* **Albany, NY: Finn Institute.**
http://www.nhtsa.gov/staticfiles/nti/ddacts/DDACTS_Theory_Practice-092009.pdf
This report details the Data-Driven Approaches to Crime and Traffic Safety (DDACTS) program, which uses data to identify areas for traffic enforcement with the goal of reducing traffic crashes and crime. DDACTS is a spatially focused program that mirrors many Byrne Criminal Justice Innovation elements. The report finds that for DDACTS to be successful, data on location and time must be used, enforcement should be varied to find the proper dosage and type, and outcomes must be continually evaluated.

Websites

Byrne Criminal Justice Innovation
http://www.lisc.org/bcji

---

[11] The Campbell Collaboration is headquartered in Norway; however, the studies referenced were conducted mainly in the United States.

White House: Neighborhood Revitalization Initiative
http://www.whitehouse.gov/administration/eop/oua/initiatives/neighborhood-revitalization

Building Neighborhood Capacity Program Resource Center
http://www.buildingcommunitycapacity.org/

U.S. Department of Education: Promise Neighborhoods Program
http://www2.ed.gov/programs/promiseneighborhoods/index.html

U.S. Department of Housing and Urban Development: Choice Neighborhoods Program
http://portal.hud.gov/hudportal/HUD?src=/program_offices/public_indian_housing/programs/ph/cn

Health Resources and Services Administration's Health Center Program
http://bphc.hrsa.gov/about/index.html

Promise Zones
https://www.hudexchange.info/promise-zones

Choice Neighborhoods
http://portal.hud.gov/hudportal/HUD?src=/program_offices/public_indian_housing/programs/ph/cn

Capital Case Litigation Initiative Program

Project Description

The Capital Case Litigation Initiative (CCLI) Program began back in 2005 through President George W. Bush's proposed initiative to fund training for capital cases. BJA convened a focus group and developed a three-pronged plan. Training programs and curricula were developed and implemented through state and local agencies. The training focuses on "investigation techniques; pretrial and trial procedures, including the use of expert testimony and forensic science evidence; advocacy in capital cases; and capital case sentencing-phase procedures."[12]

Eligible applicants are states that authorize capital punishment and conduct or will conduct prosecutions in which capital punishment is sought. For a state agency to be eligible, its state must have an "effective system" for providing competent legal representation for indigent defendants. An effective system is one that invests in the responsibility for appointing qualified attorneys to represent indigent defendants in capital cases: (1) in a public defender program that relies on staff attorneys, members of the private bar, or both, to provide representation in capital cases; (2) in an entity established by statute or by the highest state court with jurisdiction in criminal cases staffed by those with demonstrated knowledge and expertise in capital cases, except for prosecutors; or (3) pursuant to a statutory procedure enacted before the CCLI Act was established under which the trial judge is required to appoint qualified attorneys from a roster maintained by a state or regional selection committee or similar entity.[13]

CrimeSolutions.gov Ratings:
No ratings at this time

Partners and Professional Organizations:
✓ National Judicial College

✓ National District Attorneys Association

✓ National Legal Aid & Defender Association

OJP-Sponsored and Non-OJP-Sponsored Evaluations[14]

Note: No BJA program evaluations were found during the literature review. Although much has been written on capital punishment, defendants, and juries in capital cases, little was found on the program itself.

Academic Articles

Maher, R. M. (2013). "Improving State Capital Counsel Systems through Use of the ABA Guidelines." *Hofstra Law Review, 42*: 419–445.
http://www.hofstralawreview.org/wp-content/uploads/2014/04/BB.3.Maher_.final2_.pdf
The author describes how the American Bar Association (ABA) Guidelines for the Appointment and Performance of Defense Counsel in Death Penalty Cases can improve the quality of legal representation for capital defense counsel. The author suggests the ABA Guidelines for death penalty cases have been adopted, implemented, and cited by state and federal courts in every active jurisdiction in the United States.

[12–13] https://www.bja.gov/ProgramDetails.aspx?Program_ID=52

[14] For each article, a link has been provided to either the full-length document or the website where it can be accessed.

Robinson, L. (2011). National Public Defense Symposium: Keynote Address. *Tennessee Journal of Law & Policy,* **7(3): 25–34.**
http://trace.tennessee.edu/cgi/viewcontent.cgi?article=1126&context=tjlp
In this keynote address, Ms. Laurie Robinson, the former Assistant Attorney General, Office of Justice Programs, details OJP's efforts to improve indigent defense through the CCLI program and other hiring initiatives.

Other Report

Arizona Supreme Court, Capital Case Oversight Committee. (2013). *Meeting Agenda and Draft Minutes.* **Phoenix, AZ: Author.**
https://www.azcourts.gov/cscommittees/Capital-Case-Oversight-Committee/Archived-CCOC-Meetings-Minutes
The minutes from the Arizona Supreme Court Oversight Committee's 2013 meeting include status reports on programs from the Capital Case Committee.

Coordinated Tribal Assistance Solicitation Program

Project Description

The Coordinated Tribal Assistance Solicitation (CTAS) program[15] provides federally recognized tribes and tribal consortia with an opportunity to develop a comprehensive and coordinated approach to public safety and victimization issues and to apply for funding. Existing tribal government–specific programs through DOJ are included in and available through this single CTAS program. DOJ's tribal government–specific competitive grant programs outlined in this solicitation are referred to as purpose areas. Applicants may apply for funding under the purpose area(s) that best address tribal concerns related to public safety; criminal and juvenile justice; and the needs of victims and survivors of domestic violence, sexual assault, and other forms of violence. The FY16 purpose areas include the following:

CrimeSolutions.gov Ratings:
No ratings at this time

Partners and Professional Organizations:
- ✓ **National Tribal Judicial Center at the National Judicial College**
- ✓ **Fox Valley Technical College**
- ✓ **National Indian Child Welfare Association**
- ✓ **Tribal Law and Policy Institute**

1. Public Safety and Community Policing (Community Oriented Policing Services [COPS])
2. Comprehensive Tribal Justice Systems Strategic Planning (BJA)
3. Justice Systems, and Alcohol and Substance Abuse (BJA)
4. Corrections and Correctional Alternatives (BJA)
5. Violence Against Women Tribal Governments Program (Office on Violence Against Women [OVW])
6. Children's Justice Act Partnerships for Indian Communities (Office for Victims of Crime [OVC])
7. Comprehensive Tribal Victim Assistance Program (OVC)
8. Juvenile Healing to Wellness Courts (Office of Juvenile Justice and Delinquency Prevention [OJJDP])
9. Tribal Youth Program (OJJDP).

NOTE: For the purposes of the literature review, BJA-funded purpose areas listed above were included (purpose areas 2–4). Additional resources, such as programs, evaluation, or studies primarily funded in the other purpose areas (which may have been funded through OJJDP, NIJ, OVW, OVC, or COPS) were included in some cases due to the valuable background and contextual information those resources provided.

---

[15] For more background on the Coordinated Tribal Assistance Solicitation Program, please visit the following link: http://www.tribalgrants.info/GrantDetails.aspx?gid=27899

OJP-Sponsored Evaluations[16]

Arnold, A. F., Cumbie Reckess, S., & Wolf, R. V. (2011). *State and Tribal Courts: Strategies for Bridging the Divide.* **New York, NY: Center for Court Innovation. BJA sponsored.**
http://www.courtinnovation.org/sites/default/files/documents/StateAndTribalCourts.pdf
This report from the Center for Court Innovation presents information on current collaboration efforts to bridge the differences between state and tribal courts. This report notes that although state and tribal courts in many areas have overlapping jurisdictions and need to deal with local problems that have an impact on both systems, past cultural differences and inconsistent federal policies have contributed to ongoing tensions between state and tribal governments. These tensions have prevented these entities from working effectively for their communities.

Bachman, R., Zaykowski, H., et al. (2008). *Violence Against American Indian and Alaska Native Women and the Criminal Justice Response: What Is Known.* **Newark, DE, and Wilmington, NC: University of Delaware and University of North Carolina, Wilmington, Departments of Sociology and Criminal Justice. NIJ sponsored.**
http://www.ncjrs.gov/pdffiles1/nij/grants/223691.pdf
Based on a synthesis of the empirical literature and original data analyses, this report presents an overview of the epidemiology of violence against American Indian and Alaska Native women as well as a review of the criminal justice responses to this violence.

Brimley, S., Garrow, C., et al. (2005). *Strengthening and Rebuilding Tribal Justice Systems: Learning from History and Looking Towards the Future—Final Evaluation Report* **[NCJ-210893]. Cambridge, MA: Harvard Project on American Indian Economic Development. NIJ sponsored.**
http://www.ncjrs.gov/pdffiles1/nij/grants/210893.pdf
This is the final report of a process evaluation of the Comprehensive Indian Resources for Community and Law Enforcement (CIRCLE) project. The report discusses the contributions of the CIRCLE program in improving the tribal justice system and suggests ways in which to increase the value of future federal investments. The study describes tribal justice system accomplishments and challenges encountered by both tribes and the federal government. It gives a description of the federal planning and implementation process and includes process-oriented summaries of each participating tribe's implementation work. The evaluation concludes that CIRCLE made important contributions to tribal efforts to design a strong justice system.

Denman, K., & Broidy, L. (2013). *Evaluation of Dlo'ayazhi Project Safe Neighborhoods* **[NCJ-242316]. Albuquerque, NM: University of New Mexico, Institute for Social Research, New Mexico Statistical Analysis Center. DOJ sponsored.**
http://nmsac.unm.edu/psn-process-evaluation-final-report.pdf
This report summarizes a process evaluation of these expansion efforts as well as ongoing efforts of Project Safe Neighborhoods (PSN) in the Crownpoint area of the Navajo Nation. PSN is designed to be centered on the community where it is implemented, recognizing and reacting to community needs and the local resources available to address those needs. This evaluation's purpose is to determine whether the initiative isimplemented as it was intended; to understand the perceived success of the initiative; and to pinpoint facilitators and barriers to implementation, focusing especially on coordination of activities. The evaluation concluded that the PSN is making progress toward reaching its goals. Participants in the program thought that youth had become more aware of the dangers of gun violence, drugs, and gangs.

---

[16] For each article, a link has been provided to either the full-length document or a website where it is accessible.

Gottlieb, K. (2005). *Lessons Learned in Implementing the First Four Tribal Wellness Courts* **[NCJ-231168]. Washington, DC: U.S. Department of Justice. NIJ sponsored.**
http://www.ncjrs.gov/pdffiles1/nij/grants/231168.pdf
This report discusses the lessons learned from the experiences of the first four Tribal Wellness Courts (drug courts): Hualapai (AZ), Blackfeet (MT), Fort Peck reservation (MT), and Poarch Creek (AL). These tribes had unique experiences in the implementation of their wellness courts, and they exhibited similar patterns of strengths and weaknesses. The report is organized into 10 lessons learned, each of which suggests best practices in wellness courts. The report also highlights challenges in implementing the recommended practices and suggests ways to overcome these challenges.

Gottlieb, K. (2005). *Process and Outcome Evaluations of the Blackfeet Alternative Court* **[NCJ-231161]. Washington, DC: U.S. Department of Justice. NIJ sponsored.**
http://www.ncjrs.gov/pdffiles1/nij/grants/231161.pdf
This report presents the methodology, findings, and recommendations of an evaluation of the Blackfeet Alternative Court (the Court), a pilot program of the Blackfeet Tribe of Montana. The Court gave substance-abusing Tribal offenders access to holistic, structured, and phased substance abuse treatment and rehabilitation services that incorporated Tribal culture and tradition. The evaluation concluded that the Court had many strengths. The discussion included some anecdotal reports from Court participants about their experiences, particularly how it has helped improve their self-esteem and self-worth.

Gottlieb, K. (2005). *Process and Outcome Evaluations of the Fort Peck Tribes Community Wellness Court* **[NCJ-231162]. Washington, DC: U.S. Department of Justice. NIJ sponsored.**
http://www.ncjrs.gov/pdffiles1/nij/grants/231162.pdf
This report presents the methodology, findings, and recommendations of the evaluation of the Fort Peck Tribes Community Wellness Court (CWC) in northeastern Montana (Assimboine and the Sioux Tribes). This process evaluation described and analyzed how the program is operating and is meeting its administrative and procedural goals. In reviewing its key components, the evaluation found several strengths attributed to the Court's implementation as well as some weaknesses.

Gottlieb, K. (2005). *Process and Outcome Evaluations of the Hualapai Wellness Court* **[NCJ-231165]. Washington, DC: U.S. Department of Justice. NIJ sponsored.**
http://www.ncjrs.gov/pdffiles1/nij/grants/231165.pdf
This report presents the methodology, findings, and recommendations of an evaluation of the Hualapi Wellness Court (HWC) of the Hualapai Tribe in northwestern Arizona. The HWC gave access to holistic, structural, and phased substance-abuse treatment and rehabilitation services for both adults and juveniles that incorporated tribal culture and tradition. The process evaluation found several strengths and weaknesses resulting in the HWC implementation. Strengths included but were not limited to home and school liaison involvement, treatment as structure in participant lives, and traditional healing practices that were incorporated. Weaknesses were attributed to challenges in HWC operation, including a lack in team commitment because of a lack of leadership. Furthermore, the HWC's judicial side was not well integrated with the treatment side; traditional healing activities occurred irregularly.

Gottlieb, K. (2005). *Process and Outcome Evaluations of the Poarch Band of Creek Indians Drug Court* **[NCJ-231166]. Washington, DC: U.S. Department of Justice. NIJ sponsored.**
http://www.ncjrs.gov/pdffiles1/nij/grants/231166.pdf
This report presents the methodology, findings, and recommendations of an evaluation of the drug court of the Poarch Band of Creek Indians in southwestern Alabama near the Florida border. First, in evaluating outcomes from the 28 participants, the study concluded that there is no statistically significant relationship between completion status and recidivism; graduated participants are as likely to recidivate as terminated participants. However, graduates recidivate at a slower rate than the terminated participants. The evaluation found several strengths and weaknesses related to the Court operations. Strengths included positive team relationships, combined roles of counselor and probation officer, and intensive monitoring.

There was also room for improvement in the integration of treatment and forming a steering committee including tribal and community leaders to extend the integration of the Drug Court to the community.

Horne, A., & Travis, T. (2009). *Court Reform and American Indian and Alaska Native Children: Increasing Protections and Improving Outcomes.* **Portland, OR: National Council of Juvenile and Family Court Judges, and National Indian Child Welfare Association. OJJDP Sponsored.**
http://nc.casaforchildren.org/files/public/community/judges/July_2010/CourtReform_NativeChildren.pdf
This paper is a preliminary examination of recommendations from the Pew Commission on Children in Foster Care as they pertain to state and tribal court involvement in Indian child welfare matters. It also looks at State Court Improvement Program grants, challenges, and promising practices gleaned from tribal–state collaborations around court improvement, and examines opportunities for improving court systems for the betterment of American Indian and Alaska Native (AI/AN) children. The paper offers recommendations for future tribal applications designed to improve the well-being of AI/AN youth.

Joe, J. R., Chong, J., et al. (2007). *Final Report: Participatory Evaluation of the Sisseton Wahepton Oyate IASAP Demonstration Project* **[NCJ-222740]. Tucson, AZ: University of Arizona, Native American Research and Training Center. NIJ sponsored.**
http://www.ncjrs.gov/pdffiles1/nij/grants/222740.pdf
Using a participatory evaluation model, this federally supported study evaluated the Sisseton Wahpeton Oyate (SWO) Indian Alcohol Substance Abuse Program (IASAP). The IASAP program's goal was to lower alcohol-related motor vehicle fatalities and decrease access to and abuse of alcohol by tribal youth. The evaluation concluded that lack of adequate resources was a challenge for the program. Despite this, court probation officers were able to improve the supervision of the juvenile probationers by collaborating with school providers and with other community agencies to increase community awareness. The evaluation found that the SWO IASAP demonstration project could be applicable to other tribes. The project demonstrates that despite the lack of a reservation-based program for youth, it successfully called on its probation staff to help the youth access and use existing resources to improve their treatment outcomes.

Joe, J. R., Hassin, J., et al. (2008). *Final Report: Participatory Evaluation of the Lummi Nation's Community Mobilization Against Drugs Initiative/Bureau of Justice Assistance's Indian Alcohol and Substance Abuse Demonstration Project* **[NCJ-222741]. Tucson, AZ: University of Arizona, Native American Research and Training Center. NIJ sponsored.**
http://www.ncjrs.gov/pdffiles1/nij/grants/222741.pdf
This report presents the results of the federally supported participatory evaluation of the Community Mobilized Against Drugs program implemented by the Lummi Nation (LN) in Washington State. The goals of the evaluation were to determine if the LN-Indian Alcohol and Substance Abuse demonstration project successfully achieved its stated program goals, and whether its outcomes would be applicable to other ribal communities.

Lambson, S. H. (2015). *Peacemaking Circles: Evaluating a Native American Restorative Justice Practice in a State Criminal Court Setting in Brooklyn* **[2011-IC-BX-0039]. New York, NY: Center for Court Innovation. BJA sponsored.**
http://www.courtinnovation.org/sites/default/files/documents/Peacemaking%20Circles%20Final.pdf
This study was conducted by the Center for Court Innovation. A pilot project was launched at the Red Hook Community Justice Center (Brooklyn, NY) to examine the impact and effectiveness of peacemaking when applied in a state court. The pilot project made peacemaking available as a pretrial diversion option in cases that dealt with juvenile delinquency or for select misdemeanor criminal cases. Researchers found that of the defendants who successfully completed the program (average 2.74 sessions that lasted 2–3 hours per session) were more likely to have their cases dismissed. Participants who did not complete the program and their court obligations had to return for further dispositonal hearings. This report provides details regarding program implementation and model adherence as well as qualitative data in the form of stakeholder and participant views and experiences.

Tribal Law and Policy Institute. (2003). *Tribal Healing to Wellness Courts: The Key Components* [NCJ-188154]. **West Hollywood, CA: Author. BJA sponsored.**
https://www.ncjrs.gov/pdffiles1/bja/188154.pdf
This publication is organized around 10 key components, adapted for Indian Nations and Tribal justice systems, that describe the basic elements defining Tribal Healing to Wellness Courts. The purpose of each key component is explained, followed by several recommendations for implementing each component.

Tribal Law and Policy Institute. (2010). *Tribal Healing to Wellness Courts: Needs Assessment Report* [NCJ-239075]. **West Hollywood, CA: Author. BJA sponsored.**
http://www.wellnesscourts.org/files/BJAReviewWellnessNeedsAssessmentAB.pdf
This report summarizes the Tribal Healing to Wellness Courts needs assessment survey administered by the Tribal Law and Policy Institute. The survey is administered as part of the training and technical assistance for Tribal Healing to Wellness Courts.

Wakeling, S., Jorgensen, M., et al. (2007). *Strengthening and Rebuilding Tribal Justice Systems: A Participatory Outcomes Evaluation of the U.S. Department of Justice Comprehensive Indian Resources for Community and Law Enforcement (CIRCLE) Project—Final Report* [NCJ-221080]. **Tucson, AZ: University of Arizona, Udall Center for Studies in Public Policy, Native Nations Institute of Leadership, Management, and Policy. NIJ sponsored.**
http://www.ncjrs.gov/pdffiles1/nij/grants/221080.pdf
This report is an overview of the outcomes of the federally funded CIRCLE project for FY2002 and FY2003. The study sought to determine whether there were any determinants that would indicate the CIRCLE project's success. Key findings were that in the right circumstances, investments in improving criminal justice system functioning can help Native nations address pressing crime problems. Sustainability was a significant challenge at every site; however, this study suggests approaches to planning design considerations that promote sustainability.

Wood, D. (2010). *A Review of Research on Alcohol and Drug Use, Criminal Behavior, and the Criminal Justice System Response in American Indian and Alaska Native Communities.* **Vancouver, WA: Washington State University Vancouver, Program in Public Affairs. NIJ sponsored.**
http://www.ncjrs.gov/pdffiles1/nij/grants/231348.pdf
This report presents a detailed review of the existing literature on crime resulting from alcohol and other drug abuse in American Indian and Alaska Native (AI/AN) communities and the response to the problem by the criminal justice system. The discussion differentiated between studies using measures of co-occurrence and those using measures of association. Although these studies do not provide proof that alcohol use is a cause of crime in AI/AN communities, they do indicate that there are higher levels of alcohol involvement in AI/AN crime, and AI/ANs who use alcohol are more likely to be crime victims or perpetrators.

GAO Audits

U.S. Government Accountability Office. (2011). *Indian Country Criminal Justice: Departments of the Interior and Justice Should Strengthen Coordination to Support Tribal Courts.* **Washington, DC: Author.**
http://www.gao.gov/new.items/d11252.pdf
This study analyzed the challenges facing Indian tribes in adjudicating Indian Country crimes and federal efforts to address these challenges. It also examines the extent to which the Departments of the Interior and Justice and have collaborated in supporting tribal justice systems.

Academic Research

Foley, K., & Pallas, D. (2010). "Effect of Job Skills Training on Employment and Job Seeking Behaviors in an American Indian Substance Abuse Treatment Sample." *Journal of Vocational Rehabilitation, 33*(3): 181–192.
http://www.ncbi.nlm.nih.gov/pmc/articles/PMC3147294/
This study reports on the Southwest Node of the National Institute on Drug Abuse Clinical Trials Network (CTN) that conducted a single-site adaptation of its national Job Seekers Workshop (JSW) study in an American Indian treatment program, Na'Nizhoozhi Center. Results do not support the use of the costly and time-consuming JSW intervention in this population and setting. Despite the lack of a demonstrable treatment effect, this study established the feasibility of including a rural American Indian site in a rigorous CTN trial through a community-based participatory research approach.

Lowe, J., Liang, H., et al. (2012). "Community Partnership to Affect Substance Abuse Among Native American Adolescents." *American Journal of Drug and Alcohol Abuse, 38*(5): 450–455.
http://www.ncbi.nlm.nih.gov/pubmed/22931079
This study used a community-based participatory research approach to develop and evaluate an innovative school-based cultural intervention targeting substance abuse among a Native American adolescent population. Findings suggest that cultural considerations may enhance the degree to which specific interventions address substance abuse problems among this population.

Walsh, M. L., & Baldwin, J. A. (2015). American Indian Substance Abuse Prevention Efforts: A Review of Programs, 2003–2013. *American Indian Alaskan Native Mental Health Research, 22*(2): 41–68.
http://www.ncbi.nlm.nih.gov/pubmed/26053884
This review examines substance abuse prevention (SAP) efforts in American Indian and Alaska Native (AI/AN) communities during the 2003–2013 time period. Historically, many prevention programs have been unable to meet the unique cultural needs of people within the AI/AN communities due to possible inherent incompatibility between the theories used to guide development of prevention programs in AI/AN communities and culturally appropriate theoretical constructs of AI/AN worldviews. Eighteen articles ($N = 31$ programs) were examined. "Results indicated that SAP programs in AI/AN communities vary widely in their use of theory, implementation strategies, view and definition of cultural constructs, overall evaluational rigor, and reporting methods." The authors suggest that future research is needed to examine ways in which to integrate appropriate theory and cultural elements into substance abuse prevention programs to better tie them to positive and measurable outcomes for AI/AN communities.

Whitbeck, L. B., & Walls, M. L. (2012). "Substance Abuse Prevention in American Indian and Alaska Native Communities." *American Journal of Drug and Alcohol Abuse, 38*(5): 428–435.
http://www.ncbi.nlm.nih.gov/pubmed/22931077
This article reviewed three categories of American Indian/Alaska Native (AI/AN) substance abuse prevention programs: (1) published empirical trials, (2) promising programs (published and unpublished) that are in the process of development and that have the potential for empirical trials, and (3) examples of innovative grassroots programs that originate at the local level and may show promise for further development. Findings indicate that prevention scientists who are not AI/AN are largely unaware of the numerous grassroots prevention work going on in AI/AN communities.

Other Reports

Center for Court Innovation. (N.d.). *Planning a Problem-Solving Justice Initiative. A Toolkit for Tribal Communities* **[2012-IC-BX-K005]. New York, NY: Center for Court Innovation. BJA sponsored.**

http://www.courtinnovation.org/sites/default/files/documents/Planning%20a%20Problem-Solving%20Justice%20Initiative.pdf

The planning toolkit is designed to help tribal justice practitioners assess their current justice systems and develop new or enhanced approaches that build upon community traditions and strengths. The toolkit is not a training device but a practical guide to help tribal justice practitioners work through the steps of planning a problem-solving justice initiative.

Cobb, K. A., Mowatt, M. A., et al. (2011). *A Desktop Guide for Tribal Probation Personnel: The Screening and Assessment Process.* **Lexington, KY: American Probation and Parole Association. BJA sponsored.**

https://www.bja.gov/Publications/APPA_TribalProbation.pdf

This guide presents tribal probation personnel with information on how the screening and assessment process can facilitate and promote offender accountability and long-term behavior change.

Cobb, K. A., & Mowatt, M. A. (2013). *Risk-Needs Responsivity: Turning Principles into Practice for Tribal Probation Personnel.* **Lexington, KY: American Probation and Parole Association. BJA sponsored.**

https://www.bja.gov/Publications/APPA-RNR-Tribal-Probation.pdf

This bulletin is a brief introduction to the risk, need, and responsivity principles of evidenced-based community supervision. It also offers guidance on how tribal probation officers can incorporate the premise behind each principle into everyday practice.

Cobb, K., & Mullins, T. G. (2014). *Going Beyond Compliance Monitoring for Drug and Alcohol-Involved Tribal Probationers.* **Lexington, KY: American Probation and Parole Association. BJA sponsored.**

https://www.ncjrs.gov/App/Publications/abstract.aspx?ID=269188

This report was developed to assist probation officers working with drug and/or alcohol-involved probationers in Indian country. The tribal communities prefer alternatives to incarceration such as probation and community supervision programs that offer a more culturally compatible approach to punishment. This report informs probation officers on approaches to changing offender behavior to improve public safety and influence behavior change. Recommended approaches include working with the probationer to develop a plan of action, monitoring that plan, and involving the probationer's family in the supervision process.

Farrenkopf, T. M., & Bryan, C. (2013). *Overview of the Bureau of Justice Assistance's Tribal Civil and Criminal Legal Assistance Program and Resources* **[NCJ-241626]. Washington, DC: U.S. Department of Justice, Office of Justice Programs, Bureau of Justice Assistance.**

https://www.bja.gov/Publications/TCCLA_Overview.pdf

This publication presents an overview of BJA's Tribal Civil and Criminal Legal Assistance Program. The publication identifies resources and eligibility guidelines for tribes seeking to obtain or offer civil and criminal legal assistance for their communities. It also explores program sustainment strategies and outlines several promising practices for providing indigent legal assistance in tribal communities.

Folsom-Smith, C. (2015). *Enhanced Sentencing in Tribal Courts: Lessons Learned from Tribes* **[2012-AL-BX-K003]. Reno, NV: The National Tribal Judicial Center. BJA sponsored.**

https://www.bja.gov/Publications/TLOA-TribalCtsSentencing.pdf

This publication provides a brief overview of the changes under the Tribal Law and Order Act (TLOA) and how these changes specifically effect enhanced sentencing authority on and in tribal lands and communities. Furthermore, the authors offer additional considerations for correctional/detention and community corrections programs regarding enhanced sentences. Lastly a checklist is provided that is designed to encourage and guide discussions around the successful implementation of enhanced sentencing authority. The report uses interviews with tribal court judges and personnel whose involvement in establishing the provisions required to convey enhanced sentences has been instrumental to the adoption of enhanced sentencing under TLOA. The report also provides "information on financial resources available to support funding for enhanced sentencing authority implementation."

Melton, A. P. (2013). *Considerations for Developing a Program of Reentry in Tribal Communities.* *American Indian Development Associates* **[NCJ-247077]. Springdale, WA: American Indian Development Associates and Community Corrections Institute. BJA sponsored.**
http://www.communitycorrections.org/psn/publications/DevReentryinTribalComm.pdf
This resource has information about tribal participation in reentry initiatives, research, and evaluations of tribal reentry efforts, and planning and development of these reentry efforts. Re-entrants from jails or prisons need a positive support from their communities and families. The report recommends that tribes rethink the most effective ways to respond to reentrants' risks and protective factors. To develop efficient reentry systems, available programs, policies, and practices should be fully examined.

Minton, T.D. (2015). *Jails in Indian Country, 2014.* **Washington, DC: U.S. Department of Justice, Office of Justice Programs, Bureau of Justice Statistics.**
http://www.bjs.gov/content/pub/pdf/jic14.pdf
This bulletin provides an extensive breakdown of the number of inmates in Indian country jails, the number of jails operating in Indian country, and details regarding types of criminal offenses that led to incarceration in these facilities. There were 79 tribal facilities, and findings include a 4 percent increase in the number of inmates confined in Indian country facilities compared to the previous midyear point, and domestic violence or aggravated/ simple assault accounted for the largest percentage of violent offenders housed in tribal correctional facilities.

Sekaquaptewa P., & van Schilfgaarde, L. (2015). *Tribal Healing to Wellness Courts: The Policies and Procedures Guide* **[2012-AC-BX-K001]. West Hollywood, CA: Tribal Law and Policy Institute. BJA sponsored.**
http://www.wellnesscourts.org/files/Tribal%20Healing%20to%20Wellness%20Court%20Playbook%20F INAL_November%202015.pdf
This guide is part of a series developed by the Tribal Law and Policy Institute via support from BJA. It serves two main purposes: "1) to inform the tribal government, the court, service providers, participants, and the general community of the operations and authority of the court, including Healing to Wellness Court structure and processes; and 2) to serve as a guide to the team members by outlining the expectations and requirements of the participant." The publication defines the basic elements of a Tribal Healing to Wellness Court policies and procedures manual and provides numerous examples from implemented Wellness Courts. The ultimate goal of the project is to assist tribes in developing and enhancing their own Wellness Courts.

U.S. Department of Justice, Office of Justice Programs, Bureau of Justice Assistance. (2014). *BJA Strategies to Support Tribal Reentry.* **Washington, DC: Author.**
https://www.bja.gov/Publications/TribalReentryFS.pdf
This report highlights BJA strategies that support tribal reentry and highlights three tribes that have received support. Strategies include support for planning through strategic planning and grants from the Coordinated Tribal Assistance Solicitation to support reentry.

Work Group on Corrections (2011). *Tribal Law and Order Act (TLOA): Long-Term Plan to Build and Enhance Tribal Justice Systems.* **Washington, DC: U.S. Department of Justice and U.S. Department of Interior.**

https://www.bja.gov/Publications/FinalTLOATribalJusticePlan.pdf

This report discusses the plan to enhance tribal justice systems that includes ways to address incarceration and its alternatives in Indian Country. Findings indicate that TLOA has created a tremendous opportunity for tribal nations across the United States to enhance their tribal justice systems and improve safety in Indian Country.

Website

Tribal Healing to Wellness Courts
www.wellnesscourts.org

Drug Court Programs: *Including Specialized and Problem-Solving Courts*

Project Description

Drug courts are part of the larger universe of problem-solving courts. When these courts are implemented in an evidence-based manner, they have reduced recidivism and substance abuse among high-risk substance-abusing offenders and increased their likelihood of successful rehabilitation. The Drug Court Program's overall goal is to equip courts and community supervision systems with the necessary tools and resources utilizing the most current evidence-based practices and principles to intervene with substance-abusing participants while preparing them for success in the community. To accomplish this goal, grant funds will be awarded to build and/or expand drug court capacity at the state, local, and tribal levels to reduce crime and substance abuse among high-risk, high-need participants. Drug court programs do not require a research partner during implementation, but they are required to have certain key components.[17,18]

CrimeSolutions.gov Ratings:
Effective (7)
Promising (15)
No Effect (2)
Insufficient Evidence (11)

Partners and Professional Organizations:

✓ **National Association of Drug Court Professionals**

✓ **American University Drug Court Clearinghouse/Adult Technical Assistance Project**

✓ **Center for Court Innovation**

✓ **Tribal Law and Policy Institute**

Highlighted Reports

Rossman, S. B., Roman, J. K., et al. (2011). *The Multi-Site Adult Drug Court Evaluation: Executive Summary through Volume 4.* **Washington, DC: Urban Institute, Justice Policy Center.**
Executive Summary: https://www.ncjrs.gov/pdffiles1/nij/grants/237108.pdf
Volume 1: https://www.ncjrs.gov/pdffiles1/nij/grants/237109.pdf
Volume 2: https://www.ncjrs.gov/pdffiles1/nij/grants/237110.pdf
Volume 3: https://www.ncjrs.gov/pdffiles1/nij/grants/237111.pdf
Volume 4: https://www.ncjrs.gov/pdffiles1/nij/grants/237112.pdf

This evaluation report is rated on CrimeSolutions.gov as promising.
This research report funded, by NIJ, details NIJ's Multisite Adult Drug Court Evaluation, a two-phase longitudinal process, impact, and cost study of adult treatment drug courts. The report is in four volumes. Among other findings, drug courts significantly reduce drug use and criminal offending during and after participation. Participants reported less drug use and were less likely to test positive on drug tests, and they also reported less criminal activity and had fewer rearrests. Their participation in drug courts is more cost efficient than traditional case processing/supervision practices. The net benefit of drug courts is an average of $5,680 to $6,208 per participant, depending on assumptions concerning participant income estimates. The evaluation found that drug courts that target offenders with high-crime/high-substance abuse risk yield the most effective interventions and maximize return on investment.

---

[17] More information about drug courts can be found here: https://www.ncjrs.gov/pdffes1/nij/238527.pdf

[18] Programs rated in CrimeSolutions.gov are included, unless the evaluation is more than 10 years old or the *primary* focus of the program was outside of drug courts. Some programs listed under "Specialized and Problem-Solving Courts" had court-based components, but their primary strategies were other than drug courts and other problem-solving courts, such as group homes or youth court. Consequently, not all rated articles from CrimeSolutions.gov will appear in this document.

OJP-Sponsored Research

Carey, S. M., Pukstas, K., et al. (2008). *Drug Courts and State Mandated Drug Treatment Programs: Outcomes, Costs, and Consequences.* **Portland, OR: NPC Research.**
http://www.ncjrs.gov/pdffiles1/nij/grants/223975.pdf
This study examined the effectiveness of the drug court model compared with other criminal justice models for treating substance-abusing offenders, with attention to the implementation of the Substance Abuse and Crime Prevention Act of 2009 (SACPA). The findings show that the drug court model resulted in higher rates of treatment completion and lower recidivism rates than other criminal justice models for treating substance-abusing offenders in the community. The state-mandated treatment for substance-abusing offenders under SACPA succeeded in reaching a large number of eligible offenders, offering treatment for their substance abuse without incarceration.

Finigan, M. W., Carey, S. M., et al. (2007). *Impact of a Mature Drug Court Over 10 Years of Operation: Recidivism and Costs* **[Executive Summary]. Portland, OR: NPC Research.**
http://www.ncjrs.gov/pdffiles1/nij/grants/219224.pdf
This study examined the impact and costs of a drug court on the total population of drug court–eligible offenders over a 10-year period in Portland, OR. Results included reduced recidivism for drug court participants compared with eligible offenders who did not participate. Drug court judges who worked longer with the drug court had better participant outcomes. Judges who rotated through the drug court twice had better participant outcomes the second time than the first. Overall, treatment and other investment costs per participant were lower compared with traditional criminal justice system processing.

Gondolf, E. W. (2005). *Culturally Focused Batterer Counseling for African American Men.* **Washington, DC: U.S. Department of Justice, National Institute of Justice, Violence and Victimization Research Division.**
https://www.ncjrs.gov/pdffiles1/nij/grants/210828.pdf
This program was rated on CrimeSolutions.gov as having no effect.
This report details the findings of the evaluation of the Culturally Focused Batterer Counseling program in Pittsburgh, PA. The court-based program is designed for African American men who are arrested for domestic violence. The study found that participation in the program actually resulted in negative effects when compared to a racially mixed conventional counseling group program. Program participants were more likely to be rearrested than the comparison groups, even when controlling for other factors.

Gottlieb, K. (2005). *Process and Outcome Evaluations in Four Tribal Wellness Courts.* **Washington, DC: U.S. Department of Justice.**
http://www.ncjrs.gov/pdffiles1/nij/grants/231167.pdf
This is the executive summary of a report on the process and outcome evaluations of the first four tribal wellness courts funded under the Tribal Drug Court Initiative of DOJ, OJP.. The evaluations found that each court had many strengths and success stories. Success was documented as a slowing down of alcohol and drug use among adult participants. However, graduates were as likely to reoffend as nongraduates, and participants as a whole had a relatively significant 3-year recidivism rate.

Heck, C. (2006). *Local Drug Court Research: Navigating Performance Measures and Process Evaluations* **[Monograph Series 6]. Alexandria, VA: National Drug Court Institute.**
www.bja.gov/Publications/Local_Drug_Court_Research.pdf
This report from the National Research Advisory Committee recommends a national set of performance measures and a uniform research plan for drug court data collection and analysis.

GAO Audits

Government Accountability Office (GAO). (2005). *Adult Drug Courts: Evidence Indicates Recidivism Reductions and Mixed Results for Other Outcomes* **[GAO-05-219]. Washington, DC: Author.**
http://www.gao.gov/new.items/d05219.pdf
This report describes the results of a review of published evaluations of adult drug court programs, particularly relating to recidivism outcomes, substance use relapse, program completion, and costs and benefits of drug court programs. The review noted mixed results and an insufficient number of studies to determine the costs and benefits of such programs.

GAO. (2011). *Adult Drug Courts: Studies Show Courts Reduce Recidivism, But DOJ Could Enhance Future Performance Measure Revision Effort* **[GAO-12-53]. Washington, DC: Author.**
http://www.gao.gov/new.items/d1253.pdf
This study examined BJA's Adult Drug Court Discretionary Grant program. Participation in drug courts was generally associated with lower recidivism. Evaluations reporting recidivism data for 32 programs showed that drug court participants were generally less likely to be rearrested than those in a comparison group. Cost-benefit analyses showed mixed results.

Journal Articles

Meta-Analyses

Brown, R. T. (2010). "Systematic Review of the Impact of Adult Drug-treatment Courts." *Translational Research, 155*(6): 263–274.
http://www.translationalres.com/article/S1931-5244(10)00055-1/abstract
This article reviews nonexperimental and quasiexperimental literature on the impact of drug courts. It notes that randomized effectiveness studies (evaluations) of drug courts are limited.

Koetzle Shaffer, D. (2011). "Looking Inside the Black Box of Drug Courts: A Meta-Analytic Review." *Justice Quarterly, 28*(3): 493–521.
http://www.tandfonline.com/doi/abs/10.1080/07418825.2010.525222
This report combined a metaanalytic review of published and unpublished articles with a survey of drug court administrators. Findings suggest that drug courts reduce recidivism by 9 percent, on average. The study also notes that target population, program leverage and intensity, and staff characteristics explain the most variability in drug court effectiveness.

Mitchell, O., Wilson, D. B., et al. (2012). "Drug Courts' Effects on Criminal Offending for Juveniles and Adults." *Campbell Systematic Reviews, 4*: 3–86.
http://www.ndcrc.org/sites/default/files/mitchell_drugcourts_review.pdf
This article examined 154 independent evaluations of drug courts, of which 92 assessed adult drug courts, 34 examined juvenile drug courts, and 28 investigated DWI drug courts. Findings suggest that drug courts are an effective tool at reducing recidivism, but the degree of reduction depends on the type of drug court.

Sevigny, E. L., Fuleihan, B. K., et al. (2013). "Do Drug Courts Reduce the Use of Incarceration? A Meta-analysis." *Journal of Criminal Justice, 41*(6): 416–425.
http://search.ebscohost.com/login.aspx?direct=true&db=a9h&AN=91847121&site=ehost-live
This article synthesized the empirical evidence on the effectiveness of adult drug courts as an alternative to incarceration. Using metaanalyses, research found that drug courts reduced the incidence of incarceration. However, drug courts did not significantly reduce the average amount of time offenders spent behind bars. This suggests that any benefits realized from a lower incarceration rate are offset by the long sentences imposed on participants when they fail the program.

Other Evaluations

Idaho Planning and Research Administrative Office of the Courts. (2015). *Idaho Juvenile Drug Courts Evaluation*. Boise, ID: Author.
http://www.ndcrc.org/sites/default/files/idaho_juvenile_drug_court_evaluation_report_2015_courts.pdf
This evaluation compares risk of recidivism for Idaho Juvenile Drug Court (JDC) offenders and juvenile probationers, and to enhance understanding of factors that contribute to recidivism for JDC offenders. The evaluation also investigated graduation rates of JDC offenders and the factors that contribute to the likelihood of graduation.

Author (2014). *Arkansas Adult Drug Court Recidivism Study/ Cost Benefit Analysis: Measuring Recidivism and Performance*. Arkansas Community Corrections.
http://www.ndcrc.org/sites/default/files/drugcourtrecidivismperformancenov2014.pdf
This evaluation goes into the history of Arkansas' adult drug courts, and who makes up an adult drug court, and what they are designed to do. The evaluation looked at findings of Arkansas drug courts in relations to the population they are serving (graduation rate, dropout rate, etc), and the financial benefits to the state.

Anspach, D. F., & Ferguson, A. S. (2005). *Part II: Outcome Evaluation of Maine's Statewide Juvenile Drug Treatment Court Program*. Augusta, ME: University of Southern Maine.
http://www.maine.gov/dhhs/samhs/osa/pubs/correct/2005/jdtcoutcomeeval.pdf
This program was rated on CrimeSolutions.gov as promising.
This report evaluates Maine's Statewide Juvenile Drug Treatment Courts that operate in seven counties. The program targets medium- to high-risk juveniles with substance abuse problems. The evaluation found that participants in the program were less likely to recidivate during a 12-month follow-up period compared with youth on traditional probation. However, the effect on recidivism was small.

Axel, D. K., & Rosen, D. M. (2013). "Putting Two Drug Courts to the Top Ten Test: Comparing Essex and Denver Drug Courts with 'The Carey Team's' Best Practices." *Valparaiso University Law Review, 47*: 839–867.
https://litigation-essentials.lexisnexis.com/webcd/app?action=DocumentDisplay&crawlid=1&doctype=cite&docid=47+Val.+U.L.+Rev.+839&srctype=smi&srcid=3B15&key=df2046fedfed638b49579304b35b8985
This article examines two drug courts in Essex County, NJ, and Denver, CO, and their adherence to best practices.

Boles, S. M., Young, N. K., et al. (2007). "The Sacramento Dependency Drug Court: Development and Outcomes." *Child Maltreatment, 12*(2): 161–171.
http://cmx.sagepub.com/content/12/2/161.short
The evaluation examined Dependency Drug Courts (DDCs) and reports the 24-month reunification rates from the Sacramento [CA] DDC. Results indicate that DDC participation resulted in higher unification rates and higher rates of treatment than in a comparison group. Recidivism rates were similar in both the treatment and comparison groups.

Bouffard, J. A., & Richardson, K. A. (2007). "The Effectiveness of Drug Court Programming for Specific Kinds of Offenders." *Criminal Justice Policy Review, 18*(3): 274–293.
http://cjp.sagepub.com/content/18/3/274.short
This research examined whether drug courts were equally effective for offenders charged with methamphetamine-related and DWI crimes compared with other types of drug offenders. In terms of recidivism, results of drug court participation were positive for offenders of methamphetamine-related offenses, but there was no effect on DWI offenders.

Bouffard, J. A., & Smith, S. (2005). "Programmatic, Counselor, and Client-Level Comparison of Rural Versus Urban Drug Court Treatment." *Substance Use & Misuse, 40*(3): 321–342.
http://informahealthcare.com/doi/abs/10.1081/JA-200049340
This study examined two drug courts in rural areas and two in urban settings. The research found that rural clients are more likely to be White and urban clients are more likely to be Hispanic or African American. The article also found that drug courts located in rural settings had lower treatment budgets, resulting in limited treatment services.

Brown, R. (2011). "Drug Court Effectiveness: A Matched Cohort Study in the Dane County Drug Treatment Court." *Journal of Offender Rehabilitation, 50*(4): 191–201.
http://www.tandfonline.com/doi/abs/10.1080/10509674.2011.571347#.U6RufvldX6I
This article examines recidivism rates among drug treatment court participants and compares them with a matched comparison group in Wisconsin. The study found that the drug treatment group lasted longer than the comparison group before committing new crimes, particularly participants who were women, older, minorities, and those with more serious criminal histories.

Burrus, S.W.M., Mackin, J. R., et al. (2008). *Baltimore City Family Recovery Program (FRP) Independent Evaluation: Outcome and Cost Report.* **Portland, OR: NPC Research.**
http://www.npcresearch.com/Files/Baltimore_City_FRC_Outcome_and_Cost_0808.pdf

This program has been rated on CrimeSolutions.gov as promising.
The report details the finding of the Baltimore City [MD] Family Recovery Program. Like other family treatment courts, this program serves families with children in the child welfare system whose parents have substance abuse issues. The evaluation found that parents in the program were quicker to enroll in the treatment and complete treatment compared with those not in the program. It also found that children in these families generally spent less time in "nonkinship" foster care.

Byrne, F. R., Schauffler, R., et al. (2004). "California Drug Courts: A Methodology for Determining Costs and Avoided Costs." *Journal of Psychoactive Drugs, 2*: 147–156.
http://www.tandfonline.com/doi/abs/10.1080/02791072.2004.10400050#.U6Rus_ldX6I
This article presents a cost-benefit analysis (Phase I) of three drug courts in California. It found that all three sites indicate that participation in drug court, regardless of graduation status, saves taxpayers significant money over time in terms of cost avoidance due to a reduction in recidivism.

Carey, S. M., Finigan, M., et al. (2006). "California Drug Courts: Outcomes, Costs and Promising Practices: An Overview of Phase II in a Statewide Study." *Journal of Psychoactive Drugs, 3*: 345–356.
http://www.tandfonline.com/doi/abs/10.1080/02791072.2006.10400598#.U6Ru1vldX6I
This article presents a cost-benefit analysis (Phase II) on nine drug court study sites across California, with the intent of developing a methodology to calculate costs and benefits of drug court programs. This study found that participation in drug court saved California more than $9 million in criminal justice and treatment costs due to lower recidivism among drug court participants.

Carey, S. M., Fuller, B. E., et al. (2008). *Michigan DUI Courts Outcome Evaluation: Final Report.* **Portland, OR: NPC Research.**
http://council.legislature.mi.gov/files/sdtcac/mi_dui_outcome_eval_final_report_0308.pdf

This program was rated on CrimeSolutions.gov as promising.
This report details the Ottawa County [MI] Sobriety Court Program evaluation, which targets repeat DUI offenders. The study revealed that compared with traditional probation, program participants were arrested less often during the 2-year follow-up period. It also found participants spent less time in jail and that re-arrest for comparison group offenders occurred significantly earlier than for program participants.

Carey, S. M., Sanders, M. B., et al. (2010). *Jackson County Community Family Court Process, Outcome, and Cost Evaluation.* **Portland, OR: NPC Research.**
http://www.oregon.gov/CJC/docs/Jackson_Byrne_Final_Report_June_2010.pdf?ga=t
This program was rated on CrimeSolutions.gov as effective. ☑
This article presents the finding of the Jackson County [OR] Community Family Court evaluation. The program is for court-involved parents with substance abuse issues, with a goal toward family reunification, treatment/sobriety, and child safety. The evaluation found that parents in the program had higher treatment participation and completion rates compared with parents not in the program.

Carey, S. M., & Waller, M. S. (2007). *Guam Adult Drug Court Outcome Evaluation: Final Report.* **Portland, OR: NPC Research.**
http://www.npcresearch.com/Files/Guam_Adult_Drug_Court_Outcome_Evaluation_Final%20_Report
This program was rated on CrimeSolutions.gov as promising. ☑
This article presents the finding of the Guam Adult Drug Court evaluation. This program serves adult felony drug offenders with demonstrated drug problems and no prior felony convictions. The evaluation indicates that the Guam Adult Drug Court was effective at reducing the number of new case filings for the treatment group over 3 years. However, due to the small number of cases reviewed, the results must be interpreted with caution.

Carey, S. M., & Waller, M. S. (2011). *Oregon Drug Court Cost Study: Statewide Costs and Promising Practices.* **Portland, OR: NPC Research.**
http://www.oregon.gov/CJC/docs/ORDC_BJA_Cost_and_Best_Practices_Final_Report_Rerelease_March_2011.pdf
This program was rated on CrimeSolutions.gov as promising. ☑
This article presents the findings of the Oregon Drug Court and Cost Study. The statewide study assessed whether drug courts are cost beneficial and identified best practices. It found that program participants recidivated less than the comparison group, with recidivism defined as new arrests within 3 years. However, the treatment effect on recidivism seemed to fade over time. The study also identified 38 practices that helped improve graduation rates, lower recidivism rates, and produce cost savings.

Carter, W. C., & Barker, R. D. (2011). "Does Completion of Juvenile Drug Court Deter Adult Criminality?" *Journal of Social Work Practice in the Addictions, 11*(2): 181–193.
http://www.tandfonline.com/doi/abs/10.1080/1533256X.2011.571188#.U6RvAPldX6I
This study focuses on the link between juvenile drug court participation and later adult offending rates. The research looked at conviction records of 79 former juvenile drug court participants and found little impact on misdemeanors but significant impact on felonies. Differences based on race were also noted.

Conley, T. B., Allen-Blakney, H., et al. (2013). "The Development of a Standardized Drug Court Data System in the Rural Western State of Montana." *Journal of Social Work Practice in the Addictions, 13*(2): 127–142.
http://www.tandfonline.com/doi/abs/10.1080/1533256X.2013.787319#.U6RvKvldX6I
This article documents the process of standardizing and evaluating 12 unique local specialty courts in Montana. The study found that outcomes varied among populations but were positive and consistent with existing drug court literature.

Csete, J., & Catania, H. (2013). "Methadone Treatment Providers' Views of Drug Court Policy and Practice: A Case Study of New York State." *Harm Reduction Journal, 10*(1): 35–43.
http://www.biomedcentral.com/content/pdf/1477-7517-10-35.pdf
This article focuses on the exclusion of methadone treatment in drug courts in New York State. The authors found that providers believe methadone treatment is stigmatized and poorly understood by some drug court personnel.

Dakof, G. A., Cohen, J. B., et al. (2010). "A Randomized Pilot of the Engaging Moms Program for Family Drug Court." *Journal of Substance Abuse Treatment, 38*: 263–274.
http://www.journalofsubstanceabusetreatment.com/article/S0740-5472(10)00009-7/abstract

This program was rated on CrimeSolutions.gov as promising.
This article details the finding of the Engaging Moms Program (EMP), which is intended to help mothers with substance abuse problems maintain parental rights by participating in a drug court program. The study found that EMP participants had equal or better outcomes compared with those who received intensive case management services.

Dannerbeck, A., Harris, G., et al. (2006). "Understanding and Responding to Racial Differences in Drug Court Outcomes." *Journal of Ethnicity in Substance Abuse, 5*(2): 1–22.
http://www.tandfonline.com/doi/abs/10.1300/J233v05n02_01#.U6RvePldX6I
This study evaluated differences in the outcomes between White and African American drug court participants. The authors found significant differences in outcomes between Whites and African Americans in 10 Missouri adult drug courts.

Egbert, S. C., Church II, W. T., et al. (2006). "Justice and Treatment Collaboration: A Process Evaluation of a Drug Court." *Best Practice in Mental Health, 2*(1): 74–91.
http://essential.metapress.com/content/q3303x7v13444480/
This article focuses on a process evaluation of a developing drug court in Utah and offers recommendations for improvement.

Eibner, C., Morral, A. R., et al. (2006). "Is the Drug Court Model Exportable? The Cost-Effectiveness of a Driving-Under-the-Influence Court." *Journal of Substance Abuse Treatment, 31*(1): 75–85.
http://www.sciencedirect.com/science/article/pii/S0740547206000900
This evaluation examined the effectiveness and cost-effectiveness of a DUI court in California. It found that the court produced cost savings for third-time offenders. This suggests that implementing a DUI-specific court intervention for serious DUI recidivists is a worthwhile investment of public resources.

Festinger, D. S., Foltz, C., et al. (2005). "Perceived Deterrence and Outcomes in Drug Court." *Behavioral Sciences & the Law, 23*(2): 183–198.
http://onlinelibrary.wiley.com/doi/10.1002/bsl.636/abstract
This article examined perceived-deterrence theory as a possible explanation for the effects of drug court. Although the study design did not permit inferences of causality, the results suggest that perceived deterrence is a potential explanatory mechanism for the effects of drug courts.

Gallagher, J. R. (2014). "Predicting Criminal Recidivism Following Drug Court: Implications for Drug Court Practice and Policy Advocacy." *Journal of Addictions & Offender Counseling, 35*(1): 15–29.
http://onlinelibrary.wiley.com/doi/10.1002/j.2161-1874.2014.00021.x/full
This study evaluated a drug court in Texas and found that those might likely to recidivate included participants with a violation within the first 30 days of drug court as well as terminated participants. Implications for drug court practice and policy advocacy are discussed.

Galloway, A. L., & Drapela, L. A. (2006). "Are Effective Drug Courts an Urban Phenomenon? Considering Their Impact on Recidivism Among a Nonmetropolitan Adult Sample in Washington State." *International Journal of Offender Therapy and Comparative Criminology, 50*(3): 280–293.
https://www.ncjrs.gov/app/abstractdb/AbstractDBDetails.aspx?id=237608
This study evaluates the effects of intermediate sanctions in a drug court among adult offenders in a small, nonmetropolitan county in northwest Washington State. It found that rearrest rates are significantly lower among drug court graduates than probationers, even when controlling for age, race, gender, and number of days at risk in the community.

Gottfredson, D. C., Najaka, S. S., et al. (2003). "Effectiveness of Drug Treatment Courts: Evidence from a Randomized Trial." *Criminology & Public Policy, 2*(2): 171–196.
http://onlinelibrary.wiley.com/doi/10.1111/j.1745-9133.2003.tb00117.x/abstract

This program has been rated on CrimeSolutions.gov as promising.
The study examined whether drug treatment courts in Baltimore City, MD, could reduce recidivism levels among a sample of drug-addicted offenders better than other options open to the criminal justice system. Participants were randomly assigned to either the drug treatment court or treatment as usual. The study found that drug treatment court reduced rates of recidivism among its sample of offenders, primarily resulting from the use of sanctions for unacceptable behavior and the use of certified drug treatment programs.

Green, B. L., Furrer, C., et al. (2007). "How Effective Are Family Treatment Drug Courts? Outcomes from a Four-Site National Study." *Child Maltreatment, 12*(1), 43–59.
http://cmx.sagepub.com/content/12/1/43.short
This study examined four family treatment drug courts and compared participants with a sample of similar nonparticipants (control group). It found improved outcomes in terms of parent participation in substance abuse treatment, placements, and reunification compared with similar nonparticipants.

Green, B. L., Furrer, C. J., et al. (2009). "Building the Evidence Base for Family Drug Treatment Courts: Results from Recent Outcome Studies." *Drug Court Review, 6*(2): 53–82.
http://pdxscholar.library.pdx.edu/sysc_fac/4/
This review of current research on family treatment drug courts (FDTCs) found evidence for their effectiveness in assisting and supporting parents in entering, remaining in, and completing substance abuse treatment. However, different program models achieved varying outcome patterns. The findings of completed FDTC outcome studies are summarized, including one unpublished and two published reports. Results are also presented from a recently completed large-scale outcome study.

Griffin, K. (2012). "Answering the Critics: How Judges' Adherence to High Ethical Standards Increases Drug Courts' Effectiveness." *Journal of the Legal Profession, 36*(2): 245–255.
http://heinonline.org/HOL/LandingPage?handle=hein.journals/jlegpro36&div=24&id=&page=
This article focuses on the link between judicial adherence to high ethical standards and its impact on the effectiveness of the drug courts.

Guastaferro, W. P. (2012). "Using the Level of Service Inventory-Revised to Improve Assessment and Treatment in Drug Court." *International Journal of Offender Therapy and Comparative Criminology, 56*(5): 769–789.
http://ijo.sagepub.com/content/early/2011/06/18/0306624X11413879.abstract
This article examined the utility of using the Level of Service Inventory-Revised (LSI-R) to help identify treatment needs of people in drug courts. The results found empirical support for using the LSI-R as a link between assessment and treatment.

Hartman, J. L., Listwan, S. J., et al. (2007). "Methamphetamine Users in a Community-Based Drug Court: Does Gender Matter?" *Journal of Offender Rehabilitation, 45*(3/4): 109–130.
http://www.tandfonline.com/doi/abs/10.1300/J076v45n03_05#.U6Rx8_ldX6I
This article examines men and women methamphetamine users who participated in a community-based drug court. Among study participants, men were more likely to fail after an 18-month follow-up period than women.

Henggeler, S. W., Halliday-Boykins, C. A., et al. (2006). "Juvenile Drug Court: Enhancing Outcomes by Integrating Evidence-Based Treatments." *Journal of Consulting and Clinical Psychology, 74*(1): 42–54.
http://psycnet.apa.org/journals/ccp/74/1/42/
This article focuses on the integration of evidence-based treatment in juvenile drug courts, namely multisystemic therapy. It found that the use of evidence-based treatments within the drug court context improved substance-related outcomes among youth.

Hiller, M. L., Malluche, D., et al. (2010). "A Multisite Description of Juvenile Drug Courts: Program Models and During-program Outcomes." *International Journal of Offender Therapy and Comparative Criminology, 54*(2): 213–235.
http://ijo.sagepub.com/content/54/2/213.short
This article summarizes and integrates findings from process evaluations of three juvenile drug courts. Similarities and differences in the structure and design of the programs are noted.

Kleinpeter, C. B., Brocato, J., et al. (2009). "Specialty Groups for Drug Court Participants." *Journal of Groups in Addiction & Recovery, 4*(4): 265–287.
http://www.tandfonline.com/doi/abs/10.1080/15560350903340486#.U6Ryi_ldX6l
This study describes and evaluates specialty groups added to the traditional drug court services in Orange County, CA. It focused on certain outcomes, including increasing program retention and successful completion (graduation) rates for participants.

Koetzle, D., Listwan, S. J., et al. (2013, December 20). "Treating High-Risk Offenders in the Community: The Potential of Drug Courts." *International Journal of Offender Therapy and Comparative Criminology.* **[Epub ahead of print]**
http://ijo.sagepub.com/content/early/2013/12/19/0306624X13515635.abstract
This article compares recidivism rates of high-risk drug court participants and high-risk probationers. In terms of recidivism, the study found that drug court participants had significantly better outcomes than probationers.

Koob, J., Brocato, J., et al. (2011). "Enhancing Residential Treatment for Drug Court Participants." *Journal of Offender Rehabilitation, 50*(5): 252–271.
http://www.tandfonline.com/doi/abs/10.1080/10509674.2011.574204#.U6Ryx_ldX6l
This study evaluated the impact of increased access to residential treatment for high-need offenders in a California drug court. Results suggest that providing residential treatment to offenders in need of a higher level of treatment was related to positive outcomes.

Labriola, M., Cissner, A. B., et al. (2012). *Testing the Efficacy of Judicial Monitoring: A Randomized Trial at the Rochester, New York, Domestic Violence Courts.* **New York: Center for Court Innovation.**
http://www.courtinnovation.org/sites/default/files/documents/Testing_Efficacy_Judicial_Monitoring.pdf
This program was rated on CrimeSolutions.gov as having no effect. ⊘
This report discusses the evaluation of the mandatory Rochester Domestic Violence Court Judicial Monitoring program that is targeted for domestic violence offenders. The evaluation found that participation in the program had no impact on rearrest rates, program completion, or program attendance.

Lapham, S. C., Kapitula, L. R., et al. (2006). "Impaired-Driving Recidivism Among Repeat Offenders Following an Intensive Court-Based Intervention." *Accident Analysis and Prevention, 38*: **162–169.**
http://www.sciencedirect.com/science/article/pii/S0001457505001454
This report details the DUI Intensive Supervision Program in Multnomah County, OR. The 3-year program for repeat DUI offenders uses swift and certain sanctions, intensive probation and monitoring, and mandatory treatment to help change behaviors that lead to impaired driving and to reduce recidivism. The evaluation found that the program helped reduce recidivism, defined as rearrest for impaired driving.

Listwan, S. J., Shaffer, D. K., et al. (2009). "Combating Methamphetamine Use in the Community: The Efficacy of the Drug Court Model." *Crime & Delinquency, 55*(4): **627–644.**
http://cad.sagepub.com/content/55/4/627.short
This study explores whether drug courts are a viable option for treating methamphetamine-addicted offenders. It noted that drug of choice does not influence outcome in a drug court setting.

Marlowe, D. B. (2010). *Research Update on Adult Drug Courts.* **Alexandria, VA: National Association of Drug Court Professionals.**
http://www.nadcp.org/sites/default/files/nadcp/Research%20Update%20on%20Adult%20Drug%20Courts%20-%20NADCP_1.pdf
This article presents an update on research examining the cost-effectiveness of adult drug courts and identifies certain evidence-based treatments that have been proven to lead to improved outcomes.

Marlowe, D. B., Festinger, D. S., et al. (2005). "Perceived Deterrence and Outcomes in Drug Court." *Behavioral Sciences & the Law, 23*(2): **183–198.**
http://onlinelibrary.wiley.com/doi/10.1002/bsl.636/abstract
This article examined perceived-deterrence theory as a possible explanation for the effects of drug court. Although the study design did not permit inferences of causality, the results suggest that perceived deterrence is a potential explanatory mechanism for the effects of drug courts.

Marlowe, D. B., Festinger, D. S., et al. (2006). "Matching Judicial Supervision to Clients' Risk Status in Drug Court." *Crime & Delinquency, 52*(1): **52–76.**
http://cad.sagepub.com/content/52/1/52.short
This study evaluated the effectiveness of matching drug court clients to the correct service track based on their assessed risk status. The study offers support for the risk principle in drug courts and provides practical information for enhancing the efficacy and cost efficiency of drug courts.

Marlowe, D. B., Festinger, D. S., et al. (2008). "Effectiveness Trial of Contingency Management in a Felony Preadjudication Drug Court." *Journal of Applied Behavior Analysis, 41*(4): **565–577.**
http://www.ncbi.nlm.nih.gov/pmc/articles/PMC2606594/pdf/jaba-41-04-565.pdf
This study evaluated the effectiveness of a contingency management (CM) program delivered in the context of a felony preadjudication drug court. It found that the CM program did not improve outcomes.

Marlowe, D. B., Festinger, D. S., et al. (2009). "Adaptive Interventions May Optimize Outcomes in Drug Courts: A Pilot Study." *Current Psychiatry Reports, 11*(5): **370–376.**
http://link.springer.com/article/10.1007/s11920-009-0056-3
This study looked at adaptive interventions in a juvenile drug court setting. Adaptive interventions apply a priori decision rules for adjusting treatment services in response to clinical presentation or performance in treatment by participants. It found adaptive interventions improved outcomes for juvenile misdemeanor drug offenders.

McNiel, D. E., & Binder, R. L. (2007). "Effectiveness of a Mental Health Court in Reducing Criminal Recidivism and Violence." *American Journal of Psychiatry, 164*(9):1395–1403.
http://ajp.psychiatryonline.org/article.aspx?articleid=98922

This program was rated on CrimeSolutions.gov as promising. ☑
This article details the evaluation of the San Francisco Behavioral Health Court that targets both felony and misdemeanor offenders who have axis I clinical psychiatric disorders according to DSM-IV criteria. Compared with control subjects, participants in the voluntary program had longer average times before filing of new charges. Completion of the program resulted in lower recidivism over 18 months compared with people who received treatment as usual.

Patten, R., Messer, S., et al. (2014, April 30). "'I Don't See Myself as Prison Material': Motivations for Entering a Rural Drug Court." *International Journal of Offender Therapy and Comparative Criminology.* **[Epub ahead of print]**
http://ijo.sagepub.com/content/early/2014/04/28/0306624X14532321.abstract

The study used semistructured interviews to determine the reasons why former drug court participants were motivated to participate in the program. The results noted that the most important motivation for the majority of participants was trying to avoid jail or prison. The second most significant reason for participation was the desire to break the cycle of addiction.

Rempel, M., Fox-Kralstein, D., et al. (2003). *The New York State Adult Drug Court Evaluation: Policies, Participants, and Impacts.* **New York: Center for Court Innovation.**
http://www.courts.state.ny.us/whatsnew/pdf/NYSAdultDrugCourtEvaluation.pdf

These programs were rated on CrimeSolutions.gov as effective: Bronx Treatment Court, Brooklyn Treatment Court, Queens Treatment Court, and Suffolk Drug Treatment Court.[19] ☑
The article presents findings from evaluations of multiple drug treatment courts in New York state: Brooklyn, the Bronx, Manhattan, Queens, Suffolk, Syracuse, Rochester, and Buffalo. The target populations vary, but the courts are for first-time nonviolent felony or misdemeanor drug offenders. The evaluation found that drug court participants showed significant reductions in recidivism for up to 3 years after initial arrest compared with a comparison group.

Ronan, S. M., Collins, P. A., et al. (2009). "The Effectiveness of Idaho DUI and Misdemeanor/DUI Courts: Outcome Evaluation." *Journal of Offender Rehabilitation, 48*(2):154–165.
http://www.isc.idaho.gov/psc/Effectiveness_Of_ID_DUI_Courts_Outcome_Evaluation.pdf

This program was rated on CrimeSolutions.gov as promising. ☑
The article presents the findings of Idaho's DUI and Misdemeanor DUI Courts. The study looked at the state's eight Misdemeanor DUI Courts and four DUI courts and found that program participants had fewer new court filing charges compared with the comparison group.

Shaffer, D. K., Hartman, J. L., et al. (2011). "Outcomes Among Drug Court Participants: Does Drug of Choice Matter?" *International Journal of Offender Therapy and Comparative Criminology, 55*(1): 155–174.
http://ijo.sagepub.com/content/early/2010/01/28/0306624X09359648.abstract

This study examined recidivism rates of drug court clients by drug of choice. Results indicated that drug of choice does not significantly influence either successful graduation or rearrest, based on a 2-year follow-up period.

---

[19] Each court program was rated and counted separately in CrimeSolutions.gov. For brevity, they are combined here.

Shaffer, D. K., Listwan, S. J., et al. (2008). "Examining the Differential Impact of Drug Court Services by Court Type: Findings from Ohio." *Drug Court Review, 6*(1): 33–66.
https://www.ncjrs.gov/App/abstractdb/AbstractDBDetails.aspx?id=246070
This study explored the characteristics and outcomes among seven adult and three juvenile drug courts across Ohio in an attempt to understand the impact of various courts in different settings. Regardless of type of court, findings suggest that clients who receive drug court services have significantly better outcomes as a group than those who do not receive such services.

Sheidow, A. J., Jayawardhana, J., et al. (2012). "Money Matters: Cost Effectiveness of Juvenile Drug Court with and without Evidence-Based Treatments." *Journal of Child & Adolescent Substance Abuse, 21*(1): 69–90.
http://www.tandfonline.com/doi/abs/10.1080/1067828X.2012.636701#.U6Rz2PldX6I
This study examined the outcome and cost-effectiveness of drug courts and family courts with evidence-based treatment services, namely multisystemic therapy with or without contingency management. It found that adding evidence-based treatment improves outcomes and also makes family courts and drug courts more cost efficient.

Small, M. L., & Allard, S. W. (2013). "Reconsidering the Urban Disadvantaged: The Role of Systems, Institutions, and Organizations." *ANNALS of the American Academy of Political and Social Science, 647*(1): 6–20.
http://ann.sagepub.com/content/647/1/6.short
The authors examine why a relatively small pool of drug offenders participate in drug courts. They find that four factors have prevented drug courts from substantially lowering the flow of offenders into prisons and jails: tight eligibility requirements of drug courts, specific sentencing requirements, legal consequences of program noncompliance, and constraints in drug court capacity and funding.

Smith, E. P., Wolf, A. M., et al. (2004). "The Adolescent Diversion Project: 25 Years of Research on an Ecological Model of Intervention." *Prevention and Intervention in the Community, 27*(2): 29–47.
http://www.tandfonline.com/doi/abs/10.1300/J005v27n02_03#.U71jm_ldX6I
This program was rated on CrimeSolutions.gov as effective.
The article presents findings from the evaluation of the Adolescent Diversion Project (ADP), a youth court–based diversion program. ADP's intent is to strengthen youths' attachment to family and the community through tailored services. The study found that ADP was effective at reducing "official delinquency" at 1-year follow-up.

Worcel, S. D., Furrer, C. J., et al. (2008). "Effects of Family Treatment Drug Courts on Substance Abuse and Child Welfare Outcomes." *Child Abuse Review, 17*(6): 427–443.
http://onlinelibrary.wiley.com/doi/10.1002/car.1045/abstract
This article presents findings from a large-scale outcome study of family treatment drug courts. The evaluation examined whether court, child welfare, and treatment outcomes differed for families served in family treatment courts compared with a matched sample of families with substance abuse issues who received traditional child welfare services. Findings suggest improved outcomes for families in treatment courts.

Websites

Translating Drug Court Research into Practice
http://research2practice.org/

National Association of Drug Court Professionals
http://nadcp.org/

American University Drug Court Clearinghouse/Adult Technical Assistance Project
http://www.american.edu/spa/jpo/drug-court-clearinghouse.cfm

Tribal Law and Policy Institute
http://www.tribal-institute.org/
http://www.wellnesscourts.org/

Economic, High-Tech, and Cyber Crime Prevention

Project Description

The Economic, High-Tech, and Cyber Crime Prevention grants were authorized under the Consolidated Appropriations Act of 2008. This is a training and technical assistance grant program that directly supports local agencies in investigating and prosecuting cybercrimes and provides national training classes in both classroom and online settings in cyber/financial crime investigations and prosecutions.

Under this program, the National White Collar Crime Center (NW3C) provides a nationwide support system for law enforcement and regulatory agencies involved in preventing, investigating, and prosecuting economic, cyber, and high-tech crimes. NW3C delivers training in computer forensics, cyber and financial crime investigations, digital evidence, and intelligence analysis as well as investigative support to agencies investigating white-collar crimes.

CrimeSolutions.gov Ratings:
No ratings at this time

Partners and Professional Organizations:
- ✓ National White Collar Crime Center
- ✓ National Criminal Justice Training Center
- ✓ International Association of Chiefs of Police
- ✓ Police Executive Research Forum
- ✓ Cyber Shield Alliance (FBI)

NW3C produces original research on all facets of white collar crime to support training and assist law enforcement. The research is geared to a variety of audiences, from citizens to law enforcement to policy makers.[20]

Note: No program evaluations were found for the Economic, High-Tech, and Cyber Crime Prevention grants. One evaluation was found for NW3C. Most of the listed articles are additional research that illustrates the need for cybercrime training and NW3C.

NIJ-Sponsored Evaluation

Bradley, K., & Connors, E. (2007). *Training Evaluation Model: Evaluating and Improving Criminal Justice Training.* **Alexandria, VA: Institute for Law and Justice. NIJ sponsored.[21]**
https://www.ncjrs.gov/pdffiles1/nij/grants/244478.pdf
This study evaluated several criminal justice training programs, including NW3C's Foundations of Intelligence Analysis Training. The evaluation found that students learned a significant amount from the course and used their new skills in their daily jobs. The evaluation concludes that the programs fill an important void by offering free high-quality training on a topic that has few quality training options.

---

[20] For more information, see https://www.nw3c.org/docs/presskit/value-of-nw3c.pdf?sfvrsn=14
[21] This evaluation examines one portion of NW3C that supports the goals and mission of the Economic, High-Tech, and Cyber Crime Prevention grants.

Academic Articles

Basham, M. J., & Rosado, A. L. (2005). "Qualitative Analysis of Computer Security Education and Training in the United States: An Implementation Plan for St. Petersburg College." *Journal of Security Education, 1*(2/3): 81–116.

http://www.tandfonline.com/doi/abs/10.1300/J460v01n02_07

This paper examines relevant literature about computer security education and training, reviews similar programs at other community colleges, and proposes creating two certificate training programs in criminal justice and computer protection. The authors propose creating new security certificate programs at St. Petersburg College. They present a blueprint for success, along with individual course titles and a certification framework. The blueprint compares and contrasts existing programs from universities and community colleges across the country and offers predictions for the future of computer security programs.

Broadhurst, R. (2006). "Developments in the Global Law Enforcement of Cyber-Crime." *Policing: An International Journal of Police Strategies & Management, 29*(3): 408–433.

http://eprints.qut.edu.au/3769/1/3769_1.pdf

This article argues for the urgent need to reform methods of mutual legal assistance among domestic jurisdictions and nations. It finds cooperative international enforcement efforts against cybercrime are promoted and implemented through the United Nations, Interpol, and other international institutions as well as through bilateral and regional efforts. The author finds encouraging signs that the market is demanding a secure and trusted environment from software developers.

Cohen, C. L. (2007). "Growing Challenges of Computer Forensics." *Police Chief, 74*(3): 24–29.

https://www.ncjrs.gov/App/publications/abstract.aspx?ID=239917

This article describes how the Indiana State Police formed an alliance with the Purdue University Department of Computer and Information Technology and NW3C. Through NW3C participation, leads can be sent to police departments with jurisdiction over offenders linked to other offenders in an online criminal network.

Davis, J. T. (2012). "Examining Perceptions of Local Law Enforcement in the Fight Against Crimes with a Cyber-Component." *Policing: An International Journal of Police Strategies & Management, 35*(2): 272–284.

http://www.emeraldinsight.com/doi/abs/10.1108/13639511211230039

This study finds that local law enforcement in North Carolina lacks adequate training, personnel, and equipment to investigate crimes with a cyber-component. The study calls for government and law enforcement leaders to implement strategies to enhance computer crime investigations.

Harrison, W., Heuston, G., et al. (2004). "High-Tech Forensics." *Communications of the ACM, 47*(7): 49–52.

http://dl.acm.org/citation.cfm?id=1005820

The dramatic proliferation in cases involving digital evidence requires prosecutors and law enforcement agents to deal with artifacts such as computer logs, e-mail, word-processing documents, image files, and so on. Today, the overwhelming majority of police officers are unprepared to deal with crimes involving either direct or indirect use of computers. Most officers receive little or no instruction in computer forensics during police academy training .

Holt, T. J., Blevins, K. R., et al. (2012). "Examining the Stress, Satisfaction, and Experiences of Computer Crime Examiners." *Journal of Crime and Justice, 35*(1): 35–52.

https://www.ncjrs.gov/App/Publications/abstract.aspx?ID=261437

This study examined the stress and job satisfaction from a sample of law enforcement agents who completed computer training through NW3C and had experience with digital evidence handling. The results show that role conflict was the most salient factor in predicting both stress and satisfaction. Experience with digital evidence handling increased job stress but was not predictive of job satisfaction.

Hunton, P. (2011). "The Stages of Cybercrime Investigations: Bridging the Gap between Technology Examination and Law Enforcement Investigation." *Computer Law & Security Review,* *27*(1): 61–67.

http://www.sciencedirect.com/science/article/pii/S0267364910001688

The stages of cybercrime investigations discussed demonstrate the logical steps and primary considerations vital to investigating cyber-related crime and criminality. The model is intended to offer both technical and nontechnical investigative resources covering mainstream law enforcement, partner agencies, and specialist technical services, with a formal and common structure when investigating the complex technical nature of cybercrime.

Other Reports

Office of Legal Education. (2015). *Prosecuting Computer Crimes.* **Washington, DC: Executive Office for United States Attorneys, DOJ.**

http://www.justice.gov/sites/default/files/criminal-ccips/legacy/2015/01/14/ccmanual.pdf.

This manual examines the federal laws that relate to computer crimes. The focus remains on those crimes that use or target computer networks, which are interchangeably referred to as "computer crime," "cybercrime," and "network crime." Examples of computer crime include computer intrusions, denial of service attacks, viruses, and worms. This report does not cover issues of state law and does not cover every type of crime related to computers, such as child pornography or phishing.

Office of Legal Education. (2015). *Searching and Seizing Computers and Obtaining Electronic Evidence in Criminal Investigations.* **Washington, DC: Executive Office for United States Attorneys, DOJ.**

http://www.justice.gov/sites/default/files/criminal-ccips/legacy/2015/01/14/ssmanual2009.pdf.

This manual examines the federal laws that relate to computer crimes. It addresses such issues as the Fourth Amendment's "Reasonable Expectation of Privacy" in computers as storage devices, private searches, and use of specialized technology to obtain information.

U.S. Department of Justice. (2015). *Best Practices for Victim Response and Reporting of Cyber Incidents.* **Washington, DC: Author, Cybersecurity Unit, Computer Crime & Intellectual Property Section.**

http://www.justice.gov/sites/default/files/criminal-ccips/legacy/2015/04/30/04272015reporting-cyber-incidents-final.pdf

This best practices document was drafted by DOJ's cybersecurity unit to assist organizations in preparing a cyber incident response plan and, more generally, in preparing to respond to a cyber incident. It reflects lessons learned by federal prosecutors while handling cyber investigations and prosecutions, including information about how cyber criminals' tactics and tradecraft can thwart recovery. It also incorporates input from private sector companies that have managed cyber incidents. It was drafted with smaller, less well-resourced organizations in mind; however, even larger organizations with more experience in handling cyber incidents may benefit from it.

INTERPOL. (2015). *Connecting Police for a Safer World.* **Lyon, France: Author.**

http://www.interpol.int/Crime-areas/Cybercrime/Cybercrime

This website provides information about cybercrimes and how these can be combated. Specifically, it addresses three types of cybercrime: (1) Attacks against computer hardware and software (e.g., botnets, malware, and network intrusion); (2) financial crimes and corruption (e.g., online fraud, penetration of online financial services, and phishing); and (3) abuse (e.g., grooming for "sexploitation").

Department of Homeland Security. (2015). *Law Enforcement Cyber Incident Reporting.* **Washington, DC: Author.**
http://www.dhs.gov/sites/default/files/publications/Law%20Enforcement%20Cyber%20Incident%20Reporting.pdf
Cyber threats from malicious actors are a growing concern across the United States. Voluntary sharing of incident information between state, local, tribal, and territorial (SLTT) law enforcement and the federal government is important to ensuring a safe and secure cyberspace. This document details different ways SLTT law enforcement partners can report suspected or confirmed cyber incidents to the federal government. No matter which "door" SLTT law enforcement uses, information is shared within the federal government to provide an appropriate response while protecting citizens' privacy and civil liberties under the law.

Davis, J. T. (2010). *Computer Crime in North Carolina 2010: Assessing the Needs of Local Law Enforcement.* **Raleigh, NC: Governor's Crime Commission, Criminal Justice Analysis Center.**
https://www.ncdps.gov/div/gcc/pdfs/pubs/cybercrime.pdf
This study finds that around 6% of investigations in North Carolina included a cybercrime component and that 26.6% of investigators were trained in computer-related investigations. Most agencies expected an increase in computer-related crime cases in the next 5 years. The study recommends funding pilot sites for joint training sessions and equipment upgrades.

National White Collar Crime Center. (2013). *National White Collar Crime 2013 Annual Report.* **Glen Allen, VA: Author. BJA and OJJDP Sponsored.**
http://www.nw3c.org/docs/nw3c-annual-reports/2013-nw3c-annual-report.pdf?sfvrsn=6
This annual report highlights NW3C's accomplishments from January through December 2013. According to the report, NW3C delivered 435 training courses to 10,392 law enforcement professionals from 5,028 agencies in 39 states. Among other achievements, NW3C developed new courses, including Cyber Investigation 335 (Advanced Wireless Network Investigations), which focuses on techniques and methods to locate wireless devices connected to wireless networks.

Websites

National White Collar Crime Center
http://www.nw3c.org/

National Criminal Justice Training Center
https://www.ncjtc.org/BJA1/Pages/BJA1.aspx

Internet Crime Complaint Center
http://www.ic3.gov/default.aspx

The United States Department of Justice (Computer Crime and Intellectual Property Section)
http://www.justice.gov/criminal-ccips

Harold Rogers Prescription Drug Monitoring Program

Project Description

Out of increasing concern for the growing consumption and potential misuse of prescription drugs, 49 states have implemented prescription drug monitoring programs (PDMPs). PDMPs are tools that address prescription drug diversion and abuse. The programs improve patient care, supply data analysis that can identify at-risk populations and individuals, and provide critical investigation and regulatory services to reduce diversion and fraud related to controlled substance prescription medications. PDMPs have had strong support across the states, and they have expanded over time.[22] Every state but Missouri has PDMPs, as does one territory (Guam). The District of Columbia is working toward completing a PDMP.

Partners and Professional Organizations:
- ✓ Office of National Drug Control Policy
- ✓ PDMP Center of Excellence
- ✓ Substance Abuse and Mental Health Services Administration
- ✓ Drug Enforcement Administration
- ✓ Food and Drug Administration
- ✓ Centers for Disease Control and Prevention

The Harold Rogers Prescription Drug Monitoring Program supports several objectives to improve the operation and enhancement of PDMPs. The funding program enables states to better collect and analyze controlled substance prescription data through a centralized database administered by an authorized state agency. Program objectives include building a data collection and analysis system at the state level, enhancing existing programs' ability to analyze and use collected data, facilitating states' exchange of collected prescription data, and assessing the efficiency and effectiveness of the programs funded under this initiative. Furthermore, BJA provides funds to support the interstate exchange of PDMP data,[23] state and local multidisciplinary teams to develop holistic drug abuse reduction strategies, and tribal agencies to partner with existing PDMPs.

Highlighted Reports

Freeman, P. R., Goodin, A., Troske, S., & Talbert, J. (2015, March). *Kentucky House Bill 1 Impact Evaluation.* **BJA sponsored. Lexington, KY: Institute for Pharmaceutical Outcomes and Policy.**
http://www.chfs.ky.gov/NR/rdonlyres/8D6EBE65-D16A-448E-80FF-30BED11EBDEA/0/KentuckyHB1ImpactStudyReport03262015.pdf
In July 2015, the University of Kentucky's Institute for Pharmaceutical Outcomes and Policy released a BJA-funded study that examined the impact of Kentucky's HB1, which was enacted during a special session in 2012. HB1 included multiple strategies to prevent the abuse and diversion of prescription drugs, including mandatory registration with the Kentucky All Schedule Prescription Electronic Reporting (KASPER) system and the requirement to query the KASPER system under particular circumstances.

---

[22] Office of National Drug Control Policy (2011). Prescription Drug Monitoring Programs. NCJ 235722. Retrieved from https://www.ncjrs.gov/pdffiles1/ondcp/pdmp.pdf
[23] Bureau of Justice Assistance (2013). Harold Rogers Prescription Drug Monitoring Program Fact Sheet. BJA, NCJ 244536. Retrieved from https://www.bja.gov/Publications/PDMP.pdf

PDMP Center of Excellence at Brandeis (2014, September). *Briefing on PDMP Effectiveness.* **Waltham, MA: Author. BJA sponsored.**
http://www.pdmpexcellence.org/sites/all/pdfs/Briefing%20on%20PDMP%20Effectiveness%203rd%20revision.pdf
This resource highlights research studies, evaluations, surveys, and other reports demonstrating PDMP effectiveness in improving medical care, reducing doctor shopping and prescription fraud, and assisting in drug diversion investigations. The paper synthesizes findings into common themes and trends related to PDMP effects. For example, research suggests that use of PDMP data can further clinically appropriate prescribing, improve medical care, and reduce doctor shopping and its contribution to drug-related deaths. Additional findings suggest that states with PDMPs have smaller increases in opiate exposures related to abuse and misuse and lower outpatient drug claims.

PDMP Center of Excellence at Brandeis University. (2014, April). *PDMPs and Third-Party Payers Meeting, December 2012: Report of Proceedings.* **Waltham, MA: Author. BJA sponsored. NCJ 247151.**
http://www.pdmpexcellence.org/sites/all/pdfs/Brandeis_COE_PDMP_3rd_pty_payer_mtg_rpt.pdf
This ground-breaking report recommends that medical insurers use prescription monitoring data to reduce overdoses, deaths, and health care costs associated with abuse of opioids and other prescription drugs. The recommendations come from a meeting of 77 experts, including 9 PDMP directors.

PDMP Center of Excellence at Brandeis University. (2014, October). *Using PDMP Data to Guide Interventions with Possible At-Risk Prescribers.* **Waltham, MA: Author. BJA sponsored.**
http://www.pdmpexcellence.org/sites/all/pdfs/Using_PDMP_Data_Guide_Interventions_at_Risk_Prescribers.pdf
The prescription drug abuse epidemic is driven in part by a minority of prescribers who over-prescribe or misprescribe controlled substances, especially opioids and benzodiazepines. This report refers to prescribers who deviate from accepted standards of practice or whose prescribing is unusual or uncharacteristic for their specialty as *at-risk* prescribers. Identifying and intervening where appropriate with at-risk prescribers is a key strategy in efforts to control prescription drug misuse and diversion.

PDMP Center of Excellence at Brandeis University. (2015, February). *Use of PDMP Data by Opioid Addiction Treatment Programs.* **Waltham, MA: Author. BJA sponsored.**
http://www.pdmpexcellence.org/sites/all/pdfs/Use%20of%20PDMP%20data%20by%20opioid%20treatment%20programs.pdf
This briefing describes how a convenience (nonrandom) sample of opioid treatment programs and office-based opioid treatment program providers is currently using PDMP data and the benefits and limitations of such use. Although the programs described here are not necessarily representative, similar procedures are likely followed by many of the addiction treatment providers that access their state's PDMP. The objectives, in all cases, are the same: to keep patients safe and healthy, maximize the effectiveness of addiction treatment, and curtail the diversion of controlled substances.

PDMP Center of Excellence at Brandeis University. (2015, May). *COE Briefing on PDMP Delegate Account Systems.* **Waltham, MA: Author. BJA sponsored.**
http://www.pdmpexcellence.org/sites/all/pdfs/COE%20Briefing%20on%20Delegate%20Account%20Systems.pdf
As identified in a recent survey, a significant barrier to prescriber use of PDMPs is the time consumed in retrieving prescription information. To address this problem, many states allow primary or master PDMP account holders (e.g., prescribers, dispensers) to designate nonprescribing employees in their practices to access the database via delegate accounts. This saves the master account holder the time of inputting patient names and downloading PDMP data. The number of states authorizing delegate accounts has increased rapidly, from 1 state (Utah) in 2010, to 12 in 2012, to 36 in 2014. The addition of delegate accounts has been identified as a PDMP best practice. To assist states in setting up their own delegate accounts, this briefing describes well-established systems in Maine, Washington, and Kentucky.

Clark, T., Eadie, J., et al. (2012). *Prescription Drug Monitoring Programs: An Assessment of the Evidence for Best Practices.* **Waltham, MA:The Prescription Drug Monitoring Program Center of Excellence, Heller School for Social Policy and Management, Brandeis University. Prepared for The Pew Charitable Trusts.**
http://www.pdmpexcellence.org/sites/all/pdfs/Brandeis_PDMP_Report.pdf
This report covers the history of PDMPs and why they were developed. It also covers evidence-based best practices and the evidence for effectiveness and the relative strength of the methods and evidence used. The report concludes with recommendations and outlines a research agenda, suggesting the kinds of studies needed to produce a stronger evidence base for practices to improve PDMP effectiveness.

Office of National Drug Control Policy. (2011). *Epidemic: Responding to America's Prescription Drug Abuse Crisis.* **Washington, DC: Office of National Drug Control Policy Prescription Drug Abuse Prevention Plan.**
https://www.whitehouse.gov/sites/default/files/ondcp/issues-content/prescription-drugs/rx_abuse_plan.pdf
This report describes the rise in illicit use of prescription drugs amongst Americans. The report stresses that we must educate our society to the dangers of using and abusing prescriptions meds. Health care provider education to the dangers of overprescribingis also needed. The report goes into detail about the PDMP, its history, how it is used to detect and prevent the diversion and abuse of prescription drugs, and how it allows for the collection and analysis of prescription data.

NIJ-Sponsored Evaluations

Freeman, P., Blumenschein, K., Goodin, A., Higgins, G. E., Talbert, J., Vito, G. F., & Wixson, S. (2015, September). *Optimizing prescription drug monitoring programs to support law enforcement activities.* **Washington, DC: DOJ. NIJ sponsored. NCJ 249186.**
https://www.ncjrs.gov/pdffiles1/nij/grants/249186.pdf
Reduced diversion (e.g., doctor shopping; theft; prescription forgery;illegal sale by physicians, patients, or pharmacists) and abuse of prescription drugs are goals for all PDMPs. However, there is variability in how individual states implement and operationalize these programs, including policies and mechanisms for law enforcement access and utilization. This project used qualitative and quantitative methods to examine law enforcement use and perceptions of PDMPs. Findings suggest that training in how to access PDMPs and interpret PDMP reports are important factors in how law enforcement personnel perceive the utility and effectiveness of PDMPs. In addition, law enforcement personnel view lack of access to PDMP data from surrounding states as a hindrance to investigations. The variability in how states permit law enforcement access to PDMP data should be further studied to clarify the impact of various access designs on PDMP goals, including reductions in abuse, diversion, morbidity, and mortality related to illicit prescription drug use.

OJP-Sponsored Evaluations[24]

Butler, S., & Harnisch, B. (2011). *Scheduled Prescription Drug Distribution in Wyoming: Analysis of the Wyoming Prescription Drug Monitoring Program 2004–2009.* **Laramie, WY: Wyoming Survey & Analysis Center, University of Wyoming. BJA sponsored. NCJ 238746.**
http://www.jrsa.org/pubs/sac-digest/documents/wy_prescription_drug_monitoring_04-09.pdf
This report provides a focused, detailed description of prescribing patterns in Wyoming over the study period. It examined statewide prescribing patterns of Schedule II and above drugs as recorded through the Wyoming PDMP, which contains prescribing information for drugs that have high potential for abuse. This method is used to examine the data because this measure quantifies "levels of volume" in prescribing both over time and geographically (with the available data in the PDMP). With the nonpersonally identifiable data set provided by the Wyoming State Board of Pharmacy, the analyses conducted as part of this project cannot definitively determine whether variation in prescribing patterns geographically (or

---

[24] For each article, a link has been provided to either the full-length document or the link where it can be accessed.

over time) provide proof of greater or lesser abuse, diversion, addiction, or irresponsible prescribing. The data show that there is substantial variation in prescribing some drugs over time, both statewide and by county, and also by prescriber.

Garrettson, M., & Ringwalt C., et al. (2013). *An Evaluation of the North Carolina Controlled Substances Reporting System: Part I User Surveys.* **Waltham, MA:The Prescription Drug Monitoring Program Center of Excellence, Heller School for Social Policy and Management, Brandeis University Funded by BJA.**

http://pdmpexcellence.org/sites/all/pdfs/NC_control_sub_eval_pt_1.pdf

Because of an alarming increase in prescription drug overdoses in North Carolina, the PDMP was implemented to collect data on prescription drugs and to make these data available for various uses, including patient care, public health surveillance, and law enforcement investigations. The North Carolina Controlled Substances Reporting System (CSRS) was created to monitor substance abusers and to efficiently stop diversion of prescription drugs. This is the first external CSRS evaluation since its implementation in 2007. The study sample included registered prescribers. The evaluation included several important findings; for example, a quarter of the providers and pharmacists surveyed were unaware of CSRS, suggesting the need to include a module that provides instructions on how to access the system and the benefits for using such a system in North Carolina's medical, nursing, and school curricula.

OJP-Sponsored Research

PDMP Center of Excellence at Brandeis. (2014). *Guidance on PDMP Best Practices: Options for Unsolicited Reporting.* **Waltham, MA: Author. BJA sponsored.**

http://www.pdmpexcellence.org/sites/all/pdfs/Brandeis_COE_Guidance_on_Unsolicited_Reporting_final.pdf

This guidance document outlines the rationale and basic procedures for unsolicited reporting, including a discussion of criteria and thresholds in PDMP data used to select individuals for reporting, and options for reporting by current PDMP practice.

PDMP Center of Excellence at Brandeis. (2014). *Mandating PDMP Participation by Medical Providers: Current Status and Experience in Selected States.* **Waltham, MA: Author. BJA sponsored.**

http://www.pdmpexcellence.org/sites/all/pdfs/COE_briefing_mandates_2nd_rev.pdf

This briefing describes the status of state mandates and the implementation and outcomes thus far of mandates in Kentucky, Tennessee, New York, and Ohio. It also highlights policy and implementation issues for states considering mandates. Experience in the states that have implemented PDMPs shows that mandates for registration decrease prescription of commonly abused controlled substances.

PDMP Center of Excellence. (2010). *Trends in Wyoming PMP Prescription History Reporting: Evidence for a Decrease in Doctor Shopping.* **Waltham, MA: Author. BJA sponsored.**

http://www.pdmpexcellence.org/sites/all/pdfs/NFF_wyoming_rev_11_16_10.pdf

This report provides an analysis and summary of trends identified through the Wyoming PMP. The data, gathered from the reports received by PMP medical providers, reveal that a decrease in unsolicited reports is tied to a reduction in doctor shopping. This is because medical providers in Wyoming have become more informed about their patients' prescription histories and have used this information for subsequent prescriptiosn. Therefore, sending out unsolicited reports, the timeliness of prescription history data, quicker report turnaround, and what Wyoming Board of Pharmacy officials described as "good customer service" all seemed to incentivize provider use of the Wyoming PMP system, which in turn helps reduce doctor shopping among the population tracked by the program.

PDMP Center of Excellence. (2011). *Nevada's Proactive PMP: The Impact of Unsolicited Reports.* **Waltham, MA: Author. BJA sponsored.**
http://www.pdmpexcellence.org/sites/all/pdfs/nevada_nff_10_26_11.pdf
This report provides an analysis and summary of trends identified through the Nevada PMP. In reviewing the data gathered from the PMP users, the authors concluded that the decision to issue unsolicited reports paid off, both as a strategy to generate awareness and interest in the PMP and as a tool to improve clinical practice and change patient behavior. Nevada's unsolicited reporting initiative set an important precedent in the design and goals of an effective PMP, one that proactively engages the resources of the medical community in fighting prescription drug abuse.

Academic Articles

Baehren, D. F., Marco, C. A., et al. (2010). "A Statewide Prescription Monitoring Program Affects Emergency Department Prescribing Behaviors." *Annals of Emergency Medicine, 56*(1): 19–23.
http://www.ncbi.nlm.nih.gov/pubmed/20045578
This paper presents results of a study seeking to evaluate an online prescription monitoring program shortly after it was implemented in Ohio. The Ohio Automated Rx Reporting System (OARRS) was implemented to monitor controlled substance prescriptions. This study identifies the influence of OARRS data on clinical management of emergency department (ED) patients with painful conditions. OARRS data revealed that among 179 participants, high numbers of narcotics prescriptions were filled in the more recent 12 months. Numerous providers prescribed narcotics for patients. Patients had filled narcotics prescriptions at different pharmacies. Eighteen providers are represented in the study. Four providers treated 63% ($n = 114$) of the patients in the study. After review of the OARRS data, providers changed the clinical management in 41% ($n = 74$) of cases. In cases of altered management, the majority (61%; $n = 45$) resulted in fewer or no opioid medications prescribed than originally planned, whereas 39% ($n = 29$) resulted in more opioid medication than previously planned. Following the analysis, the study concluded that a statewide narcotic registry frequently altered prescribing behavior for management of ED patients with complaints of nontraumatic pain.

Brady, J.E., Wunsch, H., et al. (2014). "Prescription Drug Monitoring and Dispensing of Prescription Opioids." *Public Health Reports, 129*(2): 139–147.
http://www.ncbi.nlm.nih.gov/pubmed/24587548
Many states have implemented electronic PDMPs in an effort to deter abuse of controlled substances. This study evaluates the impact of state PDMPs on opioid dispensing. The study found that the annual MMEs dispensed per capita increased progressively until 2007 before stabilizing. Adjusting for temporal trends and demographic characteristics, implementation of state PDMPs was associated with a 3% decrease in MMEs dispensed per capita ($p = 0.68$). The impact of PDMPs on MMEs dispensed per capita varied markedly by state, from a 66% decrease in Colorado to a 61% increase in Connecticut. Based on the findings, it was concluded that implementation of state PDMPs up to 2008 did not show a significant impact on per capita opioids dispensed. The authors recommend that to control the diversion and abuse of prescription drugs, state PDMPs may need to improve their usability, implement requirements for committee oversight of the PDMP, and increase data sharing with neighboring states.

Deyo, R.A., Irvine, J.M., et al. (2013). "Measures Such as Interstate Cooperation Would Improve the Efficacy of Programs to Track Controlled Drug Prescriptions." *Health Affairs, 32*(3): 603–613.
http://www.ncbi.nlm.nih.gov/pubmed/23406570
In response to increasing abuse of prescription drugs, almost all states have implemented monitoring programs to track prescriptions of controlled medications. Although these programs were originally designed to help law enforcement officials and regulatory agencies spot possible illegal activity, health care providers have begun to use this data to help improve patient safety and quality of care. In this study, the authors reviewed government documents, expert white papers, articles from the peer-reviewed medical literature, and reports of the experiences of local health officials and concluded that PDMPs are a benefit to both law enforcement and health care delivery. However, the programs and their overall impact

on drug abuse and illegal activity remains unclear. The study recommends that improving the efficacy of PDMPs will require such changes as more standardization and interstate cooperation, better training of providers, more secure funding, and further evaluation.

Feldman, L., Williams, K. S., & Coates, J. (2012). "Influencing Controlled Substance Prescribing: Attending and Resident Physician Use of a State Prescription Monitoring Program." *Pain Medicine, 13*: 908–914.

http://www.ncbi.nlm.nih.gov/pubmed/22681237

The purpose of this study is to evaluate the influence of attending physician awareness and utilization of a state prescription monitoring program on resident physician behavior. Twenty-five attending physicians and 70 residents in emergency medicine, internal medicine, neurology, pediatrics, and psychiatry completed an 11-item questionnaire assessing awareness and utilization of a state PDMP. Residents who used the system had, on average, a higher proportion of supervising attendings using the system; residents required to utilize the system had the highest proportion of attendings using the system. Overall, almost 90% of the physicians who utilized the system did so due to concerns surrounding prescription drug abuse. More than one third of attending physicians reported increasing the quantity or amount of medication prescribed after utilizing the system, whereas no residents reported similar outcomes. Through the behavioral influence of supervising attending physicians, residents were significantly more likely to utilize the system.

Gugelmann, H., Perrone, J., & Nelson, L. (2012). "Windmills and Pill Mills: Can PDMPs Tilt the Prescription Drug Epidemic?" *Journal of Medical Toxicology, 8*(4): 378–386.

http://www.ncbi.nlm.nih.gov/pmc/articles/PMC3550255/pdf/13181_2012_Article_273.pdf

PDMPs are state-based registries of prescriptions for specific controlled substances. This overview describes the history and funding of these databases, addresses the characteristics thought to be of greatest utility for PDMPs, and reviews current literature regarding their effectiveness and potential limitations. Although more extensive research on PDMP outcomes is needed, these databases are an essential component in ongoing efforts to establish safe and compassionate prescription opioid stewardship.

Blumenschein, K., Fink, J. L., Freeman, P. R., Kirsh, K. L., Steinke, D. T., & Talbert, J. (2010). *Independent Evaluation of the Impact and Effectiveness of the Kentucky All Schedule Prescription Electronic Reporting Program (KASPER)*. **Lexington, KY: University of Kentucky**

http://www.chfs.ky.gov/NR/rdonlyres/24493B2E-B1A1-4399-89AD-1625953BAD43/0/KASPEREvaluationFinalReport10152010.pdf

This independent evaluation of KASPER consisted of five main components: a review of the current status of PMDPs in the United States; interviews with key stakeholders of the KASPER program, including professional licensure boards and law enforcement officials; a survey of KASPER system users; an analysis of KASPER usage, including the impact of KASPER on health care and law enforcement; anduse of national and other relevant data sets (including ARCOS, TEDS, and Kentucky Medicaid) to assess the potential impact of KASPER on controlled substances (CS) diversion and abuse. Insight into the value of the KASPER program was gleaned from stakeholder interviews. Analysis of national data sets revealed that the distribution of CSs to Kentucky and its contiguous states continues to rise, as does the rate of admission to substance abuse treatment facilities for opiate abuse.

Katz, N., Panas, L., et al. (2010). "Usefulness of Prescription Monitoring Programs for Surveillance Analysis of Schedule II Opioid Prescription Data in Massachusetts, 1996–2006." *Pharmacoepidemiology and Drug Safety, 19*(2): 115–123.

http://www.ncbi.nlm.nih.gov/pubmed/20014166

Electronic prescription monitoring programs (PMPs) have been developed in many states as a public health surveillance tool. The authors have analyzed 11 years of Massachusetts PMP data to evaluate trends in opioid prescribing, dispensing, and usage. The researchers found that the number of prescriptions, doses prescribed, and people receiving Schedule II prescription opioids steadily increased from 1996 to 2006. Most people (87.5%) used 1–2 prescribers, 1–2 pharmacies, and had no early refills

(2006). The greater the number of prescribers used, the greater the number of pharmacies used. When defined as the use of ≥ 4 prescribers and ≥ 4 pharmacies, questionable activity accounted for 2,748 people, 47,953 prescriptions, and 2,966,056 doses (2006). The Schedule II opioid most highly associated with questionable activity was short-acting oxycodone. The research concluded that PMPs can become a useful public health surveillance tool to monitor the medical and nonmedical use of prescription opioids and to inform public health and safety policy.

Kerlikowske, G., Jones, C.M., Labelle, R.M., & Condon, T.P. (2011). "Prescription Drug Monitoring Programs: Lack of Effectiveness or a Call to Action." *Pain Medicine,* **687–689.**
http://onlinelibrary.wiley.com/doi/10.1111/j.1526-4637.2011.01108.x/abstract
The authors reflect on the study on the effectiveness of PDMPs. They argue that the utilization of PDMPs by health care providers was not assessed or accounted for when determining the impact PDMPs had on overdose mortality or opioid consumption rates. They suggest that the findings of the study serves as a call to action for health care providers and policymakers to fully embrace PDMPs as an intervention to improve public health.

Li, G., Brady, J.E., et al. (2014). "Prescription Drug Monitoring and Drug Overdose Mortality." *Injury Epidemiology, 1*:e9–e9.
http://www.injepijournal.com/content/1/1/9
The researchers analyzed demographic and drug overdose mortality data for state-quarters with and without PDMPs in 50 states and the District of Columbia between 1999 and 2008. During the 10-year study period, there were a total of 2,040 state-quarters (10×4×51; the District of Columbia was treated as a state), including 619 in which PDMPs were operational in 31 states with varying implementation dates. They estimated adjusted risk ratios and 95% confidence intervals of drug overdose mortality associated with the implementation of state PDMPs through multivariable negative bionomial regression modeling. The study concluded that implementation of PDMPs did not reduce drug overdose mortality in most states through 2008. It further concluded that we need program enhancements that help health care practitioners access and use prescription drug monitoring data systems.

Manchikanti, L. (2006). "Prescription Drug Abuse: What Is Being Done to Address this New Drug Epidemic? Testimony Before the Subcommittee on Criminal Justice, Drug Policy and Human Resources." *Pain Physician, 9*(4): 287–321.
https://www.asipp.org/documents/PrescriptiondrugabuseWhatisbeing.pdf
This comprehensive health policy review of the prescription drug abuse epidemic is based on the written and oral testimony of witnesses at a July 26, 2006, congressional hearing, including that of Laxmaiah Manchikanti, M.D., the chief executive officer of the American Society of Interventional Pain Physicians, and additions from review of the literature. The hearing's purpose was to explore the extent to which federal efforts are aimed at reducing the incidence of prescription drug abuse and the success of such efforts. The subcommittee was particularly focused on exploring the extent to which the Food and Drug Administration and the Drug Enforcement Agency are working to minimizing the abuse and diversion of controlled substances. This is a comprehensive policy review seeking to present the causes of the prescription drug abuse epidemic, what is being done about it, and further suggestions for future research.

Morgan, L., Weaver, M., Sayeed, Z., & Orr, R. (2012). "The Use of Prescription Monitoring Programs to Reduce Opioid Diversion and Improve Patient Safety." *Journal of Pain and Palliative Care Pharmacotherapy, 27*(1): 4–9.
http://www.ncbi.nlm.nih.gov/pubmed/23190160
There has been an increase in the prescribing of opioids in an effort to improve management of chronic pain, and this has led to enhanced availability of controlled substances for diversion and abuse. Evidence suggests that the use of PMPs may help curb this growing public health issue. The current use of PMPs varies widely from state to state, but there have been important changes improving interstate interconnectivity of PMPs. This paper describes data on the effect of PMPs on reducing abuse and

diversion of controlled substances. It also offers suggestions on how PMPs may be incorporated into practice and clinical decisionmaking to ensure appropriate pain management and patient safety.

Paulozzi, L. J., Kilbourne, E. M. et al. (2011). "Prescription Drug Monitoring Programs and Death Rates from Drug Overdose." *Pain Medicine, 12*(5): 747–754.
http://www.ncbi.nlm.nih.gov/pubmed/21332934
This observational study of the United States during 1999 and 2005 seeks to determine the rates of drug overdose mortality, opioid overdose mortality, and opioid consumption by state. The researchers found that PDMPs were not significantly associated with lower rates of drug overdose or opioid overdose mortality or lower rates of consumption of opioid drugs. When compared, PDMP states consumed significantly greater amounts of hydrocodone and not significantly lower amounts of Schedule II opioids. Furthermore, during 1999 and 2005, overdose mortality rates were significantly lower in three PDMP states (California, New York, and Texas) that required use of special prescription forms. The researchers concluded that although PDMPs are an important tool to prevent the nonmedical use of prescribed controlled substances, their impact is not reflected in drug overdose mortality rates. Their effect on overall consumption of opioids appears to be minimal. They recommend that PDMP data must be used in improved ways to address the problem of prescription drug overdoses.

Paulozzi, L. J., & Stier, D. D. (2010). "Prescription Drug Laws, Drug Overdoses, and Drug Sales in New York and Pennsylvania." *Journal of Public Health Policy, 31*(4): 422–432.
http://www.ncbi.nlm.nih.gov/pubmed/21119649
Death by drug overdose has nearly doubled in the United States from 1999 to 2004, with most of the increase due to prescription drug overdoses. Studying mortality rates in states that did not experience such increases may identify successful prescription overdose prevention strategies. The authors compared New York, a state that did not experience an overdose increase, with its neighbor, Pennsylvania. New York and Pennsylvania had PDMPs, but New York's PDMP was better funded and made use of serialized, tamperproof prescription forms. Per capita usage of the major prescription opioids in New York was two-thirds that of Pennsylvania. The drug overdose death rate in Pennsylvania was 1.6 times than that of New York in 2006.

Worley, J. (2012). "Prescription Drug Monitoring Programs, a Response to Doctor Shopping: Purpose, Effectiveness, and Directions for Future Research." *Issues in Mental Health Nursing* **33:319–328.**
http://www.ncbi.nlm.nih.gov/pubmed/22545639
The following study calls for the need to develop an understanding and reach in the effects of PDMPs on prescribing practices and the perspective of health practitioners on PDMPs. The paper argues that there is a lack of research in this area, where only 11 articles were published in this topic in the last 10 years. The growing concern regarding the rise of prescription drug abuse worldwide necessitates the development of more research to help better understand behavior of health care professionals and patients toward PDMPs. Despite implementation of PDMPs, prescription drug rates for controlled substances and abuse rates have risen.

Other Articles

Durkin, C., et al. (2010). *Cost-Benefit Analysis of a Prescription Drug Monitoring Program in Wisconsin.* **Waltham, MA: PDMP Center of Excellence, Brandeis University.**
http://cbkb.org/wp-content/uploads/2012/07/Prescription_Drugs_2010.pdf
This study developed cost-benefit models that could be used to assess the potential impact of a PDMP in Wisconsin. Based on economic efficiency, the authors recommend that the pharmacy examining board contract with the vendor health information designs to implement and run Wisconsin's PDMP.

Florida Department of Health. (2013). *Florida Prescription Drug Monitoring Program (PDMP) Annual Report, 2012–2013.* **Tallahassee, FL: E-FORCE**

http://www.floridahealth.gov/statistics-and-data/e-forcse/news-reports/_documents/2012-2013pdmp-annual-report.pdf

This report highlights the accomplishments of the Florida PDMP in reducing abuse, misuse, and diversion of controlled substance prescription drugs in the program's second full year of implementation. The Florida Department of Health has collaborated with law enforcement agencies, the Attorney General's office, and privacy stakeholders to strengthen policies that protect health information. Overall, Florida has seen promising results since the implementation of the program. For example, there is a significant decrease in deaths caused by oxycodone, and overall drug deaths fell by 10 percent. Additionally, prescriptions for drugs such as oxycodone and methadone fell by 24 percent. Furthermore, the program has contributed to a decrease in doctor shopping and controlled substance-related deaths while supporting sound clinical prescribing, dispensing, and use of controlled substances.

Irvine, J. M., Hallvik, S. E., et al. (2014). "Who Uses a Prescription Drug Monitoring Program and How? Insights from a Statewide Survey of Oregon Clinicians." *The Journal of Pain: Online* **First.**

http://www.ncbi.nlm.nih.gov/pubmed/24787089

This study examined differences between PDMP users and nonusers and how clinicians in various specialties use PDMPs in practice. The study presents the results of a random sample study of Oregon providers with 1,065 respondents. Clinicians in emergency medicine, primary care, and pain and addiction specialties were the largest number of registrants but many frequent prescribers of controlled substances were not registered to use the PDMP. Among users, 95% reported accessing the PDMP when they suspected a patient of abuse or diversion, but fewer than half would check it for every new patient or every time they prescribe a controlled drug. Nearly all PDMP users reported that they discuss worrisome PDMP data with patients; 54% reported making mental health or substance abuse referrals, and 36% reported sometimes discharging patients from the practice. Clinicians reported frequent patient denial or anger, and only occasional requests for help with drug dependence. The authors recommend the need for more research to optimize how clinicians use PDMPs across settings and how clinicians and patients respond to the data. A better understanding of effective PDMP use will facilitate access to treatment for patients with pain while curbing the prescription drug epidemic, and may ultimately reduce abuse, misuse, and overdose death.

Lambert, D. (2007). *Impact Evaluation of Maine's Prescription Drug Monitoring Program.* **Portland, ME: Muskie School of Public Service, University of Southern Maine..**

http://muskie.usm.maine.edu/Publications/ihp/PrescDrugMonitoringPgrmExecSum.pdf

This is an evaluation of Maine's PDMP, seeking to assess its effect on reducing prescription drug abuse and overdose. The original intent of the state's PDMP was to act as a public health and clinical intervention tool rather than as a law enforcement tool. The researchers found that over time, the prescription monitoring program has grown steadily, with the largest growth occurring with the introduction of the Web portal.

Office of National Drug Control Policy. (2011). *Advancing a New Approach to Drug Policy: Key Accomplishments.* **Washington, DC: Author. NCJ 235714.**

https://www.ncjrs.gov/pdffiles1/ondcp/newapproach.pdf

This report outlines ONDCP's key accomplishments in coordinating a government-wide public health and public safety approach to reducing drug use and its consequences in the United States. The report identified key areas for reducing prescription drug abuse.

Program Design and Evaluation Services. (2013). *Early Assessment of the Prescription Drug Monitoring Program: A Survey of Providers, Program Design, and Evaluation Services.* **Salem, OR: Multnomah County Health Department and Oregon Health Authority.**

http://www.orpdmp.com/orpdmpfiles/PDF_Files/Reports/PDES_PDMPeval_01.10.13.pdf

The Program Design and Evaluation Services developed a survey administered to providers who used PDMP in Oregon to assess the early use of the system. The report presents the survey findings. Surveys were sent to 1,100 providers chosen randomly from board lists of licensed medical doctors, physician assistants, nurse practitioners, doctors of osteopathy, dentists, and pharmacists. The response rate was 62 percent, and the final sample size was 675. Overall, there was very positive feedback about the program. Furthermore, the report concludes that it will be useful to develop solutions for barriers to registering and using the PDMP system. Other suggestions were made to improve the system interface to improve usability.

Virginia Prescription Monitoring Program. (2010). *2010 Statistics.* **Retrieved September 11, 2012.**

www.dhp.virginia.gov/dhp_programs/pmp/docs/ProgramStats/2010PMPStatsDec2010.pdf

This is a report presenting an analysis of data from the Virginia PMP programIt indicates that the program experienced exceptional growth in 2010. The program also processed a large number of requests during the year. The number of people receiving prescriptions for controlled substances in Schedules II-IV increased slightly in 2010. This seems to demonstrate that the existence of the PMP does not prevent people from receiving controlled substances for legitimate medical purposes nor does it appear to have a "chilling effect" on the prescribing habits of physicians treating those people.

Websites

PDMP Center of Excellence
http://www.pdmpexcellence.org/

Office of National Drug Control Policy, Prescription Drug Abuse
http://www.whitehouse.gov/ondcp/prescription-drug-abuse

Substance Abuse and Mental Health Services Administration
http://www.samhsa.gov/prescription-drug-misuse-abuse

Enhanced Collaborative Model to Combat Human Trafficking

Project Description

The first law addressing human trafficking was the Trafficking Victims Protection Act (TVPA) of 2000 (P.L. 106-386). The TVPA was reauthorized through the Trafficking Victims Protection Reauthorization Act (TVPRA) of 2003 (P.L. 108-193), the TVPRA of 2005 (P.L. 109-164), and the William Wilberforce Trafficking Victims Protection Reauthorization Act of 2008 (P.L. 110-457) and 2013 (H.R. 898). The TVPA and its reauthorizations seek to combat human trafficking by punishing traffickers, protecting victims, and mobilizing U.S. government agencies to wage a global anti-trafficking campaign. The TVPA includes two forms of severe trafficking: sex trafficking and labor trafficking, defined in the TVPA as:

CrimeSolutions.gov Ratings:
No ratings at this time

Partners and Professional Organizations:
- ✓ Office for Victims of Crime
- ✓ Federal Bureau of Investigation
- ✓ National Human Trafficking Resource Center

- Sex trafficking is the recruitment, harboring, transportation, provision, or obtaining of a person for the purposes of a commercial sex act, in which the commercial sex act is induced by force, fraud, or coercion, or in which the person induced to perform such an act has not attained 18 years of age.

- Labor trafficking is the recruitment, harboring, transportation, provision, or obtaining of a person for labor or services through the use of force, fraud, or coercion for the purpose of subjection to involuntary servitude, peonage, debt bondage, or slavery.

Since 2002, when Washington was the first state to enact a state human trafficking criminal statute, all 50 states have passed legislation to combat human trafficking.

In the summer of 2004, following the first National Human Trafficking Conference, BJA began building on the efforts of the Office for Victims of Crime (OVC) to assist victims of human trafficking. BJA's efforts have been two-pronged: (1) to develop training for law enforcement and communities to identify trafficking in persons and to rescue victims by working with federal law enforcement and victims service providers, and (2) to support and fund task forces based on a sound strategy of collaboration among federal, state, and local law enforcement; trafficking victim services providers; and U.S. attorney offices. BJA has funded the training as a national initiative, through the Upper Midwest Community Policing Institute (UMCPI) and in 2015, added the International Association of Chiefs of Police (IACP), as the TTA provider for human trafficking task forces. The Enhanced Collaborative Model to Combat Human Trafficking task force initiative is jointly funded by BJA and OVC. The OVC Training and Technical Assistance Center (OVC TTAC) has put together a document that contains a directory of training and technical assistance resources for anti-human trafficking task forces and service providers. The TTA providers included in the directory have the ability to assist practitioners across the nation; they have been vetted by OVC and the BJA Planning Committee.[25]

---

[25]U.S. Department of Justice, Office of Justice Programs, Office for Victims of Crime (2012). *Directory of Training and Technical Assistance Resources for Anti-Human Trafficking Task Forces and Service Providers.* Washington, DC: Author. https://www.ovcttac.gov/downloads/TTADirectory/HT_TTA_Directory_508c_12-5-12_FINAL.pdf

NIJ-Sponsored Evaluations

Caliber Associates. (2007). *Evaluation of Comprehensive Services for Victims of Human Trafficking: Key Findings and Lessons Learned.* **Washington, DC: U.S. Department of Justice. NIJ sponsored.**
https://www.ncjrs.gov/pdffiles1/nij/grants/218777.pdf
In 2002, Caliber Associates, along with the Urban Institute, began an evaluation of the Comprehensive Services for Victims of Human Trafficking. The primary goals of the evaluation were to determine the effectiveness of the Comprehensive Services in helping trafficking victims to access appropriate and adequate services, and to document the development and implementation of coordinated service delivery networks so others can learn from this experience and implement similar programs. The evaluation findings present evidence that the three Comprehensive Services initiatives had made significant progress toward achieving their shared overarching goals of improving service provision for victims. They have done this, for example, by increasing the availability of services that adequately met most client needs as reported by service providers and victims themselves.

Gibbs, D., Walters, J.L.M., et al. (2014). *Evaluation of Services for Domestic Minor Victims of Human Trafficking: Final Report* **[2009-VF-GX-0206]. Research Triangle Park, NC: RTI International. NIJ sponsored.**
https://www.ncjrs.gov/pdffiles1/nij/grants/248578.pdf
RTI International conducted a participatory process evaluation of three programs funded by DOJ OVC to identify and provide services to victims of sex and labor trafficking who are U.S citizens and lawful permanent residents under the age of 18. The goals of the evaluation were to document program implementation in the three programs, identify promising practices for service delivery programs, and inform delivery of current and future efforts to serve this population. Key findings indicate the enormous diversity of trafficked minors, the challenges of initial and continued engagement between service providers and victims, the frequency of lifelong push/pull factors that led to the victimization of these minors, and the emphasis on the vital role of trafficking service providers.

Simich, L., Goyen, L., et al. (2014). *Improving Human Trafficking Victim Identification—Validation and Dissemination of a Screening Tool* **[NCJ-246712]. Washington, DC: Vera Institute of Justice. NIJ sponsored.**
https://www.ncjrs.gov/pdffiles1/nij/grants/246712.pdf
The Vera Institute of Justice (Vera) designed, field-tested and validated a comprehensive screening tool to improve victim identification, victim services and law enforcement efforts on a nation-wide scale. Working with 11 victim service providers, Vera collected original data on more than 230 cases from interviews with potential trafficking victims and case file reviews to determine if the screening tool could reliably identify victims, including adults and minors, and domestic and foreign-born, of sex and labor trafficking. Vera also facilitated participatory evaluation by conducting focus groups and 36 in-depth interviews with service providers, trafficking survivors and law enforcement personnel to identify best practices in implementation of the screening tool. This screening tool successfully identified good practices in victim identification while accurately providing measures across multiple targets areas. This newly developed tool has shown itself to be highly reliable in predicting victimization for both sex and labor trafficking across diverse subgroups.

OJP-Sponsored Research[26]

Human trafficking is a multifaceted issue stretching beyond international borders. Its complexity requires examination of causes, practices, and responses to the crime so that countries can work together effectively against it. The articles in this section serve as evidence of the United States' continuing efforts to eliminate human trafficking nationally and internationally. Topics for these articles include evaluation of U.S. policies and challenges in combating the issue.

---

[26] For each article, a link has been provided to either the full-length document or the website where it can be accessed.

Bales, K., & Lize, S. (2005). *Trafficking in Persons in the United States: Final Report.* **Oxford, MS: University of Mississippi, Croft Institute for International Studies. NIJ sponsored.**
http://www.ncjrs.gov/pdffiles1/nij/grants/211980.pdf
This research used case studies from 1992 to 2002 to identify intervention points at each stage of the process of trafficking in persons in the United States. The report's findings address the characteristics of trafficking victims, methods traffickers used to recruit and control victims, types of work victims were forced to perform, ways victims escaped from the control of traffickers, the nature and effectiveness of law enforcement and prosecution efforts, and the effectiveness of victims services. The study concludes that a lack of understanding of trafficking in persons as a crime, a lack of sensitivity to trafficking victims, a lack of law enforcement training for dealing with the crime, and the public's demand for cheap goods and services all contribute to the continuation of trafficking and forced labor in the United States.

Banks, D., & Kyckelhahn, T. (2011). *Characteristics of Suspected Human Trafficking Incidents, 2008–2010.* **Washington, DC: U.S. Department of Justice, Office of Justice Programs, Bureau of Justice Statistics.**
http://www.bjs.gov/content/pub/pdf/cshti0810.pdf
This report—the second in a Bureau of Justice Statistics series on the characteristics of human trafficking investigations, suspects, and victims—focuses on case outcomes, including suspect arrests and the visa status of confirmed victims. It describes the characteristics of incidents entered into the Human Trafficking Reporting System by the federally funded task force beginning in 2008.

Carpenter, A., & Gates, J. (forthcoming). *Measuring the Nature and Extent of Gang Involvement in Sex Trafficking in the San Diego-Tijuana Border Region: Executive Summary* **[2012-R2-CX-0028]. San Diego, CA: University of San Diego. NIJ sponsored.**
https://www.sandiego.edu/peacestudies/documents/Executive%20Summary%20Human%20Trafficking%20Study%202015.pdf
This study had a narrow focus on an understudied area of human trafficking found in the United States, namely street gangs and their function as facilitators of sex trafficking. Researchers gathered and analyzed data from 1,205 people, including first-time prostitution offenders, current and former gang members, schools, law enforcement agencies, and victim service providers. "The study is a large-scale model of collaborative research to impact policy and practice, and serves as a national model for future research on human trafficking more broadly." Findings indicate that sex trafficking is San Diego's second largest underground economy (after drug trafficking), at least 110 different gangs are involved in the commercial exploitation of people, and 15 years of age is the average entry in child commercial sexual exploitation. The full report should be published in the forthcoming year.

Clawson, H. J., Dutch, N., et al. (2006). *Law Enforcement Response to Human Trafficking and the Implications for Victims: Current Practices and Lessons Learned [Final Report].* **Fairfax, VA: Caliber Associates. NIJ sponsored.**
http://www.ncjrs.gov/pdffiles1/nij/grants/216547.pdf
This study examines the understanding of human trafficking among law enforcement agencies working on this criminal enterprise, describes how these agencies respond to it, and discusses the implications of this response for trafficking victims. A significant percentage of state and local law enforcement personnel in key cities with known human trafficking activity were not fully informed about the nature, prevalence, and patterns of human trafficking. By increasing law enforcement personnel's knowledge and awareness of this crime, they will be better able to seek the support and technical assistance needed to identify this crime, respond to it, and assist its victims. Respondents indicated they were benefiting from human-trafficking response protocols in their daily law enforcement work.

Clawson, H. J., Dutch, N., et al. (2008). *Prosecuting Human Trafficking Cases: Lessons Learned and Promising Practices.* **Fairfax, VA: ICF International. NIJ sponsored.**
http://www.ncjrs.gov/pdffiles1/nij/grants/223972.pdf
This study examined the effectiveness of existing U.S. federal and state legislation in providing prosecutors with the tools needed to gain convictions of those charged with human trafficking, defined as "the use of force, fraud, or coercion to exploit a person for profit." The study suggested several important findings. Just over 85 percent of the 298 cases prosecuted under the federal Trafficking Victims Protection Act during the past 7 years have resulted in convictions. Prosecutors experienced in managing human-trafficking cases have collaborated with local, state, and federal law enforcement agencies and nongovernmental organizations; assisted victims in accessing services; identified key evidence; and used proven prosecutorial techniques. Convictions are just one measure of success.

Dank, M., Khan, B., et al. (2014). *Estimating the Size and Structure of the Underground Commercial Sex Economy in Eight Major U.S. Cities* **[2010-IJ-CX-1674]. Washington, DC: Urban Institute. NIJ sponsored.**
http://www.urban.org/research/publication/estimating-size-and-structure-underground-commercial-sex-economy-eight-major-us-cities/view/full_report
This paper provides some of the most comprehensive and in-depth information regarding the underground commercial sex economy across eight major cities in the United States. The authors provide a wealth of background information regarding the prevalence of human trafficking in the United States and report their findings on sex trafficking, sex work, and child pornography. They conducted additional research into the intersections of the sex, gun, and drug economies. They conclude with policy and practice implications to try and address this growing problem of abuse on a national scale.

Farrell, A., McDevitt, J., et al. (2008). *Understanding and Improving Law Enforcement Responses to Human Trafficking: Final Report.* **Boston, MA: Northeastern University, Institute on Race and Justice. NIJ sponsored.**
https://www.ncjrs.gov/pdffiles1/nij/grants/222752.pdf
This project addresses four main areas: (1) the perceptions of trafficking held by law enforcement, and the preparation agencies have taken to address the problem; (2) the frequency in which law enforcement identifies and investigates cases of human trafficking; (3) the characteristics of those cases investigated by law enforcement; and (4) the investigation and prosecution of human trafficking cases.

Owens, C., Dank, M., et al. (2014). *Understanding the Organization, Operation, and Victimization Process of Labor Trafficking in the United States* **[2011-IJ-CX-0026]. Washington, DC: Urban Institute. NIJ sponsored.**
http://www.urban.org/sites/default/files/alfresco/publication-pdfs/413249-Understanding-the-Organization-Operation-and-Victimization-Process-of-Labor-Trafficking-in-the-United-States.PDF
This study examines labor trafficking found in many industries in the United States. Findings indicate labor trafficking investigations were not prioritized by local or federal law enforcement agencies. Analysis indicated that survivors mostly escaped on their own and lived for several months or years before being connected to a specialized service provider. A lack of awareness and outreach, coupled with the victims' fear of being unauthorized, inhibited the identification of survivors. The authors provide policy and practice recommendations to improve identification and response to labor trafficking and guide future research on labor trafficking victimization.

Reichert, J., & Sylwestrzak, A. (2013). *National Survey of Residential Programs for Victims of Sex Trafficking.* **Chicago: Illinois Criminal Justice Information Authority. BJA sponsored.**
http://www.icjia.state.il.us/assets/pdf/researchreports/nsrhvst_101813.pdf
The authors surveyed residential programs for trafficking victims for the purpose of sharing available programs and services with other jurisdictions so that they might better serve victims of trafficking. This literature would contribute to wider knowledge about the availability of these programs. The study found that 33 residential programs had been implemented, 2 of which were in Illinois. However, 28 states did

not have residential programs for victims of sex trafficking. Other important findings revealed that most programs accepted both national and international victims, and the majority of the programs were designated for minor victims of sex trafficking. The paper also included other significant findings regarding characteristics of residential programs.

Academic Articles

Chacon, J. M. (2006). "Misery and Myopia: Understanding the Failures of U.S. Efforts to Stop Human Trafficking." *Fordham Law Review, 74*: 2977–3040.
http://papers.ssrn.com/sol3/papers.cfm?abstract_id=931448
The Trafficking Victims Protection Act (TVPA) was passed in 2000 and expanded and reauthorized in 2003, 2005, 2008, and 2013. To understand why the TVPA has fallen short of its goals, it must be analyzed in the context of its legal antecedents: the labor, immigration, and sex trafficking laws that existed before the TVPA and that form the bulk of its substantive provisions. This article demonstrates that long before the TVPA was enacted, legal and policy decisions were made affecting each of goal that continue to exacerbate the domestic manifestations of human trafficking and the related exploitation of undocumented migrant workers.

Chuang, J. A. (2006). "The United States as Global Sheriff: Using Unilateral Sanctions to Combat Human Trafficking." *Michigan Journal of International Law, 27*(2): 441–493.
http://papers.ssrn.com/sol3/papers.cfm?abstract_id=990098
This article examines the significance of U.S. sanctions on the the 2000 UN Protocol to Prevent, Suppress and Punish Trafficking in Persons, Especially Women and Children. It goes on to critique the potential effectiveness and suggests a framework for assessing United States sanctions..

Farrell, A., & Pfeffer, R. (2014). "Policing Human Trafficking: Cultural Blinders and Organizational Barriers." *The ANNALS of the American Academy of Political and Social Science, 653 (1)*: 46–64.
http://ann.sagepub.com/content/653/1/46.full.pdf+html
This article uses data from case records and qualitative interviews with police, prosecutors, and victim service providers in 12 counties to highlight and discuss the challenges local police face in identifying cases of human trafficking. They found that the culture of local police agencies and the perceptions of police officials about human trafficking do not support the identification of a broad range of human trafficking cases. With local definitions of human trafficking still evolving, police focus on sex trafficking of minors, which they perceive to be the most serious problem facing their communities. Another finding was that the reluctance to differentiate between vice and sex trafficking minimizes the problem of human trafficking and makes labor trafficking seem largely nonexistent.

Frank, M.J., & Terwilliger, G.Z. (2015). "Gang-Controlled Sex Trafficking." *Virginia Journal of Criminal Law, 3*: 342–434.
http://sharedhope.org/wp-content/uploads/2015/08/Gang-Sex-Trafficking-Article.pdf
This article highlights the move from traditional gang criminal enterprises toward their involvement in sex trafficking. It discusses the various ways in which gangs recruit their victims, including their reliance upon difference "pimp" typologies, the techniques used to keep their victims under their control to be continuously exploited, and how gangs are now finding ways to market/advertise their victims to "customers." The authors draw upon multiple examples of gang-related sex trafficking cases that have been prosecuted in federal courts. They conclude that due to most gangs' ability to instill fear through violence, a ready supply of assets, and strong networks of fellow offenders, gang-related sex trafficking is likely to increase. The authors argue that investigators, prosecutors, and political leaders need to remain vigilant and at the forefront of pursuing and stopping gang-related criminal activity.

McGough, M. (2013). "Ending Modern-Day Slavery: Using Research to Inform U.S. Anti-Human Trafficking Efforts." *National Institute of Justice Journal, 271*: 26–32.
https://ncjrs.gov/pdffiles1/nij/240701.pdf
This article presents the results of a study examining the challenges facing the U.S. criminal justice system in its efforts to combat human trafficking. Findings from the study include the following: (1) identifying victims of human trafficking can be extremely difficult, because perpetrators hide and move their victims; (2) the cultural and organizational characteristics of police agencies, including a lack of proactive strategies, can hinder efforts to identify victims; (3) victims are reluctant to cooperate with investigators, because they fear retaliation from traffickers or they distrust law enforcement; (4) law enforcement officers often have negative stereotypes about victims of human trafficking, especially those involved in prostitution and drug use; and (5) many human trafficking cases are often cross-jurisdictional.

Omole, C. (2016). *Human Trafficking: The Health of Men Forced into Labor Trafficking in the United States.* **(Doctoral dissertation, Walden University).**
http://scholarworks.waldenu.edu/dissertations/1980/
This quantitative study examined archival data to identify the types of trafficking men are subjected to, their health ailments, and how these differ from the health ailments of trafficked women. Archival data from 124 men subjected to human trafficking in Florida were analyzed. Findings indicated that males were more likely to have been labor trafficked compared to other forms of trafficking, and that labor trafficked people were not more susceptible to health ailments than were sex trafficked people. Also, there was a significant difference in health conditions between male and female victims, with females reporting more issues such as malnourishment, skin rash, and anxiety. Implications for social change include increased awareness of male trafficking in health care policies and human trafficking prevention efforts.

Rand, A.M. (2014). *"It's a Marathon Not a Race": Exiting the Commercial Sex Trade* **[2013-IJ-CX-0014]. (Doctoral dissertation, University of Kansas). DOJ sponsored.**
https://www.ncjrs.gov/pdffiles1/nij/grants/248978.pdf
This study used qualitative interviews with 19 sexually exploited people to examine the ways in which men and women exit the commercial sex industry. The role of social service providers throughout the process is also discussed. The author finds that successful exit from the the commercial sex industry is often a long and complex process, where many people who wish to exit need a combination of intense personal internal resources alongwith appropriate social service support. Findings from this article suggest that this unique population is not adequately provided with available social service support. The author concludes with suggestions for future social work practice, policy, and research to address this problem.

Rieger, A. (2007). "Missing the Mark: Why the Trafficking Victims Protection Act Fails to Protect Sex Trafficking Victims in the United States." *Harvard Journal of Law & Gender, 30*: 231–256.
http://www.law.harvard.edu/students/orgs/jlg/vol301/rieger.pdf
This article outlines what human trafficking is and why the Trafficking Victims Protection Act (TVPA) fails to protect sex trafficking victims. The passage of the TVPA in 2000 identified the scope and the severity of the human trafficking problem and attempted to provide protection and relief to its victims globally and domestically. This article argues that domestic victims are not being served by the TVPA's rigid provisions and unjust requirements that must be met before relief is granted. As a result, it recommends that Congress must reexamine provisions within the Act, such as TVPA certification procedures. To improve services of trafficking victims, lawmakers and officials must understand the unique needs of this population and the complexity of their circumstances so they may accurately reflect this understanding in TVPA language and enforcement.

Wooditch, A. (2011). "Efficacy of the Trafficking in Persons Report: A Review of the Evidence." *Criminal Justice Policy Review, 22*(4): 471–493.
http://search.proquest.com/docview/1013742585/452C14A212142D0PQ/1?accountid=26333
Anti-trafficking efforts have been adopted globally to curb human trafficking, yet many nations have failed to put initiatives into practice. This exploratory study investigates the efficacy of this policy by means of a longitudinal assessment of the Trafficking in Persons report's tier classifications, a system that grades countries based on anti-trafficking initiatives and determines if U.S.-funded anti-trafficking initiatives internationally target those countries in need. The findings suggest that tier ranking has not improved over time, and the United States has failed to systematically allocate funds based on the recommendations of the tier classification system. Policy recommendations and implications for future research are discussed.

Other Reports

The articles in this section outline the results of the human trafficking task forces established nationally and internationally to combat human trafficking. Some of the task forces are the result of the Trafficking Victims Protection Act of 2000. These reports demonstrate the ongoing effort to eradicate human trafficking.

California Alliance to Combat Trafficking and Slavery Task Force. (2012). *The State of Human Trafficking in California.* **Sacramento, CA: Author.**
http://oag.ca.gov/sites/all/files/agweb/pdfs/ht/human-trafficking-2012.pdf
The Attorney General of California's Department of Justice, Kamala D. Harris, created the Human Trafficking work group in 2012 to examine the nature and scope of human trafficking in California as well as to evaluate the state's efforts in combatting it. This report reflects the work group discussions held during a 3-day meeting and includes supplemental research and investigation by the California Department of Justice.

International Justice Mission (IJM). (2006). *Independent Final Evaluation of the Thailand Sex Trafficking Task Force: Prevention and Placement Program* **[IJM Cooperative Agreement Number E-9-K-2-0076]. Washington, DC: Author. U.S. Department of Labor (USDOL) Sponsored.**
http://www.dol.gov/ilab/projects/summaries/Thailand_TraffickingTaskForce_feval.pdf
On September 30, 2002, IJM received a 3-year cooperative agreement for U.S. $702,907 from the USDOL to implement the Thailand Sex Trafficking Task Force: Prevention and Placement program. A final independent evaluation of this project was conducted in 2006 to (1) determine whether the project achieved its stated objectives, (2) assess project impacts and sustainability, (3) identify lessons learned and good practices, and (4) provide recommendations for improving future project design. The program's objective of the was to contribute to reducing victimization of minors who have been trafficked or who are at risk of being trafficked into commercial sexual exploitation in northern Thailand. The USDOL-funded components of this project focused on prevention activities to lower the vulnerability of the population at risk for trafficking and on placement activities to connect victims with educational and vocational opportunities.

New York State Interagency Task Force on Human Trafficking. (2008). *A Report by the Interagency Task Force Implementation of the 2007 Law.* **Albany, NY: Author.**
http://www.criminaljustice.ny.gov/pio/humantrafficking/human_trafficking_rpt_aug08.pdf
This report presents the task force's accomplishments during its first year its, including establishing a victims service program; offering statewide training on human trafficking to law enforcement, prosecutors, and service providers; establishing collaboration between various state government agencies, law enforcement, and nongovernmental entities; and conducting awareness-raising activities statewide.

Office of Attorney General Martha Coakley. (2013). *Massachusetts Interagency Human Trafficking Policy Task Force: Findings and Recommendations.* **Boston, MA: Author.**
http://www.mass.gov/ago/docs/ihttf/ihttf-findings.pdf
This report presents a guide to addressing the issue of human trafficking in Massachusetts. The task force makes recommendations on how to coordinate services for victims in an efficient and effective way, with the goal of developing a model for other states. The report makes recommendations concerning victim services, demand reduction, data collection and information sharing, education and training, and public awareness.

Office of the Attorney General. (2012). *Texas Human Trafficking Prevention Task Force Report 2012 to the Texas Legislature.* **Austin, TX: Author.**
https://www.texasattorneygeneral.gov/files/agency/20121912_htr_fin_3.pdf
This annual report presents information on the 2012 findings from the Texas Human Trafficking Task Force. The 82nd Legislature enacted significant improvements to Texas human trafficking prevention laws. Findings show that law enforcement training has improved. Law enforcement and prosecutors responded to human trafficking with a clear message by assisting with compassionate recovery of victims and determined prosecution of offenders. The ask force is developing guidelines for victim service providers for both adults and minors. Increasing initiatives that focus on specific populations such as at-risk youth, medical professionals, and school personnel will strengthen Texas's ability to prevent victimization and identify vulnerable victims. Future initiatives should focus on developing response systems for victims, expanding current awareness and education efforts, and implementing proven tactics across Texas.

State of Alaska Task Force on the Crimes of Human Trafficking, Promoting Prostitution and Sex Trafficking. (2013). *Final Report and Recommendations.* **Juneau, AK: Author.**
http://www.law.state.ak.us/pdf/admin/021513-TaskForceFinalReport.pdf
This report summarizes the task force's recommendations on how to better identify victims and raise public awareness of human trafficking. The report outlines several recommendations for raising awareness, including high-profile media campaigns and education for youth on human and sex trafficking. Other suggestions including training law enforcement, establishing safe shelters, and evaluating legislation to allow expungement of prior prostitution convictions of trafficking victims.

State of Hawaii Department of the Attorney General. (2010). *Report of the Hawaii Anti-Trafficking Task Force.* **Honolulu, HI: The Twenty-Fifth State Legislature Regular Session. BJA sponsored.**
http://lrbhawaii.info/reports/legrpts/ag/2010/act260_slh06_10.pdf
This resource highlights activities associated with Hawaii Anti-Trafficking Task Force and Coalition efforts established through BJA program funds.

U.S. Department of Justice, Office of Justice Programs, Office for Victims of Crime and Bureau of Justice Assistance .(2013). *Anti-Human Trafficking Task Force Strategy and Operations e-Guide.* **Washington, DC: Author.**
https://www.ovcttac.gov/taskforceguide/
This guide was developed jointly by OVC and BJA. It is intended as a resource for both established and new task forces. Established task forces can use it to enhance existing operations or as a tool to help revitalize their efforts and operations. The guide offers direction and development to form new task forces to combat human trafficking. It presents a stage-by-stage outline, from startup and needs assessment, to composition and structure of the group and task force meeting dynamics. This guide can also be used as a tool for the following: to determine the strengths and weaknesses of the group according to the recommended structures and activities described in each section, to learn about new or creative approaches, and to highlight useful task force documents and resources.

U.S. Department of State. (2007). *Trafficking in Persons Report 2007.* **Washington, DC: Author.**
http://www.state.gov/documents/organization/82902.pdf
This report outlines the efforts federal agencies undertook in 2006 to help victims of human trafficking. With assistance from grants, offenders are investigated, prosecuted, and sentenced. The U.S. commitment to combating human trafficking through various efforts, including aiding domestic and international law enforcement and NGOs, are also described.

U.S. Department of State. (2007). *Victims of Trafficking and Violence Protection Act of 2000: Trafficking in Persons Report 2007.* **Washington, DC: Author.**
http://www.state.gov/j/tip/rls/tiprpt/2007/
The *Trafficking in Persons Report* is one of the most comprehensive reviews of government efforts to fight human trafficking. This is an updated global outlook on human trafficking, outlining the impact it has on the world. It further addresses policy approaches (victim rescue, health impact, supply and demand) as well as many topics of special interest that allow for a greater understanding of the scope and nature of human trafficking.

Vera Institute of Justice. (2014). *Screening for Human Trafficking: Guidelines for Administering the Trafficking Victim Identification Tool (TVIT)* **[NCJ-246713]. Washington, DC: Author. NIJ sponsored.**
https://www.ncjrs.gov/pdffiles1/nij/grants/246713.pdf
This is a manual intended to be used by victim service agency staff and other social service providers who will administer the Trafficking Victim Identification Tool (TVIT) to clients who are potential trafficking victims. This manual was developed by the Vera Institute of Justice supported by extensive research and collaborating with leading legal and victim services agencies in the United States to develop a validated screening tool and related best practices to identify trafficked persons. The Vera Institute determined that TVIT is highly reliable in predicting both sex and labor trafficking in women and men and among U.S. and international victims.

Website

Polaris Project
http://www.polarisproject.org/

Intellectual Property Theft Enforcement Program

Project Description

The Intellectual Property Theft Enforcement Program (IPEP), administered by BJA, helps state and local criminal justice systems enhance their capacity to prevent and prosecute intellectual property (IP) crimes. The program funds IP crime enforcement, investigations, and prosecutions and also supports education about IP crime laws for law enforcement professionals and members of the public. In addition, the program funds task forces to conduct investigations and acquire equipment to conduct forensic analysis of evidence.[27]

Note: No program evaluations were found. The listed articles illustrate the need for this type of program and offer information on what action the government is taking to combat intellectual property theft.

NIJ and Other OJP-Sponsored Evaluations[28]

None at this time.

Other Academic Research

Abolsky, L. (2004). "Operation Blackbeard: Is Government Prioritization Enough to Deter Intellectual Property Criminals?" *Fordham Intellectual Property, Media and Entertainment Law Journal, 14*(2): 567–602.
http://ir.lawnet.fordham.edu/cgi/viewcontent.cgi?article=1421&context=iplj&sei-redir=1&referer=http%3A%2F%2
The article explores the inception of intellectual property crimes and current criminal penalties. It focuses on why the federal government has recently prioritized this area and is now prosecuting offenders. The author concludes that vigorous prosecution and education are effective in helping to deter these crimes.

DuBose, M. M. (2005). "Criminal Enforcement of Intellectual Property Laws in the Twenty-first Century." *Columbia Journal of Law & the Arts, 29*: 481.
http://heinonline.org/HOL/Page?handle=hein.journals/cjla29&div=30&g_sent=1&collection=journals#491
This article suggests a need for stronger domestic enforcement, more resources, updated laws, and greater international cooperation in enforcement of intellectual property rights. Moreover, without a sustained international commitment to implement these recommendations, the author believes they will have little impact on intellectual property crime.

CrimeSolutions.gov Ratings:
No ratings at this time

Partners and Professional Organizations:
- ✓ **National White Collar Crime Center**
- ✓ **Federal Bureau of Investigation: Intellectual Property Theft**
- ✓ **National Intellectual Property Rights Coordination Center**
- ✓ **U.S. Department of Justice: Intellectual Property Task Force**

---

[27] More in-depth information about the program can be found at the following website:
https://www.bja.gov/ProgramDetails.aspx?Program_ID=64
[28] For each article, a link has been provided to either the full-length document or the website where it can be accessed.

Other Reports

Government Accountability Office (GAO). (2008). *Intellectual Property: Federal Enforcement Has Generally Increased, but Assessing Performance Could Strengthen Law Enforcement Efforts.* **Washington, DC: Author.**
http://www.gao.gov/new.items/d08157.pdf
In this report, GAO (1) examines roles, priorities, and resources devoted to IP-related enforcement in key federal agencies; (2) evaluates IP-related enforcement statistics and achievements among agencies; and (3) examines the status of the National Intellectual Property Rights Coordination Center. GAO reviewed relevant documents, interviewed officials in five key agencies, and analyzed agency IP enforcement data from fiscal years 2001 through 2006.

Executive Office of the President of the United States. (2012). *2011 U.S. Intellectual Property Enforcement Coordinator Annual Report on Intellectual Property Enforcement.* **Washington, DC: Author.**
http://www.whitehouse.gov/sites/default/files/omb/IPEC/ipec_annual_report_mar2012.pdf
This report outlines the U.S. federal government's coordinated efforts to address the challenges of enforcing intellectual property of U.S. rightsholders abroad. These efforts include securing supply chains; pursuing sources of counterfeit and pirated goods; and meeting the challenges posed by emerging criminal trends, such as the online sales of counterfeit pharmaceuticals, economic espionage, and targeted theft of trade secrets.

Executive Office of the President of the United States. (2012). *2012 U.S. Intellectual Property Enforcement Coordinator Joint Strategic Plan Two Year Anniversary.* **Washington, DC: Author.**
https://www.whitehouse.gov/sites/default/files/omb/IPEC/ipec_two-year_anniversary_report.pdf
This publication highlights the accomplishments from the past 2 years (2010–2012) since the implementation of the Intellectual Property Law Enforcement Coordinator Joint Strategic Plan. Topics include an increase in law enforcement presence to combat IP violations, voluntary agreements and best practices in the field, legislative recommendations, efficiency and agency coordination, and enforcing U.S. IP laws and rights on an international market. This report provides detailed successes of the strategic plan so far as well as additional information about future actions and goals.

Executive Office of the President of the United States. (2013). *2013 Joint Strategic Plan on Intellectual Property Enforcement.* **Washington, DC: Author.**
https://www.whitehouse.gov/sites/default/files/omb/IPEC/2013-us-ipec-joint-strategic-plan.pdf
This report details the the changes and advancements to the new Joint Strategic Plan compared to the original Joint Strategic Plan from 2010. Key sections of the plan include leading by example, transparency and public outreach, ensuring efficiency and coordination, enforcing our rights abroad, securing the supply chain, and data driven government. Each section provides detailed information regarding the current status of goals and what actions will be taken in the future to ensure effective intellectual property enforcement.

Executive Office of the President of the United States. (2015). *2014 Annual Report on Intellectual Property Enforcement.* **Washington, DC: Author.**
https://www.whitehouse.gov/sites/default/files/omb/IPEC/fy2014ipecannualreportchairmangoodlatteletter.pdf
This is the annual report detailing the federal government's intellectual property enforcement during the 2014 fiscal year. The report describes the implementation around the 2013 Joint Strategic Plan and further discusses what gains were made in relation to the strategic plan's goals and initiatives.

Executive Office of the President of the United States. (2015). *Special 301 Report.* **Washington, DC: Author.**

https://www.iprcenter.gov/reports/ipr-center-reports/2015-special-301-report/view

This special report is was developed though a congressionally mandated yearly effort to describe IP protection and enforcement on a global scale. This report highlights several concerns for the United States and its trade partners regarding intellectual property, including, among other points, the reported deterioration of IP protections, enforcement, and market access. The 301 report is useful because it can be used to identify both opportunities and challenges that the United States and its trade partners may come across when protecting and enforcing IP rules and regulations. The audience of this report caninform not only the nations' trading allies but also the public about the current initiatives.

Websites

National White Collar Crime Center
http://www.nw3c.org/

Federal Bureau of Investigation: Intellectual Property Theft
http://www.fbi.gov/about-us/investigate/cyber/ipr

National Intellectual Property Rights Coordination Center
http://www.iprcenter.gov/

U.S. Department of Justice: Intellectual Property Task Force
http://www.justice.gov/iptf

Edward Byrne Memorial Justice Assistance Grant

Project Description

The Edward Byrne Memorial Justice Assistance Grant (JAG) Program, administered by BJA, is the leading source of federal justice funding to state and local jurisdictions. The JAG program provides states, tribes, and local governments with critical funding necessary to support a range of program areas, including law enforcement; prosecution, courts, and indigent defense; crime prevention and education; corrections and community corrections; drug treatment and enforcement; program planning, evaluation, and technology improvement; and crime victim and witness initiatives. Grantees conduct a broad range of activities with JAG funds, including hiring and maintaining staff, paying for overtime, training, and buying equipment and/or supplies.[29]

CrimeSolutions.gov Ratings:
No ratings at this time

Partners and Professional Organizations:
✓ **National Criminal Justice Association**

Highlighted Report

NIJ-Sponsored Evaluation[30]

Dunworth, T., Haynes, P., et al. (1997). *National Assessment of the Byrne Formula Grant Program.* **Washington, DC: U.S. Department of Justice, Office of Justice Programs, National Institute of Justice.**

http://www.ncjrs.gov/pdffiles/162203.pdf

This NIJ assessment of the Byrne program found that it was well implemented at the state level. States generally complied with statutory requirements for strategic planning and for federal review of plans and observed regulatory constraints . The strategic planning process resulted in better use of resources and gave states a valuable opportunity to introduce long-term considerations into their criminal justice systems. The assessment concluded that the Byrne program fostered advances in coordination and cooperation, in particular through multijurisdictional task forces. However, structural factors in the program made it difficult to meet program evaluation requirements.

Other Evaluation

Chettiar, I., Eisen, L.-B., et al. (2013). *Reforming Funding to Reduce Mass Incarceration.* **New York: Brennan Center for Justice at NYU School of Law.**

http://www.brennancenter.org/sites/default/files/publications/REFORM_FUND_MASS_INCARC_web_0.pdf

This research, conducted by the Brennan Center for Justice, examines a new approach for funding corrections strategies aimed at reducing mass incarceration. Current research indicates that although crime and violence rates have fallen in recent years, often to historically low levels, the rate of mass incarceration has increased, with almost $80 billion spent annually to house the nation's inmates. The JAG program provides funding to state and local governments to help them deal with rising criminal justice costs. This report proposes changing JAG criteria to more closely align with today's criminal justice goals and policies. The proposal calls for DOJ to reorient JAG's performance measures to

---

[29] More in-depth information about the program can be found at the following website:
https://www.bja.gov/ProgramDetails.aspx?Program_ID=59
[30] For each article, a link has been provided to either the full-length document or the website where it can be accessed.

encourage states to modernize their criminal justice policies and practices with more effective and successful ways proven to reduce crime while reducing mass incarceration rates.

Other Reports

Cooper, A.D., & Hyland, S.S. (2015). *Justice Assistance Grant Program Technical Report* **[NCJ-249105]. Washington, DC: U.S. Department of Justice, Office of Justice Programs, Bureau of Justice Statistics.**
http://www.bjs.gov/content/pub/pdf/jagp15.pdf
This report highlights the JAG funding model and 2015 annual allocation.

Kenyon, M.D. (2015). *State and Local Funding Allocations Report: Edward Byrne Memorial Justice Assistance Grant (JAG) Program.* **Washington, DC: Bureau of Justice Assistance.**
https://www.bja.gov/Publications/JAGAllocationsReport2013.pdf
This report highlights the funding allocations of JAG grantees for calendar year 2013. It finds that the majority of JAG money is allocated toward law enforcement purposes, reflecting the heritage of the Local Law Enforcement Block Grants.

Missouri Department of Public Safety. (2007). *Missouri Department of Public Safety—Edward Byrne Memorial Justice Assistance Grant Program: FY07 State Annual Report.* **Jefferson City, MO: Author.**
http://www.jrsa.org/pubs/sac-digest/documents/missouri-fy2007-report.pdf
This report presents data on the impact of the JAG program on state and local criminal justice systems in Missouri and updates its annual JAG strategic plan. Within the report, the Missouri Department of Public Safety evaluated programs across all JAG purpose areas, using quarterly performance measurement data.

National Criminal Justice Association. (2013). *The Impact of the Byrne Justice Assistance Grant Program: How Byrne JAG is Changing the Criminal Justice System.* **Washington, DC: Author.**
http://www.ncja.org/sites/default/files/documents/System-Change-Through-the-Byrne-JAG-Program-NCJA-10-13.pdf
This report highlights the work done in the states to bring about real and lasting change in their criminal justice systems. Specific state projects in almost every U.S. state are reviewed.

U.S. Department of Justice, Office of Justice Programs, Bureau of Justice Assistance. (2013). *Program Performance Report: Justice Assistance Grant (JAG) Program, April 2011−March 2012.* **Washington, DC: Author.**
https://www.bja.gov/Publications/JAGTFApr2011-Mar2012.pdf
This report highlights activities funded by the JAG program for the April 2011–March 2012 reporting period.

U.S. Department of Justice, Office of Justice Programs, Bureau of Justice Assistance. (2014). *Edward Byrne Justice Assistance Grant (JAG) Program Fact Sheet.* **Washington, DC: Author.**
https://www.bja.gov/Publications/JAG_Fact_Sheet.pdf
This fact sheet gives an overview of the JAG program as well as answers to several frequently asked questions.

Wyatt, L., Fender, S., and Kim, T. (2013). *Grant Activity Report: Justice Assistance Grant (JAG) Program April 2012−March 2013.* **Washington, DC: U.S. Department of Justice, Office of Justice Programs, Bureau of Justice Assistance.**
https://www.bja.gov/Publications/JAG_LE_Grant_Activity_03-13.pdf
This report highlights activities funded by the JAG program for the April 2012–March 2013 reporting period.

Websites

Bureau of Justice Assistance: State and Territory Fact Sheets
http://www.iir.com/bja-state-fact-sheets/

JAG Accountability Measures Revision Page
https://www.bjaperformancetools.org/help/JAGDocs.html

Justice and Mental Health Collaboration Program

Project Description

The Justice and Mental Health Collaboration Program (JMHCP) started in 2004 with the passage of the Mentally Ill Offender Treatment and Crime Reduction Act.[31] This was a response to requests from state government officials for improvements "to the criminal justice system's response to people with mental illness." [32]

The purpose of the program is to "increase public safety" by promoting collaboration among "criminal justice, juvenile justice, mental health treatment, and substance abuse systems to increase access to treatment" for this particular population of offenders.[33] Because a large proportion of adult and juvenile offenders have mental illness or co-occurring disorders, JMHCP focuses on training for people working in the criminal justice field on how to deal with mental illness while also offering training to mental health treatment specialists on how to deal with the criminal aspects of this population.[34] Another goal is to foster communication between the criminal justice agents and the treatment professionals to make sure that all clients receive the care and services they need.

Note: JMHCP focuses on both criminal justice agencies and mental health practitioners. Many studies look at mental illness but not necessarily at both the criminal justice system and mental health services. The research cited here incorporates both, either by evaluating JMCHP programs (or programs that fit the description) or by focusing on a need for both mental health services and criminal justice to collaborate to create treatment options for this population.

NIJ-Sponsored Evaluations

Stevens, J., Kelleher, K., et al. (2014). *Aftercare Services for Juvenile Parolees with Mental Disorders: A Collaboration Between the Ohio Department of Youth Services (DYS) and Columbus Children's Research Institute* **[NCJ-245574]. Columbus, OH: Ohio Department of Youth Services. NIJ sponsored.**[35]
https://www.ncjrs.gov/pdffiles1/nij/grants/245574.pdf
Stevens and colleagues looked at care received by juveniles reentering the community. Most of these juveniles had at least one mental health disorder. The study found that there is a need for the correctional facilities to be more involved with juvenile aftercare. The researchers found "inadequate or interrupted care" led to higher recidivism rates and stressed the need for more collaboration between the criminal

---

CrimeSolutions.gov Ratings:
Effective (3)
Promising (7)
No Effect (0)
Insufficient Evidence (0)

Partners and Professional Organizations:
- ✓ Substance Abuse and Mental Health Services Administration
- ✓ GAINS Center for Behavioral Health and Justice Transformation
- ✓ Council of State Governments Justice Center

---

[31] www.bja.gov/ProgramDetails.aspx?Program_ID=66
[32] Ibid.
[33] Ibid.
[34] Ibid.
[35] This study was included even though it does not fall under an evaluation for a JMHCP program; it does stress the need for more collaboration between correctional facilities and mental health treatment services, which is an underlying goal of the program.

justice system and community services to prevent juveniles with mental health disorders from returning to the criminal justice system.

OJP-Sponsored Evaluations

Council of State Governments Justice Center. (2007). *Increasing Collaboration between Corrections and Mental Health Organizations: Orange County Case Study* **[NCJ-217283]. New York: Author. National Institute of Corrections (NIC) Sponsored.**
http://nicic.gov/Downloads/PDF/Library/022134.pdf
This Florida case study is part of a technical assistance project launched by the Council of State Governments (CSG) and NIC to improve collaboration between corrections and mental health agencies. Even though the report does not mention JMHCP, the programs that are listed would fall under the same program categories that JMHCP funds.

OJP-Sponsored Reports[36]

Comeaux, A., & Ashley, D. (2013). *Justice and Mental Health Collaboration Program: Planning— Final Project Report* **[NCJ-247205]. Jackson, WY: Teton County Board of County Commissioners. BJA sponsored.**
http://www.tetonwyo.org/systemsofcare/docs/JMHCP%20Full%20Report%20July%202013.pdf
This report highlights the activities and outcomes from the awarding of JMHCP funds to Teton County, Wyoming.

Council of State Governments Justice Center. (2012). *Justice and Mental Health Collaboration Program.* **New York: Author. BJA sponsored.**
http://csgjusticecenter.org/wp-content/uploads/2012/11/JMHCP-Brochure.2012.pdf
This resource provides information about BJA's JMHCP, including what its purpose is, what award categories it funds, what technical assistance it offers, and how to access a program's database and learning sites.

Council of State Governments Justice Center. (2002). Criminal Justice/Mental Health Consensus Project. New York: Author. BJA sponsored.
https://www.ncjrs.gov/pdffiles1/nij/grants/197103.pdf
The criminal justice/mental health consensus project came about because of the dimensions and the complexity of serving the mental health population and the problem of those with mental illness "falling through the cracks" and landing in the criminal justice system—mainly jails and prisons. This report defines measures that state legislators, law enforcement, prosecutors, defense attorneys, judges, corrections, and those involved with victim advocacy and the mental health departments can use to improve the response to people with mental illness who are in contact with the criminal justice system. The report provides 46 policy statements that can serve as a guide or prompt an initiative to improve the criminal justice system's response to people with mental illness.

CSR, Inc. (2012). *Justice and Mental Health Collaboration Program Closeout Report: January– December 2011* **[NCJ-247181]. Washington, DC: U.S. Department of Justice, Office of Justice Programs, Bureau of Justice Assistance. BJA sponsored.**
https://www.bja.gov/Programs/JMHCP2011CloseoutReport.pdf
This document is the last of a series of reports on performance measures submitted by JMHCP grantees before the measures were revised in January 2012.

---

[36] For each article, a link has been provided to either the full-length document or the website where it can be accessed.

Lynch, S. M., DeHart, D. D., Belknap, J., & Green, B. L. (2012). *Women's Pathways to Jail: The Roles & Intersections of Serious Mental Illness & Trauma.* **Washington DC: U.S. Department of Justice, Office of Justice Programs, Bureau of Justice Assistance. BJA sponsored. Grant No. 2010-DB-BX-K048.**
https://www.bja.gov/Publications/women_Pathways_to_jail.pdf
This is a multisite study that addressed the gaps in literature by assessing the prevalence of PTSD, substance abuse, and mental disorders in women in jail. The report used a random sample collected from rural and urban jails. This report reviews the understanding of how female offenders go into offending and identifies key factors and intervening variables that may have an effect (either positive or negative) on risk.

Rueland, M., Draper, L., et al. (2010). *Improving Responses to the People with Mental Illnesses: Tailoring Law Enforcement Initiatives to Individual Jurisdictions* **[NCJ-229713]. New York: Council of State Governments Justice Center and Police Executive Research Forum. BJA sponsored.**
https://www.ncjrs.gov/pdffiles1/Archive/229713NCJRS.pdf
This report goes over innovative policies and procedures that law enforcement agencies have created while working with mental health agencies and community groups. These new programs improve encounters between law enforcement personnel and people with mental illness.

Rueland, M., Draper, L., et al. (2012). *Statewide Law Enforcement/Mental Health Efforts: Strategies to Support and Sustain Local Initiatives* **[NCJ-240786]. New York: Council of State Governments Justice Center. BJA sponsored.**
https://www.bja.gov/Publications/CSG_StatewideLEMH.pdf
This report examines how states have developed structures and standards to make police encounters with people with mental illnesses safer for all involved and to produce better mental health and criminal justice system outcomes. The report offers a starting point for policymakers, practitioners, and others interested in planning or enhancing a statewide initiative to support local-level specialized policing responses such as crisis intervention and law enforcement/mental health co-response teams.

Rueland, M., & Schwarzfeld, M. (2008). *Improving Responses to the People with Mental Illnesses: Strategies for Effective Law Enforcement Training* **[NCJ-224332]. New York: Council of State Governments Justice Center. BJA sponsored.**
https://www.bja.gov/Publications/Strategies_%20for_LE_Training.pdf
This training resource guide synthesizes the key lessons learned by several jurisdictions that have developed training for police officers to help them interact effectively and appropriately with people who have mental illnesses.

Rueland, M., Schwarzfeld, M., et al. (2009). *Law Enforcement Responses to People with Mental Illnesses: A Guide to Research-Informed Policy and Practice* **[NJC-226965]. New York: Council of State Governments Justice Center. BJA sponsored.**
http://csgjusticecenter.org/wp-content/uploads/2012/12/le-research.pdf
This guide examines studies on law enforcement interactions with people with mental illnesses and translates the findings to help policymakers and practitioners develop safe and effective interventions.

Schwarzfeld, M., Rueland, M., et al. (2008). *Improving Responses to People with Mental Illnesses: The Essential Elements of a Specialized Law Enforcement–Based Program* **[NCJ-223343]. New York: Council of State Governments Justice Center. BJA sponsored.**
https://www.bja.gov/Publications/LE_Essential_Elements.pdf
This publication identifies 10 key components found in any successful law enforcement initiative to foster better outcomes in officer encounters with people with mental illnesses. The report also discusses how these key elements can help guide people in communities interested in developing a law enforcement-based program or improving the organization and functions of an existing one.

Skowyra, K. R., & Cocozza, J. J. (2007). *Blueprint for Change: A Comprehensive Model for the Identification and Treatment of Youth with Mental Health Needs in Contact with the Juvenile Justice System* **[NCJ-226427]. Delmar, NY: National Center for Mental Health and Juvenile Justice and Policy Research Associates. OJJDP Sponsored.**

http://www.ncmhjj.com/wp-content/uploads/2013/07/2007_Blueprint-for-Change-Full-Report.pdf

This report presents a conceptual and practical framework for juvenile justice and mental health systems to use when developing strategies, policies, and services aimed at improving mental health services for youth involved with the juvenile justice system. The result is a model to identify and treat mental disorders among youth at key stages of the juvenile justice process. The authors stress the need for collaboration between the juvenile justice system and mental health facilities so that juveniles can receive the proper treatment. This will help these youth to cycle out of the criminal justice system.

Academic Research

Cloud, D., & Davis , C. (2015). *First Do No Harm: Advancing Public Health in Police Practices.* **New York, NY: Vera Institute.**

http://www.vera.org/sites/default/files/resources/downloads/public-health-and-policing.pdf

This report contains recommendations on how community health providers and police can work together to promote access to health services for marginalized populations often caught up in the criminal justice system—people who live in poverty, use drugs, or live with mental illness—while reducing the cycle of arrest and incarceration. It provides practical strategies for incorporating principles of harm reduction— which aims to remedy the negative effects of drug use and other high-risk behaviors, even when people are not ready or willing to give up the behavior—and health promotion into policing practices.

Morabito, M. S., Kerr, A. N., Watson, A. C., Draine, J., & Angell, B. (2012). "Crisis Intervention Teams and People with Mental Illness: Exploring the Factors that Influence the Use of Force." *Crime & Delinquency, 58* **(1): 57–77. DOI 10.1177/0011128710372456**

http://cad.sagepub.com/content/58/1/57.short

Data from 216 officers in 4 Chicago police districts were used to examine factors that influence use of force in encounters between police and people with mental illnesses. Findings indicate a crisis intervention team (CIT) officer is likely to respond with less force for an increasingly resistant demeanor in comparison with non-CIT officers.

Erickson, C. D. (2011). "Using Systems of Care to Reduce Incarceration of Youth with Serious Mental Illness." *American Journal of Community Psychology, 49*(3–4): 404–416.

http://forensicsocialworkandthelawblog.wordpress.com/
http://link.springer.com/article/10.1007/s10464-011-9484-4#page-1

The author identifies the "systematic factors" that contribute to the "inappropriate incarceration of youth with serious mental illness." This paper also reviews ongoing efforts to address this problem and makes recommendations on how it could be fixed. It does not cover a JMHCP program but does propose that JMHCP-type programs should be used to curb overincarceration.

Assisted Outpatient Treatment (AOT)

This program was rated on CrimeSolutions.gov as effective.

Program summary: Also known as outpatient commitment, AOT is a civil legal procedure whereby a judge can order a person with a serious mental illness to follow a court-ordered treatment plan while living in the community.

Details: http://www.CrimeSolutions.gov/ProgramDetails.aspx?ID=228

Gilbert, A. R., Moser, L. L., et al. (2010). "Reductions in Arrest Under Assisted Outpatient Treatment in New York." *Psychiatric Services, 61*(10): 1–4.

http://ps.psychiatryonline.org/article.aspx?articleID=101586
http://www.CrimeSolutions.gov/ProgramDetails.aspx?ID=228

This program was rated on CrimeSolutions.gov as effective.

Gilbert and colleagues found that the odds of arrest in any given month for participants who were currently receiving assisted outpatient treatment (AOT) were significantly lower than the odds for participants in the reference group, which included people who had signed a voluntary service agreement but not started AOT as well as those who had not signed a voluntary service agreement. The odds of arrest were nearly two-thirds lower for participants currently receiving AOT, compared with the odds of arrest for the reference group.

Link, B. G., Epperson, M. W., et al. (2011). "Arrest Outcomes Associated with Outpatient Commitment in New York State." *Psychiatric Services, 62*(5): 504–508.

http://deepblue.lib.umich.edu/bitstream/handle/2027.42/84915/LinkEpperson_2010.pdf?sequence=1
http://www.CrimeSolutions.gov/ProgramDetails.aspx?ID=228

This program was rated on CrimeSolutions.gov as effective.

Within-group analyses conducted by Link and colleagues showed that the risk of arrest was significantly higher for people during the period before assisted outpatient treatment (AOT) than during AOT. Though the risk of arrest went up slightly after AOT was discontinued, this difference was not significant. For a person who had never received AOT, the risk of any arrest was 2.66 times greater before AOT than it was while receiving AOT. The between-group results showed that the risk of arrest among people in the comparison group who were never assigned to AOT was significantly higher than the risk of arrest for the AOT group while they were assigned to AOT. Compared with people during and shortly after the period of assignment to AOT, the comparison group who never received AOT had nearly double the odds of arrest.

Swanson, J. W., Swartz, M. S., et al. (2000). "Involuntary Out-Patient Commitment and Reduction of Violent Behavior in Persons with Severe Mental Illness." *British Journal of Psychiatry, 176*: 324–331.

http://bjp.rcpsych.org/content/176/4/324.long
http://www.CrimeSolutions.gov/ProgramDetails.aspx?ID=228

This program was rated on CrimeSolutions.gov as effective.

An initial analysis performed by Swanson and colleagues found there was no significant difference in the rate of violence between the group randomly assigned to involuntary outpatient commitment (OPC) and the control group (32.3 percent in the OPC group compared with 36.8 percent in the control group). Further analysis looked at whether OPC interacts with the provision of outpatient services to reduce the risk of violent behavior. An initial analysis found that OPC alone did not significantly reduce the risk of violent behavior. Similarly, receiving frequent outpatient services alone was not associated with less violence. However, a combination of both variables (at least 6 months of OPC with an average of three or more outpatient visits per month in the community) did significantly reduce the risk of violence. The predicted probability of any violent behavior was cut in half, from 48 to 24 percent, attributable to extended OPC and regular outpatient services. Again, this result should be viewed with caution, because the amount of time on OPC was neither random nor controlled for experimentally.

Multisystemic Therapy (MST)

This program was rated on CrimeSolutions.gov as effective.
Program summary: A family and community-based treatment program for adolescent offenders who have exhibited serious antisocial, problem, and delinquent behaviors.
Details: http://www.CrimeSolutions.gov/ProgramDetails.aspx?ID=192

Borduin, C. M., Mann, B. J., et al. (1995). "Multisystemic Treatment of Serious Juvenile Offenders: Long-Term Prevention of Criminality and Violence." *Journal of Consulting and Clinical Psychology, 63*(4): 569–578.
http://www.campbellcollaboration.org/artman2/uploads/1/borduin.pdf
http://www.CrimeSolutions.gov/ProgramDetails.aspx?ID=192

This program was rated on CrimeSolutions.gov as effective.
Survival analysis by Borduin and colleagues showed significant differences between treatment and comparison groups 4 years after the end of their probation: 71.4 percent of the individual therapy (IT) comparison group participants were arrested at least once, compared with 26.1 percent of MST participants. Further analysis showed that the number of arrests among the recidivists was significantly lower for the MST treatment group: intervention group recidivists were arrested on average 1.71 times, compared with 5.43 times in the comparison IT group. The researchers also explored the severity of the crimes committed by study participants. They found that the recidivists of the MST group had also been arrested for significantly less serious crimes and significantly fewer violent crimes than IT recidivists.

Henggeler, S. W., Melton, G. B., et al. (1992). "Family Preservation Using Multisystemic Therapy: An Effective Alternative to Incarcerating Serious Juvenile Offenders." *Journal of Consulting and Clinical Psychology, 60*(6): 953–961.
http://www.campbellcollaboration.org/artman2/uploads/1/henggelermelton.pdf
http://www.CrimeSolutions.gov/ProgramDetails.aspx?ID=192

This program was rated on CrimeSolutions.gov as effective.
Results of the Henggeler and colleagues study at 59 weeks postreferral showed the multisystemic therapy (MST) treatment group had just over half the number of rearrests than the usual-services comparison group. Significant differences were also found in recidivism rates, with 42 percent for the MST group and 63 percent for the comparison group. On average, MST participants spent significantly fewer days (73) than the comparison group incarcerated in facilities run by the Department of Youth Services. At 59 weeks postreferral, 20 percent of the MST group had been incarcerated, compared with 68 percent of the comparison group. At the posttest, the comparison group self-reported delinquency-scale scores were nearly three times greater than the MST intervention group.

Timmons-Mitchell, J., Bender, M. B., et al. (2006). "An Independent Effectiveness Trial of Multisystemic Therapy with Juvenile Justice Youth." *Journal of Clinical Child and Adolescent Psychology, 35*: 227–236.
http://www.goccp.maryland.gov/msac/documents/gang-studies/MST/Timmons-Mitchell-2006.pdf
http://www.CrimeSolutions.gov/ProgramDetails.aspx?ID=192

This program was rated on CrimeSolutions.gov as effective.
At the 18-month posttreatment follow-up of the study by Timmons-Mitchell and colleagues, the 66.7 percent recidivism rate for the MST group was significantly lower than the 86.7 percent rate for the treatment-as-usual (TAU) group. MST participants were also arrested and arraigned for new charges significantly less often (on average 1.44 times) compared with the TAU group (2.29 times). Binary logistic regression showed young people in the TAU group were 3.2 times more likely to be arrested than the MST group. Although survival analysis revealed significant differences in recidivism between treatment groups, no significant differences were found between groups regarding the time until first arrest.

Multisystemic Therapy—Substance Abuse

This program was rated on CrimeSolutions.gov as effective.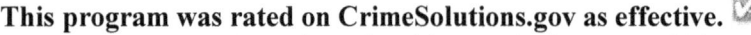
Program summary: A version of multisystemic therapy (MST) targeted to adolescents with substance abuse and dependency issues.
Details: http://www.CrimeSolutions.gov/ProgramDetails.aspx?ID=179

Henggeler, S. W., Clingempeel, W. G., et al. (2002). "Four-Year Follow-Up of Multisystemic Therapy with Substance-Abusing and Substance-Dependent Juvenile Offenders." *Journal of the American Academy of Child and Adolescent Psychiatry, 41*: 868–874.
http://www.sciencedirect.com/science/article/pii/S089085670961056X
http://www.CrimeSolutions.gov/ProgramDetails.aspx?ID=179

This program was rated on CrimeSolutions.gov as effective.
Henggeler and colleagues found significant differences for the measures of aggressive crimes, the Self-Report Delinquency Aggression scale, and the annualized conviction rates for aggressive crimes. Compared with the control participants, those receiving MST treatment had a 75 percent reduction in convictions for aggressive crimes since the age of 17. MST participants also reported committing fewer aggressive crimes in the past 12 months than the control group receiving usual services. There was no significant effect found with regard to property crimes.

Henggeler, S. W., Halliday-Boykins, C. A., et al. (2006). "Juvenile Drug Court: Enhancing Outcomes by Integrating Evidence-Based Treatments." *Journal of Consulting and Clinical Psychology, 74*: 42–54.
http://www.ncbi.nlm.nih.gov/pubmed/16551142
http://www.CrimeSolutions.gov/ProgramDetails.aspx?ID=179

This program was rated on CrimeSolutions.gov as effective.
Henggeler and colleagues found significant differences between the treatment groups (those receiving MST tailored to substance abuse) and the comparison group. Adolescents in the drug court (DC) and the drug court MST contingency management groups reported a significant decrease in alcohol use at 4-month follow-up, compared with those in the family court (FC) comparison condition. Controlling for the baseline assessment, the treatment group continued to report significantly less alcohol use at 12-month follow-up than those in the comparison condition. This shows a strong short-term effect in the first 4 months that persists up to 12 months later. For heavy alcohol use, the short-term effect was not evident. However, at 12-month follow-up, those in the treatment group reported significantly less heavy alcohol use than those in the comparison condition.

Connections

This program was rated on CrimeSolutions.gov as promising.
Program summary: A juvenile court–based program designed to address the needs of juvenile offenders on probation who have emotional and behavioral disorders as well as the needs of their families. The approach is meant to be an integrated, seamless, coordinated system of care for children with mental health problems.
Details: http://www.CrimeSolutions.gov/ProgramDetails.aspx?ID=295

Pullman, M. D., Kerbs, J., et al. (2006). "Juvenile Offenders with Mental Health Needs: Reducing Recidivism Using Wraparound." *Crime and Delinquency, 52*(3): 375–397.
http://cad.sagepub.com/content/52/3/375.abstract
https://www.ncjrs.gov/App/publications/abstract.aspx?ID=237511

This program was rated on CrimeSolutions.gov as promising.
Pullman and colleagues found that youth in the Connections program intervention, an individualized, coordinated mental health service within a juvenile department, were significantly less likely to recidivate. Connections is a community-based program first implemented in Clark County, Washington,

in 2001 that addresses the needs of juvenile offenders with emotional and behavioral disorders as well as the needs of their families. Youth in the comparison group were 2.8 times more likely to commit any type of offense compared with youth in the Connections program. Youth in the comparison group were also 3 times more likely to commit a felony offense compared with youth in the Connections program.

Front-End Diversion

This program is rated on CrimeSolutions.gov as promising.
Program summary: A preadjudication diversion program designed to divert juveniles with mental health needs away from the juvenile justice system through specialized supervision and case management.
Details: http://www.CrimeSolutions.gov/ProgramDetails.aspx?ID=357

Colwell, B., Villarreal, S. F., et al. (2012). "Preliminary Outcomes of a Preadjudication Diversion Initiative for Juvenile Justice Involved Youth with Mental Needs in Texas." *Criminal Justice and Behavior, 39*(4): 447–460.
http://cjb.sagepub.com/content/39/4/447.abstract
http://www.CrimeSolutions.gov/ProgramDetails.aspx?ID=357

This program is rated on CrimeSolutions.gov as promising.
Colwell and colleagues found that juveniles who participated in the Front End Diversion Initiative (FEDI) program were significantly less likely to face adjudication compared with those who only received traditional supervision while on probation. Only 7.7 percent of the FEDI treatment group were adjudicated, compared with 22.0 percent of the comparison group. The results from the logistic regression also found that juveniles in the comparison group were 11 times as likely to have been adjudicated in the 90 days since receiving traditional supervision while on probation, compared with the FEDI treatment group.

Mendota Juvenile Treatment Center

This program is rated on CrimeSolutions.gov as promising.
Program summary: A residential facility that provides mental health treatment to serious and violent juvenile offenders in secured correctional institutions.
Details: http://www.CrimeSolutions.gov/ProgramDetails.aspx?ID=274

Caldwell, M., Skeem, J., et al. (2006). "Treatment Responses of Adolescent Offenders with Psychopathy Features: A 2-Year Follow-Up." *Criminal Justice and Behavior, 33*(5): 571–596.
https://www.ncjrs.gov/App/publications/abstract.aspx?ID=237390
http://www.CrimeSolutions.gov/ProgramDetails.aspx?ID=274

This program is rated on CrimeSolutions.gov as promising.
Of the 141 youth with psychopathic features included in the study by Caldwell and colleagues, 10.6 percent were released directly to adult prison following treatment. For these youth, recidivism occurred in juvenile institutional settings after treatment. Therefore, the results were examined in two ways: (1) combined institutional and community recidivism, and (2) community recidivism only. Results showed that youth treated in the Mendota Juvenile Treatment Center (MJTC) in Wisconsin were significantly less likely to recidivate in general. Within 2 years of release from custody, 57 percent of treatment youth had recidivated in the institution or community, compared with 78 percent of comparison youth. Considering only cases of youth who had some community access during the follow-up period, 56 percent of MJTC–treated youth had recidivated following release compared to 73 percent of comparison youth.

Caldwell, M. F., & Van Rybroek, G. J. (2005). "Reducing Violence in Serious Juvenile Offenders Using Intensive Treatment." *International Journal of Law and Psychiatry, 28*(6): 622–636.
http://www.ncbi.nlm.nih.gov/pubmed/16112731
http://www.CrimeSolutions.gov/ProgramDetails.aspx?ID=274

This program is rated on CrimeSolutions.gov as promising. ☑
The evaluation by Caldwell and Van Rybroek showed that at the 2-year follow-up period, 52 percent of the treatment group had recidivated compared with 73 percent of the comparison group. With regard to more serious violence, 37 percent of the comparison group was charged with a violent felony (25 percent of which involved serious victim injury or death), and only 18 percent of the treatment group had been charged with a violent felony (only 7 percent of which involved serious victim injury)—all significant differences. However, there were no significant differences between the groups on misdemeanor offenses.

Modified Therapeutic Community for Offenders with Mental Illness and Chemical Abuse (MICA) Disorders

This program is rated on CrimeSolutions.gov as promising. ☑
Program summary: An adaptation of the therapeutic community models for use with offenders who have drug abuse problems and mental health disorders. This modified version uses a more flexible, more personalized, and less intense program that targets reductions in substance use and recidivism.
Details: http://www.CrimeSolutions.gov/ProgramDetails.aspx?ID=90

Sullivan, C. J., McKendrick, K., et al. (2007). "Modified Therapeutic Community Treatment for Offenders with MICA Disorders: Substance Use Outcomes." *American Journal of Drug and Alcohol Abuse, 33*: 823–832.
http://www.ncbi.nlm.nih.gov/pubmed/17994478
http://www.CrimeSolutions.gov/ProgramDetails.aspx?ID=90

This program is rated on CrimeSolutions.gov as promising. ☑
Sullivan and colleagues found that there were significantly better outcomes for all substance use variables (any substance, any illegal drug, and alcohol to intoxication) for the modified therapeutic community (MTC) participants compared with the control group. After 12 months, 69 percent of MTC participants had not used any substance, compared with 44 percent for the control group; 75 percent of MTC participants had not used an illegal drug, compared with 56 percent of control group; and 81 percent of MTC participants had not used alcohol to intoxication, compared with 61 percent of the control group.

Multisystemic Therapy–Family Integrated Transitions (MST–FIT)

This program is rated on CrimeSolutions.gov as promising. ☑
Program summary: The program provides integrated individual and family services to juvenile offenders who have co-occurring mental health and chemical dependency disorders during their transition from incarceration back into the community.
Details: http://www.CrimeSolutions.gov/ProgramDetails.aspx?ID=271

Trupin, E. J., Kerns, S.E.U., et al. (2011). "Family Integrated Transitions: A Promising Program for Juvenile Offenders with Co-Occurring Disorders." *Journal of Child & Adolescent Substance Abuse, 20*: 421–436.
http://www.tandfonline.com/doi/pdf/10.1080/1067828X.2011.614889
http://www.CrimeSolutions.gov/ProgramDetails.aspx?ID=271

This program is rated on CrimeSolutions.gov as promising. ☑
Overall, Trupin and colleagues found mixed results. Multisystemic Therapy–Family Integrated Transitions (MST–FIT) had a significant effect on felony recidivism at 36 months postrelease. However, the MST–FIT intervention did not appear to have a significant effect on overall recidivism (misdemeanor and felony), misdemeanor recidivism, and violent felony recidivism.

San Francisco (California) Behavioral Health

This program is rated on CrimeSolutions.gov as promising.
Program summary: A mental health court that aims to reduce recidivism of criminal defendants with serious mental illness. The court connects defendants with community treatment services and considers the defendant's mental illness and severity of the offense in disposition decisions.
Details: http://www.CrimeSolutions.gov/ProgramDetails.aspx?ID=39

Watson, A.C., Ottati, V.C, Morabito, M., Draine, J., Kerr, A.N., & Angell, B. (2009). "Outcomes of police contact with persons with mental illness: the impact of CIT." *Administrative Policy and Mental Health*, **DOI: 10.1007/s10488-009-0236-9**
http://www.ncbi.nlm.nih.gov/pubmed/19705277
The Crisis intervention team model (CIT) is possibly the most well known and widely adopted model to improve police response to persons with mental illness. A primary goal of CIT programs is to divert those with mental illness from the criminal justice system to mental health services. This study examines the effectiveness of fielding CIT trained and supported officers for influencing call outcomes using data from patrol officers ($n = 112$) in four Chicago police districts. Results from regression analysis indicate that CIT certified officers directed a greater proportion of people with mental illness to mental health services than their non-CIT certified peers. CIT did not have an immediate effect on arrest. Moderator analysis indicates that CIT had its biggest effect on increasing direction to services and decreasing "contact only" among officers who have a positive view of mental health services and who know someone with mental illness. Additional moderators of the CIT effect on call outcomes include level of resistance and the presence of a weapon. Findings from this study have important implications for policy, practice and future research.

Skeem, J. & Bibeau, L. (2008). "How Does Violence Potential Relate to Crisis Intervention Team Responses to Emergencies?" *Psychiatric Services, 59:201–204.*
http://risk-resilience.berkeley.edu/sites/default/files/wp-content/gallery/publications/2008.How_does_violence_potential_relate_to_crisis_intervention_team_responses_to_emergencies1.pdf
This study explored whether a crisis intervention team (CIT) promotes public safety and diversion from jail to treatment. Police reports ($N = 655$) were analyzed for CIT events that occurred between March 2003 and May 2005 to determine each subject's potential for violence to self or others. Some 45% of CIT events involved suicide crises, 26% involved a threat to others, and average violence potential ratings suggested minor to moderate risk. Officers' use of force related strongly to violence potential (eta of .54). Nevertheless, officers used force in only 15% of 189 events posing serious to extreme risk of violence and used low-lethality methods. Of events, 74% were resolved through hospitalization, whereas only 4% were resolved through arrest. Although the study lacked a comparison group, the results are consistent with some studies suggesting that CIT holds promise in meeting safety and jail diversion goals.

Watson, A. C., Schaefer Morabito, M., Draine J., & Ottati, V. (2008). "Improving Police Response to Persons with Mental Illness: A Multi-Level Conceptualization of CIT." *International Journal of Law and Psychiatry, 31: 359–368.*
http://www.ncbi.nlm.nih.gov/pmc/articles/PMC2655327/
The large numbers of people with mental illness in jails and prisons has fueled policy concern in all domains of the justice system. This includes police practice, where initial decisions to involve people in the justice system or divert them to mental health services are made. One approach is using Crisis Intervention Teams (CIT). There are more than 400 operational programs. Although the limited evidence on CIT effectiveness is promising, research on CIT is limited in scope and conceptualization; much of it focuses on officer characteristics and training. This paper reviews the literature on CIT and presents a conceptual model of police response to people with mental illness that accounts for officer, organizational, mental health system and community level factors likely to influence implementation and effectiveness of CIT and other approaches.

McNiel, D. E., & Binder, R. L. (2007). "Effectiveness of a Mental Health Court in Reducing Criminal Recidivism and Violence." *American Journal of Psychiatry, 164*(9): 1395–1403.
http://ajp.psychiatryonline.org/article.aspx?articleid=98922
http://www.CrimeSolutions.gov/ProgramDetails.aspx?ID=39

This program is rated on CrimeSolutions.gov as promising.
The outcome results from the McNiel and Binder study showed that participation (even if a participant did not complete the entire program and graduate) was associated with positive results. Participation in the Behavioral Health Court (BHC) predicted a longer time to any new charge. At 18 months, the treatment group was 26 percent less likely to be charged with a new offense compared with the treatment-as-usual group. Participation in BHC also resulted in a longer time to a new violent charge. The treatment group was 55 percent less likely to be charged with a new violent offense compared with the treatment-as-usual group.

Teller, J. L. S., Munetz, M. R., Gil, K. G., & Ritter, C. (2006). "Crisis Intervention Team Training for Police Officers Responding to Mental Disturbance Calls." *Psychiatric Services, 57:* 232–237.
http://www.ncbi.nlm.nih.gov/pubmed/16452701
As police are often the first responders for people experiencing a mental illness crisis, police departments nationally are incorporating specialized training for officers in collaboration with local mental health systems. This study examined police dispatch data before and after implementation of a crisis intervention team (CIT) program to assess the effect of the training on officers' disposition of calls. The authors analyzed police dispatch logs for 2 years before and 4 years after implementation of the CIT program in Akron, Ohio, to determine monthly average rates of mental disturbance calls compared with the overall rate of calls to the police, disposition of mental disturbance calls by time and training, and the effects of techniques on voluntariness of disposition. Since the training program was implemented, there has been an increase in the number and proportion of calls involving possible mental illness, an increased rate of transport by CIT-trained officers of people experiencing mental illness crises to emergency treatment facilities, an increase in transport on a voluntary status, and no significant changes in the rate of arrests by time or training. The study suggest that a CIT partnership between the police department, the mental health system, consumers of services, and their family members can help in efforts to assist people who are experiencing a mental illness crisis to gain access to the treatment system, where such people most often are best served.

Other Reports

Morningside Research and Consulting, Inc. (2012). *Bureau of Justice Assistance Justice and Mental Health Collaboration Program: Travis County, Texas: Phase I Strategic Plan.* **Austin, TX: Author.**
http://www.austintexas.gov/edims/document.cfm?id=183380
https://www.traviscountytx.gov/criminal_justice/Research_planning/pdfs/justice_mental_health_2012-10.pdf
This report reviews how the funds for the Travis County Criminal Justice Planning Office would be used. An outside advisory board analyzed any barriers in treatment that might be met and how they could be overcome. The grant was awarded for a Phase 1 development for a communitywide strategic plan to address the needs of people diagnosed with severe and persistent mental disorders.

Chopko, B. A. (2011). "Walk in Balance: Training Crisis Intervention Team Police Officers as Compassionate Warriors." *Journal of Creativity in Mental Health, 6*(4): 315–328.
http://www.collegecounseling.org/wp-content/uploads/The-Compassionate-Warrior-and-How-We-Can-Connect-with-Our-Student-Veterans.pdf
Crisis Intervention Teams (CIT) were developed to enable law enforcement officers to effectively and compassionately respond to calls involving people experiencing psychiatric distress. Mental health professionals responsible for training CIT officers are in a unique position to promote the compassionate treatment of those experiencing psychiatric distress as well as the well-being of the police officers. Fostering spiritual connections and a compassionate-warrior mindset may enhance the training of CIT

officers. This article includes descriptions of creative interventions, including historical compassionate-warrior comparisons, fictitious stories, and spiritual symbols. These techniques are based on warrior codes of groups such as samurai warriors, martial artists such as Shaolin Kung Fu, medieval knights, Native Americans, and the U.S. military.

Doulas, A. V., & Lurigio, A. J. (2010). "Youth Crisis Intervention Teams (CITs): A Response to the Fragmentation of the Educational, Mental Health, and Juvenile Justice Systems." *Journal of Police Crisis Negotiations, 10*(1/2): 241–262.
http://www.citinternational.org/CITINT/PDF/CITResearchBibliographyofPublishedReportsAugust2015.pdf
This article discusses CITs for youth with mental illness. Adapted from adult CIT models, youth CITs are designed to divert and refer for services adolescents with suspected psychiatric disorders who have a higher prevalence of psychiatric and substance-use disorders (and their co-occurrence), compared with youth who have no mental health problems. The authors suggest that the failure of the school, mental health, and juvenile justice systems to provide seriously distressed youth with coordinated and comprehensive assessment and treatment services has increased the likelihood that they will encounter the police and further penetrate the juvenile and adult criminal justice systems. The article provides an early look at three programs in diverse geographic areas: Denver, Chicago, and San Antonio and concludes with observations regarding the need for such programs as well as the challenges that police departments are likely to face implementing and continuing such initiatives.

Websites

GAINS Center for Behavioral Health and Justice Transformation at SAMHSA
http://gainscenter.samhsa.gov/

Council of State Governments Justice Center—Mental Health Page
http://csgjusticecenter.org/mental-health/

Justice Reinvestment Initiative

Project Description

Justice reinvestment is a data-driven approach to improve public safety, reduce corrections and related criminal justice spending, and reinvest savings in strategies that can decrease crime and strengthen neighborhoods. The purpose of justice reinvestment is to manage and allocate criminal justice populations more cost effectively, generating savings that can be reinvested in evidence-based strategies that improve public safety while holding offenders accountable. States and localities engaging in justice reinvestment collect and analyze data on what drives criminal justice populations and costs, identify and implement changes to increase efficiencies, and measure both the fiscal and public safety impacts of those changes.[37]

Justice reinvestment comprises three important activities: analyzing, developing, and measuring. Agencies *analyze* criminal justice trends to see why the population of jails and prisons grows. They *develop* and implement policies to manage the growth in correction expenditures to promote public safety and make offenders more accountable. Finally, they *measure* the impact of policy changes, reinvest resources, and hold policymakers accountable for their results.

CrimeSolutions.gov Ratings:
No ratings at this time

Partners and Professional Organizations:
- ✓ Council of State Governments Justice Center
- ✓ Urban Institute: Justice Policy Center
- ✓ Vera Institute of Justice
- ✓ Pew Charitable Trusts: Public Safety Performance
- ✓ Center for Effective Public Policy
- ✓ Crime and Justice Institute

Highlighted Reports

BJA-Sponsored Evaluation[38]

Hall, M., Hevener, G., et al. (2014). *Justice Reinvestment Act Implementation Evaluation Report.* **Raleigh, NC: North Carolina Sentencing and Policy Advisory Commission.**
http://www.nccourts.org/Courts/CRS/Councils/spac/Documents/JRIReports-2014.pdf
This report includes background on justice reinvestment in North Carolina. It summarizes major provisions of the legislation and subsequent changes and outlines recent policy and procedure changes made by agencies. Other sections include feedback and observations from the field on emerging practices obtained through site visits across the state, and available statewide Justice Reinvestment Act data for 2013.

Other Academic Articles[39]

Allen, R. (2011). "Justice Reinvestment and the Use of Imprisonment: Policy Reflections from England and Wales." *Criminology & Public Policy, 10*(3): 617–627.
http://onlinelibrary.wiley.com/doi/10.1111/capp.2011.10.issue-3/issuetoc
In this response to Todd R. Clear's "A private-sector, incentives-based model for justice reinvestment" (2011), the author examines the implementation of justice reinvestment principles in the United Kingdom's prison policy. He argues that such efforts must be made on a local level, targeting specific communities to be fully effective. The article offers support for the justice reinvestment initative model.

---

[37] This description as well as more in-depth information about the program can be found at the following website: https://www.bja.gov/programs/justicereinvestment/index.html
[38] For each article, a link has been provided to either the full-length document or the website where it can be accessed.
[39]This section includes some research conducted with funding from BJA.

Austin, J., & Cadora, E. (2013). *Ending Mass Incarceration Charting a New Justice Reinvestment.* **Washington, DC: Sentencing Project.**

http://sentencingproject.org/doc/publications/sen_Charting%20a%20New%20Justice%20Reinvestment.pdf
This report assesses the performance of the JRI over time as it relates to the ability to educate state legislators and public officials about the consequences of four decades of mass incarceration. Topics include cost-effectiveness, the role of corrections, and the need to persuade public officials to undertake reforms not previously considered.

Austin, J., & Coventry, G. (2014). "A Critical Analysis of Justice Reinvestment in the United States and Australia." *Victims & Offenders, 9*(1): 126–148.

http://www.tandfonline.com/doi/full/10.1080/15564886.2014.861687#.U8PQV5S-1cY
The authors examine the JRI experience in the United States and consider implications for Australia. Findings indicate that the two countries are currently in different phases and have different specialized needs. As a result, both countries need to think critically about their design of JRI programs.

Burch, J.H. (2011). "Encouraging Innovation on the Foundation of Evidence: On the Path to the Adjacent Possible." *Criminology & Public Policy, 30*(3): 609–616.

http://tepataka.rethinking.org.nz/eserv/rcp:177/Burch_James_Encouraging_innovation_on_.pdf
The author reports the need to invest in community corrections, explores the history of the Justice Reinvestment Initiative, and stresses the need to encourage forward-thinking ideas and innovation to advance justice in America.

Clement, M., Schwarzfeld, M., et al. (2011). *National Summit on Justice Reinvestment and Public Safety: Addressing Recidivism, Crime, and Corrections Spending.* **New York: Council of State Governments Justice Center.**

https://www.bja.gov/publications/csg_justicereinvestmentsummitreport.pdf
This report summarizes the remarks, research, and case studies highlighted during the National Summit on Justice Reinvestment and Public Safety on January 27, 2010, in Washington, DC. This report aims to assist Congress and practitioners through concise articulation of four key principles of JRI to reduce recidivism and increase public safety.

Fabelo, T. (2010). "Texas Justice Reinvestment: Be More Like Texas?" *Justice Research and Policy, 12*(1): 113–131. **doi: 10.3818/JRP.12.1.2010.113 BJA**

http://jrsa.metapress.com/content/g81758244k541h47/
This article presents a review of the Texas JRI that includes the scope and outcomes of the program across the state. Comparisons are drawn between the Texas model and California-based efforts that includes a discussion of the related financial effects.

Fox, C., Albertson, K., et al. (2011). "Justice Reinvestment: Can It Deliver More for Less?" *Howard Journal of Criminal Justice, 50*(2): 119–136. **doi: 10.1111/j.1468-2311.2010.00654.x**

http://onlinelibrary.wiley.com/doi/10.1111/hojo.2011.50.issue-2/issuetoc
This article identifies various issues relating to implementing justice reinvestment in the United Kingdom and discusses the success of the model in the United States and what this could mean for the U.K. The author also lays out an agenda for academic discourse on justice reinvestment as it relates to this effort.

Hall, M., Hevener, G., et al. (2014). *Justice Reinvestment Act Implementation Evaluation Report.* **Raleigh, NC: North Carolina Sentencing and Policy Advisory Commission.**

http://www.nccourts.org/Courts/CRS/Councils/spac/Documents/JRIReports-2014.pdf
See also: http://www.nccourts.org/Courts/CRS/Councils/spac/Documents/JRIReports-2013.pdf
This report includes background on justice reinvestment in North Carolina. It summarizes major provisions in the legislation and subsequent changes; recent policy and procedure changes made by agencies; feedback and observations from the field regarding emerging practices obtained through site visits across the state; and available statewide JRA data for CY 2013.

James, J., & Agha, S. (2013). *Justice Reinvestment in Action: The Delaware Model.* **New York: Vera Institute of Justice.**
http://www.vera.org/sites/default/files/resources/downloads/justice-reinvestment-in-action-delaware-v4.pdf.pdf
Vera Institute of Justice conducted a comprehensive examination of factors contributing to the Delaware corrections population. Based on the findings, Vera offered direction on how to address these issues in the correction system. This policy brief describes and draws lessons from Delaware's model for reorienting the use of imprisonment only for high-risk offenders and reinvesting the cost savings in corrections practices that have proven effective in reducing recidivism and holding offenders accountable.

Kleiman, M.A.R. (2011). "Justice Reinvestment in Community Supervision." *Criminology & Public Policy, 10*(3): 651−659.
http://onlinelibrary.wiley.com/doi/10.1111/capp.2011.10.issue-3/issuetoc
This article focuses on implementation of justice reinvestment. It highlights a discussion between leaders in the field about the merits of the JRI model that covers a model other than private-sector partnerships and the possible benefits of that model.

Lawrence, A., & Lyons, D. (2013). *Justice Reinvestment Crime Brief.* **Denver, CO: National Conference of State Legislatures, Criminal Justice Program.**
http://www.ncsl.org/Documents/CJ/July2013CrimeBrief.pdf
This brief highlights several state reforms and successes. The analysis includes projections of justice reinvestment savings as a result of implementation. Although this is mainly a review of progress, the financial analysis may prove useful.

Lyons, D. (2013). "High-Yield Corrections." *State Legislatures, 39*(1): 22−25.
http://www.ncsl.org/research/civil-and-criminal-justice/high-yield-corrections.aspx
The article discusses the justice reinvestment reforms carried out in the United States. It presents an overview of efforts of the Public Safety Performance Project at the Pew Center on the States. It cites the justice reinvestment changes first made by Texas and Kansas. The author shares information on the reviews and reforms performed in various states by 2010.

Maruna, S. (2011). "Lessons for Justice Reinvestment from Restorative Justice and the Justice Model Experience." *Criminology & Public Policy, 10*(3): 661−669.
http://onlinelibrary.wiley.com/doi/10.1111/capp.2011.10.issue-3/issuetoc
This essay offers lessons for justice reinvestment from restorative justice and the justice model in the United States. It also relates justice reinvestment to ideas such as community policing, drug courts and therapeutic jurisprudence, and broken-window theory.

Redondo Illescas, S., & Frerich, N. (2014). "Crime and Justice Reinvestment in Europe: Possibilities and Challenges." *Victims & Offenders, 9*(1): 13−49. **doi:10.1080/15564886.2013.864525**
http://www.tandfonline.com/doi/full/10.1080/15564886.2013.864525#.U8PDfJS-1cY
This paper reviews some of the main features and figures of crime and criminal justice in Europe, including rehabilitation and cost–benefit analyses. Victimization rates in different European countries are presented as well as some insights on the differential criminal policy and the punitive nature of distinct countries. In terms of offender treatment and cost–benefit analyses, the paper gives an overview of the European systematic reviews and meta-analyses on the topic, highlighting the main treatment strategies and countries of application; the typologies of treated offenders; and the efficiency of treatment, prisons, and alternatives.

Schwartz, M. (2010). "Building Communities, Not Prisons: Justice Reinvestment and Indigenous Over-Imprisonment." *Australian Indigenous Law Review, 14*(1): 2−17.
http://heinonline.org/HOL/Page?handle=hein.journals/austindlr14&div=7&g_sent=1&collection=journals#12
This article examines how justice reinvestment is addressed in the United States and the United Kingdom, analyzes justice reinvestment's potential to be used effectively among indigenous Australians, and discusses the aspects of justice reinvestment that distinguish it from other "decarceration" initiatives. It identifies the ways in which this approach is suited both to articulated policy aims in relation to indigenous people and to the particular circumstances of indigenous communities in the current financial climate. The author concludes that the combination of these factors makes justice reinvestment an approach worth pursuing in Australia, particularly with indigenous Australians.

Schwartz, M., Brown, D. B., et al. (2012, June 6). "The Promise of Justice Reinvestment." *Social Science Research Network.*
http://ssrn.com/abstract=2078715
This article examines the notion and practice of justice reinvestment, an emerging approach addressing the high social and economic costs of soaring incarceration rates. Key distinguishing features of justice reinvestment are briefly outlined, followed by discussion of its recent emergence and application in the United States, and to a lesser extent in the United Kingdom. The prospects for adopting these approaches in Australia are then considered, with particular reference to the high imprisonment rates of indigenous Australians.

Taxman, F. S., Pattavina, A., et al. (2014). "Justice Reinvestment in the United States: An Empirical Assessment of the Potential Impact of Increased Correctional Programming on Recidivism." *Victims & Offenders, 9*(1): 50−75. doi:10.1080/15564886.2013.860934
http://www.tandfonline.com/toc/uvao20/9/1
The authors examine the justice reinvestment model to assess different treatment methodsand offer four measures to gauge performance of systems undergoing justice reinvestment initiatives. Findings indicate that expanding correctional programming is an important if not essential component of undoing the impact of mass incarceration policies.

U.K. Ministry of Justice. (2013). *Justice Reinvestment Pilots: First Year Results.* **London: Author.**
https://www.gov.uk/government/uploads/system/uploads/attachment_data/file/194291/justice-reinvestment-pilots-y1.pdf
This brief reports on the first year results of the six Justice Reinvestment pilots programs in the United Kingdom. The goal was to incentivize local statutory partners to reduce demand on courts, legal aid, prisons, and probation and consequently reduce costs to the justice system. Early results showed a decline in demand for services, as expected.

Wall, A. T. (2010). "Rhode Island Halts Growth in the Inmate Population While Increasing Public Safety." *Corrections Today, 72*(1): 40−44.
http://www.americanbar.org/content/dam/aba/administrative/litigation/materials/sac_2012/49-2_b_ri_halts_growth.authcheckdam.pdf
The author discusses efforts by Rhode Island to implement the justice reinvestment model to reduce growth in the inmate population while continuing to increase public safety. The article reviews the efforts by the Rhode Island legislature and the governor to address the issue of overcrowding in state correctional institutions as well as the help received from the Justice Center of the Council of State Governments to foster implementation.

Wong, K., Fox, C., et al. (2014). "Justice Reinvestment in an 'Age of Austerity': Developments in the United Kingdom." *Victims & Offenders, 9*(1): 76−99. doi: 10.1080/15564886.2014.861688
http://www.tandfonline.com/toc/uvao20/9/1
Drawing on evidence from justice reinvestment experiments in the United Kingdom—including Payment by Results (PBR) pilot projects in England and Wales—this paper examines how models of justice reinvestment can be implemented in an age of austerity. The discussion is set against the backdrop of the wider application of PBR commissioning for criminal justice and related services.

Wong, K., Meadows, L., et al. (2013). "The Development and Year One Implementation of the Local Justice Reinvestment Pilot." London: U.K. Ministry of Justice.
http://shura.shu.ac.uk/7175/1/wong_Development_and_year_one_imp.pdf
This report reviews several local justice reinvestment sites in the United Kingdom. Findings showed that various sites responded in different ways and to varying degrees. This includes evidence of a more enthusiastic response in Greater Manchester compared with some London sites in terms of investing in new approaches to managing offenders.

Wood, W. R. (2014). "Justice Reinvestment in Australia." *Victims & Offenders, 9*(1): 100−119. doi: 10.1080/15564886.2013.860935
http://www.tandfonline.com/doi/full/10.1080/15564886.2013.860935#.U8PLj5S-1cY
For the complete article: http://www.academia.edu/5870963/Justice_Reinvestment_in_Australia
This article reviews justice reinvestment and highlights some of the more pertinent problems facing the justice system, offenders, victims of crime, and local communities regarding the use of punishment and incarceration in Australia. It then considers the degree to which justice reinvestment may or may not deliver on some or all of its promises, in particular problems that it faces in terms of implementation, use, and long-term viability in Australia.

Other Reports

Allen, R. (2015). *Rehabilitation Devolution: How Localising Justice Can Reduce Crime and Imprisonment.. London, England: Transform Justice.*
http://www.transformjustice.org.uk/wp-content/uploads/2015/12/TRANSFORM-JUSTICE-REHABILITATION-DEVOLUTION.pdf
The report details the JR initiatives in the United Kingdom and reviews components of the initiative and what effects it has had in the United Kingdom in crime reduction and financial savings.

Davies, E., Harvell, S., and Cramer, L. (2015). *The Justice Reinvestment Initiative: Thinking Local for State Justice Reinvestment.* **Washington, DC: Urban Institute. BJA sponsored.**
https://www.bja.gov/Publications/UI-JRIThinkingLocal.pdf
This report covers some JRI's success stories, featuring states that have implemented successful JRI programs and how they have impacted their community. It also showcases the importance of sharing data, partnering, and investing locally.

Justice Center for State Governments. (2015). *Justice Reinvestment in Montana: Overview.* **New York, NY: The Council of State Governments.**
https://csgjusticecenter.org/wp-content/uploads/2015/11/Justice_Reinvestment_in_Montana_Overview.pdf
This report looks at recent trends in Montana's criminal justice system and what the Justice Center's staff will be analyzing more closely in a following report. The report goes into the steps it will follow when approaching justice reinvestment in Montana.

Justice Center for State Governments. (2015). *Justice Reinvestment in Rhode Island: Overview.* **New York, NY: The Council of State Governments.**
https://csgjusticecenter.org/wp-content/uploads/2015/07/RhodeIslandOverview.pdf
This report looks at recent trends in Rhode Island's criminal justice system and what the Justice Center's staff will be analyzing more closely in a following report. Governor Raimondo issued an executive order to establish a Justice Reinvestment Working Group. The Justice Center will be working alongside this working group to analyze criminal justice trends and establish focus groups. The report goes into the steps it will follow when approaching Justice Reinvestment in Rhode Island.

Justice Center for State Governments. (2015). *Justice Reinvestment in Washington: Analysis and Policy Framework.* **New York, NY: The Council of State Governments.**
https://csgjusticecenter.org/jr/washington/publications/justice-reinvestment-in-washington-analysis-and-policy-framework/
This report summarizes an analyses of sentencing, corrections, and arrests data presented to the Washington State Justice Reinvestment Taskforce. It outlines strategies and policy options to "avert prison population growth by reducing property crime, holding offenders accountable with supervision, reinvesting to strengthen supervision policies and practices to reduce recidivism, and supporting victims of property crime." The report also goes over projected savings the state will gain if the policies are implemented.

Justice Center for State Governments. (2015). *Nebraska's Justice Reinvestment Approach.* **New York, NY: The Council of State Governments.**
https://csgjusticecenter.org/jr/nebraska/publications/nebraskas-justice-reinvestment-approach/
This report looks at the problems Nebraska faced with its prison population and what steps were taken to enact policies for justice reinvestment. Policymakers developed a policy framework designed to reduce prison overcrowding and expand the use of probation and parole supervision.

Cramer, L., et. al. (2014). *The Justice Reinvestment Initiative: Experiences from the Local Sites.* **Washington, DC: The Urban Institute. BJA-Sponsored.**
https://www.bja.gov/Publications/UI-JRI-Local-Sites.pdf
This report goes into detail about the JRI program and common components of the program, and it highlights certain states that initiated the program.

Clement, M., Schwarzfeld, M., et al. (2011). *The National Summit on Justice Reinvestment and Public Safety: Addressing Recidivism, Crime, and Corrections Spending.* **New York, NY: Justice Center Council for State Governments.**
https://www.bja.gov/Publications/CSG_JusticeReinvestmentSummitReport.pdf
This report summarizes the remarks, research, and case studies highlighted during the National Summit on Justice Reinvestment and Public Safety on January 27, 2010, in Washington, DC. The aim of the summit and this report is to help Congress and practitioners through a concise articulation of four key principles to reduce recidivism and increase public safety.

Justice Center for State Governments. (2014). *Justice Reinvestment in Alabama: Analysis and Policy Framework.* **New York, NY: The Council of State Governments.**
https://csgjusticecenter.org/wp-content/uploads/2015/03/JRinAlabamaPoliciesandFramework.pdf
This report summarizes the analyses of sentencing, corrections, probation, and parole data presented to Alabama's Prison Reform Task Force. It outlines strategies and policy options to reduce the prison population and recidivism in the state. The report says that "by strengthening community-based supervision" and "treatment, prioritizing prison space for violent and dangerous offenders," and providing supervision to every person released from prison, this will reduce recidivism and the prison population. The report also offers strategies for supporting victims of crime through improved victim notification.

Justice Center for State Governments. (2014). *Justice Reinvestment in Alabama: Overview.* **New York, NY: The Council of State Governments.**
https://csgjusticecenter.org/wp-content/uploads/2014/06/JR-in-Alabama-Overview.pdf
This report looks at recent trends in Alabama's criminal justice system and what the Justice Center's staff will be analyzing more closely in a following report. The report goes into the steps it will follow when approaching Justice Reinvestment in Alabama and how it will be implemented in the state.

Justice Center for State Governments. (2013). *Lessons from the States: Reducing Recidivism and Curbing Corrections Costs Through Justice Reinvestment.* **New York, NY: The Council of State Governments Justice Center.**
https://www.bja.gov/Publications/CSG_State-Lessons-Learned-Recidivism.pdf
This report presents 6 lessons learned from 17 states that have worked with the Council of State Governments Juice Center to develop reinvestment strategies that make criminal justice operations more cost effective.

Justice Center for State Governments. (2014). *Justice Reinvestment in Nebraska: Overview.* **New York, NY: The Council of State Governments.**
https://csgjusticecenter.org/wp-content/uploads/2014/06/JR_Nebraska-Overview.pdf
This report looks at recent trends in Nebraska's criminal justice system and what the Justice Center's staff will be analyzing more closely in a following report. A working group will be established based on the analysis of the crime trends. The report goes into the steps it will follow when approaching Justice Reinvestment in Nebraska and how it will be implemented in the state.

Justice Center for State Governments. (2014). *Justice Reinvestment in Washington State: Overview.* **New York, NY: The Council of State Governments.**
https://csgjusticecenter.org/wp-content/uploads/2014/06/Washington-State-Overview.pdf
This report looks at recent trends in Washington's criminal justice system and what the Justice Center's staff will be analyzing more closely in a following report. Based on the findings, a task force will be created and will use the findings to develop policy options for the state to consider. The report also goes into the steps it will follow when approaching Justice Reinvestment in Washington and how it will be implemented in the state.

Justice Center for State Governments. (2014). *West Virginia's Justice Reinvestment.* **New York, NY: The Council of State Governments.**
https://csgjusticecenter.org/wp-content/uploads/2014/06/West-Virginias-Justice-Reinvestment-Summary-Report.pdf
This report looks at what West Virginia was facing with its prison population slated to increase by 24 percent in a few years. The Justice Center ran an analysis of crime trends in the state and formed a working group to come up with policies based on the analysis's findings. This report goes over the challenges the state and working group faced and reviews the projected impact that the new policies will have on the state and its criminal justice system.

Justice Center for State Governments. (2013). *Justice Reinvestment in West Virginia: Analysis and Policy Options to Reduce Spending on Corrections and Reinvest in Strategies to Increase Public Safety.* **New York, NY: The Council of State Governments.**
https://csgjusticecenter.org/jr/west-virginia/publications/justice-reinvestment-in-west-virginia-analyses-policy-options-to-reduce-spending-on-corrections-reinvest-in-strategies-to-increase-public-safety/
This report analyzed West Virginia's crime trends, took the findings, and convened focus groups to talk about what can be done to fix these trends. This report also provides the framework for future policies to address the key issues that came about from the focus groups and anaylsis.

Justice Center for State Governments. (2014). *Justice Reinvestment in Nebraska: Overview.* **New York, NY: The Council of State Governments.**
https://csgjusticecenter.org/wp-content/uploads/2014/06/JR_Nebraska-Overview.pdf
This report looks at recent trends in Nebraska's criminal justice system and what the Justice Center's staff will be analyzing more closely in a following report. A working group will be established based on the analysis of the crime trends. The report goes into the steps it will follow when approaching Justice Reinvestment in Nebraska and how it will be implemented in the state.

Justice Center for State Governments. (2014). *Justice Reinvestment in Washington State: Overview.* **New York, NY: The Council of State Governments.**
https://csgjusticecenter.org/wp-content/uploads/2014/06/Washington-State-Overview.pdf
This report looks at recent trends in Washington's criminal justice system and what the Justice Center's staff will be analyzing more closely in a following report. Based on the findings, a task force will be created and will use the findings to develop policy options for the state to consider. The report also goes into the steps it will follow when approaching Justice Reinvestment in Washington and how it will be implemented in the state.

Justice Center for State Governments. (2014). *West Virginia's Justice Reinvestment.* **New York, NY: The Council of State Governments.**
https://csgjusticecenter.org/wp-content/uploads/2014/06/West-Virginias-Justice-Reinvestment-Summary-Report.pdf
This report looks at what West Virginia was facing with their prison population slated to increase by 24 percent in a few years. The Justice Center ran an analysis of crime trends in the state and formed a working group to come up with policies based on the analysis's findings. This report goes over the challenges the state and working group faced and reviews the projected impact that the new policies will have on the state and its criminal justice system.

Dwyer, A.M., Neusteter, R.S., et al. (2012). *Data-Driven Decisionmaking for Strategic Justice Reinvestment* **[Brief 2]. Washington, DC: Urban Institute.**
http://www.urban.org/UploadedPDF/412543-Data-Driven-Decisionmaking-for-Strategic-Justice-Reinvestment.pdf
This brief discusses the need for and use of effective data in strategic justice reinvestment at the local level. It also includes the use of performance measures to monitor the progress of the justice reinvestment at the local level process.

Ho, H., Neusteter, S.R., et al. (2013). *Justice Reinvestment: A Toolkit for Local Leaders.* **New York: Urban Institute.**
http://www.urban.org/UploadedPDF/412929-Justice-Reinvestment-A-Toolkit-for-Local-Leaders.pdf
This toolkit presents an overview of the justice reinvestment model for local leaders, including examples from localities that have implemented justice reinvestment.

Lachman, P., & Neusteter, S.R. (2012). *Tracking Costs and Savings through Justice Reinvestment.* **New York: Urban Institute. BJA sponsored.**
http://www.urban.org/UploadedPDF/412541-Tracking-Costs-and-Savings-through-Justice-Reinvestment.pdf
This brief addresses the use of justice reinvestment strategies by local criminal justice professionals and policymakers. It also explores how to document costs and demonstrate savings, track populations across systems, measure savings throughout jurisdictions, determine the best ways to reinvest, and use crime mapping to target reinvestment.

Lachman, P., Neusteter, S.R., et al. (2013). *Criminal Justice Planner's Toolkit for Justice Reinvestment at the Local Level.* **New York: Urban Institute, BJA sponsored.**
http://www.urban.org/UploadedPDF/412931-The-Criminal-Justice-Planners-Toolkit-for-Justice-Reinvestment-at-the-Local-Level.pdf
This toolkit presents planners of a local justice reinvestment initiative with the technical information to identify what drives criminal justice system costs and to design strategies addressing those changes.

LaVigne, N.G., et al. (2014). *Justice Reinvestment Initiative State Assessment Report.* **Washington, DC: The Urban Institute. BJA sponsored.**
http://www.urban.org/UploadedPDF/412994-Justice-Reinvestment-Initiative-State-Assessment-Report.pdf
This JRI State Assessment Report, funded by BJA, describes the progress, challenges, and preliminary outcomes of 17 states involved in the JRI Initiative from 2010 to summer of 2013. States that have enacted policies are showing promise in reducing prison populations or averting future growth, generating savings while enhancing public safety. In addition to population changes, justice reinvestment has encouraged states to shift toward a culture of greater collaboration, data-driven decision-making, and increased use of evidence-based practices.

LaVigne, N.G., et al. (2013). *Justice Reinvestment at the Local Level: Planning and Implementation Guide Second Edition.* **New York, NY: The Urban Institute. BJA sponsored.**
http://www.urban.org/UploadedPDF/412930-Justice-Reinvestment-at-the-Local-Level-Planning-and-Implementation-Guide-Second-Edition.pdf
This guidebook provides information for local governments to use in planning and implementing a justice reinvestment strategy in their communities.

Lawrence, A., & Lyons, D. (2013, July). *Justice Reinvestment* [Crime Brief]. **Washington, DC: National Conference of State Legislatures.**
http://www.ncsl.org/Documents/CJ/July2013CrimeBrief.pdf
This resource lists justice reinvestment reforms that have led to savings in 19 states.

Lyons, D. (2013). "High-Yield Corrections." *State Legislatures,* **39(1): 22–25.**
http://www.ncsl.org/research/civil-and-criminal-justice/high-yield-corrections.aspx
The article discusses the justice reinvestment reforms implemented in various states, including those by Texas and Kansas. It also presents an overview of efforts of the Public Safety Performance Project at the Pew Center on the States.

National Institute of Justice. (2010). *An Examination of Justice Reinvestment and its Impact on Two States.* **Washington, DC: Author.**
http://nij.ncjrs.gov/multimedia/transcripts/audio-nijconf2010-justice-reinvestment-transcript.htm
This transcript of a panel held at a 2010 NIJ conference featured representatives from two states involved in justice reinvestment—Michigan and New Hampshire. Panel participants examine details of the initiative and how it is progressing.

Rivers, J. S. (2011). *Improving Criminal Justice and Reducing Recidivism through Justice Reinvestment.* **Washington, DC: U.S. Department of Justice, Office of Justice Programs, Bureau of Justice Assistance.**
https://www.bja.gov/Publications/JRI_FS.pdf
This fact sheet explains the rationale behind the Justice Reinvestment Initiative and outlines its various features.

U.S. Department of Justice, Office of Justice Programs, Bureau of Justice Assistance. (2013). *Justice Reinvestment Initiative: Experiences from the States.* **Washington, DC: Author.**
https://www.bja.gov/Publications/UI-JRI-State-Experiences.pdf
This policy brief reports on state experiences with JRI. The brief identifies factors common to several states—namely parole and probation revocations, sentencing policies and practices, insufficient and inefficient community supervision and support, and parole system processing delays and denials. It also identifies common legislative provisions and policy reforms that have been implemented across several states.

Websites

Council of State Governments Justice Center: Justice Reinvestment
http://csgjusticecenter.org/jr/

Pew Center on the States: Public Safety Performance Project Overview
http://www.pewtrusts.org/en/projects/public-safety-performance-project

Urban Institute: Justice Reinvestment at the Local Level
http://www.urban.org/center/jpc/justice-reinvestment/

Vera Justice Reinvestment Initiative
http://www.vera.org/project/justice-reinvestment-initiative

Missing Alzheimer's Disease Patient Alert Program

Project Description

The National Initiatives: Law Enforcement and Missing Persons with Alzheimer's Disease is a grant that focuses on programs addressing community and law enforcement needs and is committed to helping first responders improve their knowledge and skills to safeguard and interact with this special population. This grant is funded under the Missing Alzheimer's Disease Patient Alert Program and was developed to support law enforcement in locating missing people who have Alzheimer's disease and other forms of dementia. More than 60 percent of those with dementia (nearly 3.1 million people) will wander at some point, and more than half of those who wander become lost and separated from their loved ones.

CrimeSolutions.gov Ratings:
No ratings at this time

Partners and Professional Organizations:
- ✓ International Association of Chiefs of Police
- ✓ National Association of States United for Aging and Disabilities
- ✓ Project Lifesaver Inc.
- ✓ University of South Florida
- ✓ University of Illinois, Chicago
- ✓ University of Louisiana at Monroe
- ✓ MedicAlert Foundation United States, Inc.

OJP-Sponsored Evaluations[40]

Note: No program evaluations were found. The listed articles illustrate the need for this type of program and offer information on what action the federal government is taking to combat this issue.

OJP-Sponsored Research

U.S. Department of Justice, Office of Justice Programs, Bureau of Justice Assistance, and Project Lifesaver International. (2014). *Lost and Found: Understanding Technologies Used to Locate Missing Persons with Alzheimer's or Dementia* **[NCJ-245653]. Washington, DC: Authors. BJA sponsored.**

https://www.bja.gov/Publications/PLI-Lost_and_Found.pdf

This report familiarizes law enforcement officers and other first responders, caregivers, families, and the community about the signs of dementia and offers information on passive identification products used to identify people with Alzheimer's. It gives suggestions for improving skills to better deal with the challenges of Alzheimer's disease or dementia as well as a broad overview of symptoms and the potential impact on people living with these diseases. A review of the passive identification techniques, public alert options, locating device technology, and current locative products in the field are also presented.

Other Academic Articles

Carr, D., Muschert, G. W., et al. (2010). "Silver Alerts and the Problem of Missing Adults with Dementia." *Gerontologist, 50*(2): 149–157.

http://www.psychologytoday.com/files/attachments/142743/silver-alerts-and-the-problem-missing-adults-dementia-carr-et-al.pdf

This study analyzes varieties of Silver Alert programs: dementia-related and AMBER extension, the dates of enactment, and the criteria and the process of activation The paper makes recommendations for future research, including examining whether Silver Alerts are an appropriate response to address the problem of

---

[40] For each article, a link has been provided to either the full-length document or a website it can be accessed.

missing adults with dementia or cognitive impairments. The costs and benefits of these programs are further examined, including discusisions on how best to balance efforts of keeping those living with cognitive impairments safe while supporting them in maintaining their autonomy and self empowerment.

Petonito, G., Muschert, G. W., et al. (2013). "Programs to Locate Missing and Critically Wandering Elders: A Critical Review and a Call for Multiphasic Evaluation." *Gerontologist, 53*(1): 17–25.
http://www.ncbi.nlm.nih.gov/pubmed/22565495

This paper describes and critically examines three prominent and widespread programs that assist older adults who go missing: Safe Return, Project Lifesaver, and Silver Alert. Despite the emergence of these programs, there has been little research on their effectiveness. More fundamentally, the nature and scope of the missing elder problem is understudied. The paper calls for further research into this issue as well as assessments of how well these programs balance individual liberties with safety concerns.

Wasser, T. D., & Fox, P. K. (2013). "For Whom the Bell Tolls: Silver Alerts Raise Concerns Regarding Individual Rights and Governmental Interests." *Journal of the American Academy of Psychiatry and the Law Online, 41*(3): 421–429.
http://www.jaapl.org/content/41/3/421.full

This paper examines the purposes of the Silver Alert system and the ways in which it helps law enforcement locate missing elders. However, it also examines the unintended consequences of the program—for example, violations of a person's right to privacy. The discussion delves into some of these consequences, concluding that procedural safeguards must be maximized to protect the privacy of people with cognitive disabilities. In particular, the eligibility parameters for Silver Alert activation in all states must be more specifically and narrowly defined, and the role of mental health providers in the activation of Silver Alerts should be more thoroughly explored and defined, especially regarding ethics-related concerns and legal and professional considerations.

Yamashita, T., Carr, D. C., et al. (2013). "Analyzing State-Based Silver Alert Programs: The Case of North Carolina." *North Carolina Medical Journal, 74*(2): 111–117.
http://www.ncmedicaljournal.com/wp-content/uploads/2013/04/74202_Yamashita-FINAL.pdf

Recent discussions about securing the autonomy and safety of older people in a cost-effective way have culminated in establishing Silver Alert media-alert policies in more than half of U.S. states over the past 5 years. However, research has not yet determined how these policies have been implemented. Data from the 587 Silver Alerts activated in North Carolina in 2008, 2009, and 2010 were analyzed using sero-inflated negative binomial regression and exploratory special analyses. Despite the policy focus on older adults and people with cognitive impairment, activation of Silver Alerts was not related to the county's proportion of people ages 65 or older or to the prevalence of poor mental health. The current mission and implementation of the Silver Alert program should be reviewed, as data did not evaluate the proportion of older adults in the county or for the prevalence of impaired mental status.

Other Reports

Advisory Board of the Missing Alzheimer's Disease Patient Initiative and IACP National Law Enforcement Policy Center. (2010). *Missing Persons with Alzheimer's Disease: Model Policy.* **Alexandria, VA: International Association of Chiefs of Police.**
http://www.theiacp.org/portals/0/pdfs/AlzheimersMissingPersonsPolicy.pdf

The purpose of this policy is to offer guidance to law enforcement and other agencies for responding to and investigating the cases of missing persons with Alzheimer's disease and related dementias.

International Association of Chiefs of Police. (2011). *Missing Persons with Alzheimer's Disease: Issues and Concepts.* **Alexandria, VA: Author.**
http://www.theiacp.org/portals/0/pdfs/AlzheimersMissingPersonsIssuesandConcepts2011.pdf

This paper complements the model policy on Missing Persons with Alzheimer's Disease. The discussion addresses best practices, response challenges, and specific search-and-rescue protocols for people with Alzheimer's disease and related dementia. This material is expected to be of value to law enforcement executives in their efforts to tailor the model policy to the requirements and needs of their agencies and communities.

International Association of Chiefs of Police and Bureau of Justice Assistance. (2013). *Drivers with Alzheimer's Disease: 10 Warning Signs a Drive May Have Alzheimer's Disease/10 Steps for Interacting with Drivers Who May Have Alzheimer's Disease or Dementia.* **Alexandria, VA: Author. BJA sponsored.**
http://www.theiacp.org/portals/0/documents/pdfs/IACP-AlzheimerPocketcard.pdf
These instructional briefs offer guidance on communication tactics for police officers interacting with drivers who have Alzheimer's disease or dementia. To facilitate appropriate interaction between patrol officers and drivers who have Alzheimer's disease, these briefs (in the form of pocket-size reminder cards) list 10 warning signs for Alzheimer's disease and 10 appropriate officer responses to drivers believed to have Alzheimer's disease or dementia. When noticing a driver who has a combination of these symptoms, patrol officers should adopt these suggested appropriate interactions.

National Association of State Units on Aging. (2010). *Silver Alert Initiatives in the States: Protecting Seniors with Cognitive Impairments.* **Washington, DC: Author.**
http://www.nasuad.org/sites/nasuad/files/hcbs/files/214/10653/SilverAlertUpdatedReportMarch2010.pdf
This report identifies each state with a Silver Alert program, how each funds it, and how each administers the program. Eighteen states have a Silver Alert program, 14 states had pending legislation, and 18 states have no related legislation. The resport gives brief summaries of the legislation that establishes the programs, and the agencies administering them, program requirements for initiating an alert, and websites for each state's Silver Alert program.

U.S. Department of Justice, Office of Justice Programs, Bureau of Justice Assistance, and the Center for Public Safety and Justice. (2015). *Alzheimer's Aware: A Guide for Implementing a Law Enforcement Program to Address Alzheimer's in the Community* **[2012-SJ-BX-K002]. Washington, DC: Author. BJA sponsored.**
https://www.bja.gov/Publications/AlzheimersAware.pdf
This publication provides an overview of the Alzheimer's Aware initiative, gives detailed information regarding the components of the three areas of the program's focus (law enforcement engagement, community involvement, and public information/awareness), and includes a recommended steps section to support law enforcement agencies in their development and program implementation.

Website

International Association of Chiefs of Police Alzheimer's Initiatives
http://www.iacp.org/Missing-Alzheimers-Disease-Patient

The National Center for Campus Public Safety

Project Description

The National Center for Campus Public Safety (NCCPS), founded in 2013 through funding from BJA, is a resource for campus security and police chiefs, public safety directors, emergency managers, and other key stakeholders engaged in campus safety activities.[41] NCCPS fosters these goals:

- Identify and prioritize the needs of the field and develop comprehensive responses.

- Connect existing federal and nonfederal resources with the needs of constituents.

- Connect major campus public safety entities with one another as well as with federal agencies to facilitate collaboration and coordination around issues of campus public safety.

- Highlight and promote best and innovative practices specific to campus public safety challenges.

- Deliver essential training and technical assistance specific to campus public safety.

CrimeSolutions.gov Ratings:
Effective (2)
Promising (2)
No Effect (3)
Insufficient Evidence (0)

Partners and Professional Organizations:
- ✓ International Association of Campus Law Enforcement Administrators
- ✓ Office of Community Oriented Policing Services
- ✓ Margolis Healy

Note: The NCCPS evaluations are not complete, as the solicitation was issued in 2013. This program's implementation and evaluation are expected to take several years from the award date. Instead, the listed articles provide evaluations and information on other campus safety programs. These articles and reports have been selected from CrimeSolutions.gov, publicly available reports, and academic journals.[42]

OJP-Sponsored Evaluations[43]

Krebs, C., Lindquist, C., Warner, T., Fisher, B. S., & Martin, S. L. (2007). *The Campus Sexual Assault (CSA) Study. Final Report.* Research Triangle Park, NC: RTI International. NIJ Funded.
https://www.ncjrs.gov/pdffiles1/nij/grants/221153.pdf
The CSA study examined the prevalence, nature, and reporting of sexual assault on college campuses to inform the development of targeted intervention strategies. Data suggest that women at universities are at considerable risk for experiencing sexual assault and that several personal and behavioral factors are associated with increased risk for sexual assault.

---

[41] For more information, please visit: http://www.nccpsafety.org.

[42] CrimeSolutions.gov program and practice areas are discussed through the articles and reports cited for each program or practice. In some cases, one article may have multiple ratings, or multiple articles may be used to determine a single rating. Therefore, the number of reports or articles given a CrimeSolutions.gov rating may not match what is found by searching CrimeSolutions.gov.

[43] For each article, a link has been provided to either the full-length document or the website where it can be accessed.

Krebs, C., Lindquist, C., & Barrick, K. (2011). *The Historically Black College and University Campus Sexual Assault (HBCU-CSA) Study. Final Report.* **Research Triangle Park, NC: RTI International,. NIJ Funded.**
https://www.ncjrs.gov/pdffiles1/nij/grants/233614.pdf
The HBCU-CSA Study was undertaken to document the prevalence of distinct forms of sexual assault. This study also examines campus police and service provider perspectives on sexual victimization and student attitudes toward law enforcement and ideas about prevention and policy. The authors found that 9.6% of undergraduate HBCU women in the sample experienced sexual assault since entering college, and campus police reported that particular victim characteristics would not make them more or less likely to believe a woman claiming she had been sexually assaulted.

Messing, T., Campbell, J., Sullivan Wilson, J., Brown, S., Patchell, B., & Shall, C. (2014). *Police Departments' Use of the Lethality Assessment Program: A Quasi-Experimental Evaluation.* **NIJ Funded.**
https://www.ncjrs.gov/pdffiles1/nij/grants/247456.pdf
This quasi-experimental evaluation examined the effectiveness of the Lethality Assessment Program (LAP), a collaboration between police and social service providers that aimed to decrease rates of repeat, severe, lethal, and near-lethal domestic violence while increasing rates of emergency safety planning and help seeking.

Reaves, B. (2015). *Special Report: Campus Law Enforcement, 2011-2012.* **Washington, DC: DOJ.**
http://www.bjs.gov/content/pub/pdf/cle1112.pdf
During the 2011–12 school year, about two-thirds of U.S. 4-year colleges and universities with 2,500 or more students used sworn police officers to provide law enforcement services on campus. Among public institutions, nearly all students were enrolled on campuses with sworn and armed officers. Among private institutions, nearly half of the students were enrolled on campuses with sworn and armed officers.

Other Academic Research

Baer, J. S., Kivlahan, D. R., et al. (2001). "Brief Intervention for Heavy-Drinking College Students: 4-Year Follow-Up and Natural History." *American Journal of Public Health, 91*(8): 1310–1316.
http://www.ncbi.nlm.nih.gov/pubmed/11499124

This program was rated on CrimeSolutions.gov as effective.
This study details a single-session, individualized prevention meeting for college freshmen with histories of heavy drinking. Results indicate that those receiving the treatment had cut down on how much they drank, though not how often. This resulted in fewer negative consequences from drinking.

Baker, K., & Boland, K. (2011). "Assessing Safety: A Campus-Wide Initiative." *College Student Journal, 45*(4): 683–699.
http://connection.ebscohost.com/c/articles/77305722/assessing-safety-campus-wide-initiative
This article is an assessment of campus safety. About 150 faculty and staff and 450 students completed a survey designed to measure their beliefs and attitudes, daily behaviors, personal safety precautions, and cases of victimization. Results showed that the majority of respondents thought their campus was safe and had satisfactory safety features. Victimization was rare.

Berry, P. J., & Sedlak, L. (2007). "Florida Governor's Task Force Releases Campus Safety Proposals." *Campus Law Enforcement Journal, 37*(3): 24.
https://www.ncjrs.gov/App/publications/abstract.aspx?ID=240809
This article details 63 recommendations for improving safety and security at Florida's institutions of higher education. Five recommendations pertain to federal action, including promoting best practices, supporting initiatives to prevent various common college crimes, and increasing funding to the COPS office for use in training campus officers.

Blake, C. (2007). "After Virginia Tech: Where Do We Go from Here?" *Campus Law Enforcement Journal, 37*(3): 14–16.

https://www.ncjrs.gov/App/publications/abstract.aspx?ID=240807

This article outlines a four-point strategy for campus safety. First, promote the use of IACLEA's Threat and Risk Assessment tool, which is designed to assist campuses in identifying and prioritizing vulnerabilities and potential threats. Second, work with federal partners and individual campuses to create multidisciplinary assessment teams to develop a structure and methodology for helping students with mental health problems and removing those students who pose risks. Third, renew efforts to offer a comprehensive tool to help campuses evaluate their physical security environment. Fourth, ensure that rapid response planning and training is made available to all campuses that need it.

Fletcher, P. C., & Bryden, P. J. (2007). "Preliminary Examination of Safety Issues on a University Campus: Personal Safety Practices, Beliefs & Attitudes of Female Faculty & Staff." *College Student Journal 41*(4): 1149 –1162.

http://connection.ebscohost.com/c/articles/36792329/preliminary-examination-safety-issues-university-campus-personal-safety-practices-beliefs-attitudes-female-faculty-staff

This study examined issues that female faculty and staff members have about safety on and around campus. The study surveyed 229 female faculty and staff and found that awareness of services on campus dealing with safety issues was high, although use of such services remained relatively low. Respondents reported taking precautions that included locking car doors when alone, planning a route with safety in mind, carrying keys in a defensive manner, and checking the back seat of the car for intruders before getting into the car.

Gidycz, C., Orchowski, L., & Berkowitz, A. (2011). "Preventing Sexual Aggression Among College Men: An Evaluation of a Social Norms and Bystander Intervention Program." *Violence Against Women, 17*(6): 720–742.

http://vaw.sagepub.com/content/17/6/720

Men and women living in randomly selected first-year dormitories participated in tailored single-sex sexual assault prevention or risk-reduction programs, respectively. An evaluation of the men's project is presented ($N = 635$). The program incorporated social norms and bystander intervention education and had an impact on self-reported sexual aggression and an effect on men's perceptions that their peers would intervene when they encountered inappropriate behavior in others. Relative to the control group, participants also reported less reinforcement for engaging in sexually aggressive behavior, reported fewer associations with sexually aggressive peers, and indicated less exposure to sexually explicit media.

Gnage, M. F., Dziagwa, C., et al. (2009). "Safety on a Rural Community College Campus Via Integrated Communications." *Community College Journal of Research and Practice, 33*(11): 948–950.

http://www.tandfonline.com/doi/abs/10.1080/10668920903153105?journalCode=ucjc20

West Virginia University at Parkersburg uses a two-way emergency system as a baseline for emergency communications. The college has found that such a system, a key component of its safety and crisis management plan, can be integrated with other communication initiatives to create focused security on the campus.

Hites, L. S., Fifolt, M., et al. (2013). "A Geospatial Mixed Methods Approach to Assessing Campus Safety." *Evaluation Review, 37* (5): 347–369.

http://www.ncbi.nlm.nih.gov/pubmed/24379450

This article describes a mixed-methods approach for assessing campus safety at a large urban campus. Student focus groups yielded data regarding perceptions of risk, and analysis was used to identify campus crime incident hot spots. Although in many cases perceived risk and actual crime incidents were associated, the two were not significantly related.

Janosik, S. M., & Plummer, E. (2005). "The Clery Act, Campus Safety and the Views of Assault Victim Advocates." *College Student Affairs Journal, 25* (1): 116–130.
http://eric.ed.gov/?id=EJ957017
This study details a survey of 147 directors of women's centers about the effectiveness of the Clery Act and their views of campus safety. The study's purpose was to assess how much victim advocates knew about the Act and what their views of campus crime prevention strategies were. Results show that respondents thought mandated summaries and annual reports are unlikely to be read or to affect behavior and that passive ad campaigns are more likely to influence behavior.

Li-Shan, C. (2009). "Design and Implementation of an Intelligent Mobile Information System for Campus Safety Management." *International Journal of Organizational Innovation, 2*(1): 320–340.
http://connection.ebscohost.com/c/articles/42958469/design-implementation-intelligent-mobile-information-system-campus-safety-management
This study is aimed at establishing an intelligent mobile information system for colleges. This includes the use of video cameras in high-traffic areas and the creation of a method to embed the mobile information system into each user's device (personal digital assistant or smart phone) to promote campus safety management.

Mastroleo, I. M. G., Grossbard, J. R., et al. (2009). "A Randomized Clinical Trial Evaluating a Combined Alcohol Intervention for High-Risk College Students." *Journal of Studies on Alcohol and Drugs, 70*: 555–567.
http://www.ncbi.nlm.nih.gov/pubmed/19515296
This program was rated on CrimeSolutions.gov as effective.
This article details a study where students with a history of heavy drinking were assigned to one of four conditions: parental intervention, a brief intervention, both parental and brief interventions, or no intervention. Results indicate that the combined interventions led to significantly lower alcohol consumption and fewer negative consequences.

Rasmussen, C., & Johnson, G. (2008). *The Ripple Effect of Virginia Tech: Assessing the Nationwide Impact on Campus Safety and Security Policy and Practice.* **Minneapolis, MN: Midwestern Higher Education Compact.**
http://www.mhec.org/sites/mhec.org/files/052308mhecsafetyrpt_hr.pdf
This report details a survey of student life officers and campus safety directors to assess the impact that the April 2007 shootings at Virginia Tech had on campus safety and security policy and practice. All respondents indicated that the relationship between their institution and municipal law enforcement and state-level agencies had remained about the same or improved since that event.

Stotzer, R. L., & Hosellman, E. (2012). "Hate Crimes on Campus: Racial/Ethnic Diversity and Campus Safety." *Journal of Interpersonal Violence, 27* (4): 644 –661.
http://www.ncbi.nlm.nih.gov/pubmed/22007114
This study examines the impact of racial diversity on the reported number of campus hate crimes. Findings suggest that schools that are most successful in attracting hard-to-recruit minorities (Black and Latino students) report fewer campus hate crimes.

Other Reports

Blair, J. P., Martaindale, M. H., et al. (2014). *Active Shooter Events from 2000–2012.* **Washington, DC: Federal Bureau of Investigation.**
http://leb.fbi.gov/2014/january/active-shooter-events-from-2000-to-2012
This report details active shooter events (ASEs) and finds they are on the rise since 2000 (from 5 per year to 16 per year). Of all ASEs from 2000 to 2012, 29 percent occurred at a school. Most (59 percent) involved a pistol, and nearly half ended before law enforcement arrived on the scene. For those events

still occurring after law enforcement arrived, 43 percent ended with the police shooting the suspect. The authors conclude that officers need to be adequately trained to deal with these situations.

Greenberg, S. (2005). *National Summit on Campus Public Safety: Strategies for Colleges and Universities in a Homeland Security Environment.* **Columbia, MD: Mid-Atlantic Regional Community Policing Institute.**
https://www.ncjrs.gov/App/publications/abstract.aspx?ID=210917
This report details 3 focus points and 25 recommendations from the national summit in Baltimore, MD, from November 29 to December 1, 2004. One focus point was the establishment of a national center for campus safety to support information-sharing, policy development, model practices, operations, and research. Recommendations included creating a national agenda on campus safety, establishing a national center for campus safety, and initiating a national advisory panel on campus safety.

Lewis, B. (2014, March/April). "School Safety: Helping Law Enforcement and Communities Meet the Challenges of the Modern School Day." *TechBeat Magazine,* **3–6. NIJ sponsored.**
https://www.ncjrs.gov/App/publications/abstract.aspx?ID=267741
This article profiles efforts by NIJ to address new training and technology needs in the wake of the 2012 school shooting in Newtown, CT. The staff at the National Law Enforcement and Corrections Technology Center worked to find free, publicly available resources and links on the Internet with information on successful new technologies implemented across the country. These efforts led to the development of the SchoolSafetyInfo.org website, dedicated to offering up-to-the-minute information and assistance to the public safety community.

International Association of Campus Law Enforcement Administrators, International Association of Chiefs of Police (IACP), National Center for Campus Public Safety, and University of Wisconsin-Madison Police Department. (2014). *Practitioners' Discussion of Implementing Clery/Title IX: Report on the Summit.*
http://www.nccpsafety.org/resources/library/practitioners-discussion-of-implementing-clery-title-ix/
In August 2014, a campus safety groups, college administrators, and law enforcement officials held a summit in Madison, WI, to discuss unresolved issues around Title IX and other related legislation, including the Clery Act and the Violence Against Women Act. Campus police administrators, deans of students, Title IX and Clery staff, and others met to work toward better compliance—not only with the letter of the law but, far more important, with the spirit of the law. Summit participants created a comprehensive list of issues and promising practices to consider.

International Association of Campus Law Enforcement Administrators (IACLEA), International Association of Chiefs of Police (IACP), National Center for Campus Public Safety (NCCPS), and Georgia Tech, (2015). *Practitioners' Discussion of Implementing Clery/Title IX: Report on the Summit II.*
http://www.nccpsafety.org/assets/files/library/NCCPS_Summit_II_Paper_FINAL051815.pdf
Summit II was the second in a series of meetings co-hosted by the National Center for Campus Public Safety), the IACP University and College Police Section, and the International Association of Campus Law Enforcement Administrators. Summit I, held in August 2014, in Madison, WI, brought together campus officials from around the country to discuss issues around Title IX and other related legislation, including the Clery Act and the Violence Against Women Act (VAWA). This summit provided rich detail on what was still needed for application of the laws in an effort to decrease sexual violence trauma. It also revealed how the victim held substantial influence on how the process should transpire. Most participants acknowledged that the process was not always clear. A criminal offense may have been committed, and campus administrators often felt that their methods of handling student violations were now pushed into the more adversarial role. With this in mind, the participants at Summit II accepted the premise and intent of Title IX and Clery; however, the details of implementation needed further clarification. The anecdotes regarding sexual offenses did not fit neatly into any preordained formula or algorithm. Summit II participants reviewed and discussed some of the issues raised in Summit I; however, the emphasis quickly

shifted from the challenges to suggesting promising practices that would address those challenges. The suggestions were not meant as final solutions to complicated issues but as starting points to form a core Title IX public safety compliance system on the respective campuses.

Nolan, J., Randazzo, M., & Deisinger, G. (2011). "Campus Threat Assessment and Management Teams: What Risk Managers Need to Know Now." *University Risk Management and Insurance Association (URMIA)* **Journal Reprint.**
http://www.nccpsafety.org/assets/files/library/Campus_Threat_Assessment_and_Management_Teams.pdf
After the shootings at Virginia Tech in 2007, many colleges and universities recognized that having threat assessment and management (TAM) teams in place to address potentially threatening behavior and situations among faculty, staff, and students on campus was a best practice. This article focuses on three main aspects of TAM teams on college campuses and what risk managers can do to encourage the success and effectiveness of those teams. The article discusses the legal duties that colleges and universities have in connection with violent incidents on campus. It also focuses on the development of a TAM process, the common challenges facing TAM team members, and how risk managers can help mitigate and minimize campus risks by assisting TAM teams.

Randazzo, M., Plummer, E. (2009). *Implementing Behavioral Threat Assessment on Campus: A Virginia Tech Demonstration Project.* **Blacksburg, VA: Virginia Polytechnic Institute and State University.**
http://www.nccpsafety.org/assets/files/library/Implementing_Behavioral_Threat_Assessment.pdf
This book documents Virginia Tech's experience in developing and implementing a behavioral threat assessment process since the campus shootings on April 16, 2007. In the course of building its behavioral threat assessment capacity, Virginia Tech created documentation to support its threat assessment team and related efforts. This documentation includes an array of institutional policies, the team's mission statement, information distributed universitywide to announce and promote the threat assessment team, wallet reference cards, position descriptions, and other materials. This information can be useful to other institutions developing a behavioral threat assessment capacity or enhancing an existing threat assessment process. It is important to note that every institution is different and these examples may not be appropriate for a particular institution, but institutions can consider them when crafting their own policies, mission statement, public awareness message, and other relevant materials. Additional resources provide general templates for use in the creation of threat assessment processes.

Scalora, M., Simons, A., et al. (2010). "Campus Safety: Assessing and Managing Threats." *FBI Law Enforcement Bulletin, 79(2): 1–10.*
http://www.fbi.gov/stats-services/publications/law-enforcement-bulletin/february-2010/campus-safety
This article discusses threat assessment and management strategies to deal with the increased demands faced by campus law enforcement, mental health services, and administration officials. A collaborative and standardized assessment protocol can be a valuable tool in addressing the various potential internal and external threats to campus.

Woolfenden, S., & Stevenson, B. (2011). *Establishing Appropriate Staffing Levels for Campus Public Safety Departments.* **Washington, DC: U.S. Department of Justice, Office of Community Oriented Policing Services.**
http://www.cops.usdoj.gov/pdf/vets-to-cops/e061122378_Est-Approp-Stfg-Levels_FIN.pdf
This article details four focus groups about staffing campus public safety departments. Staffing is typically influenced by the student population, its age and gender profile, campus location and size, and similar factors. The report concludes that staff size for campus public safety departments should be affected by the policing style used, the workload of officers, and their work schedule and its demands.

AlcoholEdu for College

http://nrepp.samhsa.gov/ProgramProfile.aspx?id=9

This program is rated effective for reducing alcohol use and disorders and promising for reducing substance use-related consequences by Substance Abuse and Mental Health Services Administration's National Registry of Evidence-Based Programs and Practices.

Bringing in the Bystander

Program Summary: Bringing in the Bystander™ is a sexual violence prevention program aimed at increasing prosocial attitudes and behaviors among potential bystanders and third-person witnesses of risky behaviors and precursors to sexual victimization. The program emphasizes that all members of the community have a role to play in preventing sexual and intimate partner violence. Bringing in the Bystander is often implemented in a university campus setting to college students.

The following evaluation of this program was used as evidence for rating this program on CrimeSolutions.gov.

This program was rated on CrimeSolutions.gov as promising.
Details: http://www.CrimeSolutions.gov/ProgramDetails.aspx?ID=159

Banyard, V. A., Moynihan, M. M., & Plante. E. G. (2007). "Sexual Violence Prevention Through Bystander Education: An Experimental Evaluation." *Journal of Community Psychology, 35*(4): 463–81.
http://www.ncdsv.org/images/Sex%20Violence%20Prevention%20through%20Bystander%20Education.pdf
The current study used an experimental design to evaluate a sexual violence prevention program that teaches women and men how to intervene safely and effectively in cases of sexual violence before, during, and after incidents with strangers, acquaintances, or friends. Undergraduates participated and were randomly assigned to one of two treatment groups or a control group. Results from the research reveal that up to 2 months after participating in either a one- or three-session version of the program, participants in the treatment conditions showed improvements across measures of attitudes, knowledge, and behavior while the control group did not. Most program effects persisted at 4- and 12-month follow-ups.

Potter, S. J., Banyard, V. L., Stapleton, J. G., Demers, J. M. , Edwards, K. M., & Moynihan, M. M. (2015). *Informing Students about Campus Policies and Resources: How They Get the Message Matters.* **Durham, NH: University of New Hampshire, Prevention Innovations Research Center.**
http://www.unh.edu/news/docs/2015/messagingmatters.pdf
This research study examines the efficacy of different methods to deliver campus sexual misconduct policy information to first-year studentsto determine if exposure to the policy increased students' knowledge of the policy and of campus resources and increased their confidence to seek help or support for themselves, friends or strangers. Researchers and practitioners from seven campuses across the United States agreed to collaborate in research examining the delivery of campus sexual misconduct policies. The diverse group of campuses included public and private institutions, a Historically Black University, and a Hispanic Serving Institution. The study concludes that campus sexual misconduct policies should be disseminated in an engaging manner and provides opportunities for students to increase their knowledge and develop skills so they can help themselves, their friends, and strangers. The methods of delivery should vary and should not be limited to one method or a single dosage. Colleges and universities seem motivated to create communities that are free of sexual assault and can reach this goal through strategic planning and resource allocation for multiple prevention and response strategies that reach students, faculty, and staff throughout each student's years on campus.

Sexual Assault Risk Reduction Program

Program Summary: The Sexual Assault Risk Reduction Program is a rape-prevention program for college students. Its goal was to reduce the occurrence of sexual assault by increasing women's use of self-protective strategies and enhancing their self-efficacy in responding to threatening situations.

The following three evaluations of this program were used as evidence for rating this program on CrimeSolutions.gov.

This program was rated on CrimeSolutions.gov as having insufficient evidence.
Details: http://www.CrimeSolutions.gov/ProgramDetails.aspx?ID=405

Gidycz, C. A., Layman, M. J., Rich, C. L., Crothers, M., Gylys, J., Matorin, A., & Jacobs, C. D. (2001). "An Evaluation of an Acquaintance Rape Prevention Program: Impact on Attitudes, Sexual Aggression, and Sexual Victimization." *Journal of Interpersonal Violence,* **16(11): 1120–38.**
https://www.ncjrs.gov/app/publications/abstract.aspx?id=209235
This study assessed the effectiveness of a sexual assault prevention program on college students' rape-related attitudes and experiences with sexual aggression and victimization. Results suggested that participants evidenced less rape myth acceptance at posttest than the comparison group. Overall, the program did not have a significant effect on attitudes toward women, rape empathy, or rates of sexual aggression or victimization.

Gidycz, C. A., Rich, C. L., Orchowski, L., King, C., & Miller. A. K. (2006). "The Evaluation of a Sexual Assault Self-Defense and Risk-Reduction Program for College Women: A Prospective Study." *Psychology of Women Quarterly,* **30(2): 173–83.**
http://onlinelibrary.wiley.com/doi/10.1111/j.1471-6402.2006.00280.x/abstract
This study evaluated the efficacy of a sexual assault risk-reduction program that included a physical self-defense component for college women. Program group women significantly increased their protective behaviors over the 6-month follow-up period compared to the waiting-list control group. There were no significant differences between the two groups regarding rates of sexual victimization, assertive communication, or feelings of self-efficacy over the follow-up periods.

Orchowski, L. M., Gidycz, C. M., & Raffle, H. (2008). "Evaluation of a Sexual Assault Risk Reduction and Self-Defense Program: A Prospective Analysis of a Revised Protocol." *Psychology of Women Quarterly,* **32(2): 204–18.**
http://onlinelibrary.wiley.com/doi/10.1111/j.1471-6402.2008.00425.x/abstract
The study extended the development and evaluation of an existing and previously evaluated sexual assault risk reduction program with a self-defense component for college women. The program was effective in increasing levels of self-protective behaviors, self-efficacy in resisting against potential attackers, and use of assertive sexual communication over a 4-month interim within the test group. Results also suggested reduction of incidence of rape among program participants over the 2-month follow-up.

Gansky, S. A., Ellison, J. A., Rudy, D., Bergert, N., Letendre, M. A., Nelson, L., Kavanagh, C., & Walsh, M. M. (2005). "Cluster-Randomized Controlled Trial of an Athletic Trainer–Directed Spit (Smokeless) Tobacco Intervention for Collegiate Baseball Athletes: Results After 1 Year." *Journal of Athletic Training,* **40(2),76–87.**
http://www.ncbi.nlm.nih.gov/pmc/articles/PMC1150230/

This program was rated on CrimeSolutions.gov as promising.
This study examined whether an athletic trainer-directed smokeless tobacco (ST) intervention could decrease initiation and promote cessation of ST use among male collegiate baseball athletes. Although at 1 year, cessation of ST use was relatively high in both groups (36%), there was no significant difference between the groups.

Websites

National Center for Campus Public Safety
http://www.nccpsafety.org/

International Association of Campus Law Enforcement Administrators
www.iaclea.org

Pay for Success Program

Project Description

The Pay for Success initiative creates performance-based contracts between the federal government and social service providers, where the government only pays providers if they achieve target outcomes instead of making reimbursement payments. The concept is simple: pay providers after they have demonstrated success, not on the promise of success, which is the usual practice.[44] The financing organization works with philanthropic and other investors to invest in innovative, data-driven service providers that can achieve results. Because the government pays only for demonstrated results, philanthropic and other investors agree to bear the primary financial risk until the providers achieve the desired outcomes. This will increase the government's return on investment in social programs that often have a weak track record of success.

OJP-Sponsored and Non-OJP-Sponsored Evaluations[45]

Note: No BJA program evaluations were found during the literature review. The listed articles and reports illustrate the need for this type of program and include related materials that show support for future evaluations of Pay for Success programs. It should be noted that Social Impact Bonds (SIBs) are mostly categorized under the Pay for Success program, and articles and evaluations on SIBs are included here. There has been some discrepancy between some publications (within the same agency) that categorize SIBs as different from the Pay for Success Program. Because Pay for Success is a relatively new program, most of the research is on the first program in the United Kingdom.

Academic Research

Aylott, M., & Shelupanov, A. (2011). "Social Impact Bonds in Criminal Justice: From Interesting Idea to Business as Usual." *Prison Service Journal*, 195: 3–8.
https://www.ncjrs.gov/App/AbstractDB/AbstractDBDetails.aspx?id=261491
This paper discusses how the criminal justice system can benefit from social impact bonds (SIBs), which are funding mechanisms that invest in social outcomes.

Baliga, S. (2013). "Shaping the Success of Social Impact Bonds in the United States: Lessons Learned from the Privatization of U.S. Prisons." *Duke Law Journal*, 63: 437–479.
http://scholarship.law.duke.edu/cgi/viewcontent.cgi?article=3403&context=dlj
This law review note details the privatization challenges that government officials will likely face as they implement SIBs. Most importantly, this note is the first to propose how government officials implementing SIBs can overcome the traditional obstacles facing privatization schemes—both through the structure of SIBs and through additional contractual solutions. The author concludes with a discussion about how elements of SIBs can be incorporated to improve existing privatization models such as private prisons, and how SIBs alter the existing debate about privatization in this country.

Deering, J. (2014). "A Future for Probation?" *Howard Journal of Criminal Justice, 53*(1): 1–15.
http://search.proquest.com/docview/1512218922?accountid=26333
The probation service in England and Wales faces its greatest challenge from four competing and differing forces: its current case management approach as influenced by moves to more law-enforcement

---

[44] More details can be found at this website: http://www.whitehouse.gov/omb/factsheet/paying-for-success.
[45] For each article, a link has been provided to either the full-length document or the website where it can be accessed.

practices; theories of desistance; new developments in offender engagement; and the emergence of Payment by Results. This article considers each of these influences and discusses how important they may be to the future of probation practice, concluding that the future of the service may be unrecognizable from its past.

Fox, C., & Albertson, K. (2011). "Payment by Results and Social Impact Bonds in the Criminal Justice Sector: New Challenges for the Concept of Evidence-Based Policy?" *Criminology and Criminal Justice, 11*(5): 395–413.

http://crj.sagepub.com/content/early/2011/08/06/1748895811415580.abstract

This article lays out the challenges likely to arise in developing payment by results models and SIBs in the criminal justice system of England and Wales. These challenges include the uncertainty from defining outcomes, estimating the potential impact of interventions, measuring and attributing change, valuing benefits, demonstrating a fiscal return, and getting interventions to scale. The authors conclude that, to a government trying to deliver "more for less," payment by results may offer an attractive solution in some parts of the public sector. However, the case for this approach in the criminal justice sector, where the evidence base is contested and potential savings are difficult to quantify and realize, is not yet proven.

Fox, C., & Albertson, K. (2012). "Is Payment by Results the Most Efficient Way to Address the Challenges Faced by the Criminal Justice Sector?" *Probation Journal, 59*(4): 355–373.

http://prb.sagepub.com/content/59/4/355.short

In recent years, the United Kingdom government has emphasized evidence-based policy, increasingly promoting the Payment by Results (PbR) approach. This article discusses the potential benefits of PbR and surveys its use across the U.K. public sector. Concentrating in particular on the criminal justice system (CJS), the authors outline three methodological challenges to PbR implementation: gaming, measuring outcomes, and identifying fiscal benefits. The authors conclude that PbR has a place in commissioning services, but its role in CJS is likely to be limited and it is unlikely to succeed as a socially efficient means of attracting new sources of funding. The authors consider two alternatives to PbR: justice reinvestment and personalization.

Humphries, K. W. (2014). "Not Your Older Brother's Bonds: The Use and Regulation of Social-Impact Bonds in the United States." *Law & Contemporary Problems, 76*(3/4): 433–452.

http://scholarship.law.duke.edu/lcp/vol76/iss3/15/

The article discusses the use and regulation of SIBs in the United States as of July 2014, focusing on juvenile delinquency, recidivism rates, and the economic aspects of efforts to reduce juvenile crime. The author states that SIBs, which are also known as pay for success bonds, use private capital to fund government projects. SIBs have also been proposed or enacted by governments to address homelessness and school attendance problems.

Leventhal, R. (2012). "Effecting Progress: Using Social Impact Bonds to Finance Social Services." *New York University Journal of Law & Business, 9*: 511–534.

http://www.nyujlb.org/wp-content/uploads/nyb_9-2_511-534_Leventhal.pdf

This article focuses on the perceived benefits of using social impact bonds to finance social outcomes and to expand the availability of services.

von Glahn, D., & Whistler, C. (2011, March). "Translating Plain English: Can the Peterborough Social Impact Bond Construct Apply Stateside?" *Community Development Investment Review, 7*(1): 58–70.

http://www.frbsf.org/community-development/files/Glahn_Whistler.pdf

This paper explores several questions:

- What is the U.K. SIB? What does it offer the social sector?
- How can SIBs be constructed to balance the priorities of the government, investors, and service providers? How will they redefine traditional relationships between these players?

- Can this construct apply to the United States? If so, what must we consider to maximize its value?

York, P. (2011). "Charities May Wind Up Paying for President's 'Pay for Success' Idea.'" *Chronicle of Philanthropy, 23*(13): 10.
http://philanthropy.com/article/Pay-for-Success-Idea-Could/127499/
The article reports on the potential impact of the "pay for success" concept proposed by President Obama on nonprofit organizations in the United States. The concept aims to change the traditional financing of social services. The discussion compares this concept and the SIBs tested in the United Kingdom. The article also discussed concerns about the future involvement of some politicians and activists in the modified social programs.

Other Reports

Callanan, L., Law, J., & Mendonca, L. (2012). *From Potential to Action: Bringing Social Impact Bonds to the U.S.* **Washington, DC: McKinsey & Company.**
http://mckinseyonsociety.com/downloads/reports/Social-Innovation/McKinsey_Social_Impact_Bonds_Report.pdf
McKinsey & Company conducted a rigorous, data-driven analysis of the potential and capacity for SIBs in the United States, focusing on how SIBs might be applied in two program areas: homelessness and criminal justice.

City of New York, Office of the Mayor. (2012). *Bringing Social Impact Bonds to New York City.* **New York: Author.**
http://www.nyc.gov/html/om/pdf/2012/sib_media_presentation_080212.pdf
This briefing outlines information about the elements of New York's social impact bonds program, including evaluation elements and payment determinations based on outcomes.

City of New York, Office of the Mayor. (2012). *The NYC ABLE Project for Incarcerated Youth: America's First Social Impact Bond.* **New York: Author.**
http://www.nyc.gov/html/om/pdf/2012/sib_fact_sheet.pdf
This fact sheet provides information about the Adolescent Behavioral Learning Experience program, which aims to reduce the reincarceration rate among adolescents at Rikers Island. It includes details of how the program is funded and how it will be evaluated to determine repayment.

Costa, K. (2014). *Investing for Success: Policy Questions Raised by Social Investors.* **Washington, DC: Center for American Progress.**
http://cdn.americanprogress.org/wp-content/uploads/2014/03/SIB-brief2-5.pdf
This issue brief presents findings from two roundtable conversations in 2013 with potential social impact bond investors—discussions that produced a series of key policy questions.

Costa, K. (2014). *Social Impact Bonds in the United States.* **Washington, DC: Center for American Progress.**
http://cdn.americanprogress.org/wp-content/uploads/2014/02/SocialImpactBonds3.pdf
This fact sheet offers information about SIBs and where they have been used in the United States.

Costa, K., & Tomasko, L. (2014). *Networking for Success: Building Networks Is Essential to Investment in Social Impact Bonds.* **Washington, DC: Center for American Progress.**
http://cdn.americanprogress.org/wp-content/uploads/2014/03/SIB-brief1-3.pdf
This issue brief presents findings from two roundtable conversations in 2013 with potential social impact bond investors, concluding that strong cross-sector relationships are key to social impact bond transactions.

Disley, E., Rubin, J., et al. (2011). *Lessons Learned from the Planning and Early Implementation of the Social Impact Bond at HMP Peterborough.* **Santa Monica, CA: RAND Corporation.**
http://www.rand.org/pubs/technical_reports/TR1166.html
This report identifies early lessons from the development and implementation of the world's first social impact bond, which is being piloted by the U.K. Ministry of Justice to promote interventions to reduce reoffending.

Kohli, J., Besharov, D. J., et al. (2012). *Inside a Social Impact Bond Agreement: Exploring the Contract Challenges of a New Social Finance Mechanism.* **Washington, DC: Center for American Progress.**
http://cdn.americanprogress.org/wp-content/uploads/issues/2012/05/pdf/sib_agreement_brief.pdf
This issue brief gives examples of what should—and should not—be included in a SIB agreement.

Kohli, J., Besharov, D. J., et al. (2012). *What Are Social Impact Bonds? An Innovative New Financing Tool for Social Programs.* **Washington, DC: Center for American Progress.**
http://cdn.americanprogress.org/wp-content/uploads/issues/2012/03/pdf/social_impact_bonds_brief.pdf
This issue brief looks at Social Impact Bonds and their value to government agencies.

Liebman, J. B. (2011). *Social Impact Bonds—A Promising New Financial Model to Accelerate Social Innovation and Improve Government Performance.* **Washington, DC: Center for American Progress.**
http://payforsuccess.org/sites/default/files/social_impact_bonds_-_a_promising_new_financing_model.pdf
This report analyzes social impact bonds, a promising new approach to the government financing of social service programs or social "interventions." By combining performance-based payments and market discipline, the approach has the potential to improve results, overcome barriers to social innovation, and encourage investment in cost-saving preventive services.

Roman, J. K. (2015). *Solving the Wrong Pocket Problem: How Pay for Success Promotes Investment in Evidence-Based Practices.* **Washington, DC: The Urban Institute..**
http://www.urban.org/sites/default/files/alfresco/publication-pdfs/2000427-Solving-the-Wrong-Pockets-Problem.pdf
The author explains the concept of "pocket problems" and the types of "pocket problems" that occur, showing how Pay for Success programs get rid of "pocket problems" and promote the government to use evidence-based practices, because Pay for Success rewards successful, evidence-based programs. The report names programs that would benefit if agencies paid for them using Pay for Success.

Roman, J. K., Walsh, K. A., et al. (2014). *Five Steps to Pay for Success: Implementing Pay for Success Projects in the Juvenile and Criminal Justice System.* **Washington, DC: The Urban Institute.**
http://www.urban.org/sites/default/files/alfresco/publication-pdfs/413148-Five-Steps-to-Pay-for-Success-Implementing-Pay for-Success Projects-in-the-Juvenile-and-Criminal-Justice-Systems.PDF
This report reviews the history of Pay for Success and initial barriers states can encounter when trying to implement this program. Although states have made positive strides using evidence-based programs, the report goes into other areas that could use improvements, showing the viability of this program.

Roman, J. K., Walsh, K. A., et al. (2014). *Sharing Risk: How Pay for Success Can Make Government More Efficient.* **Washington, DC: The Urban Institute.**
http://www.urban.org/sites/default/files/alfresco/publication-pdfs/413149-Sharing-Risk-How-Pay-for-Success-Can-Make-Government-More-Efficient.PDF
This report reviews the history of Pay for Success and the basics of the program, and covers its advantages and disadvantages. The authors discuss the "5 steps to Pay for Success," how state governments can implement them, and what the furture holds for this program.

Shah, S., & Costa, K. (2013). *Social Finance: A Primer—Understanding Innovation Funds, Impact Bonds, and Impact Investing.* **Washington, DC: Center for American Progress.**
http://cdn.americanprogress.org/wp-content/uploads/2013/11/SocialFinance-brief.pdf
This issue brief considers three prominent social financing mechanisms with the potential of unlocking new sources of capital and revolutionizing how an array of social issues is addressed.

Social Finance Ltd. (2011). *Social Impact Bonds: The One* Service, One Year On.* **London, UK: Cambridgeshire and Peterborough Probation Trust.**
http://socialfinanceus.org/pubs/social-impact-bonds-one-service-one-year
This resource highlights the first-year activities of the Peterborough Social Impact Bond project, launched in September 2010.

Von Glahn, D., & Whistler, C. (2011, June). "Pay for Success Programs: An Introduction." *Policy & Practice,* **19–22.**
http://www.thirdsectorcap.org/articles/policy_practive_pay_for_success.pdf
This issue brief looks at social impact bonds and their value to government agencies.

The White House and the Nonprofit Finance Fund. (2012). *Pay for Success: Investing in What Works.* **Washington, DC: Author.**
http://payforsuccess.org/sites/default/files/pay_for_success_report_2012.pdf
This report provides a summary of and conclusions from the Pay for Success: Investing in What Works event held in October 2011. It synthesizes and analyzes what was learned, identifying the Pay for Success challenges, opportunities, and issue areas of interest for future projects.

Websites

Urban Institute Pay for Success
http://www.urban.org/socialimpactbonds/

White House Pay for Success
http://www.whitehouse.gov/omb/factsheet/paying-for-success

Prison Rape Elimination Act Program

Project Description

The Prison Rape elimination Act (PREA) Program is funded under the Prison Rape Elimination Act, 42 USC 15601, et seq., and the Commerce, Justice, Science, and Related Agencies Appropriations Act, 2013 Public Law 113-6. PREA gives funds to demonstration projects that support comprehensive approaches to prevent, detect, and respond to sexual abuse and sexual harassment in state, tribal, and local adult and juvenile correctional facilities.

CrimeSolutions.gov Ratings:
No ratings at this time

OJP-Sponsored Evaluations

This literature review has not yielded any OJP-sponsored evaluations related to this program or research area.

OJP-Sponsored Research

NOTE: PREA requires that the Attorney General annually submits to Congress PREA data collection activities undertaken by BJS for the preceding year. BJS releases numerous estimates on the prevalence and incidence of sexual victimization in confinement facilities. Not all BJS reports are listed here, but the most recent report for each data collection series has been included. The BJS website has the full list of BJS publications and products regarding PREA:

http://www.bjs.gov/index.cfm?ty=pbtp&tid=20&dcid=0&sid=0&iid=1&sortby=dt

Beck, A. J. (2015). *PREA Data Collection Activities, 2015* [NCJ 248824]. Washington, DC: U.S. Department of Justice, Office of Justice Programs, Bureau of Justice Statistics.
http://www.bjs.gov/content/pub/pdf/pdca15.pdf
This report presents information on data collection activities for 2015 as required by the Prison Rape Elimination Act of 2003. PREA requires that BJS conduct an annual comprehensive statistical review and analysis of the incidence and effects of prison rape. This report presents highlights from these surveys.

Beck, A. J., Berzofsky, M., et. al. (2013). *Sexual Victimization in Prisons and Jail Reported by Inmates, 2011–2012.* [NCJ 241399]. Washington, DC: U.S. Department of Justice, Office of Justice Programs, Bureau of Justice Statistics.
http://www.bjs.gov/content/pub/pdf/svpjri1112.pdf
This report summarizes the findings of the third National Inmate Survey conducted by BJS. The survey was administered to 92,449 inmates ages 18 or older. The sample also included juveniles ages 16 to 17 who were held in adult prisons and jails. Findings suggest that 4% of prison inmates and 3.2% of jail inmates experience one or more incidents of sexual victimization. As required by PREA, the survey is a basis for identifying facilities with high and low rates of sexual victimization, including 12 state facilities and 9 jails.

Beck, A. J., Cantor, D., et. al. (2013). *Sexual Victimization in Juvenile Facilities Reported by Youth, 2012* [NCJ 241708]. Washington, DC: U.S. Department of Justice, Office of Justice Programs, Bureau of Justice Statistics.
http://www.bjs.gov/content/pub/pdf/svjfry12.pdf
This report summarizes the findings of the second National Survey of Youth in Custody. The survey was administered to 8,707 youth in 273 state-owned or operated juvenile facilities and 53 locally or privately operated facilities that held adjudicated youth. The study found that about 10% of youth in the surveyed facilities reported one or more incidents of sexual victimization. Adjudicated youth reported incidents involving another youth in about 2.5% of the cases, and reported incidents involving facility staff in 7.7%

of the cases. Finally, the report classified 13 facilities as "high-rate," meaning the youth in those facilities reported higher rates of victimization compared with other facilities.

Beck, A. J., & Johnson, C. (2012). *Sexual Victimizations Reported by Former State Prisoners, 2008.* **[NCJ 237363]. Washington, DC: U.S. Department of Justice, Office of Justice Programs, Bureau of Justice Statistics.**
http://www.bjs.gov/content/pub/pdf/svrfsp08.pdf
Part of the National Prison Statistics Program, the National Former Prisoner Survey collects data on people on parole and people formerly incarcerated in a local jail, state prison, or community correctional facility. Based on 18,526 completed interviews, the report indicates that 9.6% of former state prisoners experienced one or more incidents of sexual victimization during their most recent incarceration. Furthermore, 5.4% of former inmates reported experiencing an inmate-on-inmate incident, and 5.3% reported an incident with facility staff.

Beck, A. J., Rantala, R. R., & Rexroat, J. (2014). *Sexual Victimization Reported By Adult Correctional Authorities, 2009–11* **[NCJ 243904]. Washington, DC: U.S. Department of Justice, Office of Justice Programs, Bureau of Justice Statistics.**
http://www.bjs.gov/content/pub/pdf/svraca0911.pdf
This report presents counts of nonconsensual sexual acts, abusive sexual contacts, staff sexual misconduct, and staff sexual harassment reported to correctional authorities in adult prisons, jails, and other adult correctional facilities in 2009, 2010, and 2011. An in-depth examination of substantiated incidents is also presented, covering the number and characteristics of victims and perpetrators, location, time of day, nature of the injuries, impact on the victims, and sanctions imposed on the perpetrators.

Booz Allen Hamilton. (2010). *Prison Rape Elimination Act (PREA): Cost Impact Analysis.* **Washington, DC: National Prison Rape Elimination Commission.**
http://www.ojp.gov/programs/pdfs/preacostimpactanalysis.pdf
This report assesses the costs associated with implementing the PREA standards and offers a comprehensive view of implementation and compliance on a national level. The cost-impact analysis focuses on five domains of correctional operations: state prison systems, state and local juvenile facilities, community corrections, local/county jails, and police lockups. Among the 41 PREA standards, 12 have little or no effect on cost. The majority of the sites visited during this analysis (8 out of 10) were in compliance with these standards. For the sites not in compliance, there was no indication that meeting PREA standards would result in any measurable costs.

Rantala, R. R., Rexroat, J., et. al. (2014). *Survey of Sexual Violence in Adult Correctional Facilities, 2009–11—Statistical Tables* **[NCJ 244227]. Washington, DC: U.S. Department of Justice, Office of Justice Programs, Bureau of Justice Statistics.**
http://www.bjs.gov/content/pub/pdf/ssvacf0911st.pdf
The Survey of Sexual Violence conducted by BJS found that in 2011, correctional administrators reported 6,660 allegations of sexual victimization, of which 605 were substantiated claims. Local jail authorities reported 2,042 allegations in 2011, of which 284 were substantiated. The statistical tables in this report summarize allegations and substantiated incidents by type of victimization for every facility and jurisdiction surveyed in 2009, 2010, and 2011.

Other Academic Research

Brocco, M. (2013). "Facing the Facts: The Guarantee Against Cruel and Unusual Punishment in Light of PLRA, Iqbal, and PREA." *Journal of Gender, Race & Justice, 16*(3): 917–954.
http://connection.ebscohost.com/c/articles/89532323/facing-facts-guarantee-against-cruel-unusual-punishment-light-plra-iqbal-prea
The article focuses on the interpretation of the federal pleadings in the U.S. Supreme Court case Ashcroft v. Iqbal, the Prison Rape Elimination Act of 2003 (PREA), and the Prison Litigation Reform Act of 1995 for providing protection to the victims of sexual abuse in prison by the prison officials. It suggests

establishment of a Prison Rape Elimination Court, a confidential administrative court, by amending PREA to prosecute prisoners claims against sexual assault.

Corlew, K. R. (2006). "Congress Attempts to Shine a Light on a Dark Problem: An In-Depth Look at the Prison Rape Elimination Act of 2003." *American Journal of Criminal Law, 33*(2): 157–190.
http://heinonline.org/HOL/LandingPage?handle=hein.journals/ajcl33&div=11&id=&page
The article examines PREA's purpose and discusses the problem of prison rape, including its impact on inmates and society. It presents an overview of PREA and its balance between federal and state interests by looking at the implementation and effectiveness of PREA initiatives in Nebraska as a test case.

DeBraux, J. L. (2006). "Prison Rape: Have We Done Enough? A Deep Look into the Adequacy of the Prison Rape Elimination Act." *Howard Law Journal, 50* (1): 203–223.
http://heinonline.org/HOL/LandingPage?handle=hein.journals/howlj50&div=9&id=&page=
http://www.law.howard.edu/dictator/media/229/how_50_1.pdf
This article describes some of the reasons offenders give for committing sexual assault in prison. The author contends that PREA is not enough to reduce or eliminate incidences of prison rape. Instead, she suggests PREA needs to be modified and offers suggestions to help reduce occurrences of prison rape and reduce the spread of HIV/AIDS in prison.

Dumond, R. W. (2005). "Impact of Prisoner Sexual Violence: Challenges of Implementing Public Law 108-79, the Prison Rape Elimination Act of 2003." *Journal of Legislation, 32*: 101–123.
http://www.wcl.american.edu/endsilence/documents/TheImpactofPrisonerSexualViolence.pdf
This article examines the progress made since the passage of PREA, such as correctional staff training, data collection, education policies, procedures, and raised awareness. The author suggests that although substantive progress has been made in implementing policies to reduce and eliminate prison sexual assault, persistent challenges remain for adequately responding to prison sexual violence. These challenges include limits on confidentiality among correctional health care/mental health care staff; wide-ranging facility types, each with its own unique challenges; and the "myth of permissible consensual inmate-on-inmate" sexual behavior.

Gonsalves, V. M., Walsh, K., & Scalora, M. J. (2012). "Staff Perceptions of Risk for Prison Rape Perpetration and Victimization." *The Prison Journal, 92*(2): 253–273.
http://www.prearesourcecenter.org/sites/default/files/library/staffriskperceptions.pdf
This empirical study systematically explores risk factors that staff perceive as important when ascertaining risk for prison sexual perpetration and victimization. This study examined ratings from 10 staff for 315 female and 1,842 male inmates screened for admission to correctional facilities in a Midwestern state. Overall, findings indicate that a low proportion of inmates were rated medium–high risk for either perpetration or victimization. In addition, results suggest that staff perceived risk factors for sexual violence somewhat differently for female and male inmates. Furthermore, data revealed that staff considered presentation characteristics more relevant than empirically derived risk factors when determining vulnerability to prison rape. Implications for institutional policy and prison sexual assault screening are discussed.

Iyama, K. (2012). "We Have Tolled the Bell for Him: An Analysis of the Prison Rape Elimination Act and California's Compliance as It Applies to Transgender Inmates." *Tulane Journal of Law & Sexuality, 21*: 23.
http://heinonline.org/HOL/LandingPage?handle=hein.journals/lsex21&div=5&id=&page=
This article details California's efforts under PREA to reduce and eliminate prison rape of transgender inmates. The author suggests these efforts have fallen short and recommends other actions that should be taken to protect this population.

Jenness, V., C. L. Maxson, J., et al. (2010). "Accomplishing the Difficult but Not Impossible: Collecting Self-Report Data on Inmate-on-Inmate Sexual Assault in Prison." *Criminal Justice Policy Review, 21*(1): 3–30.
http://cjp.sagepub.com/content/21/1/3.short
This article describes the challenges of studying and collecting self-report data on inmate-on-inmate sexual assault in California. The authors describe their research methods and offer instructive ways for other researchers to purse similar efforts.

Moster, A. N., & Jeglic, E. L. (2009). "Prison Warden Attitudes Toward Prison Rape and Sexual Assault: Findings Since the Prison Rape Elimination Act (PREA)." *Prison Journal, 89*(1): 65–78.
http://tpj.sagepub.com/content/early/2009/01/14/0032885508329981.abstract
This study examined the attitudes and beliefs of U.S. state prison wardens toward prison rape since the enactment of PREA. The survey found that of the 60 wardens who responded to the survey (out of 500 invited to participate), the majority reported that male prison rape and sexual assault was a low base-rate occurrence. It also found that wardens believe that increased inmate supervision by staff can be effective in preventing prison rape. The wardens indicated they have policies in place designed to prevent prison rape and that about half of these policies are based on PREA or PREA-related policies. The survey's findings suggest that PREA's common standards for addressing prison rape and sexual assault are effective.

Reid, E. A. (2013). "The Prison Rape Elimination Act (PREA) and the Importance of Litigation in Its Enforcement: Holding Guards Who Rape Accountable." *Yale Law Journal, 122*(7): 2084–2097.
http://heinonline.org/HOL/LandingPage?handle=hein.journals/ylr122&div=54&id=&page=
The article discusses PREA and the reported importance of litigation in the enforcement of the law, including information on a proposal to hold prison guards accountable for their roles in sexual assaults against prisoners. A legal case involving several female inmates who were allegedly assaulted by prison guards while confined by the Washington Department of Corrections is discussed.

Struckman-Johnson, C., & Struckman-Johnson, D. (2013). "Stopping Prison Rape: The Evolution of Standards Recommended by PREA's National Prison Rape Elimination Commission." *Prison Journal, 93*(3): 335–354.
http://tpj.sagepub.com/content/93/3/335.short
This article reviews the 40 standards to stop prison rape in adult prisons and jails proposed by the National Prison Rape Elimination Commission (NPREC) in 2009, comparing their scope to solutions from past literature. The authors recommend that the effectiveness of NPREC standards be evaluated and that the search for solutions continues.

Thompson, R. A., Nored, L. S., et al. (2008). "The Prison Rape Elimination: Act (PREA) An Evaluation of Policy Compliance with Illustrative Excerpts." *Criminal Justice Policy Review, 19*(4): 414–437.
http://cjp.sagepub.com/content/early/2008/04/04/0887403408315442.short
This article examines the policies of 28 states plus the Federal Bureau of Prisons ($n = 29$) to assess how they comply with PREA using 8 evaluative dimensions. The authors then excerpted language from various policy statements for the benefit of those institutions that are still developing their own documentation. They emphasized identifying core dimensions of comprehensive policy statements, along with observations and conclusions regarding future implications of prison rape abatement measures.

Other Reports

International Association of Chiefs of Police and National Council on Crime and Delinquency. (2012). *Prison Rape Elimination Act (PREA) Needs Assessment of Lockups.* **Alexandria, VA: Author. BJA sponsored.**
http://www.prearesourcecenter.org/sites/default/files/library/preaneedsassessmentreportfinal.pdf
This report examines the current practices related to sexual abuse in local jails and lockups as they relate to PREA and the PREA standards for these facilities. Findings suggest that smaller and midsized agencies

generally lack awareness and understanding of what PREA standards are and how they apply to local jail and lockup operations.

Kristiansson, V. (2014). *Justice for Victims Behind Bars: Improving the Response to Cases of Sexual Abuse in Confinement.* **Washington, DC: AEquitas.**
http://www.prearesourcecenter.org/sites/default/files/library/justiceforvictimsbehindbars-improvingtheresponsetocasesofsexualabuseinconfinement.pdf
AEquitas wrote this report detailing the development of the Victims Behind Bars project with the goal of clearly identifying barriers and solutions that could be applied to this jurisdiction and others across the country. The Victims Behind Bars project, undertaken during a 4-month period in the fall/winter of 2013, involved four steps: 1) identifying and interviewing jurisdictional participants, 2) conducting an on-site multidisciplinary meeting, 3) following up with participants and field experts, and 4) analyzing current practices and barriers to responding to sexual abuse in confinement and developing strategies for promising practices for responding to sexual abuse in confinement across the criminal justice continuum.

Maccarone, R. M. (2007). "Community Corrections and the Prison Rape Elimination Act." *Corrections Today, 69*(5): 82−85.
http://www.aca.org/publications/pdf/Maccarone.pdf
The article focuses on PREA's role in community corrections. PREA directly affects federal, state, and local prisons and jails as well as community corrections agencies. It established a National Prison Rape Elimination Commission that has as its primary mission to carry out a comprehensive legal and factual study of the penal, physical, mental, medical, social, and economic impacts of prison rape in the United States.

National Center for Transgender Equality. (2012, July). *LGBT people and the Prison Rape Elimination Act.* **Washington, DC: Author.**
http://www.prearesourcecenter.org/sites/default/files/library/preajuly2012.pdf
The application of PREA standards to situations involving LGBT people is explained, providing a great overview for correctional staff. Sections of this document address the following areas: a crisis of sexual abuse in confinement; the most important protections for LGBT offenders are screening and classification, housing transgender people, protective custody, segregated LGBT pods or units, searches, minors in adult facilities, staff training, reporting abuse, support for survivors of abuse, consensual sex compared with sexual abuse, grievances and access to courts, and compliance and enforcement; correctional settings PREA applies to; pressing for implementation at the local level; ensuring compliance and protecting detained immigrants; and how one can get legal help.

National Prison Rape Elimination Commission. (2009). *National Prison Rape Elimination Commission Report.* **Washington, DC: Author.**
http://www.ncjrs.gov/pdffiles1/226680.pdf
This report discusses the scope and seriousness of the problems related to sexual assault in correctional institutions, ways of solving these problems, and the issues at stake. The report discusses the Commission's nine findings on the problems of sexual abuse in correctional facilities and outlines policies and practices that should be mandatory in all facilities to address these problems.

National Prison Rape Elimination Commission. (2009). *Standards for the Prevention, Detection, Response, and Monitoring of Sexual Abuse in Community Corrections.* **Washington, DC: Author.**
http://www.ncjrs.gov/pdffiles1/226683.pdf
This report presents standards for the prevention, detection, response, and monitoring of sexual abuse in community corrections. The standards are presented in four categories that address prevention and response planning; prevention, detection, and response; and monitoring.

Pihl-Buckley, H. (2008). "Tailoring the Prison Rape Elimination Act to a Juvenile Setting." *Corrections Today, 70*(1): 44–47.
http://www.aca.org/publications/pdf/Pihl-Buckley.pdf
The article discusses how the Massachusetts Department of Youth Services (DYS) adapted PREA to fit juvenile correctional facilities. The DYS offers training to correctional personnel on the proper institutional culture and orientations for juvenile prisoners regarding their rights and sexual behavior. The DYS also reformed the procedure for prisoners reporting incidents.

The Annie E. Casey Foundation. (2014). *A guide to Juvenile Detention Reform: Juvenile Detention Facility Assessment* **(Publication No. 2). Baltimore, MD: Author.**
http://www.aecf.org/m/resourcedoc/aecf-juveniledetentionfacilityassessment-2014.pdf
This publication provides a guide to help Juvenile Detention Alternatives Initiaitve (JDAI) sites improve conditions in juvenile detention facilities. Since 2004, officials in JDAI sites have assessed, improved, and monitored conditions in juvenile detention facilities using a set of standards the Foundation published. The Foundation has issued this revised version of the standards to acknowledge and incorporate regulations that affect the full range of facility operations. This includes the U.S. Department of Justice regulations for the prevention, detection, and response to sexual misconduct in juvenile facilities as part of its implementation of the Prison Rape Elimination Act.

U.S. Department of Justice, Office of the Inspector General. (2014). *Progress Report on the Department of Justice's Implementation of the Prison Rape Elimination Act.* **Washington, DC: Author.**
http://www.justice.gov/oig/reports/2014/e151.pdf
The U.S. Department of Justice is responsible for overseeing federal, state, and local implementation for the National Standards to Prevent, Detect, and Respond to Prison Rape (the Standards). This OIG report examines DOJ's efforts to implement the Standards. The OIG found issues related to intergovernmental agreements with the U.S. Marshal Services, investigative entities within DOJ that conduct investigations of sexual abuse in confinement settings, and PREA audits at Bureau of Prisons institutions. Recommendations were withheld since PREA Standards compliance is ongoing. However, OIG encouraged DOJ to take appropriate actions to address identified issues.

U.S. Department of Justice, Office of Legal Policy. (2012). *Regulatory Impact Assessment: United States Department of Justice Final Rule National Standards to Prevent, Detect, and Respond to Prison Rape Under the Prison Rape Elimination Act (PREA).* **Washington, DC: Author.**
http://www.prearesourcecenter.org/sites/default/files/library/prearia.pdf
This report examines the financial impact of full nationwide compliance with the PREA standards on prisons, jails, tribal facilities, and juvenile correctional facilities. In particular, it assesses the monetary benefits of eliminating prison sexual assault. The report also summarizes the comments relating to the costs and benefits of the standards that DOJ received in response to the Notice of Proposed Rulemaking and Initial Regulatory Impact Assessment.

Website

National PREA Resource Center
http://www.prearesourcecenter.org/

Project Honest Opportunity Probation and Enforcement/Swift & Certain Sanctions

Project Description

There are multiple states, counties, cities, and tribes that are interested in implementing "swift, certain, and fair" (SCF) models of supervision with offenders in the community. This interest has grown out of the potential promise that these SCF models have shown in effectively reducing recidivism and preventing crime. SCF approaches are intended to: 1) improve supervision strategies that reduce recidivism; 2) promote and increase collaboration among agencies and officials who work in community corrections and related fields; 3) enhance the offenders' perception that the supervision decisions are fair, consistently applied, and have transparent consequences; and 4) improve the outcomes of people participating in these initiatives.

CrimeSolutions.gov Ratings:
Effective (0)
Promising (2)
No Effect (0)
Insufficient Evidence (1)

Partners and Professional Organizations:
- ✓ RTI, International
- ✓ Hawaii HOPE
- ✓ Pepperdine University

One of the SCF models is the Hawaii Opportunity Probation with Enforcement (HOPE) model, which is a community supervision strategy for substance-abusing probationers. HOPE's main goals are to reduce drug use, recidivism, and incarceration. HOPE was designed with a theoretical foundation that emphasizes clearly defined behavioral expectations for probationers, swift and certain sanctions when probationers fail to comply with those expectations, and elements of procedural justice that make it clear to probationers that courtroom members want them to succeed.[46]

Note: The Honest Opportunity Probation and Enforcement evaluations have not yet been completed, because the solicitation was issued in 2011. BJA and NIJ are in the process of completing a demonstration field experiment (DFE) in the area of probation. DFEs work to produce new knowledge in key areas of criminal justice by applying the rigor of science to program implementation and then 1) evaluating those programs through randomized controlled experiments, 2) tracking and coaching for program fidelity, and 3) strengthening data collection and analysis. In the HOPE DFE, BJA is funding the demonstration sites, and NIJ is funding evaluation efforts. The HOPE DFE is replicating a program that has shown evidence of success. The four sites selected for this DFE are being rigorously tested to determine whether the HOPE probation model can promote the successful widespread completion of probation for high-risk probationers. The results from this DFE are expected in spring 2016.

OJP-Sponsored Research

Harrell, A., Mitchell, O., et al. (2003). *Evaluation of Breaking the Cycle.* Washington, DC: Urban Institute. NIJ Funded.
http://www.urban.org/UploadedPDF/410659_BreakingtheCycle.pdf
This report evaluates Breaking the Cycle, a program aimed at reducing drug use among offenders. One portion of the program is focused on regular drug testing and certain and swift punishments for those who test positive. The program was found to reduce drug use at two of three sites and to reduce criminal

---

[46] https://www.CrimeSolutions.gov/ProgramDetails.aspx?ID=49

activity and family problems at all three sites. A cost-benefit analysis found that for every $1 invested in the program, it saved between $2.30 and $5.30.

Hawken, A., & Kleiman, M. (2009). *Managing Drug Involved Probations with Swift and Certain Sanctions: Evaluating Hawaii's HOPE.* **Washington, DC: U.S. Department of Justice, Office of Justice Programs, National Institute of Justice.**
http://www.ncjrs.gov/pdffiles1/nij/grants/229023.pdf

This program was rated on CrimeSolutions.gov as promising.
This study presented a process and outcome evaluation of Hawaii's HOPE Program. The process evaluation found that the program decreased the workload of probation officers but greatly increased the workload of court staff. The outcome evaluation used a randomized, controlled trial to assign probationers to either the HOPE program or traditional probation. The results showed that those in the HOPE group were more likely to keep their probation appointments, less likely to have a positive drug test, less likely to be arrested for a new crime, and less likely to have their probation revoked.

Hawken, A., Davenport, S., & Kleiman, M. A. R. (2014). *Managing Drug-Involved Offenders.* **Report produced for the U.S. Department of Justice.**
http://www.scfcenter.org/resources/Research/201407%20Managing%20Drug-Involved%20Offenders.pdf
Effectively managing drug-involved offenders is an essential step to reduce crime and drug abuse. Many of the most active criminals and heaviest-using drug abusers are supervised by the criminal justice system; conversely, drug-using parolees and probationers are disproportionately responsible for both crime and drug abuse in America. As crime and drugs are at least somewhat synergistic—criminal behavior can lead to drug abuse, and vice versa—resolving the drug habits of the most chronic criminal offenders and the criminal habits of the most habitual drug abusers may be an integral element of a successful approach to either problem. Fortunately, many of these people are already supervised by probation or parole programs, subjecting them to additional monitoring and discipline. For decades, probation and parole programs have largely failed to wean participants off of either crime or drugs. In a nutshell, current programs have attempted to stretch insufficient resources across overwhelming numbers of parolees and probationers. However, innovations based on the Swift and Certain testing-and-discipline paradigm (SAC), as successfully implemented in Hawaii's HOPE project, can break this pattern (Hawken and Kleiman, 2009). A phenomenon called "behavioral triage" allows program resources to be allocated to the offenders whose poor behavior most requires them (Hawken 2010). The quick and efficient identification of egregious offenders—rather than the slow and conventional process of waiting until they compile an extensive list of violations—is combined with swift and consistent punishments. When punishments follow within days of the violation, they have much greater correctional effect on the offender.

Academic Reports[47]

Grommon, E., Cox, S. M., Davidson, W. S., & Bynum, T. S. (2013) "Alternative Models of Instant Drug Testing: Evidence from an Experimental Trial." *Journal of Experimental Criminology,* *9:***145-168.**
http://link.springer.com/article/10.1007/s11292-012-9168-6
This study describes and provides relapse and recidivism outcome findings related to an experimental trial evaluating the viability of frequent, random drug testing with consequences for use. The sample consisted of 529 offenders released on parole. An experimental design with random assignment to one of three groups was employed. The study found frequent monitoring of drug use with randomized testing protocols, immediate feedback, and certain consequences is effective in lowering rates of relapse and recidivism. The effectiveness is particularly salient in the short term during the period of exposure to

---

[47] Links to abstracts are provided when full articles are not available.

testing conditions. The findings lend support to the use of randomized testing with swift and certain sanctions with parolees.

Kilmer, B., Nicosia, N., et al. (2013). "Efficacy of Frequent Monitoring with Swift, Certain, and Modest Sanctions for Violations: Insights from South Dakota's 24/7 Sobriety Project." *American Journal of Public Health, 103*(1): e37–e43.

http://www.ncbi.nlm.nih.gov/pubmed/23153129

This study evaluated South Dakota's 24/7 Sobriety project for those convicted of alcohol-involved offenses. The program requires offenders to submit to breathalyzer test twice a day or wear a continuous alcohol-monitoring bracelet. Those who test positive are subject to swift and certain punishments. Results showed a 12 percent reduction in repeat DUI arrests and a 9 percent reduction in domestic violence arrests in counties adopting the program.

Kleiman, M.A.R., & Hawken, A. (2008). "Fixing the Parole System." *Issues in Science & Technology 24*(4): 45–52.

http://issues.org/24-4/kleiman/

The article discusses the possibility of COPE, a version of the HOPE program for parolees in California. When the article was published, this was a theoretical program and had not been implemented. Although this article came out before the final results of the NIJ-funded HOPE study, it shows support for swift and certain punishment programs. The authors argue that a HOPE-type program can work for parolees, though they provide no data to back up this claim.

Shannon, L. M., Hulbig, S. K., Birdwhistell, S., Newell, J., & Neal, C. (2015). "Implementation of an Enhanced Probation Program: Evaluating Process and Preliminary Outcomes." *Evaluation and Program Planning, 49*, 50–62.

http://www.sciencedirect.com/science/article/pii/S0149718914001268

Supervision, Monitoring, Accountability, Responsibility, and Treatment (SMART) is Kentucky's enhanced probation pilot program modeled after Hawaii's Opportunity Probation with Enforcement (HOPE). SMART is proposed to decrease substance use, new violations, and incarceration-related costs for high-risk probationers by increasing and randomizing drug testing, intensifying supervision, and creating linkages with needed resources (i.e., mental health and substance use). SMART adopts a holistic approach to rehabilitation by addressing mental health and substance abuse needs as well as life skills for fostering deterrence of criminal behavior compared with punitive action only. A mixed methods evaluation was used to assess program implementation and effectiveness. Qualitative interviews with key stakeholders (i.e., administration, judges, attorneys, and law enforcement/corrections) suggested successful implementation and collaboration to facilitate the pilot program. Quantitative analyses of secondary Kentucky Offender Management System data (grant Year 1: 07/01/2012–06/30/2013) also suggested program effectiveness. Specifically, SMART probationers showed significantly fewer: violations of probation (1.2 vs. 2.3), positive drug screens (8.6% vs. 29.4%), and days incarcerated (32.5 vs. 118.1) than comparison probationers. Kentucky's SMART enhanced probation shows preliminary success in reducing violations, substance use, and incarceration. Implications for practice and policy will be discussed.

Lapham, S. C., Kapitula, L. R., et al. (2006). "Impaired-Driving Recidivism Among Repeat Offenders Following an Intensive Court-Based Intervention." *Accident Analysis and Prevention, 38*: 162–169.

http://www.ncbi.nlm.nih.gov/pubmed/16202465

This program was rated on CrimeSolutions.gov as promising.
The study evaluated a swift and certain sanction program aimed at those convicted of DUI. The program reduces jail time but requires electronic monitoring, random urinalysis, mandatory treatment, self-help group attendance, and maintaining full-time employment. Those who chose to take the program were less likely to be arrested for a new DUI offense, driving with a revoked or suspended license offense, or any other traffic violation.

Zettler, H. R., Morris, R. G., Piquero, A. R., & Cardwell, S. M. (2015). "Assessing the Celerity of Arrest on 3-Year Recidivism Patterns in a Sample of Criminal Defendants." *Journal of Criminal Justice, 43*(5), 428-436.
http://www.sciencedirect.com/science/article/pii/S0047235215000471.
In an effort to build on celerity research, the researchers used longitudinal data to examine whether celerity, as measured by the amount of time from the commission of an offense to the time of arrest, impacts the likelihood of recidivism. Findings were consistent with assumptions of deterrence theory; experiencing a shorter time between offense and arrest date was related to a significantly lower risk of recidivism, although the effect diminished beyond 30 days. Results suggest that celerity of arrest may have a small, short-term deterrent effect–a finding that is similar to one from the research on sanction certainty.

Other Reports

American Probation and Parole Association (APPA)/National Center for State Courts. (2013). *Effective Responses to Offender Behavior: Lessons Learned for Probation and Parole Supervision.* **Lexington, KY: APPA.**
http://www.appa-net.org/eWeb/docs/APPA/pubs/EROBLLPPS-Report.pdf
This report examines several lessons learned from HOPE and similar probation programs. First, legal issues can arise because there is little case law in this area. Second, incentives must be used at least as much as sanctions to keep the program in balance. Third, key stakeholders, such as the judicial system, must be on board. Fourth, consistent and proportionate responses to infractions must be delivered. Finally, any program should be evaluated for fidelity and outcomes.

Carns, T. W., & Martin, S. (2011). *Anchorage PACE (Probation Accountability with Certain Enforcement): A Preliminary Evaluation of the Anchorage Pilot PACE Project.* **Anchorage, AK: Alaska Judicial Council.**
http://www.ajc.state.ak.us/reports/pace2011.pdf
This report describes the progress of Anchorage [AK] PACE, a probation program modeled after Project HOPE. Because of data issues, the PACE probationers were compared with HOPE probationers and not a control group. The report found that over half of the PACE probationers did not have a positive drug test in the first year, but their probation violations increased after starting the program. There were not enough data to draw any significant conclusions about program effectiveness.

Hawken, A., & Kleiman, M. A. R. (2011). *Washington Intensive Supervision Program: Evaluation Report* **[Report to Seattle City Council]. Seattle, WA: City of Seattle.**
http://www.seattle.gov/council/burgess/attachments/2011wisp_draft_report.pdf
This report evaluates WISP, a HOPE-based program piloted in Seattle, WA, after 6 months of operation. Parolees were randomly assigned to WISP or parole-as-usual. Those on WISP were less likely to test positive for drugs, and those that did were more likely to be issued a warrant for a violation. Those on WISP were also less likely to be arrested for a new felony crime and spent less time in jail.

Loudenburg, R., Drube, G., et al. (2010). *South Dakota 24/7 Sobriety Program Evaluation Findings Report.* **Salem, SD: Mountain Plans Evaluation, LLC.**
http://apps.sd.gov/atg/dui247/AnalysisSD24.pdf

This program was rated on CrimeSolutions.gov as having insufficient evidence.
This study evaluated South Dakota's 24/7 Sobriety Project for those convicted of alcohol-involved offenses. As with a previous article (see Kilmer et al., 2013), it found lower recidivism rates and declared the program very successful. Crimesolutions.gov rated the program as having insufficient evidence because of inadequate design quality.

Snell, C. (2007). *Fort Bend County Community Supervision and Corrections Special Sanctions Court Program: Evaluation Report.* **Richmond, TX: Fort Bend County Commission.**
http://s3.amazonaws.com/static.texastribune.org/media/documents/SANCTIONS_COURT_FINAL_REP
ORT.pdf?preview
This paper is an overview of Texas's Sanctions Court, later renamed SWIFT (Supervision With Intensified enForcemenT). It is similar to HOPE in that it calls for random drug tests, with swift and certain punishments for those who test positive. It differs from HOPE in that it provides many more positive incentives for good behavior. Those in the SWIFT program were less likely to violate probation, have probation revoked, and be convicted of new crimes than those under traditional probation.

Vermont Center for Justice Research. (2011). *Bennington County Integrated Domestic Violence Docket Project: Outcome Evaluation.* **Northfield Falls, VT: Vermont Center for Justice Research.**
http://www.vcjr.org/reports/reportscrimjust/reports/idvdreport_files/IDVD%20Final%20Report.pdf
This report evaluates the Integrated Domestic Violence Docket (IDVD) program from 2007 through 2010. The IDVD program has multiple parts, but it focuses on offender accountability through immediate arrest for any violations of a criminal law or protective order for those convicted of domestic violence. Those offenders in the IDVD program were less likely to recidivate (be convicted of DV or any crime) than those not in it. The IDVD program also allowed for cases to be processed twice as quickly.

Virginia Criminal Sentencing Commission. (2014). *Immediate Sanction Probation Pilot Project.* **Richmond, VA: Author.**
http://www.vcsc.virginia.gov/Mar_10/Immediate%20Sanction%20Probation%20-
%20Status%20Report%2004-14-2014%20FINAL.ppt
This presentation provides information about the Immediate Sanction Probation program established through a 2012 directive in four Virginia locations and modeled after the HOPE program. Preliminary results indicate that more than two-thirds of those currently in the program have violated probation, with only five successfully completing the program. This is attributed to the growing pains of a new program.

Wright, V. (2010). *Deterrence in Criminal Justice: Evaluating Certainty vs. Severity of Punishment.* **Washington, DC: The Sentencing Project.**
http://www.sentencingproject.org/doc/deterrence%20briefing%20.pdf
This report reviews the literature on deterrence theory and concludes that the certainty of punishment is more important than its severity in determining a deterrent effect. This idea is central to HOPE and similar programs. All are based on the idea that punishment should be more certain rather than more severe.

Naus, T. J. (2013). *Measuring Evidence-Based Practices in Probation: Does Timing of Sanctions Impact Probation Termination Status?* **(Doctoral Dissertation, Alliant University.)**
http://gradworks.umi.com/35/99/3599627.html
The focus of this study investigates the evidenced-based principle of applying sanctions in a swift manner. Implementing punishments immediately as a method of decreasing unwanted behavior derives from operant conditioning and the psychological principles of behaviorism. The current research investigates a sample of probationers under the jurisdiction of the San Diego County Probation Department who exited probation in the calendar year 2010. The study sought to investigate if the amount of time between a probation violation and a sanction improved the predictability of whether an offender was revoked to prison. Significant results at alpha level .05 suggest that the time between probation violation and agency response significantly improves the ability to predict if an offender was revoked to prison.

National Center for State Courts. (2013). Arkansas SWIFT Courts: Implementation Assessment and Long-Term Evaluation Plan.
http://ncsc.contentdm.oclc.org/cdm/ref/collection/criminal/id/219

In 2011, the Arkansas legislature provided for the establishment of five pilot programs, known as SWIFT Courts. These pilots are modeled after the successful Hawaii HOPE program and are designed to reduce probation failure among high-risk probationers by concentrating on a small number of easily verifiable behaviors (drug use and showing up for appointments) to ensure compliance. The five pilot SWIFT Courts became operational between March and October 2012. An implementation review of the SWIFT Courts, conducted by the National Center for State Courts, suggests that the programs have successfully implemented the majority of the HOPE benchmarks. Preliminary data suggests the programs are having a positive short-term impact on the probationers enrolled in the program. A number of suggestions for strengthening the pilot programs are offered throughout this review. Finally, the report concludes with a long-term evaluation plan for the SWIFT Court programs.

Websites

RTI, International, Honest Opportunity Probation with Enforcement Project
http://www.rti.org/newsroom/news.cfm?obj=36F6E9F3-5056-B100-319D5F71B2FC878B

Hawaii's State Judiciary's HOPE Probation Program
http://hopehawaii.net/

Swift, Certain, and Fair Resource Center
http://scfcenter.org/index.html

Example of a Warning Hearing
http://www.nij.gov/topics/corrections/community/drug-offenders/documents/229023-appendix-2-example-warning-hearing.pdf

HOPE: Hawaii's Opportunity Probation with Enforcement Program
http://hopehawaii.net/

HOPE: Theoretical Underpinnings and Evaluation Findings
www.crimevictimsunited.org/issues/treatment/hope/hawken090410.pdf

National Institute of Justice "Swift and Certain" sanctions
http://www.nij.gov/topics/corrections/community/drug-offenders/pages/hawaii-hope.aspx

National Network for Safe Communities: Swift, Certain, and Fair
http://nnscommunities.org/our-work/strategy/swift-certain-fair

Swift, Certain, and Fair
http://www.swiftcertainfair.com/

Project Safe Neighborhoods

Project Description

Project Safe Neighborhoods (PSN) is a nationwide commitment to reduce gun and gang crime in America at the local level. The core of PSN involves the funding of local programs coupled with increased federal prosecution of illegal gun use and possession. Since its inception in 2001, $2 billion has been committed to this initiative. This funding is used to hire new federal and state prosecutors, support investigators, provide training, distribute gun lock safety kits, deter juvenile gun crime, and develop and promote community outreach efforts as well as to support other gun and gang violence reduction strategies.[48]

Each year, the 94 U.S. Attorney districts are eligible for PSN grants to develop and sustain the 5 core elements of PSN. This includes partnerships with local and state agencies, strategic planning with a research partner, training on laws or crime trends, community outreach and public awareness campaigns, and accountability through progress reports.

Note: The evaluations that follow include not only PSN evaluations but also evaluations of programs similar to PSN that have been developed at a local or state level. All programs included share a goal of gun or gang crime reduction and have core elements similar to PSN. Evaluations fitting these criteria have been selected from CrimeSolutions.gov, publicly available reports, and academic journals.[49]

CrimeSolutions.gov Ratings:
Effective (3)
Promising (7)
No Effect (2)
Insufficient Evidence (2)

Partners and Professional Organizations:
- ✓ Michigan State University
- ✓ National District Attorneys Association
- ✓ International Association of Chiefs of Police
- ✓ American Probation and Parole Association
- ✓ National Crime Prevention Council
- ✓ National Gang Center
- ✓ Regional Information Sharing Systems

OJP Evaluations[50]

NIJ-Sponsored Evaluations

Bynum, T., & Decker, S. H. (2006). *Chronic Violent Offenders Lists: Case Study 4.* **Washington, DC: U.S. Department of Justice, Office of Justice Programs, National Institute of Justice.**
https://www.bja.gov/Publications/Chronic_Violent_Offenders.pdf
This report discusses chronic violent offender lists, which include those offenders who are wanted or are involved in multiple gun crimes. The goal is for the lists to increase awareness of the offenders throughout the criminal justice system, coordinate information sharing, and enhance deterrence through enforcement and prosecution of repeat offenders. An evaluation of chronic offender lists has not been done, but data suggest that it could be an effective tool leading to the arrest of chronic offenders.

---

[48] More information on Project Safe Neighborhoods can be found at the following link: https://www.psn.gov

[49] CrimeSolutions.gov program and practice areas are discussed in the articles and reports are cited for each program or practice. In some cases, one article may have multiple ratings, or multiple articles may make be used to determine a single rating. Therefore, the number of reports or articles given a CrimeSolutions.gov rating in this report may not match what is found by searching CrimeSolutions.gov.

[50] The full report for each evaluation or article can be found in the link provided.

Bynum, T. S., Grommon, E., et al. (2014). *Evaluation of a Comprehensive Approach to Reducing Gun Violence in Detroit.* Washington, DC: U.S. Department of Justice, Office of Justice Programs, National Institute of Justice.
https://www.ncjrs.gov/pdffiles1/nij/grants/244866.pdf
This report examines the PSN program in Detroit, MI. The Detroit program followed the standard PSN model with mixed-agency task forces and case reviews. The process evaluation found a significant increase in the number of charges for carrying a concealed weapon. The outcome evaluation found a significant decrease in the number of fatal and nonfatal shootings in the target areas.

Decker, S. H., Huebner, B. M., et al. (2007). *Eastern District of Missouri: Case Study 7.* Washington, DC: U.S. Department of Justice, Office of Justice Programs, National Institute of Justice.
https://www.bja.gov/Publications/ED_Missouri.pdf
This report discusses the PSN program in the eastern district (St. Louis area) of Missouri. The program identified areas of high gun crime, then focused enforcement and prosecution on these areas. Implementation data show an increase in information sharing and federal prosecutions for gun crimes. Violent gun crime in the target areas decreased significantly, though it is not clear if the PSN program caused the decrease.

Decker, S. H., & McDevitt, J. (2006). *Gun Prosecution Case Screening: Case Study 1.* Washington, DC: U.S. Department of Justice, Office of Justice Programs, National Institute of Justice.
https://www.bja.gov/Publications/Gun_Prosection_Case_Screening.pdf
This report describes the screening process for possible PSN cases. This includes keeping the case in state court, sending it to federal court, or using state court with federal backing. Results show that a review system of cases led to better information sharing, increased federal prosecution, and enhanced public safety.

Decker, S. H., McGarrell, E. F., et al. (2007). *Strategic Problem-Solving Responses to Gang Crime and Gang Problems: Case Study 8.* Washington, DC: U.S. Department of Justice, Office of Justice Programs, National Institute of Justice.
https://www.bja.gov/Publications/Strategic_Prob_Solving.pdf
This report examines gang-focused strategies as part of PSN. It references Operation Cease Fire, which offers three successful strategies to reduce gang violence. First, the intervention must be based on local police data. Second, data must be continually collected and used to refine the intervention as needed. Third, the intervention must combine local, state, and federal efforts.

Hipple, N. K., Corsaro, N., & McGarrell, E. F. (2010). *The High Point Drug Market Initiative: A Process and Impact Assessment, Project Safe Neighborhoods Case Study 12.* East Lansing, MI: Michigan State University, School of Criminal Justice.
http://www.psnmsu.com/documents/PSN_CaseStudy12.pdf
This program was rated on CrimeSolutions.gov as having insufficient evidence.
This report details the PSN and Drug Market Initiative (DMI) program in High Point, NC. The DMI program focuses deterrence strategies on specific open-air drug markets and the related violence. Results of the study show a decrease in violent crime of more than 7% and a decrease in drug and nuisance crimes by more than 5%.

Hipple, N. K., Frabutt, J. M., et al. (2007). *Middle District of North Carolina: Case Study 11.* Washington, DC: U.S. Department of Justice, Office of Justice Programs, National Institute of Justice.
https://www.ncjrs.gov/pdffiles1/nij/grants/241729.pdf
This report details the PSN program in the middle district of North Carolina (Durham/Greensboro/Winston-Salem/Salisbury area). A series of task forces were used in each city, coordinated by the U.S. Attorney's Office. The program had two components: a deterrence-based strategy

and access to services and resources. The results show that total gun crime declined in all four cities studied, though this decline was only significant in two of the cities.

Hipple, N. K., O'Shea, T., et al. (2007). *Southern District of Alabama: Case Study 10.* **Washington, DC: U.S. Department of Justice, Office of Justice Programs, National Institute of Justice.**
https://www.ncjrs.gov/pdffiles1/nij/grants/241728.pdf
This report details the PSN program in the southern district of Alabama (around Mobile). This program did not use a traditional task force but instead had officials stay within their agencies while working together. It relied on increased federal prosecution and a media campaign of deterrence messages. Analysis showed a significant decrease in total gun crime, violent gun crime, armed robberies, and assaults with a gun. There was no significant change in gun homicides.

Hipple, N. K., Perez, H. A., et al. (2007). *District of Nebraska: Case Study 9.* **Washington, DC: U.S. Department of Justice, Office of Justice Programs, National Institute of Justice.**
https://www.ncjrs.gov/pdffiles1/nij/grants/241727.pdf
This report discusses the PSN program in Nebraska. The main focus of this program was a task force in Omaha. The task force, made up of federal, state, and local authorities, used a strategic problem-solving approach with regular incident reviews. Data show a significant 20 percent reduction in firearms offenses after the start of the PSN intervention.

Kellermann, A. L., Fuqua-Whitley, D., et al. (2006). *Reducing Gun Violence: Community Problem Solving in Atlanta.* **Washington, DC: U.S. Department of Justice, Office of Justice Programs, National Institute of Justice.**
https://www.ncjrs.gov/pdffiles1/nij/209800.pdf
This report evaluates a program in Atlanta, GA, aimed at reducing youth gun violence. The program focused on reducing the supply of illegal firearms, strengthening enforcement of illegal carrying, and rehabilitating youth gun offenders. Although homicides fell, this was part of a continuing trend also seen in nonprogram areas. The authors conclude the program did not have an effect. It has since been rolled into PSN.

Klofas, J., & Hipple, N. K. (2006). *Crime Incident Reviews: Case Study 3.* **Washington, DC: U.S. Department of Justice, Office of Justice Programs, National Institute of Justice.**
https://www.bja.gov/Publications/Crime_Incident_Reviews.pdf
This report examines crime incident reviewswhich is a way to share detailed crime-related information between local agencies to help in solving crime problems. Success requires good cooperation and collaboration, sound analysis and quality research, and demonstrating linkages between incidents and strategic interventions. The goal of the crime incident review is to develop focused deterrent strategies to reduce gun violence. No evaluation of their effectiveness is presented.

McDevitt, J., Braga, A. A., et al. (2007). *Lowell, District of Massachusetts: Case Study 6.* **Washington, DC: U.S. Department of Justice, Office of Justice Programs, National Institute of Justice.**
https://www.bja.gov/Publications/Lowell_MA.pdf
This report takes a look at the PSN program in Lowell, MA. This program focused on identifying and prosecuting serious chronic offenders. Outcome data show a significant reduction in assaults with a firearm, but no reduction in armed robberies or gun-related calls for service. The reduction in firearm assaults was sustained for over 2 years.

McDevitt, J., Decker, S. H., et al. (2006). *Offender Notification Meetings: Case Study 2.* **Washington, DC: U.S. Department of Justice, Office of Justice Programs, National Institute of Justice.**
https://www.bja.gov/Publications/Offender_Notification_Meetings.pdf
This report looks at offender notification meetings, a program developed in Operation Cease Fire. The meetings focus on communicating a deterrent message, promising an aggressive response to gun violence, and offering support services for those on the verge of violence. Showing a causal connection between

notification meetings and a decrease in violence is difficult, but the evaluation shows that the meetings are effective at getting the message across.

McGarrell, E. F., Hipple, N. K., et al. (2007). *Middle District of Alabama: Case Study 5.* **Washington, DC: U.S. Department of Justice, Office of Justice Programs, National Institute of Justice.**
https://www.bja.gov/Publications/MD_Alabama.pdf
This report examines the PSN program in middle Alabama (the area around Montgomery). Implementation data show an increase in the number of federal prosecutions for gun crimes, with a focus on those with extensive criminal histories. Outcome data show a significant decrease in assault with a firearm and a marginal decrease in homicide.

McGarrell, E. F., Hipple, N. K., et al. (2009). *Project Safe Neighborhoods—A National Program to Reduce Gun Crime: Final Project Report.* **Washington, DC: U.S. Department of Justice, Office of Justice Programs, National Institute of Justice.**
https://www.ncjrs.gov/pdffiles1/nij/grants/226686.pdf
This report examines the PSN program on a national level by evaluating implementation and outcomes. Implementation was successful when the U.S. Attorney's office took a leadership role, resources were focused on high-gun-crime areas, and crime data were readily available. To determine outcomes, two research methodologies were used. First, several case studies were conducted. Second, an analysis of violent crime in cities with populations over 100,000 was conducted. This analysis showed that as the level of PSN increased, a greater decrease in crime occurred.

McGarrell, E. F., Corsaro, N., et al. (2011). *An Assessment of the Comprehensive Anti-Gang Initiative: Final Project Report.* **Washington, DC: U.S. Department of Justice, Office of Justice Programs, National Institute of Justice.**
https://www.ncjrs.gov/pdffiles1/nij/grants/240757.pdf
This report presents the findings of a national evaluation of the Comprehensive Anti-Gang Initiative (CAGI). CAGI involved comprehensive strategies aimed at reducing gang violence through enforcement, intervention, re-entry, and prevention. The evaluation found that in cities where comprehensive strategies were implemented with sufficient intensity, levels of violence declined in comparison to similar U.S. cities that were not part of the CAGI effort.

McGarrell, E. F., Hipple, N. K., et al. (2013). *Promising Strategies for Violence Reduction: Lessons from Two Decades of Innovation.* **Washington, DC: U.S. Department of Justice, Office of Justice Programs, National Institute of Justice.**
https://www.bja.gov/Publications/MSU_PromisingViolenceReductionInitiatives.pdf
This article examines several PSN-based programs—Operation Ceasefire, Cure Violence, PSN, and DMI. The authors conclude that all of these programs focus on establishing new partnerships and rely on a data-driven approach to addressing violent crime issues. They suggest jurisdictions tailor their program based on specific needs, since each of these four programs has a slightly different focus.

Roehl, J., Rosenbaum, D. P., et al. (2005). *Strategic Approaches to Community Safety Initiative (SACSI) in 10 U.S. Cities: The Building Blocks for Project Safe Neighborhoods.* **Washington, DC: U.S. Department of Justice, Office of Justice Programs, National Institute of Justice.**
https://www.ncjrs.gov/pdffiles1/nij/grants/212866.pdf
This report examines the SACSI program, a precursors to PSN based on Boston's Operation Ceasefire. The program took place in 10 midsized cities, all with violent crime rates much higher than average. It focused on collaboration, strategic planning, and pulling levers. The results show that both homicide and violent crime dropped in the 10 sites, while these measures rose in other cities. All sites have since been rolled into PSN programs.

Skogan, W. G., Hartnett, S. M., et al. (2009). *Evaluation of Cease-Fire Chicago.* **Washington, DC: U.S. Department of Justice, Office of Justice Programs, National Institute of Justice.**
https://www.ncjrs.gov/pdffiles1/nij/grants/227181.pdf

This program was rated on CrimeSolutions.gov as promising.
This report details Project Ceasefire in Chicago, IL. This program aims to identify those at risk of being the victim or offender of a shooting and using "interrupters" (specially trained workers with local knowledge) to prevent a shooting. The evaluation found that shootings decreased and gun crime hot spots shrank after the program was implemented.

Tita, G. E., Riley, K. J., et al. (2005). *Operation Ceasefire in Los Angeles.* **Washington, DC: U.S. Department of Justice, Office of Justice Programs, National Institute of Justice.**
https://www.ncjrs.gov/pdffiles1/nij/192378.pdf
This report discusses the Los Angeles Ceasefire program. The program borrowed heavily from Boston's Operation Ceasefire: work groups that included police, researchers, and community groups; various sanctions and rewards; and stepped-up patrols. The program saw a 37 percent decrease in violent crime, and smaller decreases in gun- and gang-related crime.

Other OJP-Sponsored Evaluations

Cahill, M., Coggeshall, M. B., et al. (2008). *Community Collaboratives Addressing Youth Gangs: Interim Findings from the Gang Reduction Program.* **Washington, DC: Urban Institute, Justice Policy Center. OJJDP Sponsored.**
http://www.urban.org/UploadedPDF/411692_communitycollaboratives.pdf
This program was rated on CrimeSolutions.gov as having no effect in
one location (Richmond, VA) and promising in another (Los Angeles).
This research evaluates the Gang Reduction Program (GRP), an OJJDP-sponsored program to reduce youth street gang crime in four cities. Results from two cities are discussed on CrimeSolutions.gov. In Los Angeles, the GRP provided prevention, reentry, and suppression services to combat youth gangs. Results showed a significant decrease in shots-fired calls and gang-related incidents. In Richmond, VA, many of the same services were offered. Results showed an increase in drug incidents, serious violent incidents, and gang-related incidents.

Radtke, T., Sousa, W., et al. (2008). *Operation Ceasefire in Clark County, Nevada: Evaluating a Cross-Jurisdictional Approach to Reducing Gun Violence.* **Las Vegas, NV: University of Nevada, Las Vegas, Center for the Analysis of Crime Statistics. BJS Sponsored.**
http://cacs.unlv.edu/pdf/OCF.pdf
This report examines the Safe Village Initiative program in Las Vegas, NV. It is a replication of Boston's Operation Ceasefire and focuses on collaboration and community mobilization to decrease gun crime. The report examined calls for service from 1 year before and 1 year after the program. Results showed a significant decrease in all calls for service, person-with-a-gun calls, assaults with a gun, and illegal shooting.

Roman, C. G., Cahill, M., et al. (2005). *The Weed and Seed Initiative and Crime Displacement in South Florida: An Examination of Spatial Displacement Associated with Crime Control Initiatives and the Redevelopment of Public Housing.* **Washington, DC: Urban Institute, Justice Policy Center. CCDO Sponsored.**
http://www.jrsa.org/ws-eval/studies_other/displacement-final-report.pdf
This program was rated on CrimeSolutions.gov as having no effect.
This report details the Weed and Seed program in Miami, FL. This program seeks to "weed" out the criminals and "seed" the community by revitalizing the neighborhood. In Miami, this program also runs the PSN program, and efforts for both programs are focused on the same target areas. The results show no significant decrease in violence and an increase in drug offenses in the target areas.

Thornton, R. L., Burrell, W. D., et al. (2006). *Guns, Safety, and Proactive Supervision: Involving Probation and Parole in Project Safe Neighborhoods.* **Lexington, KY: Council of State Governments, American Probation and Parole Association. BJA sponsored.**
http://www.appa-net.org/eweb/docs/appa/pubs/GSPS.pdf
This report details how probation and parole officers can be involved in PSN. First, officers can make unannounced home visits to high-risk probationers to ensure they are complying with the conditions of their probation. Second, officers need to notify probationers of the enhanced penalties associated with carrying a firearm. Finally, officers should practice proactive supervision, where they seek to uncover information about illegal firearms.

Other Academic Articles[51]

Boyle, D. J., Lanterman, J. L., et al. (2010). "The Impact of Newark's Operation Ceasefire on Trauma Center Gunshot Wound Admissions." *Justice Research and Policy, 12*(2): 105–123.
http://ubhc.rutgers.edu/vinjweb/publications/articles/Boyle%20et%20al%202010%20Final.pdf

This program was rated on CrimeSolutions.gov as having insufficient evidence.
This article evaluated Operation Ceasefire in Newark, NJ, by examining hospital admissions for gunshot wounds. The results showed no significant decrease in the rate of gunshot wounds after the program began. This was rated as insufficient evidence due to limited or inconsistent outcome evidence.

Braga, A. A., Apel, R., et al. (2013). "The Spillover Effects of Focused Deterrence on Gang Violence." *Evaluation Review, 37*(3/4): 314–342.
http://www.ncbi.nlm.nih.gov/pubmed/24569771
This article examines the diffusion of benefits from a focused deterrent program such as PSN. The article finds that when certain gangs are targeted for enforcement, other gangs take notice and can be deterred as well. Total shootings went down for both gangs targeted and those targeted vicariously (allies and rivals of targeted gangs).

Braga, A. A., Hureau, D. M., & Papachristos, A. V. (2014). "Deterring Gang-Involved Gun Violence: Measuring the Impact of Boston's Operation Ceasefire on Street Gang Behavior." *Journal of Quantitative Criminology, 30:*113–139.
http://link.springer.com/article/10.1007/s10940-013-9198-x
This article asserts that the original evaluation of Boston's Ceasefire program had a relatively weak design, leading to uncertainty about the results. To remedy this, this revised study used a more rigorous design to find that the total number of shootings involving Boston gangs dropped by 31% when subjected to Operation Ceasefire. This result helps to bolster the findings in previous studies.

Braga, A. A., Kennedy, D. M., et al. (2001). "Problem-Oriented Policing, Deterrence, and Youth Violence: An Evaluation of Boston's Operation Ceasefire." *Journal of Research in Crime and Delinquency, 38*(3): 195–225.
http://www.pacinst.org/wp-content/uploads/sites/11/2013/05/Braga-et-al-2001.pdf

This program was rated on CrimeSolutions.gov as effective.
This research evaluated Boston's Operation Ceasefire, a PSN-type program that focused attention on chronic, gang-involved offenders who were responsible for much of the youth homicide in Boston. Results show that the program was associated with significant reductions in youth homicide, shots-fired calls, and firearm assaults.

---

[51] Links to abstracts are provided when full articles are not available.

Braga, A. A., & Pierce, G. L. (2005). "Disrupting Illegal Firearms Markets in Boston: The Effects of Operation Ceasefire on the Supply of New Handguns to Criminals." *Criminology & Public Policy, 4*(4): 717–748.
https://www.ncjrs.gov/App/publications/abstract.aspx?ID=233777

This program was rated on CrimeSolutions.gov as effective.
This research examines a second element of Operation Ceasefire in Boston: the crackdown on firearms traffickers that supplied youth with guns. This program brought ATF and Boston authorities together to crack down on those trafficking firearms commonly used by gang members—usually new, small-caliber, low-quality semiautomatic handguns. The study found that the program resulted in a significant decrease in the number of new handguns seized by the police. However, it appears that criminals simply used older handguns in response to the crackdown.

Braga A. A., McDevitt J., & Pierce G. L. (2006). "Understanding and Preventing Gang Violence: Problem Analysis and Response Development in Lowell, Massachusetts." *Police Quarterly, 9*: 20–46.
https://www.ncjrs.gov/App/AbstractDB/AbstractDBDetails.aspx?id=237093
This article reported results from a Project Safe Neighborhoods initiative in Lowell, MA. The problem analysis revealed that gun violence was concentrated among 19 active street gangs. This led to a focused deterrence strategy combined with outreach and support. This article provides an excellent example of a collaborative problem-solving model and systematic problem analysis and presents promising findings from the intervention.

Braga, A. A. (2008). "Pulling Levers Focused Deterrence Strategies and the Prevention of Gun Homicide." *Journal of Criminal Justice, 36*: 332–343.
https://www.ncjrs.gov/App/AbstractDB/AbstractDBDetails.aspx?id=245874
This article presents the results of an evaluation of Stockton, California's Operation Peacekeeper. This initiative involved the focused deterrence "pulling levers" strategy to address gang member gun violence. The results indicated significant declines in gun homicide.

Braga, A. A., Piehl, A. M., and Hureau, D. (2009). "Controlling Violent Offenders Released to the Community: An Evaluation of the Boston Reentry Initiative." *Journal of Research in Crime and Delinquency, 46*: 411–436.
https://www.ncjrs.gov/App/AbstractDB/AbstractDBSearchResults.aspx?Title=controlling+violent+offenders&Author=braga&Journal=&NCJNum=&General=&StartDate=&EndDate=&SearchMode=All&SortBy=4&Offset=0
This article reports the results of a study of the use of parolee call-in forums with parolees who have prior histories of violence. The results indicate a significant reduction in reoffending among parolees attending the forums.

Braga, A. A., & Weisburd, D. L. (2012). "The Effects of 'Pulling Levers' Focused Deterrence Strategies on Crime." *Campbell Systematic Reviews, 8*(6).
http://campbellcollaboration.org/lib/project/96/

This practice was rated on CrimeSolutions.gov as promising.
This study examines focused deterrence or "pulling levers," a strategy used in Operation Ceasefire and at the heart of PSN. Focused deterrence relies on targeting chronic offenders and informing them of heightened penalties if they do not stop. It is usually backed up by crackdowns on those who continue committing crimes. This meta-analysis found a significant, medium-size crime reduction from these strategies.

Corsaro, N., Hunt, E. D., et al. (2012). "The Impact of Drug Market Pulling Levers Policing on Neighborhood Violence: An Evaluation of the High Point Drug Market Intervention." *Criminology and Public Policy, 11*(2):167–199.
http://onlinelibrary.wiley.com/doi/10.1111/j.1745-9133.2012.00798.x/abstract

This program was rated on CrimeSolutions.gov as effective.
This report details the DMI program in High Point, NC, that concentrated resources on problem areas and chronic offenders involved in the drug markets. The program focused on identifying these areas, notifying offenders of the harsh sanctions, and offering community resources. Areas targeted by the program saw an almost 8 percent drop in violence, whereas a comparison area had a similar increase in violence.

Corsaro, N., Brunson, R. K., & McGarrell, E. F. (2010). "Evaluating a Policing Strategy Intended to Disrupt an Illicit Street-Level Drug Market." *Evaluation Review, 34* (6): 513–548.
http://erx.sagepub.com/content/early/2010/12/15/0193841X10389136.abstract
This study examined the implementation of the Drug Market Intervention (DMI) in a neighborhood in Nashville, TN that had long experienced open air drug dealing. The results indicated a significant reduction in drug and narcotics incidents and reports of large increases in the perceived quality of neighborhood life.

Corsaro, N., Brunson, R., and McGarrell, E. F. (2013). "Problem-Oriented Policing and Open-Air Drug Markets: Examining the Pulling Levers Deterrence Strategy in Rockford, Illinois."*Crime and Delinquency, 59* (7): 1085–1107.
https://www.ncjrs.gov/App/AbstractDB/AbstractDBDetails.aspx?id=267149
This article presents the results of the Drug Market Intervention (DMI) strategy conducted in Rockford, IL. The results indicated a significant reduction in crime, drug, and nuisance offenses in the DMI neighborhood.

Corsaro, N., & McGarrell, E. (2009). "Testing a Promising Homicide Reduction Strategy: Reassessing the Impact of the Indianapolis 'Pulling Levers' Intervention." *Journal of Experimental Criminology, 5*(1):63–82.
https://www.ncjrs.gov/App/publications/abstract.aspx?ID=248740

This program was rated on CrimeSolutions.gov as promising.
This article evaluates the Indianapolis "Pulling Levers" program, modeled after Boston's Operation Ceasefire. The program focused on reducing gang homicide by targeting chronic offenders. The results show an overall decrease in homicides. However, when the data are disaggregated, the authors show that the program had a greater effect on gang homicides than nongang homicides. This supports the proposition that the program caused the decrease.

Corsaro, N., and E.F. McGarrell. (2010). "Reducing Homicide Risk in Indianapolis between 1997 and 2000." *Journal of Urban Health 87*(5): 851–64.
http://link.springer.com/article/10.1007/s11524-010-9459-z
This article analyzes the Indianapolis Violence Reduction Partnership from the perspective of homicide risk reduction. The findings indicate that the focused deterrence strategy produced the highest reduction in gun homicides among the populations at highest risk of victimization.

Engel, R. S., Tillyer, M. S., & Corsaro, N. (2013). "Reducing Gang Violence Using Focused Deterrence: Evaluating the Cincinnati Initiative to Reduce Violence (CIRV)." *Justice Quarterly, 30* (3): 403–439.
http://www.tandfonline.com/doi/abs/10.1080/07418825.2011.619559
This article presents the findings of the evaluation of the Cincinnati Initiative to Reduce Violence. It describes the nature of the initiative and reports significant declines in group-member involved homicides and violent firearm incidents.

Klofas, J., Hipple, N. K., & McGarrell, E. F. (2010). *The New Criminal Justice.* **New York: Routledge.**
https://www.routledge.com/products/9780415997287
This book summarizes the findings of the research on Project Safe Neighborhoods. Chapters include information about the foundations of the PSN model, strategic problem solving, and partnerships. Additional chapters present the results of case studies of PSN initiatives and the lessons learned on establishing effective practitioner-researcher partnerships.

McGarrell, E. F., Corsaro, N., Hipple, N. K., & Bynum T. S. (2010). "Project Safe Neighborhoods and Violent Crime Trends in U.S. Cities: Assessing Violent Crime Impact." *Journal of Quantitative Criminology, 26:* **165–190.**
https://www.ncjrs.gov/App/AbstractDB/AbstractDBDetails.aspx?id=253426

This program was rated on CrimeSolutions.gov as promising.
This article presents the results of the national evaluation of Project Safe Neighborhoods. The findings indicate that PSN target cities experienced significant reductions in violent crime compared to other U.S. cities that were not the focus of a PSN intervention. The results were most pronounced where PSN was implemented with the most intensity and fidelity to the core PSN principles.

McGarrell, E. F., Chermak, S., Wilson, J. M., & Corsaro, N. (2006). "Reducing Homicide Through a 'Lever-Pulling' Strategy." *Justice Quarterly, 23:* **214–231.**
https://www.ncjrs.gov/App/AbstractDB/AbstractDBDetails.aspx?id=236020
The Indianapolis Violence Reduction Partnership represents one of the first replications of Boston's Operation Ceasefire. Problem analyses revealed that much of the gun violence in Indianapolis involved people involved in gangs and groups of chronic offenders. The pulling levers strategy was utilized, and the results indicated a significant reduction in homicides.

McGarrell, E. F., Corsaro, N., Melde, C., Hipple, N., Bynum, T., & Cobbina, J. (2013) "Attempting to Reduce Firearms Violence Through a Comprehensive Anti-Gang Initiative (CAGI): An Evaluation of Process and Impact." *Journal of Criminal Justice, 41:* **33–43.**
https://www.ncjrs.gov/App/AbstractDB/AbstractDBDetails.aspx?id=264734
This article presents the results of an evaluation of the Comprehensive Anti-Gang Initiative (CAGI). The results did not indicate a consistent impact on gang violence but rather reductions in violent crime were limited to those jurisdictions that were able to successfully implement the enforcement components of the strategy. Suggestions for addressing implementation challenges are presented.

Papachristos, A. V., Meares, T. L., et al. (2007). "Attention Felons: Evaluating Project Safe Neighborhoods in Chicago." *Journal of Empirical Legal Studies, 4(2):* **223–272.**
http://papers.ssrn.com/sol3/papers.cfm?abstract_id=860685

This program was rated on CrimeSolutions.gov as promising.
This research evaluated four interventions associated with the PSN program in Chicago, IL. The authors found a significant decline in homicide between the PSN areas and comparison areas. The greatest decline in homicide was attributed to the offender notification meetings. However, the PSN areas also received attention from Operation Ceasefire, so it is possible that this caused some of the decrease.

Rosenfeld, R., Fornango, R., et al. (2005). "Did Ceasefire, Compstat, and Exile Reduce Homicide?" *Criminology & Public Policy, 4(3):* **419–449.**
http://thehumanist.com/wp-content/uploads/sites/11/2013/01/Rosenfeld-et-al-Did-Ceasefire-Compstat-and-Excile-Reduce-Homicide.pdf

This program was rated on CrimeSolutions.gov as promising.
This research examines three programs touted as reducing homicides in three cities. The analysis compares the claimed reductions with 95 other cities to determine what truly decreased crime. The authors find that Boston's Operation Ceasefire did result in a drop in homicide, though not enough to

reach a strong conclusion. Project Exile in Richmond, VA, had a significant drop in homicides consistent with the claims of the program.

Wallace, D., Papachristos, A. V., Meares, T., & Fagan, J. (2015). "Desistance and Legitimacy: The Impact of Offender Notification Meetings on Recidivism among High Risk Offenders." *Justice Quarterly.*
http://dx.doi.org/10.1080/07418825.2015.1081262
Chicago's Project Safe Neighborhoods program has included parolee forums with high-risk offenders returning to the community as a key component of its overall violence- reduction strategies. This study presents the results of an evaluation of the forums and finds significant reductions in reoffending among the parolees attending the forums.

Webster, D., Whitehill, J., et al. (2013). "Effects of Baltimore's Safe Streets Program on Gun Violence: A Replication of Chicago's Ceasefire Program." *Journal of Urban Health, 90*(1): 27–40.
http://www.ncbi.nlm.nih.gov/pmc/articles/PMC3579298/
This research examines Baltimore's Safe Streets program, a replication of the Ceasefire program in Chicago. The only major difference was the lack of "interrupters" in the Baltimore program. The program was implemented in four areas with high gun crime. Three of these areas had a significant decrease in one or more measures of gun violence. The authors estimate the program prevented about 35 shootings and 5 homicides over about 9 years.

Other Reports

MacDonald, J. M., Wilson, J. M., et al. (2005). *Data-Driven Homicide Prevention: An Examination of Five Project Safe Neighborhoods Target Areas.* **Washington, DC: RAND.**
http://www.rand.org/content/dam/rand/pubs/working_papers/2005/RAND_WR284.pdf
This research examines the PSN program in California by examining five target areas. The research provides four suggestions for enhancing the PSN projects to combat youth homicide. First, patrols should be directed to specific places and times based on data analysis. Second, enforcement of firearms laws should be increased by using federal prosecutions. Third, entire gangs should be held responsible for the actions of the members by pulling levers against gangs. Finally, education and treatment should be provided.

Matz, A. K., & Mowatt, M.A. (2013). *Research Brief: Feedback from APPA Membership on PSN T/TA.* **New York: Council of State Governments. BJA-funded.**
http://www.appa-net.org/psn/docs/PSN_TTA_Survey_Bulletin.pdf
This survey looked at APPA members' involvement in PSN and TTA for PSN. It found that only 30% of members were involved in PSN but that 56% were interested in PSN TTA support. This high level of desire for TTA most likely comes from agencies involved in other collaborative programs, such as Operation Ceasefire, which 58% of respondents participated in.

Matz, A. K., & Mowatt, M. A. (2014). *PSN Update: Gang Members in Small-Town and Rural Communities.* **New York: Council of State Governments. BJA-funded.**
http://www.appa-net.org/Perspectives/Perspectives_V38_N1_P52.pdf
This report examines the literature surrounding gangs in small towns and rural areas. It finds that historically, most youth gangs are concentrated in urban areas, and that the differences between urban and rural gangs must be considered when examining the feasibility of an intervention program. The report concludes that rural gang issues have not been adequately studied and that programs in rural areas have not been sufficiently documented.

Picard-Fritsche, S., Swaner, R., & Lambson, S. H. (2014). *Deterrence and Legitimacy in Brownsville, Brooklyn.* **New York: Center For Court Innovation.**
http://justideasonline.org/sites/default/files/documents/BAVP_Report.pdf
This report details the implementation of the Brownsville antiviolence project, which is based on the Chicago PSN program. A major part of the Brownsville program is the use of offender call-in meetings. The report found that these meetings were mostly carried out with fidelity to the Chicago model, with three main exceptions: the lack of a strong antigun message from the NYPD, the infrequent representation of the ATF, and a lack of specificity surrounding the services being offered. Regardless, the study found adherence to the model to be moderately strong.

Virginia Department of Criminal Justice Services. (2003). *Evaluation of the Virginia Exile Program.* **Richmond, VA: Author.**
https://www.dcjs.virginia.gov/research/documents/exileFinal.pdf
This report details Virginia's Exile program, a series of grants to help localities enforce new state laws requiring mandatory minimums for certain gun crimes. It is based on Richmond's Project Exile and aims to reduce gun crime. Results showed an increase in most violent crimes after the program began. The report concludes that this could be because the program was simply not effective.

Websites

Project Safe Neighborhoods
http://www.psn.gov/

National Crime Prevention Council
http://www.ncpc.org/

National Gang Center
http://www.nationalgangcenter.gov

National District Attorneys Association
http://www.ndaa.org

International Association of Chiefs of Police
http://www.iacp.org

American Probation and Parole Association
http://www.appa-net.org/eweb/

Regional Information Sharing Systems
http://www.riss.net/

Michigan State University–Project Safe Neighborhoods
http://psnmsu.com

Michigan State University–Drug Market Intervention
http://dmimsu.com

Public Safety Officers' Benefits Program

Project Description[52]

First enacted in 1976, the Public Safety Officers' Benefits (PSOB) Program is designed to provide death, disability, and education benefits to catastrophically injured public safety officers or the survivors of fallen law enforcement officers, firefighters, and other first responders.[53] The program was created to help recruit qualified personnel, emphasize the value placed on those who serve the community in dangerous circumstances, and foster peace of mind in those who seek to work in public safety.[54]

The PSOB Program is divided into three distinct areas. First, it provides death benefits in the form of a one-time financial payment to eligible survivors of public safety officers whose deaths are the direct and proximate result of a personal injury sustained in the line of duty. Second, the program offers benefits to public safety officers who are permanently and totally disabled because of injuries sustained in the line of duty (i.e., catastrophically injured). Finally, the program provides financial assistance to help pay higher education costs for the spouses and children of public safety officers for whom PSOB death or disability benefits have been paid.

CrimeSolutions.gov Ratings:
No ratings at this time

Partners and Professional Organizations:
- ✓ Badge of Honor Memorial Foundation
- ✓ Concerns of Police Survivors
- ✓ Correctional Peace Officers Foundation
- ✓ National Fallen Firefighters Foundation

NIJ-Sponsored and Other OJP-Sponsored Evaluations[55]

Office of the Inspector General. (2015). *Audit of the Office of Justice Programs' Processing of Public Safety Officer' Benefit Programs Claims.* Washington, DC: Author.
https://oig.justice.gov/reports/2015/a1521.pdf
This audit of PSOB evaluated the timeliness of PSOB claims processing.

Academic Research

Violanti, J. M. (1995). "Survivors' Trauma and Departmental Response Following Deaths of Police Officers." *Psychological Reports, 77*(2): 611–615.
http://www.amsciepub.com/doi/abs/10.2466/pr0.1995.77.2.611?journalCode=pr0
This article examined line-of-duty deaths and how police departments supported spouses after line-of-duty deaths. The report found that traumatic stress was lower in spouses when the department was supportive, such as when assisting with death benefits. The author concludes that departments should institute policies that offer assistance to spouses after a death.

Other Research

BJA (2015, July). *Public Safety Officers' Benefits Program* [FS 000359]. Washington, DC: Author.
https://www.bja.gov/Publications/PSOB_FS.pdf
This fact sheet presents information about activities associated with the PSOB Program.

---

[52] https://www.bja.gov/Funding/12PSOBLawEnfSupportSol.pdf
[53] https://www.bja.gov/Publications/PSOB_FS.pdf
[54] Ibid.
[55] For all articles, a link has been provided to either the full-length document or the website it can be accessed.

Fahy, F. R., LeBlanc, R. P., & Molis, L. J. (2014). *Firefighter Fatalities in the United States—2013.* **Quincy, MA: National Fire Protection Association, Fire Analysis and Research Division.**
http://www.nfpa.org/~/media/Files/Research/NFPA%20reports/Fire%20service%20statistics/osfff.pdf
This report details the 97 on-duty firefighter deaths in the United States in 2013. One-third of the deaths resulted from overexertion, stress, and other medical-related issues. Of the 32 deaths in this category, 29 were classified as sudden cardiac deaths (usually heart attacks), one was a cerebral aneurysm, one was a stroke, and one was a suicide.

Government Accountability Office. (2009). *Public Safety Officers' Benefit Program: Performance Measurement Would Strengthen Accountability and Enhance Awareness among Potential Claimants* **[GAO-10-5]. Washington, DC: Author.**
http://www.gao.gov/new.items/d105.pdf
This report reviewed PSOB Program claims opened during fiscal years 2006 to 2008 for all three types of claims (death, disability, and education). The report found that education and death claims were usually processed in a reasonable amount of time but that disability claims were often complex and sometimes took years. GAO recommended that the PSOB Program establish appropriate performance measures and use reliable data to monitor and report on the program's performance.

James, N. (2010). *Public Safety Officers' Benefits (PSOB) Program.* **Washington, DC: Congressional Research Service.**
http://assets.opencrs.com/rpts/RL34413_20100105.pdf
This informational article offers an outline and specific breakdown of the PSOB Program. It describes the history of the initiative, details the process of filing claims, and presents an overview of the program's funding. It does not evaluate the program or suggest ways of improving it.

National Law Enforcement Officers Memorial Fund. (2014). *Law Enforcement Officer Deaths: 2013.* **Washington, DC: Author.**
http://www.nleomf.org/assets/pdfs/reports/2013-EOY-Fatality-Report.pdf
This report details the circumstances of 100 law enforcement officers who died in the United States in 2013. The leading cause of death was traffic crashes (43 officers), followed by firearms-related fatalities (31 officers). Twenty-one of the officers involved in firearms-related fatalities were shot with a handgun.

Office of the Inspector General. (2008). *The Office of Justice Programs' Implementation of the Hometown Heroes Survivors Benefits Act of 2003.* **[Evaluation and Inspections Report I-2008-005]. Washington, DC: Author.**
http://www.justice.gov/oig/reports/OJP/e0805/final.pdf
This report examines the implementation of the Hometown Heroes Act, which allowed for PSOB Program benefits to be granted to those who died in the line of duty from heart attacks or strokes. It found a backlog of claims and long wait times for case processing. Policy changes in 2007 helped to fix some of these problems.

Websites

PSOB Program
https://www.psob.gov/

Badge of Honor Memorial Foundation
http://bohmf.org/

Concerns of Police Survivors
http://www.nationalcops.org/

Correctional Peace Officers Foundation
http://cpof.org/

National Fallen Firefighters Foundation
http://www.firehero.org

Reentry Courts

Project Description

Reentry courts are common across the United States. There are three types: Reentry Drug Courts, Reentry Courts, and Federal Reentry Courts. Reentry Drug Courts use the Drug Court model, as defined in the 10 Key Components,[56] and facilitate the reintegration of drug-involved offenders into the community after their release from jail or prison.[57] Reentry Courts are similar to Reentry Drug Courts but do not focus on drug-addicted offenders. Federal Reentry Courts are post-incarceration and are a "cooperative effort of the U.S. District Courts, U.S. Probation Office, Federal Public Defender, and U.S. Attorney's Office."[58] Common to all these courts is that the offender is involved in "regular judicial monitoring, intensive treatment, community supervision, and drug testing." The participants are offered specialized services with the goal of successful reentry into the community.[59]

CrimeSolutions.gov Ratings:
No ratings at this time

Partners and Professional Organizations:
- ✓ National Association of Drug Court Professionals
- ✓ Center for Court Innovation
- ✓ U.S. Probation Office
- ✓ Federal Probation Office

Highlighted Reports

Lindquist, C., Hardison, J., et al. (2003). *Reentry Courts Process Evaluation (Phase 1): Final Report.* Research Triangle Park, NC: RTI International. Prepared for NIJ.
https://www.ncjrs.gov/pdffiles1/nij/grants/202472.pdf
This document presents an evaluation of the Reentry Court Initiative from the Office of Justice Programs, which establishes a system of offender accountability and support services throughout the reentry process.

Lindquist, C., Hardison Walters, J., et al. (2013). *The National Institute of Justice's Evaluation of Second Chance Act Adult Reentry Courts: Program Characteristics and Preliminary Themes from Year 1.* Research Triangle Park, NC: RTI International, Center for Court Innovation, and NNPC Research.
https://www.ncjrs.gov/pdffiles1/nij/grants/241400.pdf
This report presents the program characteristics and preliminary themes from NIJ's evaluation of Second Chance Act Adult Reentry Courts. The evaluation looked at eight courts and assessed their participants, treatment, and other variables important to reentry.

NIJ-Sponsored Evaluations

Goldkamp, J. S., & White, M. D. (2003). *Nevada Reentry Drug Court Demonstration.* Philadelphia: Crime and Justice Research Institute.
https://www.ncjrs.gov/pdffiles1/nij/grants/202559.pdf
This report describes the development and implementation of the nation's first reentry drug courts in Nevada (Clark County and Washoe County), which release prison inmates to drug courts within 2 years of their expected parole dates.

---

[56] FAQs. What Is a Reentry Court? www.ndcrc.org
[57] Ibid.
[58] FAQs. What Is a Federal Reentry/Drug Court? www.ndcrc.org
[59] FAQs. What Is a Reentry Court? www.ndcrc.org

Lindquist, C., Hardison, J., et al. (2004). *The Reentry Court Initiative: Court-Based Strategies for Managing Released Prisoners.* **Research Triangle Park, NC: RTI International. Prepared for NIJ.**
https://www.rti.org/publication/reentry-court-initiative-court-based-strategies-managing-released-prisoners
The article describes RCI programs. Telephone interviews were conducted with contacts from each site. Semistructured personal interviews were held at 3 sites with 28 key stakeholders, including judges, program directors, supervision officers, case managers, and program participants. Several barriers were common across the RCI sites, particularly the difficulties program participants had in obtaining employment and in finding appropriate, affordable housing.

BJA-Sponsored Evaluations[60]

Farole, D. J. (2003). *The Harlem Parole Reentry Court Evaluation: Implementation and Preliminary Impacts.* **New York: Center for Court Innovation.**
https://www.ncjrs.gov/pdffiles1/Digitization/204132NCJRS.pdf
This article presents a process and preliminary impact evaluation of the Harlem Parole Reentry Court established in 2001 in New York City. The evaluation focuses on the first 20 months of operation and on nonviolent adult felony offenders convicted of drug charges.

BJA Reports

Council of State Governments Justice Center. (2013). *Reentry Matters: Strategies and Successes of Second Chance Act Grantees Across the United States.* **New York: Author.**
http://csgjusticecenter.org/wp-content/uploads/2013/11/ReentryMatters.pdf
This report presents information on strategies and successes of Second Chance Act grantees, including the Harlem Parole Reentry Court.

Devers, L. (2013). *Program Performance Report: Second Chance Act—Reentry Court Grant Program, July 2011 to June 2012.* **Arlington, VA: U.S. Department of Justice, Office of Justice Programs, Bureau of Justice Assistance.**
https://www.bja.gov/Publications/SCAReentryCourt_PPR_06-12.pdf
This report covers four quarters of data collected from July 2011 to June 2012 for the Second Chance Act Reentry Courts grantees.

Rivers, J. L., & Anderson, L. (2009). *Back on Track: A Problem-Solving Reentry Court.* **Washington, DC: U.S. Department of Justice, Office of Justice Programs, Bureau of Justice Assistance.**
https://www.bja.gov/Publications/BackonTrackFS.pdf
This fact sheet highlights the BJA-funded Back on Track program, a San Francisco reentry initiative aimed at reducing recidivism among low-level drug trafficking defendants. The report outlines the type of participants they serve, their program requirements, and their successes.

Wolf, R. V. (2011). *Reentry Courts: Looking Ahead—A Conversation about Strategies for Offender Reintegration.* **New York: Center for Court Innovation.**
https://www.bja.gov/Publications/CCI_ReentryCourts.pdf
This report summarizes the discussions of a focus group on the status of reentry courts as viewed by policymakers, court practitioners, parole and probation administrators, and researchers.

---

[60] For each article, a link has been provided to either the full-length document or the website where it can be accessed.

Academic Articles

Fetsco, D. M. (2013). "Reentry Courts: An Emerging Use of Judicial Resources in the Struggle to Reduce the Recidivism of Released Offender." *Wyoming Law Review, 13*(2): 591–613.
http://www.uwyo.edu/law/_files/docs/wy%20law%20review/v13%20n2/fetsco.pdf
The article focuses on creation and development of reentry courts in the United States as of February 2014. It discusses Wyoming's reentry courts, spread of drug courts in the United States, OJP's national reentry court initiative, and the role of social ties in preventing future crimes by an offender. Also discussed is the Court Assisted Recovery Effort program that Massachusetts launched in 2006.

Hamilton, Z. (2010). *Do Reentry Courts Reduce Recidivism? Results from the Harlem Parole Reentry Court.* **New York: Center for Court Innovation.**
http://www.courtinnovation.org/sites/default/files/Reentry_Evaluation.pdf
This evaluation assessed the impact of the Harlem Parole Reentry Court following program modifications implemented after an initial formative evaluation. The Reentry Court seemed to have had a positive effect on preventing new crimes.

Knollenberg, L., & Martin, V. A. (2008). "Community Reentry Following Prison: A Process Evaluation of the Accelerated Community Entry Program." *Federal Probation ,72*(2): 54–60.
http://www.uscourts.gov/uscourts/federalcourts/pps/fedprob/2008-09/09_community_reentry.html
This article presents the methodology and findings of a process evaluation of the Accelerated Community Entry (ACE) program in the Federal Western District of Michigan, which uses the reentry court model to offer more structure to offenders reentering the community from prison. Despite identified limitations in the methodology, the evaluation identified areas where the ACE program has excelled as well as areas where it could improve.

O'Hear, M. M. (2007). "The Second Chance Act and the Future of Reentry Reform." *Federal Sentencing Reporter, 20:*75. **Marquette University Faculty Publications, Paper 117.**
http://scholarship.law.marquette.edu/cgi/viewcontent.cgi?article=1108&context=facpub
The author reviews the Second Chance Act and the potential significance SCA has over sentencing, expressing his concerns about the reentry movement and whether it can live up to expectations and fulfill its goals.

Petersilia, J. (2001). "Prisoner Reentry: Public Safety and Reintegration Challenges." *Prison Journal, 81*(3): 360–375.
http://jthomasniu.org/class/Temp/reentry112.pdf
This article analyzes collateral consequences of recycling parolees in and out of families and communities. The future of parole is also discussed. The author urges a rethinking of discretionary parole release.

Pinard, M. (2010). "Reflections and Perspectives on Reentry and Collateral Consequences." *Journal of Criminal Law and Criminology, 100*(3): 1213–1224.
http://digitalcommons.law.umaryland.edu/cgi/viewcontent.cgi?article=2040&context=fac_pubs
This article gives a brief history of collateral consequences and reentry. It then describes the expansion these consequences have had on reentry. The author concludes with trying to help readers better understand the scope of the collateral consequences of reentry.

Taylor, C. J. (2013). "Tolerance of Minor Setbacks in a Challenging Reentry Experience: An Evaluation of a Federal Reentry Court." *Criminal Justice Policy Review, 24*(1): 49–70.
http://cjp.sagepub.com/content/24/1/49.full.pdf+html
The Federal Probation Office and the Board of Judges for the Eastern District of Pennsylvania initiated a pilot reentry court program in 2007, the Supervision to Aid Reentry (STAR) program. The impact evaluation used a quasiexperimental research design to compare the reentry success of the first 60 STAR participants to a matched comparison group of 60 probationers in the 18 months postrelease. Although

results indicated that STAR participants were no less likely to be arrested than the comparison group, STAR participation was associated with a significant reduction in the likelihood of supervision revocation. Implications of these findings for the STAR program and other reentry programs are discussed.

Thelin, R., & Nunn, S. (2009). *Marion County Reentry Court Program Assessment: January 2005 through September 2008.* **Indianapolis, IN: Center for Criminal Justice Research.**
http://policyinstitute.iu.edu/Uploads/ProjectFiles/MCRC%20Program%20Assessment%20Complete.pdf
The Marion County Reentry Court Program in Indiana contracted with the Center for Criminal Justice Research to conduct a baseline program assessment and to compare participant profiles between the initial 2 years of the program and associated court program modifications. This report outlines the program assessment over its 3-year, 9-month run.

Thompson, A. C. (2004). "Navigating the Hidden Obstacles to Ex-Offender Reentry." *Boston College Law Review, 45*(2): 255–306.
http://lawdigitalcommons.bc.edu/bclr/vol45/iss2/1/
The article first examines the last two decades of incarceration and the political trends that have influenced it. It then moves into the reentry period and how that has affected offenders and the judicial system, concluding with two suggestions on how the legal community might improve offender reentry.

Travis, J. (2007). "Reflections on the Reentry Movement." *Federal Sentencing Reporter, 20*(2): 84–87.
http://www.jjay.cuny.edu/extra/president_articles/ReflectionsOntheReentryMovement.pdf
This report examines the history of the reentry movement, the changes it has made, reentry's resulting impact, and where the movement is headed.

Vance, S. E. (2011). "Federal Reentry Court Programs: A Summary of Recent Evaluations." *Federal Probation, 75*(2).
http://www.uscourts.gov/uscourts/FederalCourts/PPS/Fedprob/2011-09/federal_reentry.html
This article summarizes evaluations of federal reentry court programs in the federal districts of Oregon, Massachusetts, and Western Michigan established over the past 6 years. Such programs enable the court to impose graduated sanctions and positive reinforcement administered by a team that typically involves a judge, a probation officer, an assistant U.S. attorney, an assistant federal defender, and a contract services provider. Within this general model, there is considerable variation. This article describes the features of the court reentry program in each of the three districts and provides an overview of an evaluation conducted of each program.

Wilkinson, R. A., Bucholtz, G. A., et al. (2004). "Prison Reform Through Offender Reentry: A Partnership Between Courts and Corrections." *Pace Law Review, 24*(2): 609–629.
http://digitalcommons.pace.edu/cgi/viewcontent.cgi?article=1206&context=plr
This article outlines the history of prisoner reform and the concept of prisoner reentry. It examines offender reentry and the role that courts and corrections play. It also discusses the role played by reentry courts.

Other Reports

The Council of State Governments Justice Center. (2015). *Reducing Recidivism and Improving Other Outcomes for Young Adults in the Juvenile and Adult Criminal Justice System.* **New York: Author.**
https://csgjusticecenter.org/wp-content/uploads/2015/11/Transitional-Age-Brief.pdf
This report reviews the research and identifies unique needs of the young adult criminal justice population; it is designed to help state and local officials better support this population in their criminal justice systems. This report goes over what works and makes suggestions to help improve outcomes for young adults involved in the criminal justice system.

Close, D. W., Alltucker, K., et al. (2009). *The District of Oregon Reentry Court: Evaluation, Policy Recommendations, and Replication Strategies.* **Salem, OR: U.S. Probation Office, District of Oregon.**
http://www.orp.uscourts.gov/documents/ReentryCourtDoc.pdf
This document describes the model reentry court program, its basis in evidence, and its evaluation. It is divided into three main sections: the development of the District of Oregon Reentry Court, the program's components, and guidance for replicating and customizing the model.

Korber, D. (2011). *"A Courtroom Unlike Any Other": Santa Clara County's Parolee Reentry Court Is a Case Study in Reducing Prison Recidivism* **[Report 1496-S]. Sacramento, CA: California Senate Office of Oversight and Outcomes.**
http://sooo.senate.ca.gov/sites/sooo.senate.ca.gov/files/a%20courtroom%20unlike%20any%20other.pdf
This case study of Santa Clara County's Parolee Reentry Court explains its rationale and describes its operation, personnel, and impact on parolee recidivism.

Restrepo, L. F., & Rice, T. R. (2013). *Annual Report—Reentry Court Program.* **Harrisburg, PA: Pennsylvania Board of Judges.**
http://www.portal.state.pa.us/portal/server.pt/document/1376125/2013_annual_report_pdf
This report outlines the progress of Pennsylvania's Reentry Court Program, also known as the Supervision to Aid Re-entry (STAR) program, since its inception in September 2007. The report details the number of STAR graduates, how many recidivated, and how the court and its participants are doing overall.

Ndrecka, M. (2014). *The Impact of Reentry Programs on Recidivism: a Meta-Analysis.* **(Doctoral dissertation, Univeristy of Cincinnati.)**
http://cech.uc.edu/content/dam/cech/programs/criminaljustice/docs/phd_dissertations/Ndrecka.pdf
This dissertation reviewed 53 studies to see the impact that reentry programs have on recidivism, addressed at the problems prisoners face when reentering society, and suggested how to solve these specific problems. The author found that on average, reentry programs reduced recidivism by 6 percent.

Taylor, C. J. (2014). *Program Evaluation of the Federal Reentry Court in the Eastern District of Pennsylvania: Report on Program Effectiveness for the First 164 Reentry Court Participants.* **Federal Probation Department and U.S. District Court, Eastern District of Pennsylvania.**
http://digitalcommons.lasalle.edu/soc_crj_faculty/1/
This report describes the latest evaluation of the Supervision to Aid Reentry (STAR) program. The success of the Reentry Court is assessed by comparing the first 164 Reentry Court participants to a group of similarly situated participants under supervised release and analyzing services offered or received, sanctions imposed, employment status, supervision revocation, and new arrests in the 18 months following prison release.

Websites

Center for Court Innovation
www.courtinnovation.org

National Association of Drug Court Professionals
www.nadcp.org

Regional Information Sharing System

Project Description

The Regional Information Sharing Systems (RISS) is a program that serves local, state, federal, tribal and territorial law enforcement agencies. Established more than 40 years ago, it is considered a valuable and cost-effective program trusted by more than 117,000 individual users representing nearly 9,000 agencies in all 50 states, the District of Columbia, U.S. territories, Australia, Canada, England, and New Zealand.[61]

RISS offers secure information sharing and communications capabilities through RISSNET, a secure sensitive but unclassified law enforcement information-sharing cloud provider. RISSNET provides access to millions of pieces of data; offers bidirectional sharing of information; and connects disparate state, local, and federal systems.[62] RISS provides critical analytical and investigative support services for efforts against organized and violent crime, gang activity, drug activity, terrorism, human trafficking, identity theft, and other regional priorities.

A priority of the RISS program is officer safety, and through RISSafe, a comprehensive and nationwide deconfliction system, RISS users have the capability to deconflict operational events not only in RISSafe but also through the HIDTA systems, Case Explorer and SAFETNet, as part of the Nationwide Office Safety Event Deconfliction project.[63]

CrimeSolutions.gov Ratings:
No ratings at this time

Partners and Professional Organizations:

✓ **National Information Exchange Federation**

✓ **United States Attorneys' Offices**

✓ **FBI Joint Automated Booking System**

✓ **National Gang Intelligence Center**

✓ **Homeland Security Information Network**

✓ **United States Secret Service**

✓ **National Center for Missing and Exploited Children**

NIJ-Sponsored Evaluation

Institute for Intergovernmental Research. (1987). *The RISS Program Analysis of Activity: Analysis of Data Relating to Membership and Service Activities of the Regional Information Sharing Systems Projects 1984−1986.* **Tallahassee, FL: Author. NIJ sponsored.**
https://www.ncjrs.gov/pdffiles1/Digitization/126223NCJRS.pdf
This evaluation of RISS focused on a process analysis. It found that overall membership was increasing though funding remained constant. It also found growth in all of the RISS program areas, including training programs, database inquiries, and equipment loans. No analysis as to the effect or outcomes of the program was conducted.

---

[61] https://www.ncjrs.gov/pdffiles1/bja/192666.pdf
[62] http://www.riss.net/Default/Overview
[60] For more information, see https://www.ncirc.gov/Deconfliction

Academic Research

Boba, R., Weisburd, D., et al. (2009). "Limits of Regional Data Sharing and Regional Problem Solving Observations from the East Valley, CA COMPASS Initiative." *Police Quarterly, 12*(1): 22–41.

https://www.ncjrs.gov/App/Publications/Abstract.aspx?id=263433

This article examines regional data sharing for regional problem solving using the process evaluation findings of the East Valley COMPASS initiative. The study found that the development of a data system for regional problem solving ignores specific problems and the practical barriers inherent in accessing diverse databases. The study concluded that regional data sharing is important but may be better tailored toward sharing data for short-term tactical purposes or for simply identifying problems.

Chermak, S., Carter, J. G., et al. (2013). "Law Enforcement's Information Sharing Infrastructure: A National Assessment." *Police Quarterly, 16*(2): 211–244.

http://pqx.sagepub.com/content/16/2/211.full.pdf+html

This article discusses a national survey examining the experiences of state, local, and tribal law enforcement agencies as well as fusion centers in building intelligence capacity. The authors found that officials from federal, state, and local government believed the process of sharing information is neither "effective" nor "very effective." The officials surveyed thought the information they routinely received was neither helpful in protecting the public nor reliable, as they claimed that such information was often not timely and not effective enough to prevent terrorist attacks.

Lewandowski, C., & Carter, J. G. (2014). "End-User Perceptions of Intelligence Dissemination from a State Fusion Center." *Security Journal, Advance online publication.*

http://www.palgrave-journals.com/sj/journal/vaop/ncurrent/full/sj201438a.html

This article examines how users experience information sharing systems in law enforcement agencies. Of the 270 rank-and-file officers surveyed, only 1 stated that he manually looked up an intelligence product through RISS or a similar network. Most rank-and-file offers received intelligence information from e-mails (63%) and roll call meetings (20%).

Serrao, S. (2009). "Info-Sharing Techniques: Bridging the Gaps with Technology, Analysis." *Law Enforcement Technology, 36*(7): 58–61.

https://www.ncjrs.gov/App/publications/abstract.aspx?ID=250692

This article states that intelligence coordination between federal, state, and local agencies varies in consistency and effectiveness from jurisdiction to jurisdiction. However, the Regional Information Sharing System Network continues to act as a facilitator in the sharing of intelligence, and it helps coordinate efforts to combat criminal networks that operate across jurisdictions.

Other Research

Carter, D., Chermak, S., et al. (2011). *Understanding the Intelligence Practices of State, Local, and Tribal Law Enforcement Agencies* **[NCJ 238561]. East Lansing, MI: Michigan State University. NIJ sponsored.**

https://www.ncjrs.gov/pdffiles1/nij/grants/238561.pdf

Using a survey and case study design, this study examined the intelligence practices of state, local, and tribal law enforcement agencies. The authors found that although significant progress had been made since 9/11, there was still room for improvement. Respondents indicated that RISSNET and other services did not fully meet their needs.

Center for Technology Commercialization, Inc. (1999). *Law Enforcement/Criminal Justice Multi-Jurisdictional Information Systems Study: Phase II Final Report.* **Westborough, MA: Author. NIJ sponsored.**
https://www.ncjrs.gov/pdffiles1/nij/grants/181054.pdf
This report summarizes the results of onsite evaluations of 17 regional, state, and local multijurisdictional information systems for law enforcement/criminal justice. RISS was not included in this evaluation. The evaluation found that success came from effective leadership, strategic planning, partnerships with users and the vendor community, and the ability to identify funding sources.

Jackson, B.A. (2014). *How Do We Know What Information Sharing Is Really Worth?* **Washington, DC: RAND Corporation.**
http://www.rand.org/content/dam/rand/pubs/research_reports/RR300/RR380/RAND_RR380.pdf
This report states that there are very few evaluations of information sharing programs, such as RISS. The report concludes that evaluations focused on the outcomes of information sharing cases are needed and can be conducted using a suggested set of measures and systematic approaches, such as the "but-for" analysis.

Noblis. (2007). *Comprehensive Regional Information System Project, Volume 1: Metrics for the Evaluation of Regional Law Enforcement Information-Sharing Systems* **[MTR-2006-035; NCJ 219377]. Falls Church, VA: Center for Criminal Justice Technology. NIJ sponsored.**
http://www.ncjrs.gov/pdffiles1/nij/grants/219377.pdf
This study looked at the use of metrics to evaluate a regional information-sharing system. It found that a combination of metrics should be used to assess each objective and that qualitative data should be collected in conjunction with quantitative data.

Noblis. (2007). *Comprehensive Regional Information System Project, Volume 2: Concept of Operations* **[MTR-2006-036; NCJ 219378]. Falls Church, VA: Center for Criminal Justice Technology. NIJ sponsored.**
http://www.ncjrs.gov/pdffiles1/nij/grants/219378.pdf
This Concept of Operations report gives an overview of best practices, recommendations, and ideas for planning, implementing, and operating a RISS. The results come from a national survey as well as site visits. The researchers noted that the system must be developed and designed for the specific intended use, training must be provided, and operating procedures must be put in place.

Noblis. (2007). *Comprehensive Regional Information System Project, Volume 3: A Practitioner's Handbook for Law Enforcement Information-Sharing Systems: Preliminary Requirements* **[MTR-2006-037; NCJ 219379]. Falls Church, VA: Center for Criminal Justice Technology. NIJ sponsored.**
http://www.ncjrs.gov/pdffiles1/nij/grants/219379.pdf
This handbook offers a clear, documented set of requirements and guidelines for law enforcement agencies undertaking a RISS. It focuses on functional and operational requirements, program organization, and program evaluation.

Simms, T. H. (1991). *Sharing of Criminal Investigation Information Among California Law Enforcement Agencies by the Year 2000* **[NCJ 134345]. Sacramento, CA: California Commission on Peace Officer Standards and Training, Command College. NIJ sponsored.**
https://www.ncjrs.gov/pdffiles1/Digitization/134345NCJRS.pdf
This article is based on a study of issues and management strategies related to automated sharing of criminal information by California police agencies. The results revealed great uncertainty about the future of law enforcement funding in general and of computer systems in particular. The study concluded that two elements are essential to a successful system: state funding and a better system for identifying individuals.

U.S. Department of Justice, Office of Justice Programs, Bureau of Justice Assistance. (2002). *Regional Information Sharing Systems Program* **[Program Brief, NCJ 192666]. Washington, DC: Author.**
https://www.ncjrs.gov/pdffiles1/bja/192666.pdf
This report discusses the background, key elements, and accomplishments of the RISS program. According to the report, from 1991 to 2001, RISS centers assisted with almost 58,000 arrests by offering information, analytical services, equipment loans, and confidential funds to member agencies. RISS center services made possible approximately $10 billion in drug seizures and $21 million in civil Racketeer Influenced and Corrupt Organizations seizures.

U.S. Department of Justice, Office of Justice Programs, Bureau of Justice Assistance. (2003). *The National Criminal Intelligence Sharing Plan: Solutions and Approaches for a Cohesive Plan to Improve Our Nation's Ability to Develop and Share Criminal Intelligence.* **Washington, DC: Author.**
https://it.ojp.gov/documents/National_Criminal_Intelligence_Sharing_Plan.pdf
This report outlines a nationwide plan for the sharing of intelligence among law enforcement agencies. The plan establishes a backbone of information sharing by using the combined RISS network and the FBI Law Enforcement Online system. This system merge in 2002 enabled a fully encrypted connection for intelligence sharing.

U.S. Government Accountability Office. (2013). *Information Sharing: Agencies Could Better Coordinate to Reduce Overlap in Field-Based Activities* **[GAO-13-471]. Washington, DC: Author.**
http://www.gao.gov/assets/660/653527.pdf
Five types of field-based information-sharing entities are supported, in part, by the federal government: Joint Terrorism Task Forces, Field Intelligence Groups, RISS, fusion centers in states and major urban areas, and High Intensity Drug Trafficking Area investigative support centers. They have distinct missions, roles, and responsibilities. However, GAO identified 91 instances of overlap in some analytical activities, such as producing intelligence reports; and 32 instances of overlapping investigative support activities, such as identifying links between criminal organizations. GAO recommended that these systems be connected as soon as possible to reduce this overlap.

Website

Regional Information Sharing Systems
https://www.riss.net/

Residential Substance Abuse Treatment Program

Project Description

The Residential Substance Abuse Treatment for State Prisoners (RSAT) Formula Grant Program assists states and units of local government in developing and implementing RSAT programs in state and local correctional and detention facilities.

RSAT programs offer individual and group treatment activities for offenders and must meet these requirements:

- Last between 6 and 12 months;

- Be provided in residential treatment facilities set apart from the general correctional population;

- Focus on the inmate's substance abuse problems; and

- Develop the inmate's cognitive, behavioral, social, vocational, and other skills to solve the substance abuse and related problems.[64]

Note: The RSAT program has been evaluated multiple times, but these evaluations do not appear on CrimeSolutions.gov. The programs listed on CrimeSolutions.gov are similar to the RSAT in structure and have the same requirements. The rest of the sources listed were found on publicly available websites and published in academic journals.

CrimeSolutions.gov Ratings:
Effective (0)
Promising (5)
No Effect (0)
Insufficient Evidence (1)

Partners and Professional Organizations:
✓ Advocates for Human Potential

NIJ-Sponsored Evaluations

Austin, J., Dedel Johnson, K., et al. (2000). *Process Evaluation of the Michigan Department of Corrections' Residential Substance Abuse Treatment (RSAT) Program* **[NCJ-181650]. Washington, DC: The George Washington University, Institute on Crime, Justice and Corrections; and the National Council on Crime and Delinquency. NIJ sponsored.**
http://www.ncjrs.gov/pdffiles1/nij/grants/181650.pdf
A process evaluation of the Cooper Street residential drug treatment program in the Jackson, MI, state prison focused on the central components of the program's design, implementation, and operation. The study was designed to answer the first part of this call for action. The overall goals of this research were to (1) conduct a process evaluation that examined the integrity of program evaluation, and (2) make specific recommendations about program structure and eligibility criteria that could better prepare the program for an impact evaluation. This report highlights key implementation issues that could create substantial barriers to a rigorous outcome evaluation, and it makes several recommendations for overcoming these barriers.

---

[64] This description about the program can be found on the following website:
https://www.bja.gov/ProgramDetails.aspx?Program_ID=79

BOTEC Analysis Corporation. (2002). *Outcome Evaluation of a Residential Substance Abuse Program: Barnstable House of Corrections* **[NCJ-196142]. Waltham, MA: BOTEC Analysis Corporation. NIJ sponsored.**
http://www.ncjrs.gov/pdffiles1/nij/grants/196142.pdf
This report presents the methodology and findings of an outcome analysis of the Barnstable House of Corrections RSAT program in Massachusetts designed to reduce the likelihood of inmate recidivism. This is part two of a two-part series and looks at the process outcomes; part one looked at the program process.

Fulton, B., Latessa, E., et al. (2001). *Mohican Youth Center: RSAT Process Evaluation, Final Report* **[NCJ-188868]. Cincinnati, OH: University of Cincinnati, Division of Criminal Justice. NIJ sponsored.***
http://www.ncjrs.gov/pdffiles1/nij/grants/188868.pdf
*On CrimeSolutions.gov list of programs, reviewed but not rated.
This report presents the methodology and findings of a process evaluation of the Mohican Youth Center (MYC), a 160-bed secure facility operated by the Ohio Department of Youth Services as a substance abuse treatment facility for drug-involved youth convicted of a felony. Youth assessed as needing long-term residential treatment are sent to MYC for the last 6 months of their sentence.

Fulton, B., Latessa, E., et al. (2001). *MonDay Community Correctional Institutions: RSAT Process Evaluation, Final Report* **[NCJ-188871]. Cincinnati, OH: University of Cincinnati, Division of Criminal Justice. NIJ sponsored.**
http://www.ncjrs.gov/pdffiles1/nij/grants/188871.pdf
This report presents the methodology and findings of a process evaluation of the MonDay Community Correctional Institution's RSAT in Dayton, OH. This evaluation looks at everything in the program, from offender demographics to solving problems the report found.

Fulton, B., Latessa, E., et al. (2001). *Noble Choices: RSAT Process Evaluation Final Report* **[NCJ-188870]. Cincinnati, OH: University of Cincinnati, Division of Criminal Justice. NIJ sponsored.**
http://www.ncjrs.gov/pdffiles1/nij/grants/188870.pdf
This report presents the methodology and findings of a process evaluation of Ohio's Nobel Choices program, a residential substance abuse treatment program within the Noble Correctional Institution, a medium-security prison. The process evaluation involved a descriptive analysis of a sample of program participants and a qualitative analysis of the nature of services provided. The sample consisted of 33 cases. The study period extended from the date of first admission (October 18, 1998) through March 31, 1999.

Fulton, B., Latessa, E., et al. (2001). *Ohio RSAT Process Evaluation, Summary Report* **[NCJ-188869]. Cincinnati, OH: University of Cincinnati, Division of Criminal Justice. NIJ sponsored.**
http://www.ncjrs.gov/pdffiles1/nij/grants/188869.pdf
This report presents the methodology and findings of process evaluations of three RSAT programs in Ohio. This is a summary of all of the findings from the previous three reports.

Guerin, P., Hyde, R., et al. (1999). *Process Evaluation of the Genesis Program at the Southern New Mexico Correctional Facility* **[NJC-179986]. Albuquerque, NM: University of New Mexico, Institute for Social Research. NIJ sponsored.**
http://www.ncjrs.gov/pdffiles1/nij/grants/179986.pdf
This report is part 1 of a 2-part series and presents the methodology and findings of a process evaluation of the RSAT program at the Southern New Mexico Correction Facility in Las Cruces, NM. It focuses on the Genesis program.

Guerin, P. (2002). *Outcome Evaluation of the New Mexico Corrections Department Genesis Residential Substance Abuse Treatment Program for State Prisoners, Final Summary Report* [NCJ-203277]. **Albuquerque, NM: University of New Mexico, Institute for Social Research. NIJ sponsored.**
http://www.ncjrs.gov/pdffiles1/nij/grants/203277.pdf
This federally funded study is part 2 of a 2-part series; it explored the effectiveness and enhances the understanding of the RSAT Genesis in-prison therapeutic community at the Southern New Mexico Correctional Facility. The Genesis program uses social learning theory as its theoretical approach, which views the social environment as the most important source of reinforcement. The study examines the program's effectiveness in treating and rehabilitating participants, in successfully integrating recovering inmates into their communities, in reducing postrelease substance use, and in increasing social stability.

Harrison, L., & Martin, S. (2000). *Residential Substance Abuse Treatment (RSAT) for State Prisoners Formula Grant: Compendium of Program Implementation and Accomplishments—Final Report.* **Newark, DE: University of Delaware, Center for Drug and Alcohol Studies. NIJ sponsored.**
http://www.ncjrs.gov/pdffiles1/nij/grants/187099.pdf
This report explains the nature and evaluation results of the inmate drug treatment programs established by the RSAT for State Prisoners Formula Grant Program under the Violent Crime Control and Law Enforcement Act of 1994. The treatment philosophy and approach is that of a therapeutic community environment grounded in behavioral and social learning concepts.

Harrison, L., & Martin, S. (2003). *Residential Substance Abuse Treatment for State Prisoners, Implementation Lessons Learned* [NIJ Special Report]. **Washington, DC: U.S. Justice Department, Office of Justice Programs, National Institute of Justice. NIJ sponsored.**
https://www.ncjrs.gov/pdffiles1/nij/195738.pdf
NIJ drafted this evaluation report to review several programs, compare different theoretical methods, and measure what impact the RSAT program had on inmates.

Lipton, D. S., Pearson, F. S., et al. (1999). *National Evaluation of the Residential Substance Abuse Treatment for State Prisoners Program from Onset to Midpoint—Final Report* [NCJ-182219]. **Washington, DC: U.S. Department of Justice, Office of Justice Programs, National Institute of Justice.**
https://www.ncjrs.gov/pdffiles1/nij/grants/182218.pdf
This is the final report on the national evaluation of the RSAT for State Prisoners Program from onset to midpoint. It looks at all RSAT programs across the country as of December 1998.

Love, C. T. (2001). *Process Evaluation of the Rhode Island Residential Substance Abuse Treatment Program (RSAT): The Operations of a Minimum-Security Residential Substance Abuse Treatment Program—Final Report.* **Providence, RI: Brown University. NIJ sponsored.**
http://www.ncjrs.gov/pdffiles1/nij/grants/184953.pdf
This final report provided a process evaluation of the Rhode Island Department of Corrections Minimum Security RSAT. It examined the inner workings of a cognitive behavioral residential treatment program for male inmates in a minimum-security facility. The evaluation combines qualitative and quantitative methods in assessing the program and its operations. The Rhode Island Department of Correction's minimum security unit for men worked with Brown University's Center for Alcohol and Addictions Studies to conduct a thorough evaluation of the RSAT program. The review consisted of 30 cases, what inmates had to say about the program, and how the information was presented in the class.

McCormack, R. J. (2001). *Process Evaluation of the Residential Substance Abuse Treatment Programs at New Jersey Correctional Facilities, Final Report* **[NCJ-189249]. Washington, DC: U.S. Department of Justice, Office of Justice Programs, National Institute of Justice.**
http://www.ncjrs.gov/pdffiles1/nij/grants/189249.pdf
This document presents three publications related to a process evaluation of inmate drug treatment programs in New Jersey correctional facilities. These publications include a cover letter from the Department of Corrections explaining concerns about the evaluation, a critique of the evaluation, and the evaluation report itself.

McMurphy, S., Butynski, W., et al. (2002). *Process Evaluation of Summit House: A Residential Substance Abuse Treatment Program of the New Hampshire Department of Corrections.* **Durham, NH: University of New Hampshire. NIJ sponsored.**
http://www.ncjrs.gov/pdffiles1/nij/grants/195795.pdf
This evaluation, which was conducted by the New Hampshire Department of Corrections from June to September 2001, focuses its findings of the RSAT program base on three categories: content and structure of the RSAT program, quality of staff and training, and individualities of the prisoners compared with another group.

McNeece, C. A. (1999). *Evaluation of the Florida Department of Corrections Residential Substance Abuse Treatment (RSAT) for State Prisoners Program: Final Technical Report* **[NCJ-194060]. Tallahassee, FL: Florida State University, Institute for Health and Human Services Research. NIJ sponsored.**
http://www.ncjrs.gov/pdffiles1/nij/grants/194060.pdf
This report presents the methodology and findings of an evaluation of Florida's Dual Diagnosis Treatment Program, a residential substance abuse treatment program for state inmates. This report also outlines difficulties the FDOC encountered and makes recommendations on how others implementing the program can avoid these difficulties.

Miller, J. M., & Koons-Witt, B. (2002). *Outcome Evaluation of the South Carolina Residential Substance Abuse Treatment.* **Columbia, SC: University of South Carolina. NIJ sponsored.**
http://www.ncjrs.gov/pdffiles1/nij/grants/199407.pdf
The South Carolina RSAT program, also known as the Correctional Recovery Academy, provides educational treatment for incarcerated males ages 17–24 who are not charged with violent crimes. This evaluation consisted of several components: a comparison group, the CRA as an independent variable, criterion measures, and a 12-month follow-up period. The outcome was that the RSAT program did not reduce the recidivism rate but actually increased it slightly.

Miller, J. M., & Ventura Miller, H. (2011). **"Considering the Effectiveness of Drug Treatment Behind Bars: Findings from the South Carolina RSAT Evaluation."** *Justice Quarterly* **28(1): 70–86. NIJ sponsored.**
http://www.tandfonline.com/doi/pdf/10.1080/07418825.2010.506880
This study examined the effectiveness of offender drug treatment programs. It used a quasi-experimental design to specify impact as indicated by recidivism, relapse, and parole revocation. Although analyses revealed no statistically significant difference between treatment and control group participants on these outcome measures, implications of the efficacy of the treatment modality are ambiguous, as implementation failure masked determination of program effects. However, drug testing frequency after release was found to be a significant factor precluding failure, contrary to the conventional view that increased testing identifies greater use.

Moffett, A. (2000). *Process Analysis of GDC RSAT Program, Draft Final Report* **[NCJ-189586]. Stone Mountain, GA: Wellsys Corporation. NIJ sponsored.**
http://www.ncjrs.gov/pdffiles1/nij/grants/189586.pdf
This report described findings of the process evaluation of the RSAT program operating within the Georgia Department of Corrections. Its overall goal was to examine the RSAT program in sufficient detail that the GDC had the information necessary to assess the program's quality, efficiency, and effectiveness and to provide the needed contextual framework for an outcome evaluation of the program.

Young, D., & Porter, R. (1999). *Collaborative Evaluation of Pennsylvania's Program for Drug Involved Parole Violators* **[NCJ-180165]. New York: Vera Institute of Justice. NIJ sponsored.**
http://www.ncjrs.gov/pdffiles1/nij/grants/180165.pdf
In 1998, Pennsylvania established two 60-bed drug treatment programs in state prisons under the federal RSAT initiative that targets technical parole violators. This report looked over Pennsylvania's RSAT program and presents findings from the process evaluation from the first year of RSAT implementation. The three key findings are in (1) program admissions and participants, (2) program retention and completion, and (3) program implementation. This is part one of a three-part series.

Porter, R. (2002, August). *Breaking the Cycle: Technical Report* **[NCJ-197057]. New York: Vera Institute of Justice. NIJ sponsored.**
http://www.ncjrs.gov/pdffiles1/nij/grants/197057.pdf
This report describes outcomes from three phases of Pennsylvania's RSAT program, comparing RSAT program participants and a group of technical parole violators who returned to prison after violating parole. This is part two of a three-part series.

Porter, R. (2002, August). *Breaking the Cycle: Outcomes from Pennsylvania's Alternative to Prison for Technical Parole Violators* **[NCJ-197056]. New York: Vera Institute of Justice. NIJ sponsored.**
http://www.ncjrs.gov/pdffiles1/nij/grants/197056.pdf
This report describes Pennsylvania's efforts at reforming the parole system through the RSAT program. It reviews the three phases in the RSAT program and how the program works as well as why RSAT was created and the outcomes of two studies of comparison groups. This is part three of a three-part series.

Rocheleau, A. M., Mennerich, A., et al. (December 2000). *Barnstable House of Correction Residential Substance Abuse Treatment: A Process Evaluation* **[NCJ-186736]. Cambridge, MA: BOTEC Analysis Corporation. NIJ sponsored.**
Executive Summary (NCJ 186733): http://www.ncjrs.gov/pdffiles1/nij/grants/186733.pdf
Full Report: http://www.ncjrs.gov/pdffiles1/nij/grants/186736.pdf
A process evaluation of the drug treatment program in the Barnstable House of Correction in Massachusetts used both quantitative and qualitative methodologies to describe and assess the program, the participants and selection process, program completions and terminations, and compliance with known principles of effective drug treatment.

Ruefle, W., & Miller, J. M. (1999). *Evaluation of the South Carolina Residential Substance Abuse Treatment Program for State Prisoners—Final Report* **[NCJ-181050]. Columbia, SC: University of South Carolina, College of Criminal Justice. NIJ sponsored.**
http://www.ncjrs.gov/pdffiles1/nij/grants/181050.pdf
This is an overview of the South Carolina RSAT Program for state prisoners. This report goes over problems the reserachers found during the evaluation and includes suggested solutions.

Stohr, M. K., Hemmens, C., et al. (2001). *Residential Substance Abuse Treatment for State Prisoners (RSAT) Partnership Process Evaluation: Final Report.* **Boise, ID: Boise State University, Department of Criminal Justice. NIJ sponsored.**
http://www.ncjrs.gov/pdffiles1/nij/grants/187352.pdf
The South Idaho Correctional Institution began implementing the RSAT program in May 1997 to create a structured environment with three treatment modalities, including cognitive self-change and behavioral

12-step programming set within a therapeutic community. The authors' research questions were centered on whether the program delivery met various criteria. This included matching its stated goals and objectives; being consistent with identified successes in the literature; addressing the targeted population; being likely to result in reduced recidivism, lower costs, and greater abstinence, or measurable behavioral changes; being solidly established so that an outcome evaluation might be conducted; being marred by any communication or other implementation barriers; and being enhanced by development of cooperative remedies to address any real or perceived barriers to successful implementation.

Stohr, M. K., Hemmens, C., et al. (2003). *Residential Substance Abuse Treatment for State Prisoners: Breaking the Drug-Crime Cycle Among Parole Violators.* **NIJ sponsored. Washington, DC: U.S. Department of Justice, Office of Justice Programs, National Institute of Justice.**
http://www.ncjrs.gov/pdffiles1/nij/199948.pdf
This report presents the methodology and findings of an evaluation of the RSAT program at the South Idaho Correctional Institution, which targets parole-violating inmates with substance abuse problems. The research team believed that the Idaho RSAT program, even without improvements they thought were needed, is likely to result in less recidivism in program graduates and therefore lower cost to taxpayers.

Taxman, F., & Bouffard, J. A. (2000). *Residential Substance Abuse Treatment (RSAT) in Jail: A Comparison of Six Sites in Virginia.* **College Park, MD: University of Maryland. NIJ sponsored.**
http://www.ncjrs.gov/pdffiles1/nij/grants/182858.pdf
This report compares residential substance abuse treatment in jail at six Virginia sites. The six programs successfully graduated relatively few clients, ranging from 3 to 13 clients. Many of the sites experienced problems with the clients being transferred to other facilities.

Taxman, F. S., Silverman, R. S., & Bouffard, J. A. (2000). *Residential Substance Abuse Treatment (RSAT) in Prison: Evaluation of the Maryland RSAT Program.* **College Park, MD: University of Maryland. NIJ sponsored.**
https://www.ncjrs.gov/pdffiles1/nij/grants/184953.pdf
This process evaluation examined the implementation of the Maryland RSAT program by observing the therapeutic community program in the prison, conducting structured interviews with treatment and administrative staff members, and tracking client progress through both the treatment and criminal justice systems. It features observations of the treatment program in the prison setting to understand the nature of the substance abuse services offered and how the programs address development of each inmate's cognitive, behavioral, social, and vocational skills.

Van Stelle, K. R., & Moberg, D. P. (2000). *Outcome Evaluation of the Wisconsin Residential Substance Abuse Treatment Program: The Mental Illness-Chemical Abuse (MICA) Program at Oshkosh Correctional Institution 1998−2000* **[NCJ-186190]. Madison, WI: University of Wisconsin Medical School, Department of Preventive Medicine, Center for Health Policy and Program Evaluation. NIJ sponsored.**
http://www.ncjrs.gov/pdffiles1/nij/grants/186190.pdf
This report presents the methodology and findings of a 2-year outcome evaluation of a component of Wisconsin's RSAT for State Prisoners project; the methodology included the collection of qualitative and quantitative evaluation research data to assess the effectiveness of the Mental Illness-Chemical Abuse (MICA) Program at Oshkosh Correctional Institution, which was implemented with RSAT funds. MICA is a residential substance abuse treatment program that utilizes a modified therapeutic community model to provide 8 to 12 months of residential treatment to male inmates who are determined to be dually diagnosed with both substance abuse and mental health disorders. This outcome study documented important aspects of program implementation and effectiveness, including institutional (intermediate) outcomes and community outcomes of mentally ill offenders involved in the MICA program.

Other Academic Articles

Amity In-Prison Therapeutic Community

Program summary: Provides intensive treatment to male inmates with substance abuse problems during the last 9 to 12 months of their prison term. The volunteer participants must reside in a dedicated program housing unit during treatment.

The following three evaluations of this program were used as evidence for rating this program on CrimeSolutions.gov.

This program was rated on CrimeSolutions.gov as promising. ☑
Details: http://www.CrimeSolutions.gov/ProgramDetails.aspx?ID=54

Wexler, H. K., De Leon, G., et al. (1999). "The Amity Prison TC Evaluation: Reincarceration Outcomes." *Criminal Justice and Behavior, 26*(2): 147–167.
http://cjb.sagepub.com/content/26/2/147.abstract
The reincarceration rates and days until reincarceration show a similar pattern of positive results. The full intent-to-treat group showed significantly more positive effects than the no-treatment control group. Within the intent-to-treat group, the postrelease outcomes are generally related to increased involvement in treatment. Inmates with the most favorable outcomes completed both the prison therapeutic community (TC) and the aftercare TC program.

Wexler, H. K., Melnick, G., et al. (1999). "Three-Year Reincarceration Outcomes for Amity In-Prison Therapeutic Community and Aftercare in California." *Prison Journal, 79*(3): 321–336.
http://www.CrimeSolutions.gov/ProgramDetails.aspx?ID=54
The authors found that at 36 months, the intent-to-treat group showed lower rates of reincarceration than the control group; however, the difference was not statistically significant. A significant difference does emerge when looking at the intent-to-treat subgroups. Only 27 percent of the aftercare completers were reincarcerated, compared with more than three-fourths of the prison TC completers (with no aftercare), prison dropouts, and controls. When controlling for background variables, there was a significant relationship between increasing the amount of treatment and the amount of time until reincarceration. Thus, the longer the treatment duration, the longer the inmate remained on parole before a first return to prison.

Prendergast, M. L., Hall, et al. (2003). "Amity Prison-Based Therapeutic Community: 5-Year Outcomes." *Prison Journal, 84*(1): 36–60.
http://www.CrimeSolutions.gov/ProgramDetails.aspx?ID=54
Although the authors found some significant differences between the groups when examining the outcomes of reincarceration using bivariate analysis, multivariate analysis did not find significant differences. Instead, other factors (age and postrelease treatment) became significant predictors of reincarnation. Also, there were no significant differences on measurements of heavy drug use and employment over the 5-year follow-up period. There were some significant differences on employment and reincarceration rates when looking at the subgroups, but no significant differences on heavy drug use.

Delaware KEY/Crest Substance Abuse Programs

Program summary: A prison-based therapeutic community for offenders with a history of substance abuse and a residential work release center that allows offenders to continue their treatment as they transition to the community. Both programs are part of the Delaware Department of Correction substance abuse treatment continuum.

The following two evaluations of this program were used as evidence for rating this program on CrimeSolutions.gov.

The program was rated on CrimeSolutions.gov as promising. ☑
Details: http://www.CrimeSolutions.gov/ProgramDetails.aspx?ID=55

Martin, S. S., Butzin, C. A., et al. (1999). "Three-Year Outcomes of Therapeutic Community Treatment for Drug-Involved Offenders in Delaware: From Prison to Work Release to Aftercare." *Prison Journal, 79*(3): 294–320.

http://www.CrimeSolutions.gov/ProgramDetails.aspx?ID=55

When looking at the new grouping of study participants (Crest dropouts, Crest graduates with aftercare, and Crest graduates without aftercare), the results are somewhat different. Crest dropouts are just as likely to be arrested on a new charge as the comparison group. However, those who complete Crest do much better, and those who complete Crest and receive aftercare are the least likely to have a new arrest. For drug-free status, Crest dropouts are more than 3 times as likely to be drug-free, Crest completers more than 5 times as likely, and Crest completers with aftercare 7 times more likely to be drug free compared with the comparison group.

Inciardi, J. A., Martin. S. S., et al. (2004). "Five-Year Outcomes of Therapeutic Community Treatment of Drug-Involved Offenders After Release From Prison." *Crime & Delinquency, 50*(1): 88–107.

http://www.CrimeSolutions.gov/ProgramDetails.aspx?ID=55
http://cad.sagepub.com/content/50/1/88.short

The authors found that participation in the transitional treatment program more than quadrupled the odds of remaining drug-free at 42 months. Treatment participation was also a significant predictor of criminal recidivism. There was a 70 percent reduction in the odds of a new arrest for those assigned to treatment. The results for drug use and rearrests at 60 months were similar to the results at 42 months. Participation in the transitional treatment program still more than tripled the odds of remaining drug free. Study participants with no previous treatment were also more likely to relapse, whereas those who received treatment were significant less likely to. Treatment participation was also a significant predictor of having no new arrests at 60 months.

Forever Free

Program summary: The first comprehensive, in-prison, residential substance abuse treatment program designed for incarcerated women.

The following two evaluations of this program were used as evidence for rating this program on CrimeSolutions.gov.

The program was rated on CrimeSolutions.gov as promising.
Details: http://www.CrimeSolutions.gov/ProgramDetails.aspx?ID=40

Hall, E. A., Prendergast, M. L., et al. (2004). "Treating Drug-Abusing Women Prisoners: An Outcome Evaluation of the Forever Free Program." *Prison Journal, 84*(1): 81–105.

http://www.CrimeSolutions.gov/ProgramDetails.aspx?ID=40

Hall and colleagues found that for measures of crime and recidivism, the bivariate analyses showed that significantly fewer Forever Free participants reported being arrested or convicted during parole compared to the comparison group. About half of the Forever Free group had been arrested since their release from CIW, and half had been convicted since release. By comparison, 75 percent of women in the comparison group reported arrests since release, and 71 percent reported convictions. Although a smaller percentage of Forever Free participants reported being reincarcerated in jail or prison than the comparison group (50 percent versus 62 percent), the difference was not statistically significant.

Prendergast, M., Hall, E., et al. (1999). *An Outcome Evaluation of the Forever Free Substance Abuse Treatment Program: One Year Post-release Outcomes.* **Los Angeles, CA: University of California at Los Angeles, Drug Abuse Research Center. NIJ sponsored.**

https://www.ncjrs.gov/pdffiles1/nij/grants/199685.pdf

This study demonstrates the effectiveness of the Forever Free program, which has a cognitive-behavioral orientation. Most research on prison-based treatment involves programs based on the therapeutic community model. The authors recommend further research on the effectiveness of psychoeducational or cognitive-behavioral models of treatment, in contrast to therapeutic community (TC) treatment within criminal justice settings. In addition, TC treatment programs typically are 9 to 12 months long. That the Forever Free program, which at the time of the study took only 6 months, was able to demonstrate its effectiveness may indicate that considerable cost savings could be achieved by shorter programs.

Minnesota Prison-Based Chemical Dependency Treatment

Program summary: Prison-based chemical dependency treatment for offenders who are chemically abusive or dependent.

The following evaluation of this program was used as evidence for rating this program on CrimeSolutions.gov.

The program was rated on CrimeSolutions.gov as promising.
Details: http://www.CrimeSolutions.gov/ProgramDetails.aspx?ID=150

Duwe, G. (2010). "Prison-Based Chemical Dependency Treatment in Minnesota: An Outcome Evaluation." *Journal of Experimental Criminology,* **6: 57–81.**
http://www.CrimeSolutions.gov/ProgramDetails.aspx?ID=150
The analyses by Duwe found that, compared with untreated offenders, those offenders who received prison-based chemical dependency (CD) treatment provided by the Minnesota Department of Corrections had significantly lower rates of reoffending across all three recidivism measures (rearrest, reconviction, and reincarceration). Among offenders that received CD treatment, program completers had lower recidivism rates compared to program dropouts across all three measures. In addition, offenders who participated in medium-term programs had the lowest recidivism rates, followed by long-term program participants. The Cox regression analysis, which can control for other factors that may impact the outcome results, showed the same result: participation in prison-based CD treatment significantly reduced the hazard ratio for all three recidivism measures. Treated offenders recidivated less often and more slowly compared to nontreated offenders.

Clark, H. W. (2001). "Residential Substance Abuse Treatment for Pregnant and Postpartum Women and Their Children: Treatment and Policy Implications." *Child Welfare, 80*(2): 179–198.
http://europepmc.org/abstract/MED/11291900
In FY 1993 and FY 1995, the federal government awarded 27 5-year grants that supported 35 residential treatment projects for substance-abusing pregnant and postpartum women and their children. These projects provided comprehensive culturally and gender-specific treatment. Preliminary aggregated data collected in a national cross-site evaluation of 24 of these projects are encouraging with respect to infant mortality and morbidity, treatment retention and completion rates, and behavioral changes in the participating mothers at 6 months post discharge. Local evaluations reflect other benefits of treatment. Cost data are expected to demonstrate the efficiencies and benefits of these projects compared to no treatment.

Daughters, S. B.; Lejuez, C. W., et al. (2005). "Distress Tolerance as a Predictor of Early Treatment Dropout in a Residential Substance Abuse Treatment Facility." *Journal of Abnormal Psychology, 114*(4): 729–734.
http://psycnet.apa.org/psycinfo/2005-15138-023
A large percentage of people who enter residential substance abuse treatment drop out before completing treatment. Given that early treatment dropout places them at an increased risk for relapse, identifying the mechanisms underlying treatment dropout would have several important theoretical and clinical implications. In this study, the authors examined levels of psychological and physical distress tolerance as a predictor of early treatment dropout in a residential substance abuse treatment facility. In a sample of 122 participants entering a residential substance abuse treatment facility, level of psychological distress tolerance was predictive of early treatment dropout above and beyond relevant self-report variables. There was no relationship between physical distress tolerance and early treatment dropout. Implications for future studies and treatment development or modification are discussed.

Knight, D. K., Logan, S. M., et al. (2001). "Predictors of Program Completion for Women in Residential Substance Abuse Treatment." *American Journal of Drug and Alcohol Abuse, 27*(1): 1–18.

http://informahealthcare.com/doi/abs/10.1081/ADA-100103116

Although there is increasing emphasis on providing drug treatment programs for women that address their specific needs (including parenting and childcare), some women still fail to complete treatment. Because of the limited information about the barriers involved, this study examines pretreatment characteristics as predictors of program completion for 87 women who were pregnant or who entered residential treatment with their children. By using a multivariate prediction model, three significant predictors of treatment completion were identified: education level, recent arrests, and peer deviance. Women who completed program requirements were more likely to have a high school degree or equivalent, no arrests in the 6 months before admission, and friends who were less socially deviant. These findings support the need for specialized education and services that address social deviancy of pregnant and/or parenting women.

Mears, D. P., Kelly, W. R., et al. (2001). "Findings from a Process Evaluation of a Statewide Residential Substance Abuse Treatment Program for Youthful Offenders." *Prison Journal, 81*(2): 246–270.

http://tpj.sagepub.com/content/81/2/246.full.pdf

Using data collected on youthful offenders with chemical dependency treatment needs in the Texas Youth Commission, this article presents a systematic and empirical process evaluation of factors associated with successful program progress in the Texas Youth Commission's Chemical Dependency Treatment program. Analyses focus on appropriate program placement and whether and to what extent risk, dynamic or criminogenic need, and behavioral and treatment amenability factors are related to several key measures of program process. These include completion or expulsion, days to completion or expulsion, and performance as well as variation among these outcomes across treatment sites.

Mitchell, O., Wilson, D. B., et al. (2007). "Does Incarceration-Based Drug Treatment Reduce Recidivism? A Meta-Analytic Synthesis of the Research." *Journal of Experimental Criminology, 3*(4): 353–375.

http://link.springer.com/article/10.1007/s11292-007-9040-2

This research synthesized results from 66 published and unpublished evaluations of incarceration-based drug treatment programs using meta-analysis. Incarceration-based drug treatment programs fell into five types: therapeutic communities, RSAT, group counseling, boot camps specifically for drug offenders, and narcotic maintenance programs. The authors examined the effectiveness of each of these types of interventions in reducing post-release offending and drug use. They also examined whether differences in research findings could be explained by variations in methodology, sample, or program features. The authors found support for the effectiveness of RSAT and group counseling programs in reducing re-offending, but the effects of these programs on drug use were ambiguous.

Pease, S. E., Tafrate, R. C., et al. (2001). *Process Evaluation of Tier IV Connecticut Department of Correction Residential Substance Abuse Treatment Programs: Final Report.* **New Britain, CT: Central Connecticut State University, Department of Criminology and Criminal Justice.**

https://www.ncjrs.gov/pdffiles1/Digitization/193426NCJRS.pdf

This evaluation spans three RSAT programs: the Time Program at the Carl Robinson Correctional Institution, the New Horizons Program at the Osborn Correctional Institution, and the Marilyn Baker House at the York Correctional Institution. This evaluation focused on finding the differences among the three programs and then identifying what contributed to the successes and failures of each program's group of inmates, with the goal of making the programs more effective.

Perez, D. M. (2009). "Applying Evidence-Based Practices to Community Corrections Supervision: An Evaluation of Residential Substance Abuse Treatment for High-Risk Probationers." *Journal of Contemporary Criminal Justice, 25*(4): 442–458.

http://ccj.sagepub.com/content/25/4/442.abstract

This study used a quasiexperimental research design in evaluating the effectiveness of residential substance abuse treatment in reducing recidivism among high-risk offenders under community corrections supervision. The findings show that the treatment group was more likely to be charged with a probation violation, whereas controls were significantly more likely to be arrested for a criminal offense during the 18-month follow-up period. This confirms the literature's consistent finding that intensive supervision significantly increases rates of technical violations. For example, among the offenders on intensive probation supervision, treatment participants were drug tested an average of 18 times compared with a mean of 11.5 for the control group. The treatment group experienced a larger reduction in mean incarcerations compared to the control group, again suggesting a positive effect of residential drug treatment.

Porter, R. (2002). *Treating Repeat Parole Violators: A Review of Pennsylvania's Residential Substance Abuse Treatment (RSAT) Program.* **New York: Vera Institute of Justice.**

http://www.portal.state.pa.us/portal/server.pt?open=18&objID=350378&parentname=Dir&parentid=4&mode=2

This study examined the planning, implementation, and outcome of Pennsylvania's coordinated use of RSAT funding from the outset of the initiative. This report follows the previous reports and presents new information about the program's ongoing implementation and insight into the reasons why the participants violated parole. It also gives an overview of the first 5 years of Pennsylvania's RSAT program along with lessons from the program for policymakers.

Other Reports

U.S. Department of Justice, Office of Justice Programs, Bureau of Justice Assistance. (2005). *Residential Substance Abuse Treatment for State Prisoners (RSAT) Program.* **Washington, DC: Author.**

https://www.ncjrs.gov/pdffiles1/bja/206269.pdf

This program update offers a brief description and history of the RSAT program. The update also discusses the program components; any recent changes to the RSAT program; a national and state-level evaluation; and several RSAT activities in the 2003 and 2002 fiscal years for each state, including the five U.S. territories.

U.S. Department of Justice, Office of Justice Programs, Bureau of Justice Assistance. (2012). *Program Performance Report: Residential Substance Abuse Treatment (RSAT) Program.* **Washington, DC: Author.**

https://www.bja.gov/Publications/RSAT_PPR_Jan-Jun13.pdf

This report includes grant activity performance information reported by recipients of BJA RSAT funds for 2013. It outlines key metrics such as program enrollment, completion rate, risk and needs assessments, and treatment services for jail- and prison-based program participants as well as people in aftercare.

U.S. Department of Justice, Office of Justice Programs, Bureau of Justice Assistance. (2012). *Program Closeout Report: Residential Substance Abuse Treatment (RSAT) Program.* **Washington, DC: Author.**

https://www.bja.gov/Publications/RSAT0312CloseoutReport.pdf

This closeout report presents an overview on what the RSAT program entails. It presents comprehensive data on RSAT grantees for January 2010 to March 2012. This shows in detail how each grantee must allocate the grant amount across several categories and what positive outcomes result from implementing the program.

U.S. Department of Justice, Office of Justice Programs, Bureau of Justice Assistance. (2012). *Program Performance Report: Residential Substance Abuse Treatment (RSAT) Program, April–September 2012.* **Washington, DC: Author.**
https://www.bja.gov/Publications/RSAT_PPR_09-12.pdf
This resource includes grant activity performance information reported by recipients of BJA RSAT funds. It includes key metrics such as program enrollment, completion rate, risk and needs assessments, and treatment services for jail- and prison-based program participants as well as people in aftercare.

Website

Advocates for Human Potential
http://www.ahpnet.com
http://www.rsat-tta.com

National Sexual Assault Kit Initiative

Project Description

The National Sexual Assault Kit Initiative (SAKI) is a brand new program within BJA. The SAKI program provides funding to support community response teams engaged in "the comprehensive reform of jurisdictions' approaches to sexual assault cases resulting from evidence found in previously untested sexual assault kits (SAKs)."[65, 66] The goal of the SAKI program is the "creation of a coordinated community response that ensures just resolution to these cases whenever possible through a victim-centered approach, as well as to build jurisdictions' capacity to prevent the development of conditions that lead to high numbers of unsubmitted SAKs in the future."[67] The program will provide jurisdictions with resources to address their unsubmitted kit issue, including providing support for conducting inventory, testing, and tracking of SAKs; creating performance metrics; accessing necessary training; and improving practices related to investigation, prosecution, and victim engagement and support relating to new evidence and new cases resulting from the testing process.

Note: There have not been any evaluations on the SAKI program yet, but there are studies on unsubmitted kits and backlogs.

NIJ-Sponsored Evaluations[68]

NIJ funded the Houston Police Department to form a multidisciplinary team to study the problem of SAKs being collected but never sent off to a crime lab to be tested. The Action-Research working group was created to investigate. Several reports were written in response to the findings, discussed below.

Busch-Armendariz, N., & Sulley, C. (2015). *Does the Justice Advocate Position Enhance Sex Crimes Investigations?* **Austin, TX: Institute on Domestic Violence and Sexual Assault, School of Social Work, The University of Texas at Austin. NIJ sponsored.**
http://www.houstonsakresearch.org/resources/documents/IDVSA_justice.pdf
This report goes over the position of the Justice Advocate (JA) and if it has a positive impact on the SAKs investigations. The JA's role is to engage and re-engage victims by helping them participate in their investigation. The report found that JAs had an overwhelmingly positive outcome on the investigation. They supported victims, increased victim participation, shared information from the investigator and prosecutor with the victims, and served as liaison between the two, among other things.

Busch-Armendariz, N., et al. (2015). *How to Notify Victims about Sexual Assault Kit Evidence: Insight and Recommendations from Victims and Professionals.* **Austin, TX: Institute on Domestic Violence and Sexual Assault, School of Social Work, The University of Texas at Austin. NIJ sponsored.**

Partners and Professional Organizations:
✓ **New York County District Attorney's Office**

---

[65] https://www.bjs.gov/Funding/15SAKIsol.pdf
[66] Unsubmitted kits are those found in police custody that have never been submitted to a crime laboratory for testing. Untested kits are those that have been submitted to a crime lab but are delayed for testing longer than 30 days as a result of the backlog of work in the laboratory. These are separate but distinct issues, and the focus of the SAKI program is on the unsubmitted kits that have never been submitted to a crime laboratory.
[67] Ibid.
[68] For each article, a link has been provided to either the full-length document or the website where it can be accessed.

http://www.houstonsakresearch.org/resources/documents/IDVSA_victims.pdf
This report describes the victim and professional perspectives on the delivery of victim notification procedures, implementation of new victim notification processes, and victim engagement within the criminal justice system, and goes over improvements to the current system. The report finds that victims want to decide whether or not they should be notified and are not happy when it is just assumed what their decision will be.

Busch-Armendariz, N., Sulley, C., & Morris, L. (2015). *Key Components of Building a Successful Victim Notification Protocol.* **Austin, TX: Institute on Domestic Violence and Sexual Assault, School of Social Work, The University of Texas at Austin. NIJ sponsored.**
http://www.houstonsakresearch.org/resources/documents/IDVSA_success.pdf
This report presents findings about the process, development, and implementation of the Houston Police Department's protocols. The report encourages working groups to constantly reassess their protocols to discover feedback and suggestions for ongoing improvement efforts.

Busch-Armendariz, N., Sulley, C., & McPhail, B. (2015). *Sexual Assault Victims' Experiences of Notification After a CODIS Hit. Austin, TX:* **Institute on Domestic Violence and Sexual Assault, School of Social Work, The University of Texas at Austin. NIJ sponsored.**
http://www.houstonsakresearch.org/resources/documents/IDVSA_CODIS.pdf
This report goes over what is involved in reestablishing contact with victims whose cases are reopened. The report discusses victim's responses to being notified that their cases were being reopened and the implementation of the Complainant Notification and Hotline protocols. The report found that the Complainant Notification and Hotline Protocols were well received by victims interviewed and followed up with recommendations for the Houston Team.

Campbell, B., & Wells, W. (2014). *Sexual Assault Investigator Training: Perceptions from Juvenile and Adult Sex Crimes Investigators.* **Huntsville, TX: College of Criminal Justice, Sam Houston State University. NIJ sponsored.**
http://www.houstonsakresearch.org/resources/documents/investigator.pdf
This report goes over recommendations for the Houston team regarding training for their investigators. The working group held several discussions about providing specialized training for criminal investigators. This report covers the criminal investigators' perceptions of their training. The results show that many investigators have not received training that is specific to sex crimes investigations and that many investigators believe additional sex-crime—specific training would be valuable.

Campbell, B., & Wells, W. (2014). *Testing Sexual Assault Kits in Cold Cases and Follow-Up Investigations: Practices Used in Agencies in the United States.* **Hunstville, TX: College of Criminal Justice, Sam Houston State University. NIJ sponsored.**
http://www.houstonsakresearch.org/resources/documents/testing.pdf
This report shares information about practices used in law enforcement agencies to test unsubmitted SAKs and investigate cold sexual assault cases. The articles were screened and determined if the practices implemented would be useful to the Houston team. Two recommendations came out of the research: case follow-up protocols and case monitoring.

Campbell, R., Fehler-Cabral, G., et al. (2015). *The Detroit Sexual Assault Kit (SAK) Action Research Project (ARP), Final Report.* **Washington, DC: Department of Justice, Office of Justice Programs, National Institute of Justice.**
https://www.ncjrs.gov/pdffiles1/nij/grants/248680.pdf
NIJ funded this study to determine long-term strategies for solving the problem of untested SAKs. The goals from this study were to 1) inventory all the kits, 2) study the "underlying reasons" why there were so many unsubmitted SAKs, 3) develop a plan for testing the unsubmitted SAKs, and 4) develop and evaluate a victim notification protocol. The results of this study helped in creating several changes in

policy and practice in Detroit, including training, policy changes in local police departments, and passage of new state-wide legislation.

Nelson, M., Chase, R., & DePalma, L. (2013). *Making Sense of DNA Backlogs, 2012-Myths vs. Reality.* **Washington DC: National Institute of Justice (NCJ: 243347).**
http://www.nij.gov/publications/page/publication-detail.aspx?ncjnumber=243347
This special report provides a definition for "backlog cases" and updates the previous reports with this new definition. The report suggests that laboratories use this new definition when tracking the cases tested in their labs.

Peterson, J., et al. (2012). *Sexual Assault Kit Backlog Study.* **Los Angelec, CA: California State University, Los Angeles, School of Criminal Justice and Criminalistics. Department of Justice, Office of Justice Programs, National Institute of Justice.**
https://www.ncjrs.gov/pdffiles1/nij/grants/238500.pdf
This report goes into detail about the backlogged cases in Los Angeles. Researchers were interested in both the results of scientific testing of backlogged cases and whether the results had any effect on the criminal justice outcomes of these and other cases. The findings from this study resulted in the following recommendations: 1) forensic testing of all kits is not recommend, stranger cases should take priority; 2) Advisory Committees should establish specific criteria for future SAK testing; 3) crime laboratories should routinely receive case files, medical examination reports, and CODIS status information so they can begin their analysis of sexual assault evidence; 4) all victims should report sexual assault; and 5) CODIS should be updated regularly with new profiles so when entering DNA evidence, the most updated files are available.

Ritter, N. (2013). "New Orleans Sexual Assault Evidence Project: Results and Recommendations." *NIJ Journal, 272.* **Washington DC: National Institute of Justice.**
https://www.nij.gov/Journals/272/Pages/sexual-assault-evidence.aspx
The author goes over the 1-year project in New Orleans and the testing and outcomes of 1,000 sexual assault kits. The tested kits were loaded into CODIS and 139 hits came about. The report covers the importance of proper evidence collection and chain of custody and describes CODIS and the type of hits that can be found. The report closes with recommendations for New Orleans.

Ritter, N. (2012). "The Case for Testing All Sexual Assault Kits." *NIJ Journal, 270.* **Washington DC: National Institute of Justice.**
https://www.nij.gov/journals/270/pages/publication-detail.aspx?ncjnumber=243347
The author goes into the pros of testing all sexual assault kits regardless of whether they are stranger or nonstranger cases. The author says that mandatory testing can yield findings such as serial rapists, affirm the victim's version of events, discredit the assailant, or exonerate an innocent suspect.

Ritter, N. (2012). "Solving Sexual Assaults: Finding Answers Through Research." *NIJ Journal, 270.* **Washington DC: National Institute of Justice.**
https://www.ncjrs.gov/pdffiles/nij/238483.pdf
The author details the findings of the Los Angeles study of severe SAK backlog in their jurisdiction. The author covers the questions raised as well as the challenges that jurisdictions face. To help LA's backlog problem, a better data management system was the most important aspect.

Ritter, N. (2011). *The Road Ahead: Unanalyzed Evidence in Sexual Assault Cases.* **Washington DC: National Institute of Justice (NCJ No: 233279).**
http://www.nij.gov/publications/page/publication-detail.aspx?ncjnumber=233279
This special report goes over the ramifications for police, crime laboratories, the courts, and victims when untested SAKs remain untested and stored in evidence rooms. The report poses questions to why these kits remain untested and how this should be remedied.

Ritter, N. (2010). "Solving the Problem of Untested Evidence in Sexual Assaults." *NIJ Journal, 267.* **Washington DC: National Institute of Justice**
https://www.nij.gov/journals/267/Pages/evidence.aspx
The author reviews the background for the NIJ study into SAK backlogs in Los Angeles, Houston, and Detroit. The author also covers such aspects as understanding the evidence and victim notification within the SAKI program.

Wells, W., Gaines, C., & Fallik, S. (2014). *Prosecutors' and Investigators' Perspectives on Collaborating with Victim Advocates.* **Huntsville, TX: College of Criminal Justice, Sam Houston State University. NIJ sponsored.**
http://houstonsakresearch.org/resources/documents/perspectives.pdf
NIJ funded the Houston Police Department to form a multidisciplinary team to study the problem of SAKs being collected but never sent off to a crime lab to be tested. The Action-Research working group was created to investigate. Several reports were created in response to the findings. This report provides information that can be used when planning to implement new models for involving victim advocates in investigations and prosecutions of sexual assault cases. The report found that prosecutors and investigators have different views of the role victim advocates play in the criminal justice system. Prosecutors see them positively, and investigators have a negative view. The study reviews recommendations working groups can implement to ensure those involved create a closer working relationship with all parties.

Academic Articles

Fallik, S., & Wells, W. (2015). "Testing Previously Unsubmitted Sexual Assault Kits: What Are the Investigative Results?" *Criminal Justice Policy Review, 26(6).*
https://cjp.sagepub.com/content/26/6/598.full.ppdf+html
This study examines the existence of potentially valuable forensic evidence never submitted to a crime laboratory for examination. The study reviews the investigative activities that occur after a forensic screening that was not submitted for testing. The study finds that testing has minimal impact; testing larger numbers of SAKs may not have a big effect on criminal justice outcomes. The study encourages policy makers and others to consider a triage approach to this issue.

Other Reports

The White House Office of the Press Secretary. (2015). *Fact Sheet: Investments to Reduce the National Rape Kit Backlog and Combat Violence Against Women.* **Washington DC: The White House.**
https://www.whitehouse.gov/the-press-office/2015/03/16/fact-sheet-investments-reduce-national-rape-kit-backlog-and-combat-viole
This fact sheet covers the Vice President's remarks about the SAKI Program. It goes through the budget allocated for the program and the reason why it was created.

Ritter, N. (2013). "Untested Evidence in Sexual Assault Cases: Using Research to Guide Policy and Practice." *Sexual Assault Report, 16(3).* **Civic Research Institute.**
https://www.ncjrs.gov/pdffiles1/nij/241356.pdf
The author details the recently found group of untested sexual assault kits, how this discovery will burden the criminal justice system to get all these kits tested, and how to keep this from happening again. The author suggests that policy makers turn to new research to guide their policy and procedure decisions with testing new and backlogged kits. She reviews specific reasons as to why kits are not tested, from bad tracking (or no tracking), to lack of knowledge/training with how to properly handle these kits. The author goes into specifics regarding stranger and nonstranger cases, backlogged compared with untested kits, and statute of limitations, among other items.

Websites

Houston Project
www.houstonsakresearch.org

Second Chance Act

Project Description

The Second Chance Act (SCA) was created to provide grants to state and local government agencies and community organizations for employment and housing assistance, substance abuse treatment, family programming, mentoring, victim support, and other services that help people returning from prison and jail to safely and successfully reintegrate into the community. This legislation supports eligible applicants in developing and implementing comprehensive and collaborative strategies that address reentry challenges by increasing public safety, reducing recidivism, and cutting correctional spending. BJA funds six separate programs that offer reentry services in employment, family relationships, substance abuse, and mental health among the reentry population:

CrimeSolutions.gov Ratings:
Effective (0)
Promising (13)
No Effect (2)
Insufficient Evidence (0)

Partners and Professional Organizations:
✓ **Council of State Governments Justice Center**

- Co-Occurring Substance Abuse and Mental Health Problems
- State, Local, and Tribal Reentry Courts
- Family-Based Prisoner Substance Abuse Treatment Programs
- Technology Careers Programs
- Adult Mentoring Programs
- Adult Offender Reentry Demonstration Programs

Although the six programs differ in population served and/or services provided, they all have certain characteristics in common—mainly, all programs MUST offer both pre-release and post-release services.

Note: When looking through the research, many studies and evaluations came up for "reentry courts." However, it was still limited when considering what is required of a SCA grantee (providing both pre- and post-release services). All research listed below meets this one requirement, along with all other requirements as specified in the grant application.[69] This report will also be divided by type of program and the research found for each program.

Co-Occurring Substance Abuse and Mental Health Program[70]
NIJ-Sponsored Evaluations

Owens, C., Rossman, S., et al. (2012). *FY 2011 Second Chance Act Adult Offender Reentry Demonstration Projects: Evaluability Assessment of the Hudson County (NJ) Community Reintegration Program* **[NCJ-243986]. Washington, DC: Urban Institute, Justice Policy Center. NIJ sponsored.**
https://www.ncjrs.gov/pdffiles1/nij/grants/243986.pdf
This study conducted an evaluability assessment (determination of whether a project is a candidate for meaningful evaluation) of the Hudson County Community Reintegration Program (CRP), a FY 2011 SCA demonstration site in New Jersey.

Willison, J. B., Walsh, K., et al. (2012). *FY 2011 Second Chance Act Adult Offender Reentry Demonstration Projects: Evaluability Assessment of the Beaver County (PA) ChancesR: Reentry,*

---

[69] https://www.bja.gov/search_results.aspx?x=0&y=0&search=SCA+Funding
[70] For each article, a link has been provided to either the full-length document or the website where it can be accessed.

Reunification, and Recovery Program **[NCJ-243988]. Washington, DC: Urban Institute, Justice Policy Center. NIJ sponsored.**

https://www.ncjrs.gov/pdffiles1/nij/grants/243988.pdf

This study conducted an evaluability assessment (determination of whether a project is a candidate for meaningful evaluation) of the Beaver County (PA) ChancesR: Reentry, Reunification, and Recovery Program, a FY 2011 SCA demonstration site.

Other Academic Articles

San Francisco (CA) Behavioral Health Court

This program was rated on CrimeSolutions.gov as promising.

Program summary: A mental health court that aims to reduce recidivism of criminal defendants with serious mental illness. The court connects defendants with community treatment services and considers the defendant's mental illness and severity of the offense in disposition decisions.

McNiel, D. E., & Binder, R. L. 2007. "Effectiveness of a Mental Health Court in Reducing Criminal Recidivism and Violence." *American Journal of Psychiatry, 164*(9): 1395–1403.

http://www.CrimeSolutions.gov/ProgramDetails.aspx?ID=39

This program was rated on CrimeSolutions.gov as promising.

The outcome results from this study showed participation (even if a participant did not complete the entire program and graduate) was associated with positive results.

- *Time until a new charge:* Participation in the Behavioral Health Court (BHC) predicted a longer time to any new charge. At 18 months, the treatment group was 26 percent less likely to have been charged with a new offense compared with the treatment-as-usual group.

- *Time until a new violent charge:* Participation in BHC also resulted in a longer time to a new violent charge. The treatment group was 55 percent less likely to have been charged with a new violent offense compared with the treatment-as-usual group.

Pogorzelski, W., Wolff, N., Pan, K., & Blitz, C. (2005). "Behavioral Health Problems, Ex-Offender Reentry Policies, and the 'Second Chance Act.'" *American Journal of Public Health*, *95*(10): 1718–1724.

http://www.ncbi.nlm.nih.gov/pmc/articles/PMC1449426/

The federal Second Chance Act of 2005 calls for expanding reentry services for people leaving prison, yet existing policies restrict access to needed services for those with criminal records. The authors examined the interaction between individual-level characteristics and policy-level restrictions related to criminal conviction and the likely effects on access to resources upon entry, using a sample of prisoners with Axis I mental disorders ($n = 3,073$). The authors identified multiple challenges related to convictions, including restricted access to housing, public assistance, and other resources. Invisible punishments embedded within existing policies were inconsistent with the call for second chances. Without modification of federal and state policies, the ability of reentry services to foster behavioral health and community reintegration is limited.

Baillargeon, J., Binswanger, I. A., Penn, J. V., Williams, B. A., & Murray, O. J. (2009). "Psychiatric Disorders and Repeat Incarcerations: The Revolving Prison Door." *American Journal of Psychiatry*, *166*(1): 103–109.

http://www.ncbi.nlm.nih.gov/pubmed/19047321/

It is unclear whether mental illness is a risk factor for multiple episodes of incarceration. The authors examined this association in a retrospective cohort study of the nation's largest state prison system. The study population included 79,211 inmates who began serving a sentence between September 1, 2006, and August 31, 2007. Data on psychiatric disorders, demographic characteristics, and history of incarceration for the preceding 6-year period were obtained from statewide medical information systems and analyzed. Inmates with major psychiatric disorders (major depressive disorder, bipolar disorders, schizophrenia, and nonschizophrenic psychotic disorders) had substantially increased risks of multiple incarcerations over the 6-year study period. The greatest increase in risk was observed among inmates with bipolar disorders, who were 3.3 times more likely to have had four or more previous incarcerations compared with inmates who had no major psychiatric disorder. Prison inmates with major psychiatric disorders are more likely than those without to have had previous incarcerations.

Fazel, S., & Yu, R. (2011). "Psychotic Disorders and Repeat Offending: Systematic Review and Meta-Analysis." *Schizophrenia Bulletin*, *37*(4): 800–810.

http://www.ncbi.nlm.nih.gov/pubmed/19959703

This study was a systematic review and meta-analysis on the risk of repeat offending in people with psychosis and an assessment of the effect of potential moderating characteristics on risk estimates. A systematic search was conducted in six bibliographic databases from January 1966 to January 2009, supplemented with correspondence with authors. Studies that reported risks of repeat offending in people with psychotic disorders ($n = 3,511$) compared with people with other psychiatric disorders ($n = 5,446$) and healthy people ($n = 71,552$) were included. Risks of repeat offending were calculated using fixed- and random-effects models to calculate pooled odds ratios (ORs). Subgroup and meta-regression analyses were conducted to examine how risk estimates were affected by various study characteristics, including mean sample age, study location, sample size, study period, outcome measure, duration of follow-up, and diagnostic criteria. Twenty-seven studies, which included 3,511 people with psychosis, were identified. Compared with people without any psychiatric disorders, there was a significantly increased risk of repeat offending in people with psychosis (pooled OR = 1.6, 95% confidence interval [CI] = 1.4-1.8), although this was only based on four studies. In contrast, there was no association when people with other psychiatric disorders were used as the comparison group (pooled OR = 1.0, 95% CI = 0.7-1.3), although there was substantial heterogeneity. Higher risk estimates were found in female-only samples with psychosis and in studies conducted in the United States. The association between psychosis and repeat offending differed depending on the comparison group. Despite this, the authors found no support for the findings of previous reviews that psychosis is associated with a lower risk of repeat offending.

Kesten, K. L., Leavitt-Smith, E., Rau, D. R., Shelton, D., Zhang, W., Wagner, J., & Trestman, R. L. (2012). "Recidivism Rates Among Mentally Ill Inmates: Impact of the Connecticut Offender Reentry Program." *Journal of Correctional Health Care*, *18*(1): 20–28. **Doi: 10.1177/1078345811421117.**

http://www.ncbi.nlm.nih.gov/pubmed/22095006/

This study compares data from the Connecticut Offender Reentry Program (CORP) and retrospective data for inmates who received standard treatment planning services from the Connecticut Department of Mental Health and Addictions Services (DMHAS). Analysis of DMHAS data investigated characteristics (demographic, psychiatric, and prison classification scores) and recidivism rates of 883 people. A program evaluation was later completed on a separate cohort of 88 people who participated in CORP. Comparison of the study results found that 14.1% of the CORP participants were rearrested within 6 months of discharge, compared to 28.3% of the DMHAS group. This study concluded that younger age and having a co-occurring substance use disorder appear to be predictors of recidivism. A distinctly smaller percentage of CORP participants were recidivistic, indicating support for specialized reentry programs.

Lynch, S. M., Heath, N. M., Matthews, K. C., & Cepeda, G. J. (2012). "Seeking Safety: An Intervention for Trauma-Exposed Incarcerated Women?" *Journal of Trauma and Dissociation*, *13*(1): 88–101. **DOI: 10.1080/15299732.2011.608780**

http://www.tandfonline.com/doi/abs/10.1080/15299732.2011.608780

Recent guidelines for incarcerated women's programming have called for interventions that address offenders' traumatic experiences, posttraumatic stress disorder (PTSD), and substance use in an integrated manner. Seeking Safety (SS) is an empirically supported cognitive behavioral manualized treatment for people with PTSD and substance use disorders. This study examined the effectiveness of SS with 59 incarcerated women who completed the intervention and 55 who were waitlisted. Participants in SS demonstrated greater symptom improvement in PTSD and depression as well as improved interpersonal functioning and coping compared to waitlisted offenders. These findings provide preliminary support for the use of this intervention with incarcerated women.

Other Reports

Devers, L. (2013). *Program Performance Report: Second Chance Act—Targeting Offenders with Co-Occurring Substance Abuse and Mental Health Grant Program.* **Washington, DC: U.S. Department of Justice, Office of Justice Programs, Bureau of Justice Assistance. BJA sponsored.**
https://www.bja.gov/Publications/SCACoOccurring_PPR_06-12.pdf
This report covers four quarters of data collected from July 2011 to June 2012 for the Second Chance Act Co-Occurring Substance Abuse and Mental Health Reentry Program grantees.

Feucht, T. E., & Gfroerer, J. (2011). *Mental and Substance Use Disorders among Adult Men on Probation or Parole: Some Success against a Persistent Challenge.* **Washington, DC: National Institute of Justice and Substance Abuse and Mental Health Services Administration.**
https://www.ncjrs.gov/pdffiles1/nij/235637.pdf
This report presents data on mental and substance use disorders among adult males on correctional supervised release–parole or probation–from local, state and federal prisons and jails. It examines issues that have grown increasingly salient with the rising costs associated with managing the growing community- and facility-based criminal justice population. Changes over time in substance abuse and mental health measures among males ages 18 to 49 were studied by comparing 2009 estimates to estimates from each prior year (2002 to 2008). The analysis reveals several significant findings. First, rates of substance dependence or abuse among probationers and parolees were found to be significantly lower than rates in prior years. Second, the percentage of parolees who reported receiving substance use treatment was significantly higher in 2009 than in 2005. Third, significantly lower percentages of probationers and parolees had more of an unmet need for substance use treatment in 2009 than in previous years. Overall, from 2002 to 2009, illegal drug use among people on probation and parole remained a persistent challenge, with rates of drug abuse and dependence remaining two to three times as high as rates among nonprobationers and nonparolees. The number of probationers and parolees with mental or substance use disorders whose treatment needs are not being met by community treatment and supportive services is significant. As a result, they are placed at greater risk for parole or probation failure leading to reincarceration. The findings suggest the ongoing need for broader implementation of effective treatment and reentry services for this high-risk, mostly nonviolent population, such as those provided under ongoing federal grant programs focused on reentering offenders. The ability to promote community reentry and reintegration for parolees and probationers with mental or substance use disorders requires a release plan that includes timely and readily accessible community-based treatment and appropriate support services.

State, Local, and Tribal Reentry Court Program

NIJ-Sponsored Evaluations

D'Amino, R., Geckeler, C., et al. (2013). *Evaluation of the Second Chance Act (SCA) Adult Demonstration 2009 Grantees: Interim Report* **[NCJ-243294]. Oakland, CA: Social Policy Research Associates. NIJ sponsored.**
https://www.ncjrs.gov/pdffiles1/nij/grants/243294.pdf
This report presents the methodology and findings of an evaluation of the implementation of 10 SCA adult demonstration grants for programs intended to improve reentry services for adult offenders.

Willison, J. B., Cramer, L., et al. (2012). *FY 2011 Second Chance Act Adult Offender Reentry Demonstration Projects: Evaluability Assessment Overview of the Johnson County (KS) Reentry Project* [NCJ-243983]. Washington, DC: Urban Institute, Justice Policy Center. NIJ sponsored.
https://www.ncjrs.gov/pdffiles1/nij/grants/243983.pdf
This study conducted an evaluability assessment (determination of whether a project is a candidate for meaningful evaluation) of the Johnson County (KS) Reentry Project, a FY 2011 SCA demonstration site.

Other Academic Articles

Preventing Parolee Crime Program (PPCP)

This program was rated on CrimeSolutions.gov as promising.
Program summary: A multidimensional, parole-based reintegration program that aims to reduce parolee crime and reincarceration by providing parolees with services to facilitate their successful reintegration into society following release from prison.
Details: http://www.CrimeSolutions.gov/ProgramDetails.aspx?ID=72

Zhang, S. X., Roberts, R.E.L., et al. (2006). "Preventing Parolees from Returning to Prison Through Community-Based Reintegration." *Crime & Delinquency, 52*(4): 551–571.
http://www.CrimeSolutions.gov/ProgramDetails.aspx?ID=72

This program was rated on CrimeSolutions.gov as promising.
The authors found that participants of the Preventing Parolee Crime Program (PPCP), as a whole, had a recidivism rate 8 percentage points lower than non–PPCP parolees (44.8 percent compared with 52.8 percent, respectively). In addition, increasing levels of participation in PPCP services was associated with an even lower recidivism rate.

Yamatani, H., & Spjeldnes, S. (2009). "Saving Our Criminal Justice System: The Efficacy of Collaborative Social Service." *Social Work, 56*(1): 53–61.
http://sw.oxfordjournals.org/content/56/1/53.short
This 3-year study investigated the effects of collaboration-based in-jail services and post-release transitional services provided by the Allegheny County Jail Collaborative in Pennsylvania. The results included a significantly lower recidivism rate among inmate participants, similar service benefits across racial groups, and successful reintegration into community life among a large majority of participants.

Other Reports

Devers, L. (2013). *Program Performance Report: Second Chance Act—Adult Demonstration Reentry Grant Program, July 2011–June 2012.* Washington, DC: U.S. Department of Justice, Office of Justice Programs, Bureau of Justice Assistance. BJA sponsored.
https://www.bja.gov/Publications/SCAReentryDemo_PPR_06-12.pdf
This report covers four quarters of data collected from July 2011 to June 2012 for Second Chance Act Adult Reentry grantees.

Ayoub, L. H., & Pooler, T. (2015). *Coming to Harlem: A Randomized Controlled Trial of the Harlem Parole Reentry Court.* New York: Center for Court Innovation.
http://www.courtinnovation.org/research/fact-sheet-coming-home-harlem-randomized-controlled-trial-harlem-parole-reentry-court
This study of the Harlem Parole Reentry Court compares participants in a neighborhood-based reentry program to similar parolees on traditional parole. Results indicate that the reentry court, which implemented a validated and reliable tool for assessing the risks and needs of people returning from prison, produced a 22% reduction in the reconviction rate and a 60% reduction in the felony reconviction rate over an 18-month follow-up period. The reentry court also produced a 45% reduction in revocations. Interview findings indicate that reentry court parolees were significantly more likely to be in school or employed and to have positive perceptions of their parole officer.

Hamilton, Z. (2010). *Do Reentry Courts Reduce Recidivism? Results from the Harlem Parole Reentry Court.* **New York: Center for Court Innovation.**
http://www.courtinnovation.org/sites/default/files/Reentry_Evaluation.pdf
This report documents the results of the first ever rigorous test of a specialized reentry court. Among the findings, reentry court parolees (including both graduates and failures) were less likely to be rearrested or reconvicted than a comparison group of parolees. Impact findings include:

    (a) Rearrests: Reentry Court parolees (including both graduates and failures) were less likely to be rearrested, although only some effects approached statistical significance (misdemeanor rearrests over the first year and drug-related rearrests over the first 2 years).

    (b) Reconvictions: Reentry Court parolees were less likely to be reconvicted, and the effects were significant at 1, 2, and 3 years (43 percent compared with 53 percent at three years).

    (c) Revocations: Reentry Court parolees were more likely to be revoked and returned to prison. Notably, revocations for technical violations were significantly higher at 1, 2, and 3 years (15 percent compared with 8 percent at e years). Also, revocations (for any reason) were significantly higher after 2 and 3 years (56 percent compared with 36 percent at 3 years).

Family-Based Substance Abuse Treatment Program

NIJ-Sponsored Evaluations

Fontaine, J., Cramer, L., et al. (2013). *FY 2011 Second Chance Act Adult Offender Reentry Demonstration Projects: Evaluability Assessment of the Ohio Department of Rehabilitation and Correction Healthy Environments, Loving Parents (HELP II) Program* **[NCJ-243987]. Washington, DC: Urban Institute, Justice Policy Center. NIJ sponsored.**
https://www.ncjrs.gov/pdffiles1/nij/grants/243987.pdf
This study was an evaluability assessment (determination of whether a project is a candidate for meaningful evaluation) of the Ohio Department of Rehabilitation and Correction Healthy Environment, Loving Parents program, a FY 2011 SCA demonstration site.

Willison, J. B., Owens, C., et al. (2012). *FY 2011 Second Chance Act Adult Offender Reentry Demonstration Projects: Evaluability Assessment of the Missouri Department of Corrections Second Chance in Action (SCIA) Program* **[NCJ-243985]. Washington, DC: Urban Institute, Justice Policy Center. NIJ sponsored.**
https://www.ncjrs.gov/pdffiles1/nij/grants/243985.pdf
This report presents an evaluability assessment (determination of whether a project is a candidate for meaningful evaluation) of the Missouri Department of Corrections Second Chance in Action (SCIA) program, a FY 2011 SCA demonstration site. Missouri's SCIA program is an innovative approach to community-based reentry services for female offenders released from incarceration into rural communities.

Other Reports

Devers, L. (2013). *Program Performance Report: Second Chance Act—Family-Based Prisoner Substance Abuse Treatment Grant Program, July 2011–June 2012.* **Washington, DC: U.S. Department of Justice, Office of Justice Programs, Bureau of Justice Assistance.**
https://www.bja.gov/Publications/SCAFamily-Based_PPR_06-12.pdf
This report covers four quarters of data collected from July 2011 to June 2012 for the Second Chance Act Family-Based grantees.

Miller, M. J., Miller, H. V., & Barnes, J. C. (2015). "Outcome Evaluation of a Family-Based Jail Reentry Program for Substance Abusing Offenders." *The Prison Journal.*
DOI:10.1177/0032885515605482
http://tpj.sagepub.com/content/early/2015/09/30/0032885515605482.abstract?rss=1
Offender reentry programs have proliferated since the passage of the Second Chance Act in 2008. This study examines the effectiveness of one such jail-based reentry program for male inmates diagnosed with

substance dependency and who have minor children, the Delaware County (OH) Jail Substance Abuse Treatment program. This program served 34 offenders and their families over 2 years and was based on the Community Reinforcement and Family Training model, a treatment modality for substance abuse involving both operant conditioning and family-based therapy for behavioral modification. Results from a quasiexperimental design indicate that program participants were significantly less likely to be rearrested within 1 year after release relative to a comparison group of similarly situated offenders and more likely to comply with child support orders following release. Findings also revealed the treatment group had significantly more days to failure for those who did recidivate.

Liddle, H. A., Rowe, C. L., Dakof, G. A., & Henderson, C. E. (2009). "Multidimensional Family Therapy for Young Adolescent Substance Abuse: Twelve-Month Outcomes of a Randomized Controlled Trial." *Journal of Consulting and Clinical Psychology*, *77*(1): 12–25.
http://psycnet.apa.org/journals/ccp/77/1/12/
Research has established the dangers of early onset substance use for young adolescents and its links to a host of developmental problems. Because critical developmental detours can begin or be exacerbated during early adolescence, specialized interventions that target known risk and protective factors in this period are needed. This controlled trial ($n = 83$) provided an experimental test comparing multidimensional family therapy (MDFT) and a peer group intervention with young teens. Participants were clinically referred, were of low income, and were mostly ethnic minority adolescents (average age = 13.73 years). Treatments were manual guided, lasted 4 months, and were delivered by community agency therapists. Adolescents and parents were assessed at intake, at 6-weeks post-intake, at discharge, and at 6 and 12 months following treatment intake. Latent growth curve modeling analyses demonstrated the superior effectiveness of MDFT over the 12-month follow-up in reducing substance use (effect size: substance use frequency, $d = 0.77$; substance use problems, $d = 0.74$), delinquency ($d = 0.31$), and internalized distress ($d = 0.54$), and in reducing risk in family, peer, and school domains ($d = 0.27$, 0.67, and 0.35, respectively) among young adolescents.

Liddle, H. A., Dakof, G. A., Henderson, C. E., & Rowe, C. (2010). "Implementation Outcomes of Multidimensional Family Therapy-Detention to Community: A Reintegration Program for Drug-Using Juvenile Detainees." *International Journal of Offender Therapy and Comparative Criminology*. **DOI: 10.1177/0306624X10366960.**
http://ijo.sagepub.com/content/early/2010/04/27/0306624X10366960.abstract
Responding to urgent calls for effective interventions to address young offenders' multiple and interconnected problems, a new variant of an existing empirically-validated intervention for drug-using adolescents, Multidimensional Family Therapy (MDFT)–Detention to Community (DTC) was tested in a two-site controlled trial. This article (a) outlines the rationale and protocol basics of the MDFT-DTC intervention, a program for substance-using juvenile offenders that links justice and substance abuse treatment systems to facilitate adolescents' postdetention community reintegration; (b) presents implementation outcomes, including fidelity, treatment engagement and retention rates, amount of services received, treatment satisfaction, and substance abuse–juvenile justice system collaboration outcomes; and (c) details the implementation and sustainability challenges in a cross-system (substance abuse treatment and juvenile justice) adolescent intervention. Findings support the effectiveness of the MDFT-DTC intervention, and the need to develop a full implementation model in which transfer and dissemination issues could be explored more fully, and tested experimentally.

Liddle, H. A. (2013). "Multidimensional Family Therapy: A Science-Based Treatment System." *Australian and New Zealand Journal of Family Therapy*, *31*(2): 133–148.
http://onlinelibrary.wiley.com/doi/10.1375/anft.31.2.133/abstract
Multidimensional Family Therapy (MDFT) is a family-based intervention for adolescent substance abuse and associated mental health and behavioural problems (Liddle, 2010). Integrative in several ways, MDFT uses an ecological or contextual conceptual framework to understand the developmental tasks of teens and their families. Research-derived knowledge about risk and protective factors, and proximal causes, correlates, and contributors to adolescent drug and related problems inform clinical thinking and

interventions with every case. A multisystems approach, MDFT assesses and intervenes in four areas: (1) the adolescent as an individual *and* a member of a family and peer network; (2) the parent(s), both as individual adults and in his or her role as mother, father, or caregiver; (3) the family environment and family relationships, as manifested in day-to-day family transactional patterns; and (4) extrafamilial sources of influence such as peers, school, and juvenile justice. Interventions are made within and coordinated across domains. Progress in one area or with one person has implications for and use in others. Individual meetings with parent(s) and teen set the stage for family sessions, and family meetings may offer content and new outcomes that need to be brought to extrafamily meetings with juvenile justice or school personnel. MDFT was developed and tested as a *treatment system* rather than a one-size-fits-all approach. A treatment system offers different versions of a clinical model that vary according to factors such as clinical sample characteristics (older compared with younger adolescents, juvenile justice involved compared with no involvement in juvenile justice systems), and treatment parameters (type of clinical setting and treatment dose).

Technology Careers Program
NIJ-Sponsored Evaluations

No NIJ-sponsored evaluations were found that met the requirements under Technology Grants for Second Chance Act grantees.

Other Academic Articles

Corrections-Based Vocational Training Programs.

This program was rated on CrimeSolutions.gov as promising.
Practice summary: Vocational training or career technical education programs in prison that are designed to teach inmates about general employment skills or skills needed for specific jobs and industries. Details: http://www.CrimeSolutions.gov/PracticeDetails.aspx?ID=24

Davis, L. M., Bozick, R., et al. (2013). *Evaluating the Effectiveness of Correctional Education: A Meta-Analysis of Programs That Provide Education to Incarcerated Adults.* **Washington, DC: Department of Justice, Office of Justice Programs, Bureau of Justice Assistance.**
http://www.CrimeSolutions.gov/PracticeDetails.aspx?ID=24

This program was rated on CrimeSolutions.gov as promising.
Davis and colleagues conducted a meta-analysis of evaluations examining the effectiveness of programs that provide education to incarcerated adults. A comprehensive literature search was done that covered the period from January 1, 1980, through December 31, 2011. To be included in the review, a study needed to (1) evaluate an eligible intervention, (2) measure success of the program using an eligible outcome measure, and (3) employ an eligible research design.

Aos, S., Miller, M., et al. (2006). *Evidence-Based Adult Corrections Programs: What Works and What Does Not.* **Olympia, WA: Washington State Institute for Public Policy.**
http://www.wsipp.wa.gov/ReportFile/924

This program was rated on CrimeSolutions.gov as promising.
This meta-analysis updated and extended an earlier 2001 review by Aos and colleagues. The review's overall goal was to present policymakers in Washington State with a comprehensive assessment of adult corrections programs and policies that can affect crime rates. This meta-analysis concentrated exclusively on adult corrections programs.

Wilson, D. B., Gallagher, C. A., et al. (2000). "A Meta-Analysis of Corrections-Based Education, Vocation, and Work Programs for Adult Offenders." *Journal of Research in Crime and Delinquency, 37*(4):347–368.
http://www.CrimeSolutions.gov/PracticeDetails.aspx?ID=24

This program was rated on CrimeSolutions.gov as promising.
The authors examined the effectiveness of corrections-based education, vocation, and work programs for adult offenders through a meta-analysis of 33 experimental and quasi-experimental evaluations.

Postsecondary Correctional Education (PSCE)

This program was rated on CrimeSolutions.gov as promising.
Practice summary: Postsecondary correctional education is academic or vocational coursework taken beyond a high school diploma or equivalent that allows inmates to earn credit while they are incarcerated. Details: http://www.CrimeSolutions.gov/PracticeDetails.aspx?ID=23

Chappell, C. A. (2004). "Postsecondary Correctional Education and Recidivism: A Meta-Analysis of Research Conducted 1990–99." *Journal of Correctional Education*, 55(2):148–169.
http://www.CrimeSolutions.gov/PracticeDetails.aspx?ID=23

This program was rated on CrimeSolutions.gov as promising.
The author conducted a meta-analysis of studies examining the effects of postsecondary correctional education (PSCE) on recidivism. Only published articles and unpublished research finalized between 1990 and 1999 were included in the review. PSCE was defined as any type of education beyond high school, or its equivalency, that has inmates in prisons or jails for students (including vocational, academic, undergraduate, graduate, certificate, or degree programs). If studies combined data on inmates participating in PSCE with inmates in adult basic education and GED courses, they were eliminated. Studies had to include recidivism rates of program participants to be included. Studies were found through literature reviews and requests of information from the Correctional Education Association. The review included correlational and quasi-experimental studies.

Davis, L. M., Bozick, R., et al. (2013). *Evaluating the Effectiveness of Correctional Education: A Meta-Analysis of Programs that Provide Education to Incarcerated Adults.* Washington, DC: Department of Justice, Office of Justice Programs, Bureau of Justice Assistance.
https://www.bja.gov/Publications/RAND_Correctional-Education-Meta-Analysis.pdf

This program was rated on CrimeSolutions.gov as promising.
The authors conducted a meta-analysis of evaluations examining the effectiveness of programs that offer education to incarcerated adults. A comprehensive literature search was done that covered the period from January 1, 1980, through December 31, 2011. To be included in the review, a study needed to (1) evaluate an eligible intervention, (2) measure success of the program using an eligible outcome measure, and (3) employ an eligible research design.

Other Reports

Devers, L. (2013). *Program Performance Report: Second Chance Act—Technology Careers Grant Program, July 2011–June 2012.* Washington, DC: Department of Justice, Office of Justice Programs, Bureau of Justice Assistance. BJA sponsored.
https://www.bja.gov/Publications/SCATechCareers_PPR_06-12.pdf
This report covers four quarters of data collected from July 2011 to June 2012 for the Second Chance Act Technology Careers grantees.

Adult Mentoring Program

Linquist, C., Hardison, J., et al. (2003). *Reentry Courts Process Evaluation (Phase 1): Final Report* **[NCJ-202472]. Research Triangle Park, NC: RTI International. NIJ sponsored.**
http://www.ncjrs.gov/pdffiles1/nij/grants/202472.pdf
This document presents an evaluation of the Reentry Court Initiative (RCI) from OJP, which establishes a system of offender accountability and support services throughout the reentry process.

NIJ-Sponsored Evaluations

Walters, J. H., Kennedy, E., et al. (2012). *FY 2011 Second Chance Act Adult Offender Reentry Demonstration Projects: Evaluability Assessment of the Boston Reentry Initiative* **[NCJ-243979]. Washington, DC: Department of Justice, Office of Justice Programs, Bureau of Justice Assistance. NIJ sponsored.**
https://www.ncjrs.gov/pdffiles1/nij/grants/243979.pdf
This study conducted an evaluability assessment (determination of whether a project is a candidate for meaningful evaluation) of the Boston Reentry Initiative, a FY 2011 Second Chance Act demonstration site.

Walters, J. H., Kennedy, E., et al. (2012). *FY 2011 Second Chance Act Adult Offender Reentry Demonstration Projects: Evaluability Assessment of the Palm Beach County (FL) Regional and State Transitional Ex-Offender Reentry (RESTORE) Initiative* **[NCJ-243982]. Washington, DC: Urban Institute, Justice Policy Center. NIJ sponsored.**
https://www.ncjrs.gov/pdffiles1/nij/grants/243982.pdf
This study conducted an evaluability assessment (determination of whether a project is a candidate for meaningful evaluation) of the Palm Beach County (FL) Regional and State Transitional Ex-Offender Reentry (RESTORE) Initiative, a FY 2011 SCA demonstration site. The RESTORE Initiative is a coordinated countywide approach to providing reentry services to moderate-risk and high-risk offenders returning to Palm Beach County from Florida Department of Corrections correctional facilities.

Willison, J. B., Hardison Walters, J., et al. (2012). *FY 2011 Second Chance Act Adult Offender Reentry Demonstration Projects Evaluability Assessment, Executive Summary* **[NCJ-243978]. Washington, DC: Urban Institute, Justice Policy Center. NIJ sponsored.**
https://www.ncjrs.gov/pdffiles1/nij/grants/243978.pdf
This study conducted an evaluability assessment (determination of whether a project is a candidate for meaningful evaluation) of eight FY 2011 SCA demonstration sites. These sites shared the goals of increasing reentry programming for returning prisoners and their families, reducing recidivism of program participants by 50 percent over 5 years, reducing parole violations, and improving reintegration outcomes.

Willison, J. B., Steffey, D., et al. (2012). *FY 2011 Second Chance Act Adult Offender Reentry Demonstration Projects: Evaluability Assessment of the Solano County (CA) Women's Reentry Achievement Program* **[NCJ-243980]. Washington, DC: Urban Institute, Justice Policy Center. NIJ sponsored.**
https://www.ncjrs.gov/pdffiles1/nij/grants/243980.pdf
This study conducted an evaluability assessment (determination of whether a project is a candidate for meaningful evaluation) of the Solano County (CA) Women's Reentry Achievement Program (WRAP), a FY 2011 SCA demonstration site. WRAP uses a gender-responsive, evidence-based, offender-informed approach to address the barriers facing female offenders as they transition from jail to the community.

Willison, J. B., Walsh, K., et al. (2012). *FY 2011 Second Chance Act Adult Offender Reentry Demonstration Projects: Evaluability Assessment of the New Haven (CT) Reentry Initiative* **[NCJ-243981]. Washington, DC: Urban Institute, Justice Policy Center. NIJ sponsored.**
https://www.ncjrs.gov/pdffiles1/nij/grants/243981.pdf
This study conducted an evaluability assessment (determination of whether a project is a candidate for meaningful evaluation) of the New Haven (CT) Reentry Initiative, a FY 2011 Second Chance Act demonstration site.

Other Academic Articles[71]

Auglaize County (Ohio) Transition (ACT) Program

This program was rated on CrimeSolutions.gov as promising.
Program summary: One of the nation's first jail reentry programs, working to reduce recidivism of jail inmates once they reenter the community, in part by linking inmates to various resources.
Details: https://www.CrimeSolutions.gov/ProgramDetails.aspx?ID=130

Miller, H. V., & Miller, J. M. (2010). "Community In-Reach Through Jail Reentry: Findings from a Quasi-Experimental Design." *Justice Quarterly, 27*(6): 893–910.

This program was rated on CrimeSolutions.gov as promising.
The study found the Auglaize County Transition Program in Ohio was successful in reducing recidivism rates among program participants. Bivariate analysis showed that only 12.3 percent of program participants were rearrested during the 12-month follow-up period, compared with 82 percent of the control group.

Boston (MA) Reentry Initiative (BRI)

This program was rated on CrimeSolutions.gov as promising.
Program summary: An interagency public safety initiative to help incarcerated violent adult offenders transition back to their Boston neighborhoods following release from jail through mentoring, social service assistance, and vocational development.
Details: http://www.CrimeSolutions.gov/ProgramDetails.aspx?ID=42

Braga, A. A., Piehl, A. M., et al. (2009). "Controlling Violent Offenders Released to the Community: An Evaluation of the Boston Reentry Initiative." *Journal of Research in Crime and Delinquency, 46*(4): 411–436.
http://www.CrimeSolutions.gov/ProgramDetails.aspx?ID=42

This program was rated on CrimeSolutions.gov as promising.
The first analysis by these authors found consistently and significantly lower failure rates for the participants of the Boston Reentry Initiative compared with the control group, though the differences between the two groups narrowed somewhat over time. Arrests for violent crimes presented a similar pattern over the course of the study. The second analysis that looked at the effects of treatment on time to failure also found statistically significant differences between the treatment and control groups.

Delaware KEY/Crest Substance Abuse Programs

This program was rated on CrimeSolutions.gov as promising.
Program summary: A prison-based therapeutic community for offenders with a history of substance abuse and a residential work release center that allows offenders to continue their treatment as they transition to the community—both part of the Delaware Department of Correction's substance abuse treatment continuum.
Details: https://www.CrimeSolutions.gov/ProgramDetails.aspx?ID=55

---

[71] The following programs are listed in both the adult mentoring and adult reentry demonstration sections, as both programs share components.

Martin, S. S., Butzin, C. A., et al. (1999). "Three-Year Outcomes of Therapeutic Community Treatment for Drug-Involved Offenders in Delaware: From Prison to Work Release to Aftercare." *Prison Journal, 79*(3): 294–320.
http://www.CrimeSolutions.gov/ProgramDetails.aspx?ID=55

This program was rated on CrimeSolutions.gov as promising.
When looking at the new grouping of study participants (Crest dropouts, Crest graduates with aftercare, and Crest graduates without aftercare), the results are somewhat different. Crest dropouts are just as likely to be arrested on a new charge as the comparison group. However, those who complete Crest do much better, and those who complete Crest and receive aftercare are the least likely to have a new arrest. For drug-free status, Crest dropouts are more than three times as likely to be drug-free, Crest completers more than five times as likely, and Crest completers with aftercare are seven times more likely to be drug-free compared with the comparison group.

Inciardi, J. A., Martin, S. S., et al. (2004). "Five-Year Outcomes of Therapeutic Community Treatment of Drug-Involved Offenders After Release From Prison." *Crime & Delinquency, 50*(1): 88–107.
http://www.CrimeSolutions.gov/ProgramDetails.aspx?ID=55
http://cad.sagepub.com/content/50/1/88.short

This program was rated on CrimeSolutions.gov as promising.
The authors found that participation in the transitional treatment program more than quadrupled the odds of remaining drug-free at 42 months. Treatment participation was also a significant predictor of criminal recidivism. There was a 70 percent reduction in the odds of a new arrest for those assigned to treatment. The results for drug use and rearrests at 60 months were similar to the results at 42 months. Participation in the transitional treatment program still more than tripled the odds of remaining drug-free. Study participants with no previous treatment were also more likely to relapse, and those who received treatment were significant less likely to. Treatment participation was also a significant predictor of no new arrests at 60 months.

Martin, S. S., Butzin, C. A., et al. (1995). "Assessment of a Multistage Therapeutic Community for Drug-Involved Offenders." *Journal of Psychoactive Drugs, 27*(1): 109–116.
https://www.CrimeSolutions.gov/ProgramDetails.aspx?ID=55

This program was rated on CrimeSolutions.gov as promising.
The analyses by these authors showed that the KEY–Crest and Crest–only groups were significantly more likely to be drug free and arrest free at follow-up than the KEY–only and the no-treatment groups. However, the differences between the KEY–only group and the comparison group on both measures were not statistically significant.

Forever Free

This program was rated on CrimeSolutions.gov as promising.
Program summary: The first comprehensive, in-prison, residential substance abuse treatment program designed for incarcerated women.
Details: https://www.CrimeSolutions.gov/ProgramDetails.aspx?ID=40

Hall, E. A., Prendergast, M. L., et al. (2004). "Treating Drug-Abusing Women Prisoners: An Outcome Evaluation of the Forever Free Program." *Prison Journal*, 84(1): 81–105.
http://www.CrimeSolutions.gov/ProgramDetails.aspx?ID=40

This program was rated on CrimeSolutions.gov as promising.
The authors found that for measures of crime and recidivism, the bivariate analyses showed that significantly fewer Forever Free participants reported having been arrested or convicted during parole compared with the comparison group. About half of the Forever Free group had been arrested since their release from CIW, and half had been convicted since release. By comparison, 75 percent of women in the

comparison group reported arrests since release and 71 percent reported convictions. Although a smaller percentage of Forever Free participants reported being reincarcerated in jail or prison than the comparison group (50 percent versus 62 percent), the difference was not statistically significant.

InnerChange Freedom Initiative (Minnesota)

This program was rated on CrimeSolutions.gov as promising.
Program summary: A voluntary faith-based prisoner reentry program that attempts to prepare inmates for reintegration into the community through employment as well as family and other significant relationships, using educational, values-based programming.
Details: https://www.CrimeSolutions.gov/ProgramDetails.aspx?ID=353

Duwe, G., & King, M. (2012). "Can Faith-Based Correctional Programs Work? An Outcome Evaluation of the InnerChange Freedom Initiative in Minnesota." *International Journal of Offender Therapy and Comparative Criminology, 57*(7): 813–841.
http://www.ncbi.nlm.nih.gov/pubmed/22436731

This program was rated on CrimeSolutions.gov as promising.
Overall, the authors found that InnerChange Freedom Initiative participants had lower recidivism rates than nonparticipants for three of the four recidivism measures. They also found varying levels of recidivism rates for program participants. For example, completers had lower recidivism rates than dropouts, and participants who continued to meet with their mentors had lower rates than participants who did not meet with their mentors at all or who did only while in prison.

Other Reports

Council of State Governments Justice Center. (2013). *Integrated Reentry and Employment Strategies: Reducing Recidivism and Promoting Job Readiness* **[NCJ-243628]. New York: Author. BJA sponsored.**
https://www.bja.gov/Publications/CSG-Reentry-and-Employment.pdf
This report presents a set of strategies for reducing recidivism and improving employment opportunities for recently released inmates. It is intended for use by policymakers and practitioners who recognize the need for improved collaboration between the corrections and workforce development fields.

Department of Justice, Office of Justice Programs, Bureau of Justice Assistance. (2013). *Program Performance Report: Second Chance Act—Adult Mentoring Grant Program, July 2011–June 2012.* **Washington, DC: Author. BJA sponsored.**
https://www.bja.gov/Publications/SCAMentoring_PPR_06-12.pdf
This report covers four quarters of data collected from July 2011 to June 2012 for Adult Mentoring Second Chance Act grantees.

Nelson-Dusek, S., Atella, J., & Meyerson, J. (2012). *Volunteers of America Texas Second Chance Mentoring Program: Progress and Successes.* **St.Paul, MN: Wilder Foundation.**
http://www.wilder.org/Wilder-Research/Publications/Studies/VOA%20Texas%20Second%20Chance%20Mentoring%20Program/VOA%20Texas%20Second%20Chance%20Mentoring%20Program%20-%20Progress%20and%20Successes,%20Summary.pdf
In 2009, Volunteers of America Texas (VOA-TX) received a Second Chance Act Adult Mentoring Grant from the Department of Justice, Bureau of Justice Assistance. The Second Chance Act was designed to authorize grants for mentoring projects to promote the safe and successful reintegration of adults who have been incarcerated. Using this funding, VOA-TX developed the Second Chance Mentoring Program for incarcerated mothers, matching them with community members for one-on-one mentoring during incarceration and after reentry. Over the course of the program, 61 mentees participated; their ages range from ages 17 to 60. The program has also done well in maintaining a low recidivism rate. Over 3 years, only 7 out of 61 mentees were reincarcerated on a technical violation (11%), and no one has been

reincarcerated for a new crime. In looking at Texas as a whole, 21 percent of women located at in-prison therapeutic communities were re-incarcerated over the course of 3 years (2005 to 2007).

Adult Offender Reentry Demonstration Program
NIJ-Sponsored Evaluations

Hardison Walters, J., Cramer, L., et al. (2012). *FY 2011 Second Chance Act Adult Offender Reentry Demonstration Projects: Evaluability Assessment of the Minnesota Department of Corrections High Risk Recidivism Reduction Demonstration Project* **[NCJ-243984]. Washington, DC: Urban Institute, Justice Policy Center. NIJ sponsored.**
https://www.ncjrs.gov/pdffiles1/nij/grants/243984.pdf
This study conducted an evaluability assessment (determination of whether a project is a candidate for meaningful evaluation) of the Minnesota Department of Corrections High Risk Recidivism Reduction (HRRR) Demonstration Project, a FY 2011 SCA demonstration site. The HRRR Demonstration Project aims to reduce recidivism in a high-risk population of parole violators through collaborative case management and the co-location of services supported by DOC and community agency partnerships.

Linquist, C., Hardison Walters, J., et al. (2013). *The National Institute of Justice's Evaluation of Second Chance Act Adult Reentry Courts: Program Characteristics and Preliminary Themes from Year 1* **[NCJ-211400]. Research Triangle Park, NC: RTI International, Center for Court Innovation, and NPC Research. NIJ sponsored.**
https://www.ncjrs.gov/pdffiles1/nij/grants/241400.pdf
This report presents the program characteristics and preliminary themes from the National Institute of Justice's evaluation of Second Chance Act Adult Reentry Courts.

Other Academic Articles

Auglaize County (OH) Transition (ACT) Program

This program was rated on CrimeSolutions.gov as promising.
Program summary: One of the nation's first jail reentry programs working to reduce recidivism of jail inmates once they reenter the community, in part by linking inmates to various resources.
Details: http://www.CrimeSolutions.gov/ProgramDetails.aspx?ID=130

Miller, H. V., & Miller, J. M. (2010). "Community In-Reach Through Jail Reentry: Findings from a Quasi-Experimental Design." *Justice Quarterly, 27*(6): 893–910.
http://www.tandfonline.com/doi/abs/10.1080/07418825.2010.482537#.U_doAfldUQE

This program was rated on CrimeSolutions.gov as promising.
This study found the Auglaize County Transition Program in Ohio was successful in reducing recidivism rates among program participants. Bivariate analysis showed that only 12.3 percent of program participants were rearrested during the 12-month follow-up period, compared with 82 percent of the control group.

Community and Law Enforcement Resources Together (ComALERT)

This program was rated on CrimeSolutions.gov as promising.
Program summary: A reentry program in Brooklyn, NY, that provides substance abuse treatment, employment, and housing services for parolees transitioning from prison back into the community.
Details: http://www.CrimeSolutions.gov/ProgramDetails.aspx?ID=114

Jacobs, E., & Western, B. (2007). *Report on the Evaluation of the ComALERT Prisoner Reentry Program.* **Albany, NY: New York State Division of Criminal Justice Services.**
http://scholar.harvard.edu/files/brucewestern/files/report_1009071.pdf

This program was rated on CrimeSolutions.gov as promising.
The authors examined the recidivism rates between Community and Law Enforcement Resources Together participants and a matched control group. They found statistically significant and nonsignificant treatment effects on several outcome measures: rearrest, reconviction, reincarceration by parole violation, reincarceration by new sentence, any reincarceration, employment and earning, co-residence and contact with children, and drug and alcohol use.

Serious and Violent Offender Reentry Initiative (SVORI)

This program was rated on CrimeSolutions.gov as having no effect.
Program summary: A collaborative federal effort that concentrated on improving criminal justice, employment, education, health, and housing outcomes of adult and juvenile offenders upon their release from incarceration.
Details: https://www.CrimeSolutions.gov/ProgramDetails.aspx?ID=167

Lattimore, P. K., & Visher, C. A. (2009). *The Multisite Evaluation of SVORI: Summary and Synthesis.* **Research Triangle Park, NC: RTI International.**
https://www.ncjrs.gov/pdffiles1/nij/grants/230421.pdf

This program was rated on CrimeSolutions.gov as having no effect.
The authors found that the Serious and Violent Offender Reentry Initiative (SVORI) significantly increased access to a variety of services for program participants. However, the results suggest that the number of participants who reported receiving services was smaller than the number of participants who reported needing the services. The overall results of the impact evaluation did not show many significant differences between SVORI participants and non–SVORI participants using measures of housing, substance use, and criminal behavior/recidivism for adult male and female offenders and juvenile male offenders.

Other Reports

Devers, L. (2013). *Program Performance Report: Second Chance Act—Adult Demonstration Reentry Grant Program, July 2011–June 2012.* **Washington, DC: U.S. Department of Justice, Office of Justice Programs, Bureau of Justice Assistance. BJA sponsored.**
https://www.bja.gov/Publications/SCAReentryDemo_PPR_06-12.pdf
This report covers four quarters of data collected from July 2011 to June 2012 for the Second Chance Act Adult Reentry grantees.

Research and Evaluations for the SCA Program
OJP-Sponsored Evaluation

Council of State Governments Justice Center. (2013). *Reentry Matters: Strategies and Successes of Second Chance Act Grantees Across the United States.* **Council of State Governments [NCJ-244087]. New York: Author. BJA sponsored.**
http://csgjusticecenter.org/wp-content/uploads/2013/11/ReentryMatters.pdf
This report presents information on the strategies and successes of Second Chance Act grantees, highlighting the following recipients that have received funds and implemented successful programs: the New York City Office of the Criminal Justice Coordinator—Harlem Parole Reentry Court; Ottawa County, MI, West Shoreline Second Chance Connections program; the Comprehensive Community Cross-System Reentry Support Project run by the Department of Human Services in Oakland, CA; the New Haven Reentry Initiative run by the Connecticut Department of Corrections; the Springfield Community Mentoring Project, Springfield, MA; the Co-Occurring Program at Minnesota Correctional

Facility—Lino Lakes, run by the Minnesota Department of Corrections; the Ohio Department of Youth Services; the Gang Intervention Treatment: Reentry Development for Youth program in Harris County, TX; Project Reconnect in Tulsa, OK, run by the Girl Scouts of Eastern Oklahoma; the Family Supports for Treatment and Reentry Success: Center for Family Success in Multnomah County, OR; and the Wisconsin Tribal Community Reintegration Program, run by the Oneida Tribe of Indians of Wisconsin.

NIJ-Sponsored Evaluations

Altschuler, D.M., Hussemann, J., Zweig, J., Banuelos, I., Ross, C., & Liberman, A. (2016). *The Sustainability of Juvenile Programs beyond Second Chance Act Funding: The Case of Two Grantees.* **Washington, DC: The Urban Institute.**
http://www.urban.org/sites/default/files/alfresco/publication-pdfs/2000611-The-Sustainability-of-Juvenile-Programs-beyond-Second-Chance-Act-Funding-The-Case-of-Two-Grantees.pdf

In FY 2012, the Urban Institute was funded to evaluate Second Chance Act federal grantees of juvenile reentry programs. The study looks at "process and outcome evaluation of juvenile demonstration program grantees, including initial assessments of sites' feasibility for inclusion in the full outcome evaluation." As part of the study, the Urban Institute paid visits to five selected sites, but only two sites–Houston, TX, and Sacramento, CA–are discussed in this brief. Data were collected between 2013 and 2015. Semistructured interviews, telephone conversations, and document assessments were employed with grantees and community and state stakeholders during site visits. The Urban Institute addressed important components of the sites in the study: "the contexts in which they operated, their activities, lessons learned, and aspects of the grant programming that were sustained beyond Second Chance Act funding." Additionally, the facts on the ground were assessed for both sites. Overall, SCA Demonstration programs may point to a wide array of possibilities in designing and implementing reentry programs in various communities across the country.

Houston, TX

"In response to the increasing number of youth who were placed in correctional facilities for committing serious, gang-related crimes and the unique challenges associated with gang member reentry, the Texas Juvenile Justice Department (TJJD) implemented the Gang Intervention Treatment: Re-Entry Development for Youth Initiative (GitRedy)." During a 3-year span—2011 to 2014—GitRedy provided services to over 450 young people. C-PACT (Community Positive Achievement Change Tool) and R-PACT (Residential Positive Achievement Change Tool) were the formal risk assessment tools used to tailor services to participant needs. Participants were also classified into two separate categories, depending on level of need. As the number of employees in the Houston District Parole Office fell, however, officer caseloads increased, and the "GitRedy staff struggled to maintain prerelease engagement, which diminished the frequency of visits with GitRedy youth and involvement in institutional case planning meetings." Despite the challenges, GitRedy has been successful in several ways, including its ability to raise awareness about "gang-related issues in Harris County and throughout the state." Although certain aspects of GitRedy had existed before funds were awarded, GitRedy was a turning point for how state agencies and parole offices taught gang awareness and reentry strategies to program participants to help them turn their lives around.

Sacramento, CA

Sacramento's Juvenile Reentry Program (JRP) was funded from January 2010 to January 2014. The program employed an array of strategies to help moderate- and high-risk participants, ages 16 and 17, to safely return to their homes from local detention facilities. The pilot program was meant to undergo an expansion as part of the Second Chance Act grant funding, but during FY 2009 and FY 2010, the Sacramento County Probation Department had its budget slashed, which led to a decline in the number of employees available to provide services. "Youth were assessed as eligible for the program—moderate- and high-risk youth were targeted—on their arrival at the facility and during the intake process using PACT (Positive Achievement Change Tool). The services focused on counseling and family therapy, education, and participation in prosocial activities." Despite the Second Chance Act funding coming to an end, the Sacramento County Probation Department continued with the JRP, even if parts of it needed modification. Program participants are still housed in the same unit, and the program remains viable by keeping some of the most loyal probation officers in the program. To widen eligibility requirements for the JRP program, participants could now be between 17.5 and 18 years of age, which has increased the number of people participating in the program. Participants who had electronic monitoring have also been added to the list of service recipients.

Ritter, N. (2013). *"Cultural Shift" Is Among Findings of Second Chance Act Evaluation* **[NCJ-244147]. Washington, DC: U.S. Department of Justice, Office of Justice Programs, National Institute of Justice. NIJ Funded.**
http://nij.gov/journals/273/pages/second-chance-act-evaluation.aspx
The evaluation of 10 state and local governments from around the nation, which first received SCA funding, determined that reentry programs are moving toward a rehabilitative philosophy and an acceptance of evidence-based practices.

Wells, D., & Hernon, J. (2013). *Federal Initiatives Seek to Reduce Recidivism Rates* **[NIJ Update; NCJ-244916]. Washington, DC: U.S. Department of Justice, Office of Justice Programs, National Institute of Justice. NIJ Funded.**
https://ncjrs.gov/pdffiles1/nij/244916.pdf
This report, which is reprinted from *Corrections Today*, briefly discusses two federal initiatives aimed at reducing recidivism among offenders: the Serious and Violent Offender Reentry Initiative and the Second Chance Act (SCA). Analysis of SCA was begun in 2010 and is ongoing. The goal of the evaluation is to compare recidivism rates for offenders both during and after their participation in reentry court programs.

Other Academic Articles

Council of State Governments Justice Center. (2014). *Reducing Recidivism: States Deliver Results.* **New York: Author.**
http://csgjusticecenter.org/wp-content/uploads/2014/06/ReducingRecidivism_StatesDeliverResults.pdf
From 2005 to 2007, NRRC reported that seven states had achieved recidivism reduction. In this report for 2007 to 2010, NRRC notes that eight new states have been added to the recidivism reduction list.

O'Hear, M. M. (2007). *The Second Chance Act and the Future of Reentry Reform* **[Paper 117]. Milwaukee, WI: Marquette University Law School, Faculty Publications.**
http://scholarship.law.marquette.edu/facpub/117
The author comments on SCA itself and then discusses the potential significance of a reentry focus at sentencing. He suggests some concerns about the ability of the reentry movement to live up to its potential. In brief, he is troubled by the tendency to frame and evaluate reentry initiatives as solely (or even primarily) recidivism reduction measures. The author states that although decreased crime rates are certainly a plausible and desirable consequence of devoting more attention and resources to offenders during their transition from prison, he conceptualizes the reentry "problem" as a crime prevention issue that misses many important social welfare and social justice concerns implicated in the treatment of returning prisoners and threatens to reinforce, rather than supplant, the legalist mindset that fuels mass incarceration.

Staff Training Aimed at Reducing Rearrest (STARR)

This program was rated on CrimeSolutions.gov as promising.
Program summary: A training program for federal community supervision officers providing direct service to clients (i.e., offenders under supervision), with the goal of improving one-on-one officer–client interactions to reduce risk and thereby client recidivism.
Details: http://www.CrimeSolutions.gov/ProgramDetails.aspx?ID=236

Robinson, C. R., VanBenschoten, S. W., et al. (2011). "A Random (Almost) Study of Staff Training Aimed at Reducing Rearrest (STARR): Reducing Recidivism Through Intentional Design." *Federal Probation, 75*(2): 57–63.
http://www.uscourts.gov/uscourts/FederalCourts/PPS/Fedprob/2011-09/starr.html

This program was rated on CrimeSolutions.gov as promising.
This study used an experimental pretest/posttest design to examine the impact of Staff Training Aimed at Reducing Rearrest (STARR). Federal probation officers who volunteered to participate in STARR were randomly assigned to the experimental (trained) and control (untrained) groups. The randomization procedure was completed so that 66 percent of the officers were randomly assigned to the experimental group and the remaining officers were assigned to the control group.

Strategic Training Initiative in Community Supervision (STICS)

This program was rated on CrimeSolutions.gov as promising.
Program summary: A job training program for probation officers to help them apply the risk–need–responsivity model with probationers to reduce recidivism.
Details: http://www.CrimeSolutions.gov/ProgramDetails.aspx?ID=47

Bonta, J., Bourgon, G., et al. (2010). *The Strategic Training Initiative in Community Supervision: Risk–Need–Responsivity in the Real World.* **Ottawa, Ontario, Canada: Public Safety Canada.**
http://www.CrimeSolutions.gov/ProgramDetails.aspx?ID=47

This program was rated on CrimeSolutions.gov as promising.
The results of the study by Bonta and colleagues revealed significant changes in the officer population, but nonsignificant though positive differences in subsequent recidivism among offenders.

Transitional Case Management

This program was rated on CrimeSolutions.gov as having no effect.
Program summary: A strengths-based case management intervention that provided expanded case management services during an inmate's transition from incarceration to the community.
Details: https://www.CrimeSolutions.gov/ProgramDetails.aspx?ID=222

Prendergast, M., Frisman, L., et al. (2011). "A Multisite, Randomized Study of Strengths-Based Case Management With Substance-Abusing Parolees." *Journal of Experimental Criminology, 7*: 225–253.
https://www.CrimeSolutions.gov/ProgramDetails.aspx?ID=222

This program was rated on CrimeSolutions.gov as having no effect.
The authors failed to find statistically significant differences between the groups at 3 months or 9 months with regard to participation in services. Compared with those in the standard referral group, those in the transitional case management group did report significantly more nights in residential substance abuse treatment at 3 months; however, the difference was not significant at 9 months. There were no other differences in treatment or other services received by both groups.

Other Reports

Lindquist, C., Willison, J.B., Rossman, S., Walters, J. H., & Lattimore, P. K. (2015). *Second Chance Act Adult Offender Reentry Demonstration Programs: Implementation Challenges and Lessons Learned.* **Research Triangle Institute and the Urban Institute.**
https://www.ncjrs.gov/pdffiles1/nij/grants/249188.pdf
Seven grantees were included in the Cross-Site Evaluation of the BJA FY 2011 SCA Adult Offender Reentry Demonstration Programs (AORDP). Each program targets adult offenders who are under state or local custody (and who are about to return to the community) for comprehensive reentry programing, with substantial variation in target populations and service delivery approaches. Designed to meet the multiple challenges facing former inmates upon their return to the community, the AORDP programs provide an

array of pre- and post-release services, including education and literacy programs, job placement, housing services, and mental health and substance abuse treatment. Risk and needs assessments, transition case planning, and case management are key elements of grantees' SCA projects.

Implementation Challenges. The programs became fully operational fairly early in their grant periods and remained largely stable over time, with modifications commonly including increased in-reach activities and expansions of service delivery networks through additional partners. The most common cross-site implementation challenges included staff turnover and program administrative barriers; barriers to effective collaboration between corrections and community partners; enrollment, recruitment, and retention of participants; and service provision challenges, mainly the need for greater customization of service delivery and additional resources to fill specific service gaps (e.g., in housing, employment, and behavioral health services).

Lessons Learned. Grantees considered pre-release engagement with community-based service providers (followed by immediate post-release support) and intensive case management to be the most effective strategies for promoting successful reentry. Recommendations offered by grantees to assist similar programs pertained to **program administration and partnerships** (e.g., gain early buy-in from policymakers, administer the program as a community rather than law-enforcement based program, fully engage community service providers), **staffing** (e.g., cross-train staff, formalize program policies and procedures, hire staff and volunteers who have criminal histories or a personal connection to incarceration), and **service delivery approaches** (e.g., tailor the program to address participant characteristics and needs, ensure that the location of services is easy for participants to access). Site-specific features and innovations are highlighted in the full report.

U.S. Department of Justice, Office of the Inspector General (2010). *Office of Justice Programs' Management of Its Offender Reentry Initiatives* [Audit Report 10-34]. Washington, DC: Author.
http://www.justice.gov/oig/reports/OJP/a1034.pdf
The objective of this audit was to examine OJP's design and management of its three prisoner reentry grant programs: the Serious and Violent Offender Reentry Initiative (SVORI), the Prisoner Reentry Initiative (PRI), and the Second Chance Act Prisoner Reentry Initiative (SCA). Because the initial SCA grants were awarded in September 2009, OIG could not evaluate the monitoring and effectiveness of the SCA grant program. Discussion related to the SCA grant program is limited to the adequacy of the performance measures designed to monitor the program's progress.

NIJ-Pending Resources

The following articles are ongoing evaluations. Preliminary results, where available, are discussed, and links are provided to publicly available project descriptions.

Lindquist, C., Ayoub, L.H., Dawes, D., Harrison, P.M., Malsch, A.M., Walters, J.H. et al. (2014). *The National Institute of Justice's Evaluation of Second Chance Act Adult Reentry Courts from Year 2*. Portland, OR; NPC Research.
https://www.ncjrs.gov/pdffiles1/nij/grants/248187.pdf
The project is studying eight adult reentry courts. Early results indicate that a majority of program participants were male, their average age was 33, and their ethnicity varied greatly depending on site location. Follow up found that 52% of participants reported being steadily employed since their release from incarceration. Many participants reported that they were currently living in a house or apartment (80%), and smaller percentages (0%–12%) stated they had experienced homelessness since their release. Participants reported being pleased with their experiences in the reentry program but cited room for improvement in housing, employment, public assistance, and transportation.

Lindquist, C., Walters, J. H., Rempel, M., & Carey, S. M. (2013). *The National Institute of Justice's Evaluation of Second Chance Act Adult Reentry Courts: Program Characteristics and Preliminary Themes from Year 1.* **Research Triangle Park, NC; RTI International, Center for Court Innovation, NPC Research.**
https://www.ncjrs.gov/pdffiles1/nij/grants/241400.pdf
This report documented the first year of implementation across eight reentry court program sites. The sites shared common core characteristics, including an emphasis on post-release services, the range of services offered, use of case management techniques, reliance on the court to monitor participant progress, drug testing, and creation of a team approach when giving rewards or sanctions. All eight sites used reentry court participation as a special condition of a participant's community supervision. A majority of sites served moderate- to high-risk individuals. Many reentry programs excluded sex offenders or those with serious mental illness.

D'Amico, R., Geckeler, C., Henderson-Frakes, J., & Moazed, T. (2013). *Evaluation of the Second Chance Act (SCA) Adult Demonstration 2009 Grantees: Interim Report.* **Oakland, CA: Social Policy Research Associates.**
https://www.ncjrs.gov/pdffiles1/nij/grants/243294.pdf
This implementation study focused on 10 grantees awarded SCA adult demonstration grants. All grantees reported that they limited enrollment to offenders who scored at moderate or high risk for recidivism. Early results indicate that grantees experienced several challenges, such as low community support, few employment opportunities for participants, difficulty coordinating services, and the lengthy time needed for the program to begin running smoothly. Other barriers included participants with low educational levels, poor coping skills, and high instances of substance abuse and mental illness. Sites able to overcome some of these challenges indicated that they gained significant experience in needs-based planning and coordination for pre- and post- services, strengthened government and community partnerships, and embraced a rehabilitative philosophy.

The following resources currently do not offer any additional publications for inclusion in this literature review. Literature reviews are updated annually, and subsequent editions will include any final evaluations or reports from these resources.

NIJ Award Detail: Evaluation of the Multi-Site Demonstration Field Experiment: What Works in Reentry Research (DFE)
http://nij.gov/funding/awards/pages/award-detail.aspx?award=2010-RY-BX-0002
This research project will examine the effectiveness of a newly designed model, Demonstration Field Experiment, which seeks to promote a successful transition from prison back into the community. The follow-up period will be 12 months to assess if significant differences emerge between experimental and control groups. Key subgroups based on risk level will also be analyzed. A supplemental award will examine three sites and analyze whether specially trained parole officers and service providers influence offender outcomes post-release.

Websites

American Correctional Association
http://www.aca.org/

Council of State Governments Justice Center
http://csgjusticecenter.org

National Institute of Corrections
http://nicic.gov/

Smart Policing Initiative

Project Description

The Smart Policing Initiative (SPI) supports law enforcement agencies in testing innovative, evidenced-based solutions to serious crime problems. Smart Policing supports a strategic approach that incorporates science into police planning and operations. To do this, law enforcement agencies are encouraged to leverage innovative applications of analysis, technology, and evidence-based practices. The overall goal of the SPI is to improve policing performance and effectiveness while containing costs, an important consideration in today's fiscal environment.[72]

Note: The evaluations that follow include SPI evaluations as well as evaluations of specific strategies that fit into SPI.[73] This includes hot spots policing and problem-oriented policing. Evaluations have been selected from CrimeSolutions.gov, publicly available reports, and academic journals.[74]

CrimeSolutions.gov Ratings:
Effective (1)
Promising (2)
No Effect (0)
Insufficient Evidence (0)

Partners and Professional Organizations:

✓ CNA Corporation
✓ International Association of Chiefs of Police
✓ Police Executive Research Forum

OJP-Sponsored Evaluation[75]

Barthe, E., Venzon, M., et al. (2013). *Reno, Nevada Smart Policing Initiative: Reducing Prescription Drug Abuse.* **Arlington, VA: CNA Corporation.**
http://www.smartpolicinginitiative.com/sites/all/files/spotlights/Reno%20Program%20Profile%20FINAL%202013.pdf
Preliminary findings suggest that through engagement and education of community agencies and members, progress in process-related goals have been made. Positive process goals include increases in prescription drug abuse education, reductions in prescription drug availability, and enhanced suppression in reducing illegal prescription drug abuse.

Braga, A. A., Hureau, D. M., et al. (2011). "An Ex Post Facto Evaluation Framework for Place-Based Police Interventions." *Evaluation Review, 35*(6): 592–626. doi: 10.1177/0193841X11433827
http://erx.sagepub.com/content/35/6/592
See also: http://erx.sagepub.com/content/early/2012/01/03/0193841X11433827

This program is rated on CrimeSolutions.gov as promising.
This article presents findings from the impact evaluation on the Boston Police Department's Safe Street Team (SST) program, summarizing an early evaluation of an SPI award site from the hot spots policing program. The SST was determined by Crime Solutions to be promising. This evaluation was conducted with funding from BJA under SPI. The program was associated with a statistically significant reduction in violent index crimes at the treatment places relative to comparison sites, without displacing crime into nearby areas.

---

[72] For more background on the Smart Policing Program, please visit the following link:
http://www.smartpolicinginitiative.com/sites/all/files/ta/Smart%20Policing%20two%20pager%20all%20sites.pdf
[73] Many policing programs fall under the category of "smart" programs and are not included here. This review seeks to describe the theory of SPI, not provide evaluations of all "smart" policing programs.
[74] CrimeSolutions.gov program and practice areas are discussed through the articles and reports cited for each program or practice. In some cases, one article may have multiple ratings, or multiple articles may be used to determine a single rating. Therefore, the number of reports or articles given a CrimeSolutions.gov rating in this report may not match what is found by searching CrimeSolutions.gov.
[75] For each article, a link has been provided to either the full-length document or the website where it can be accessed.

Braga, A. A., & Schnell, C. (2013). "Evaluating Place-Based Policing Strategies: Lessons Learned from the Smart Policing Initiative in Boston." *Police Quarterly, 16*(3): 339–357.
http://pqx.sagepub.com/content/16/3/339
This article summarizes the process and impact evaluations of the SPI Safe Street Teams (SST) strategy implemented in the City of Boston. Findings upheld the effectiveness of the SSTs and the value of research, as the evaluation assisted Boston police in strengthening the program's implementation . Results of the process evaluation suggested the program was on target in addressing areas with high levels of violence. The impact evaluation determined that the SST intervention strategies were related to a reduction in violent crime in treatment areas.

Braga, A. A., Webster, D. W., et al. (2014). *Smart Approaches to Reducing Gun Violence: Smart Policing Initiative Spotlight on Evidence-Based Strategies and Impacts.* **Arlington, VA: CNA Corporation.**
http://www.smartpolicinginitiative.com/sites/all/files/SPI%20Gun%20Violence%20Spotlight%20FINAL.pdf
The authors review the success of the SPI program and the findings of evaluations at reducing gun violence from several SPI sites. Implications of these successes are discussed as well as plans for future research.

Bryant, K. M., Collins, G. M., et al. (2015). *Shawnee, Kansas, Smart Policing Initiative.* **Arlington, VA: CNA Corporation. BJA sponsored Spotlight Report.**
http://www.smartpolicinginitiative.com/sites/all/files/Shawnee%20Site%20Spotlight%20FINAL%202015.pdf
This report highlights the Data-Driven Approaches to Crime and Traffic Safety (DDACTS) SPI program in Shawnee, KS. The evaluation found that the DDACTS response led to significant decreases in robbery (88%), commercial burglary (84%), and vehicle crashes (24%), helping to stem an increase in violent crime.

Cork, J. W., Gaffney, M. J., et al. (2014). *The City of Pullman Safety Camera Initiative: Resolving Neighborhood Disorder Through Innovative Technology and Community Collaboration.* **Pullman, WA: City of Pullman. BJA sponsored.**
http://www.pullman-wa.gov/docman/doc_download/3845-spi-final-report
This report details the Pullman, WA, SPI project, focusing on the installation of five safety cameras in crime hot spots near the Washington State University campus. Due to a low number of crimes, an evaluation of the cameras's effectiveness at reducing crime was not completed. However, a survey of community members showed satisfaction with the camera project, despite an increase in respondents' fear of crime after the project's implementation.

Katz, C. M., Choate, D. E., et al. (2015). *Evaluating the Impact of Officer Worn Body Cameras in the Phoenix Police Department.* **Phoenix, AZ: Center for Violence Prevention & Community Safety, Arizona State University. BJA sponsored.**
https://publicservice.asu.edu/sites/default/files/ppd_spi_feb_20_2015_final.pdf
This evaluation of Phoenix's body-worn camera (BWC) system SPI grant found mixed results about the use of BWCs. Most incidents were not recorded, and technical issues led to difficulties in court. However, there was a significant decline in the number of complaints in general and sustained complaints against officers.

Keaton, S., Correia, D., et al. (2014). *CJ Bulletin: SMART Policing Initiative.* **San Diego, CA: Criminal Justice Research Division, SANDAG.**
http://www.sandag.org/uploads/publicationid/publicationid_1850_17574.pdf
This report highlights the SPI project in San Diego and discusses an evaluation of the impact of associated police operations to target gang activity. Although this was not a long-term evaluation and only

focused on the grant period, various findings are discussed, including a decrease in crime in the target areas and a substantial increase in gang intelligence about how gangs operate in San Diego.

Ratcliffe, J. H., Groff, E. R., et al. (2013). *Philadelphia, Pennsylvania Smart Policing Initiative: Testing the Impacts of Differential Police Strategies on Violent Crime.*[76] **Arlington, VA: CNA Corporation.**
http://www.smartpolicinginitiative.com/sites/all/files/Philadelphia%20Site%20Spotlight%20FINAL%202013.pdf

See also: Ratcliffe, J. H., Taniguichi, T., et al. (2011). "The Philadelphia Foot Patrol Experiment: A Randomized Control Trial of Police Patrol Effectiveness in Violent Crime Hotspots." *Criminology,* **49(3): 795–831.**
http://dx.doi.org/10.1111/j.1745-9125.2011.00240.x[77]
http://www.temple.edu/cj/footpatrolproject/documents/pfpe_full_paper.pdf
This report documents the results of the Smart Policing Initiative experiment in Philadelphia, which was funded through the SPI BJA grant. Study activities included pre- and post-experiment surveys of officers and residents. Findings showed that offender focus areas were successful in reducing all violent crimes by 22 percent and violent felonies by 31 percent compared with the equivalent control areas.

See also: Sorg, E.T., Haberman, C. P., et al. (2012). "Foot Patrol in Violent Crime Hot Spots: The Longitudinal Impact of Deterrence and Posttreatment Effects of Displacement." *Criminology,* **51(1):65–101.**
http://onlinelibrary.wiley.com/doi/10.1111/j.1745-9125.2012.00290.x/abstract [Abstract]
The study revisited the Philadelphia Foot Patrol Experiment and explored the longitudinal deterrent effects of foot patrol in violent crime hot spots using Sherman's (1990) concepts of initial and residual deterrence decay as theoretical framework. The study found that it is theoretically possible that previously displaced offenders returned to the original target areas, causing inverse displacement.

Uchida, C. D., & Swatt, M. L. (2013). "Operation Laser and the Effectiveness of Hot Spot Patrol: A Panel Analysis." *Police Quarterly, 16***(3): 287–304. doi: 10.1177/1098611113497044**
http://pqx.sagepub.com/content/16/3/287

See also: Uchida, C. D., Swatt, M. L., et. al. (2012). *Los Angeles, California Smart Policing Initiative: Reducing Gun-Related Violence through Operation LASER.*[78] **Washington, DC: Department of Justice, Office of Justice Programs, Bureau of Justice Assistance.**
http://www.smartpolicinginitiative.com/sites/all/files/spotlights/LA%20Site%20Spotlight%20FINAL%202012.pdf
Both articles present findings from an evaluation conducted on the Strategic Extraction Restoration (Operation LASER) program in Los Angeles. The program is designed to reduce gun violence as part of the Smart Policing Initiative. In the current study, the effectiveness of Operation LASER was assessed at the reporting district level using a panel design. Initial results indicated a significant reduction in gun crime in treatment areas compared with reporting districts from other divisions. Specifically, results show that Part I violent crimes, homicide, and robbery all decreased significantly after Operation LASER began. After the program was implemented, Part I violent crimes dropped by an average of 5.4 crimes per month, and homicides dropped by 22.6 percent per month. It is worth noting that the declines in crime did

---

[76] Citations for the CNA "Spotlight" articles are included when there is more than one report written on the same program evaluation with the same outcomes.
[77] An additional version of this report is available: Ratcliffe, J., Groff, E., et al. (2012). *Smart Policing Initiative Final Report.* Philadelphia: Temple University, Center for Security and Crime Science.
http://webcastium.net/wp-content/uploads/2013/05/Smart-1-final-report-Temple-University.pdf
[78,8] Citations for the CNA "Spotlight" articles are presented in addition to journal articles when there is more than one piece written on the same program evaluation with the same outcomes.

not occur outside of the treatment area, which presents strong evidence that Operation LASER caused these declines.

White, M. D., Ainbinder, D., et al. (2012). *Palm Beach County, Florida Smart Policing Initiative: Increasing Police Legitimacy and Reducing Victimization in Immigrant Communities.* **Washington, DC: Department of Justice, Office of Justice Programs, Bureau of Justice Assistance.**
http://www.smartpolicinginitiative.com/sites/all/files/spotlights/Palm%20Beach%20Program%20Profile%20FINAL%202012.pdf
This report highlights the early results from a program evaluation of Palm Beach County, FL. Findings suggest positive progress has been made, including improved relations between the police and the immigrant community as well as a reduction in robbery.

White, M. D., & Katz, C. M. (2013). "Policing Convenience Store Crime: Lessons from the Glendale, Arizona Smart Policing Initiative." *Police Quarterly, 16*(3): 305–322. **doi: 10.1177/1098611113497045**
http://pqx.sagepub.com/content/16/3/305

See also: White, M. D., & Balkcom, F. (2012). *Glendale, Arizona Smart Policing Initiative: Reducing Convenience Store Theft.*[79] **Washington, DC: Department of Justice, Office of Justice Programs, Bureau of Justice Assistance.**
http://www.smartpolicinginitiative.com/sites/all/files/spotlights/Glendale%20Site%20Spotlight%20FINAL%202012.pdf
These articles discuss problem-oriented policing in Glendale, AZ. The department received funding in 2009 through BJA's SPI. Results indicate that crime dropped significantly (42 percent) at the SPI target stores from the year preceding the intervention to the year after. This decline is inconsistent with crime patterns witnessed at the remaining convenience stores in Glendale.

Non-OJP Sponsored Evaluation

Bond, B. J., & Hajjar, L. M. (2013). "Measuring Congruence between Property Crime Problems and Response Strategies: Enhancing the Problem-Solving Process." *Police Quarterly, 16*(3): 323–338. **doi: 10.1177/1098611113497041**[80]
http://pqx.sagepub.com/content/16/3/323

See also: Bond, B. J., Hajjar, L., et al. (2014). *Lowell, Massachusetts Smart Policing Initiative: Reducing Property Crime in Targeted Hot Spots.*[81] **Washington, DC: SMART Policing Initiative.**
http://www.smartpolicinginitiative.com/sites/all/files/SPI%20Lowell%20Spotlight%20FINAL.pdf
The article and spotlight report discuss how Lowell, MA, operationalized problem-solving in crime hot spots. It focuses on the alignment between property crime problems and response strategies selected to achieve results. The authors found a high degree of congruence between the SPI problem-solving components, which likely produced the positive crime reductions observed in the outcome data.

---

[80] Bond & Hajjar (2013) is not sponsored by BJA. The evaluation conducted by Bond and colleagues (2014) is of a sponsored SPI BJA program, and funds were used to conduct the evaluation.
[81] CNA "Spotlight" articles are presented in addition to journal articles when there is more than one piece written on the same program evaluation with the same outcomes. In this case, the *Police Quarterly* article was not funded by BJA, but the program evaluation was.

Other Academic Articles[82]

Braga, A. A. (2008). "Pulling Levers Focused Deterrence Strategies and the Prevention of Gun Homicide." _Journal of Criminal Justice, 36_(4): 332–343.[83]

http://www.nnscommunities.org/Braga_Stockton_pulling_levers_2008.pdf

This article reports the results of an impact evaluation of the focused deterrence strategy known as pulling levers. Findings suggest that the pulling levers strategy was associated with a statistically significant decrease in the monthly number of gun homicide incidents in Stockton, CA. A comparative analysis of gun homicide trends in Stockton relative to other midsize California cities also supports a unique program effect associated with the pulling levers intervention.

Braga, A., Papachristos, A., et al. (2012). "Hot Spots Policing Effects on Crime." _Campbell Systematic Reviews, 8._ doi: 10.4073/csr.2012.884

http://campbellcollaboration.org/lib/download/2350/Braga_Hot_Spots_Policing_Review.pdf

This article reports the results of a systematic review of the hot spots policing innovation. Results showed that 20 of 25 tests of hot spots policing interventions reported noteworthy reductions in crime and disorder. The extant evaluation research offers fairly robust evidence that hot spots policing is an effective crime prevention strategy.

Braga, A., & Weisburd, D. (2012). "The Effects of 'Pulling Levers' Focused Deterrence Strategies on Crime." _Campbell Systematic Reviews, 8_(6). doi: 10.4073/csr.2012.6

http://campbellcollaboration.org/lib/download/1918/

This practice was rated on CrimeSolutions.gov as promising.

This analysis examined the use of pulling levers-focused deterrence strategies to reduce crime. This report presents the results of a meta-analysis of evaluations of 10 programs that used pulling levers-focused deterrence strategies to prevent gang and group-involved violence. The analysis found that 9 of the 10 programs evaluated reported statistically significant reductions in crime. Findings showed that focused deterrence strategies are highly effective at producing statistically significant, medium-sized reductions in crime.

Corsaro, N., Brunson, R. K., et al. (2013). "Problem-Oriented Policing and Open-Air Drug Markets: Examining the Rockford Pulling Levers Deterrence Strategy." _Crime & Delinquency, 59_(7): 1085–1107.

http://cad.sagepub.com/content/59/7/1085

This study examines the effect of a strategic, pulling levers intervention that was implemented by law enforcement officials in Rockford, IL, to address drug markets in a high-crime neighborhood. Study findings suggest that the Rockford strategy was associated with a statistically significant and substantive reduction in crime, drug, and nuisance offenses in the target neighborhood.

Corsaro, N., Hunt, E. D., et al. (2012). "Overview of the Impact of Drug Market Pulling Levers Policing on Neighborhood Violence: An Evaluation of the High Point Drug Market Intervention." _Criminology & Public Policy, 11_(2): 165–166. doi: 10.1111/j.1745-9133.2012.00797.x

http://onlinelibrary.wiley.com/doi/10.1111/j.1745-9133.2012.00797.x/abstract

This program was rated on CrimeSolutions.gov as effective.

---

[82] These articles serve as evidence of the successful elements of SPI. As SPI can include several different types of policing methods, this research demonstrates a portion of the evidence base in support of various SPI techniques. These references are not direct SPI evaluations but may be an important resource as part of the background regarding SPI's success. Examples include crime analysis, intelligence-led policing, hot spots policing, pulling levers, and problem-oriented policing.

[83] This evaluation was sponsored by DOJ before the SPI grant program. This is supporting evidence for the need of SPI programs.

[84] The Campbell Collaboration (C2) is in Oslo, Norway. However, the reported findings are based on a program conducted in the United States.

This study examines a drug market intervention using the pulling levers method. Findings showed a statistically significant reduction in violent offenses in specific high-crime locations across the targeted neighborhoods compared with the rest of High Point, NC, and relative to comparable nontargeted areas. The citywide violent crime rate actually increased after a series of interventions unfolded, which may suggest limitations to the approach. Finally, trend analyses indicated the strategy had different levels of violent crime impact throughout unique geographic contexts.

Groff, E. R., Ratcliffe, J. H., et al. (2015). "Does What Police Do At Hot Spots Matter? The Philadelphia Policing Tactics Experiment." *Criminology, 53*(1): 23–53.
http://onlinelibrary.wiley.com/doi/10.1111/1745-9125.12055/abstract
This article details a randomized controlled trial of three police tactics at crime hot spots to evaluate their effectiveness: foot patrol, problem-oriented policing, and offender-focused policing. The results found that offender-focused tactics resulted in a 42% reduction in violent crime, whereas the sites receiving foot patrol and problem-oriented policing did not have a significant reduction in violent crime.

Hansen, J. A., Alpert, G. P., & Rojek, J. J. (2014). "The Benefits of Police Practitioner–Researcher Partnerships to Participating Agencies." *Policing, 8 (4)* 307–320.
http://policing.oxfordjournals.org/content/8/4/307
This study uses an interview of 90 police practitioners about their partnerships to determine the benefits to a police agency of partnering with a researcher. It finds many benefits among police—research partnerships including gaining new perspectives and ideas, improved policies and procedures, better community relations, and a perception of objectivity and validity.

Jang, H., Lee, C.-B., et al. (2012). "Dallas' Disruption Unit: Efficacy of Hot Spots Deployment." *Policing, 35*(3): 593–614. doi: 10.1108/13639511211250811
http://www.emeraldinsight.com/journals.htm?articleid=17048129
This report examines policing activities in hot spots to determine if the various types of crimes were affected when deployment was applied on a rotation basis. It was found that the hot spots policing of the Dallas Police Department's Disruption Unit immediately affected violent crimes, nuisance offenses, and total index crimes, although there were no residual effects of hot spots policing.

Massarotti, M. (2012). "Intelligence-Led Policing: The Evaluation of the Denver Police Department's Policy." *Journal of Applied Security Research, 7*(2): 268–283.
http://www.tandfonline.com/doi/abs/10.1080/19361610.2012.656259#.VMlFpWjF_6I [Abstract]
This study assesses the intelligence-led policing model used by the Denver Police Department (DPD). This study focuses on the crimes of burglary, motor vehicle theft, and robbery to identify the impact an intelligence-led policing model implemented by the DPD has on the cited crimes.

Santos, R. B. (2014). "The Effectiveness of Crime Analysis for Crime Reduction: Cure or Diagnosis?" *Journal of Contemporary Criminal Justice, 30*(2): 147–168.
doi: 10.1177/1043986214525080
http://ccj.sagepub.com/content/30/2/147.abstract
This article examines the role of crime analysis as a component in specific police strategies to reduce crime. Findings show that crime analysis clearly plays a significant role in effective police approaches. It is just as apparent that crime analysis plays a very limited role in policing approaches that are ineffective. These findings show that crime analysis is a key component in successful crime-reduction efforts.

Weisburd, D., Telep, C. W., et al. (2010). "Is Problem-Oriented Policing Effective in Reducing Crime and Disorder? Findings from a Campbell Systematic Review." *Criminology & Public Policy, 9*(1): 139–172.
http://www.smartpolicinginitiative.com/sites/all/files/POP%20Weisburd_et_al.pdf
This study reports on the outcome of a systematic review examining the effectiveness of problem-oriented policing (POP) in reducing crime and disorder. Findings show that POP has an overall modest but statistically significant impact on crime and disorder.

Other Reports[85]

Braga, A. A., Davis, E. F., et al. (2012). *Boston, Massachusetts Smart Policing Initiative: Evaluating a Place-Based Intervention to Reduce Violent Crime.* **Arlington, VA: CNA Corporation.**
http://www.smartpolicinginitiative.com/sites/all/files/spotlights/Boston%20Site%20Spotlight%20FINAL%202012.pdf
This summary article discusses the findings from the process and impact evaluations conducted in Boston, MA, on its Smart Policing Initiative, Safe Street Teams. Articles listed previously present more in-depth information on the evaluation of this site-specific evaluation.

Center for Community Safety, Winston-Salem State University. (2013). *Winston-Salem Intelligent-Led Policing: A Blueprint for Implementing Smart Policing Building Blocks.* **Washington, DC: Department of Justice, Office of Justice Programs, Bureau of Justice Assistance.**
https://www.bja.gov/Publications/WSSU-PB4-WinstonSalem-ILP.pdf
This blueprint document describes the Project Safe Neighborhoods Winston-Salem Intelligent-Led Policing Initiative. This initiative was a collaborative effort for creating a systemic change in how police departments reduce crime in the Winston-Salem community. The document outlines the steps to implement the project and guidelines on how to replicate it in other communities. The report highlights development of the team and its approach and includes goals and objectives as well as strategies for implementing the initiative.

Chu, V., & Coldren, Jr., J. R. (2011). "Smart Policing: Meeting the Challenge." *JRSA Forum, 29 (3),* **1–3.**
https://www.ncjrs.gov/App/Publications/abstract.aspx?ID=262197
This article discusses the Smart Policing Initiative program, including an overview of the SPI sites and some highlights of early experiences. This includes a focus on research partnerships, collaborating with other agencies, and the value of data and analysis in the implementation of policing programs.

Rickman, S., Stewart, J., et al. (2011). *Smart Policing: Addressing the Twenty-first Century Need for a New Paradigm in Policing* **[NCJ-240122]. Arlington, VA: CNA Corporation.**
http://www.smartpolicinginitiative.com/sites/all/files/ta/SPI%20Twenty%20First%20Century%20Article.pdf
This research paper addresses the need for a new strategy for today's policing practices as a result of fiscal and demographic changes in American society. The paper examines current strategies used in policing and discusses how smart policing can be used a problem-solving approach. Seven steps that law enforcement can use to develop new policing strategies are outlined in the paper.

U.S. Department of Justice, Office of Justice Programs, Bureau of Justice Assistance. (2012). *Reducing Crime through Intelligence-led Policing.* **Washington, DC: Author.**
https://www.bja.gov/Publications/ReducingCrimeThroughILP.pdf
This report documents the use of intelligence-led policing (ILP) as a crime reduction strategy by various law enforcement agencies across the nation. Its focus was to determine the commonalities, challenges, and best practices of ILP programs so that they could be replicated in other jurisdictions. The study reports on the commonalities that are a critical part of successful ILP programs.

Websites

CNA Smart Policing Initiative
http://www.smartpolicinginitiative.com

---

[85] Some of the reports listed in this section are related to a previous article or evaluation. These reports are listed because the evaluations were conducted on the same program.

International Association of Chiefs of Police
http://www.theiacp.org/

Police Executive Research Forum
http://www.policeforum.org/

Smart Prosecution Initiative Program

Project Description

BJA's Smart Prosecution Initiative (SPI) program is designed to promote effective data-driven research-based approaches to prosecution and prosecutor-led justice system innovations and reforms. The Smart Prosecution model builds on the lessons learned from BJA's "Smart Suite" of crime-fighting programs— Smart Policing, Smart Supervision, and Smart Prosecution. Smart Prosecution pairs an operational, results-focused researcher with a prosecutor's office to develop data-driven solutions for effective, efficient, and just prosecution strategies to improve public safety. The program offers valuable resources designed to equip a prosecutor's office with access to data across various information systems in criminal justice and related fields. BJA hopes that the lessons learned will promote a rich body of evidence prosecutors can use nationwide as they work with communities to solve chronic problems and fight violent crime.[86]

CrimeSolutions.gov Ratings:
Effective (0)
Promising (1)
No Effect (0)
Insufficient Evidence (0)

Partners and Professional Organizations:
✓ Association of Prosecuting Attorneys

NIJ-Sponsored and Other OJP-Sponsored Evaluations

Note: There were no BJA program evaluations found in the literature review since the inception of this program. The listed articles provide background on smart prosecution initiatives and include related materials intended to show support for future evaluations.

Academic Research[87]

Franklin, T. W. (2010). "The Intersection of Defendants' Race, Gender, and Age in Prosecutorial Decision Making." *Journal of Criminal Justice, 38*(2): 185–192.
http://www.sciencedirect.com/science/article/pii/S0047235209001482
This study employed a nationally representative sample of felony drug defendants and examined whether age and gender mitigate the effect of race on prosecutorial decisions to dismiss criminal charges. The study found that race did not affect the decision to dismiss a charge. However, the results did indicate that middle-aged White defendants were treated more punitively than young Black defendants.

Miles, T. J. (2013). "Does the 'Community Prosecution' Strategy Reduce Crime? A Test of Chicago's Experience." *American Law and Economics Review, 16*(1): 117–143.
http://aler.oxfordjournals.org/content/early/2013/08/14/aler.aht012.full.pdf+html
"This article presents the first estimates of community prosecution's impact on crime. Over a 15-year period, Chicago's top prosecutor twice applied the community prosecution strategy in some (but not all) neighborhoods, and this sequence of two 'off/on' policy episodes permits plausible identification of the strategy's impact. Differences-in-differences estimates show that community prosecution reduced certain categories of crime, such as aggravated assault, but had no effect on other categories, such as larceny." Due to the diversity in implementation acros the community, generalization is difficult. However, using the strategies gleaned from Chicago, the potential to make cost-justified reductions in crminial activity appears promising.

---

[86] More in-depth information about the program can be found in the program solicitation:
https://www.bja.gov/Funding/14SmartProsSol.pdf
[87] For each article, a link has been provided to either the full-length document or the website where it can be accessed.

Zlatic, J. M., Wilkerson, D. C., et al. (2010). "Pretrial Diversion: The Overlooked Pretrial Services Evidence-Based Practice." *Federal Probation, 74*(1): 28–33.
www.uscourts.gov/file/document/federal-probation-journal-june-2010
The article focuses on pretrial diversion (PTD), a program that deals with juvenile offenders as an alternative to prosecution. The study found that program success was dependent on an open-systems management style and the collaboration of multiple agencies through the use of effective communication. It concludes that PTD should be evaluated as a possible evidence-based practice.

Other Reports

Crank, K. (N.d.). *Community Courts, Specialized Dockets, and Other Approaches to Address Sex Trafficking.* **New York, NY: Center for Court Innovation.**
http://www.courtinnovation.org/sites/default/files/documents/Community_Courts_Trafficking_0.pdf
"In recent years, staff in many community courts and specialized dockets have been developing an expertise in identifying trafficking victims and responding to their needs by connecting them to social services and other supports." As victims of sex trafficking are often induced to engage in illegal activities and therefore are more likely to be arrested and treated as criminals, this article highlights several example of ways in which courts can change their approach to better respond to victims of sex trafficking. The approaches highlighted in the article seek to prevent trafficked people from cycling through the justice system. Using the approaches found within the document may help victim defendants of trafficking find safe pathways out of the sex trade, with the potential of avoiding future re-arrests and/or incarceration.

Dahmann, J. (1983). *An Evaluation of Operation Hardcore: A Prosecutorial Response to Violent Gang Criminality.* **Washington, DC: U.S. Department of Justice, Office of Justice Programs, National Institute of Justice.**
https://www.ncjrs.gov/pdffiles1/Digitization/91553NCJRS.pdf
This program was rated on CrimeSolutions.gov as promising.[88]
Operation Hardcore is a special prosecution unit for gang-related offenses. The unit focuses on working with victims and witnesses to help eliminate the gang problem. Result show that the program resulted in a decrease in dismissals, an increase in convictions, and an increase in the rate of incarceration.

Janson, S., & Hood, R. (2011). *A Framework for High Performance Prosecutorial Services [Prosecutor's Report III].* **Washington, DC: Association for Prosecuting Attorneys. BJA sponsored.**
http://www.prosecutingattorneys.org/wp-content/uploads/APA-High-Performance-Framework-FINAL.pdf
This paper serves as a guide to understanding the framework for high performance prosecutorial services. Included are tools meant to assist prosecutors as they shift from their traditional roles into that of a more community guided and focused member of the justice system. It highlights four key components for the community prosecutor and provides details of real-life case studies for each of the components.

Mac Donald, H. (2014). "Prosecution Gets Smart: Intelligence-Driven Crime-Fighting Comes to the D.A.'s Office." *City Journal,* **Summer 2014.**
http://www.city-journal.org/2014/24_3_intelligence-driven-crime-fighting.html
This article describes an intelligence-driven program used by prosecutors in New York City. The program centers around a database of known gang members, some of whom have not been arrested or convicted. When a gang member on the watch list is arrested, prosecutors seek harsher penalties to keep that person off the street. In some cases, minor charges that normally would be dropped lead to convictions and jail time.

---

[88] This program is included as an example of a smart prosecution program that shows promise.

McGarrell, E. F., Hipple, N. K., et al. (2009). *Project Safe Neighborhoods—A National Program to Reduce Gun Crime: Final Project Report.* **Washington, DC: U.S. Department of Justice, Office of Justice Programs, National Institute of Justice.**

https://www.ncjrs.gov/pdffiles1/nij/grants/226686.pdf

Project Safe Neighborhoods (PSN) is a gun crime–reduction program focused around increased federal prosecution for gun offenses. This evaluation of PSN found that prosecution increased in many but not all jurisdictions as a direct result of program implementation. An analysis of their crime data found that as PSN implementation increased, a bigger drop in gun-related crime also occurred.[89]

Nugent, M. E., Fanflik, P., et al. (2004). *The Changing Nature of Prosecution: Community Prosecution vs. Traditional Prosecution Approaches.* **Alexandria, VA: American Prosecutors Research Institute. BJA sponsored.**

http://www.ndaa.org/pdf/changing_nature_of_prosecution.pdf

This study examined the community prosecution approach, which brings prosecutors together with the community to identify problems and develop solutions. It found that there is a difference between community prosecution and traditional prosecution in practice but that there is no real philosophical difference between the two approaches.

Weinstenin, S.P. (2011). *Community Prosecution: A Decade into the 21st Century [Prosecutors Report I].* **Washington, DC: Association of Prosecuting Attorneys. BJA sponsored.**

https://www.prosecutingattorneys.org/wp-content/uploads/CP-Decade-into-21st-Century-FINAL1.pdf

This paper discusses the roles and responsbilities of the modern prosecutor and how this should be reflected in community prosecution. This serves as a guide to the principles and philosophies of community prosecution and how those can be applied to the justice system of today.

Williams, R. S., & Stewart, W. (2013). *Implementing a Geographic Community-Based Prosecution Model in Philadelphia* **[Prosecutor's Report V]. Washington, DC: Association of Prosecuting Attorneys. BJA sponsored.**

http://www.apainc.org/wp-content/uploads/Philadelphia-Implementation-Guide1.pdf

This study examined the community-based prosecution model, which categorizes incoming cases based on the charges, complexity, and likely time to disposition. This leads to better use of limited judicial resources. Preliminary results show that felony cases are being disposed of more quickly, and fewer are being dismissed.[90]

---

[89] For more information on PSN, please see BJA's PSN literature review.
[90] A one-page summary of the program and its preliminary results is available at http://www.apainc.org/html/Philadelphia%20One%20Page%20Summary.pdf

Smart Supervision Program

Project Description

BJA's Smart Supervision Program (SSP) uses evidence-based practices to improve adult probation and parole.[91] The program's main goal is to improve the success rate for those on probation or parole. This in turn can lead to improved public safety and fewer prison and jail admissions. A secondary SSP goal is to enroll uninsured parolees in Medicaid.

By improving supervision practices through innovative or evidence-based strategies, SSP hopes to reduce recidivism among probationers and parolees. Grantees are encouraged to collaborate with agencies and officials across all sectors of the justice system. They are also required to incorporate a research partner to assist with data analysis, strategy development, and evaluation.

Note: Process and outcome evaluations of the SSP program and its grantees have not yet been completed and are not included in this report. Instead, the articles listed offer evaluations and information on the core aspects of SSP: evidence-based practices, research partnerships, and data-driven approaches in corrections.[92] Evaluations fitting these criteria have been selected from CrimeSolutions.gov, publicly available reports, and academic journals.[93]

CrimeSolutions.gov Ratings:
Effective (1)
Promising (0)
No Effect (0)
Insufficient Evidence (0)

Partners and Professional Organizations:
✓ Council of State Governments

OJP-Sponsored Research[94]

NIJ Evaluations

Jalbert, S. K., Rhodes, W., et al. (2011). *A Multi-Site Evaluation of Reduced Probation Caseload Size in an Evidence-Based Practice Setting.* Cambridge, MA: Abt Associates. NIJ sponsored.
http://www.ncjrs.gov/pdffiles1/nij/grants/234596.pdf
This program was rated on CrimeSolutions.gov as effective.
This study explores the characteristics of caseload size among probation officers to determine whether smaller caseloads improve probation outcomes. The results suggest that reduced caseloads can lead to less recidivism. Officers trained in evidence-based practices who have reduced caseloads are better able to identify treatment needs among their clientele, and they are better able to direct resources to those most in need.

Meredith, T., & Prevost, J. (2009). *Developing Data Driven Supervision Protocols for Positive Parole Outcomes: Final Project Report 2005-IJ-CX-0029.* Washington, DC: Department of Justice, Office of Justice Programs, National Institute of Justice.
http://www.ncjrs.gov/pdffiles1/nij/grants/228855.pdf
This study evaluates various parole methods in Georgia for their effectiveness. The report reaches some noteworthy general conclusions about supervision: adherence to evidence-based supervision can improve the odds of a positive outcome, and there is promise in using data to develop supervision strategies.

---

[91] For more information on SSP, see the 2015 solicitation at https://www.bja.gov/Funding/15SmartSupervisionSol.pdf
[92] For information on specific practices that fall under SSP, see the literature reviews of Project HOPE, JRI, and the Second Chance Act.
[93] CrimeSolutions.gov program and practice areas are discussed in the articles and reports cited for each program or practice. In some cases, one article may have multiple ratings, or multiple articles may be used to determine a single rating. Therefore, the number of reports or articles given a CrimeSolutions.gov rating in this report may not match what is found by searching CrimeSolutions.gov.
[94] For each article, a link has been provided to either the full-length document or the website where it can be accessed.

Ritter, N. (2013). "Predicting Recidivism Risk: New Tool in Philadelphia Shows Great Promise." *NIJ Journal, 271:* **4–13.**

https://ncjrs.gov/pdffiles1/nij/240696.pdf

This article discusses the use of a data-driven tool to identify probationers tracked through Philadelphia's Adult Probation and Parole Department who are likely to reoffend. Co-developed with a research partner from the University of Pennsylvania, the tool rates the risk of a probationer as high, medium, or low, then the appropriate level of supervision is assigned based on this ranking. This kind of assessment can lead to increased public safety and lower costs.

Other OJP-Sponsored Research

Crime & Justice Institute. (2004). *Implementing Evidence-Based Principles in Community Corrections: Collaboration for Systemic Change in the Criminal Justice System.* **Washington, DC: U.S. Department of Justice, National Institute of Corrections.**

http://www.in.gov/idoc/files/BASICS2-EBP.pdf

This article touches on the need for a collaboration mindset in the implementation of evidence-based principles in community corrections. The collaborative process is intended to move participants away from the traditional definition of power as control or domination, and toward a definition that allows for shared authority. Working collaboratively with all stakeholders in the planning and implementation of systemic change in community corrections can result in a more coherent continuum of care, using evidence-based principles to reduce recidivism.

Rempel, M. (2014). *Evidence-Based Strategies for Working with Offenders.* **Washington, DC: U.S. Department of Justice, Office of Justice Programs, Bureau of Justice Assistance.**

http://www.courtinnovation.org/sites/default/files/documents/Evid%20Based%20Strategies.pdf

This publication summarizes a growing body of research about evidence-based strategies in five areas for reducing recidivism among criminal offenders: (1) assessment that uses validated screening and assessment tools to determine offender risk and needs; (2) treatment that applies risk-need-responsivity principles when matching offenders to interventions; (3) deterrence that imposes certain and consistent consequences in response to noncompliance; (4) procedural justice that establishes fair and consistent procedures and treats offenders respectfully; and (5) collaboration that obtains the buy-in and participation of multiple criminal justice agencies, including both top-level officials and line staff.

Academic Reports[95]

Fabelo, T. (2010). "Texas Justice Reinvestment: Be More Like Texas?" *Justice Research and Policy,* **12(1): 113–131.**

http://jrsa.metapress.com/content/g81758244k541h47/?p=8c617f224682491db83e2621d8ece053&pi=4

In 2007, elected officials in Texas faced a major dilemma: spend $500 million to build and operate new prisons to accommodate the surging number of people expected to be incarcerated, or explore options to control that growth. The Texas legislature adopted a budget that included greater treatment capacity in the prison system and expansion of diversion options in the probation and parole system. The final budget adopted by the legislature for the 2008–2009 biennium reflected an increase of $241 million in funding for additional diversion and treatment capacity. The expansion of these programs translated into a net savings of $443.9 million. The increase in treatment capacity and intermediate sanction facilities funded by the initiative has helped to increase the number of people on probation connected to services and reduce the number revoked to prison.

---

[95] Links to abstracts are provided when full articles are not available.

Kulkarni, S. P., Baldwin, S., et al. (2010). "Is Incarceration a Contributor to Health Disparities? Access to Care of Formerly Incarcerated Adults." *Journal of Community Health, 35*(3): 268−274.
http://link.springer.com/article/10.1007/s10900-010-9234-9
This study examines the link between incarceration and access to health care and found that those who had been incarcerated had less access to health care compared with those who had not been incarcerated. The authors conclude that this can be fixed through programs to enable access to health care for those who were formerly incarcerated.

Lane, J., Turner, S., et al. (2004). "Research-Practitioner Collaboration in Community Corrections: Hurdles for Successful Partnerships." *Criminal Justice Review, 29*(1): 97−114.
http://cjr.sagepub.com/content/29/1/97.refs
This article describes lessons learned from one group of researchers after partnerships with practitioners. Most of the conflict came from differing priorities throughout the process. In general, research partners wanted a robust study with data that could be used in academic reports and to inform the field. In contrast, practitioners wanted a study that helped the agency, used funds and staff effectively, and prioritized practitioner needs over general research. These seemingly conflicting needs were overcome through respect and open communication that allowed both sides to find solutions.

MacKenzie, D. L. (2000). "Evidence-Based Corrections: Identifying What Works." *Crime & Delinquency, 46*(4): 457−471.
http://canatx.org/rrt_new/professionals/articles/MACKENZIE-EVIDENCE%20BASED%20CORRECTIONS.pdf
This article emphasizes the importance of using evidence-based corrections to reduce crime in the community. The article examines which programs work, which ones don't, and which are promising. Although a variety of community-based programs work or are promising, intensive supervision and shock probation programs do not work.

Sabet, K., Talpins, S., et al. (2013). "Smart Justice: A New Paradigm for Dealing with Offenders." *Journal of Drug Policy Analysis, 6*(1): 1−17.
http://www.alcoholandcrime.org/the-voice/issues/dec12/SmartJustice-TheVoice-DEC2012.pdf
New ways of thinking about community corrections are necessary to reduce both the economic impact and the public safety consequences of offenders cycling in and out of prison and jail. Several new paradigms for dealing with offenders have recently emerged and are expanding throughout the United States. All of these approaches involve using sanctions that are swift, certain, and modest rather than random and severe, which is the status quo.

Skeem, J. L., & Manchak, S. (2008). "Back to the Future: From Klockars' Model of Effective Supervision to Evidence-Based Practice in Probation." *Journal of Offender Rehabilitation, 47*(3): 220−247.
https://www.ncjrs.gov/App/publications/Abstract.aspx?id=245881
This paper compares three contemporary models of probation supervision: surveillance (protecting community safety), treatment (promoting offender rehabilitation), or hybrid (both surveillance and treatment). Results indicate that a hybrid model is more effective than either surveillance or treatment alone. However, most agencies focus on surveillance and have not included an evidence-based treatment element.

Taxman, F. S., Pattavina, A., et al. (2014). "Justice Reinvestment in the United States: An Empirical Assessment of the Potential Impact of Increased Correctional Programming on Recidivism." *Victims & Offenders, 9*(1): 50–75.[96]
http://www.tandfonline.com/doi/abs/10.1080/15564886.2013.860934#.U-EK8vldX6I
Efforts to use evidence-based practices will likely have limited success altering the outcomes from incarceration unless more attention is paid to the principles of effective interventions and access to efficacious treatment services. The most comprehensive survey of services, conducted in 2005–2006, found that less than 10% of offenders can participate in treatment services on a given day. Expanding access and participation rates in programs can yield reductions in recidivism, and adding treatment matching will accelerate the recidivism reduction. By offering risk-need-responsivity programming, the reincarceration rate can be reduced by 3% to 6%.

Waters, K., Moreno, M., et al. (2013). "Capitalizing on Collaboration in Arizona: Working Together to Advance the Use of Evidence-Based Officer Skills at All Levels of Community Corrections." *Federal Probation, 77*(2): 59–63.
http://www.uscourts.gov/uscourts/FederalCourts/PPS/Fedprob/2013-09/capitalizing.html
This article reports on the development and operation of a multijurisdictional collaboration of probation agencies in Arizona. This effort facilitates rational planning for and implementation of evidence-based policies and practices for reducing recidivism. The shared vision of this ongoing project is to train officers in evidence-based tools to reduce recidivism as well as to support and learn from community corrections partners in Arizona as knowledge and skill acquisition progresses.

Other Reports

Burrell, W. D. (2005). "Trends in Probation and Parole in the States." In *The Book of the States 2005,* **pp. 595–600. Washington, DC: Council of State Governments.**
http://www.csg.org/knowledgecenter/docs/BOS2005-ProbationParoleTrends.pdf
This article describes several trends in probation and parole, including the establishment of formal, high-level partnerships with other agencies and researchers and the use of data in the evaluation of programs. This results-driven system relies on performance measurement to prove success.

Carter, M. M., & Sankovitz, R. J. (2015). *Dosage Probation: Rethinking the Structure of Probation Sentences.* **Washington, DC: National Institute of Corrections.**
https://s3.amazonaws.com/static.nicic.gov/Library/027940.pdf
This report outlines the dosage probation model, which is designed to reduce recidivism and the cost of extended supervision by promoting probation based on a variable dosage. It asserts that the length of supervision should be determined by the number of hours of intervention necessary to reduce recidivism risk, rather than an arbitrarily or customarily established amount of time.

Latessa, E. J., Lowenkamp, C. T., et al. (2009). *Community Corrections Centers, Parolees, and Recidivism: An Investigation into the Characteristics of Effective Reentry Programs in Pennsylvania— Executive Summary.* **Cincinnati, OH: University of Cincinnati, Center for Criminal Justice Research.**
http://www.uc.edu/content/dam/uc/ccjr/docs/reports/project_reports/PA_Reentry_executivesummary.pdf
This study examined which community corrections centers in Pennsylvania were effective in reducing recidivism. A total of 54 programs were evaluated, scored, and rated on program content and capacity based on the Evidence-Based Correctional Program Checklist. The study found that of the 54 sites, 93 percent were ineffective or needed improvement. Of the two types of facilities examined, the community contract facilities (CCFs) offered more treatment programs than the community corrections centers (CCCs), yet the CCC programs had lower rates of recidivism than the CCF programs.

---

[96] For more information on the Justice Reinvestment Initiative, please see the JRI literature review.

Regenstein, M., & Nolan, L. (2014). *Implications of the Affordable Care Act's Medicaid Expansion on Low-Income Individuals on Probation.* **Washington, DC: George Washington University, School of Public Health and Health Services, Department of Health Policy.**
http://hsrc.himmelfarb.gwu.edu/cgi/viewcontent.cgi?article=1296&context=sphhs_policy_facpubs
This report examines how the Affordable Care Act will change health coverage for those on probation, many of whom have unmet health, mental health, and substance abuse problems. By offering health insurance for these people, it may be possible for more people to successfully complete probation.

Website

Council of State Governments Justice Center
http://www.csgjusticecenter.org/

State and Local Anti-Terrorism Training

Project Description

The State and Local Anti-Terrorism Training (SLATT) program is dedicated to providing critical training and resources to our nation's law enforcement professionals, who face the challenges presented by the terrorist/violent criminal extremist threat. To help confront this threat, the SLATT program provides specialized multiagency anti-terrorism detection, investigation, and interdiction training and related services to state, local, and tribal law enforcement and prosecution authorities.

The SLATT program has been proactively involved in anti-terrorism research and training since 1996. SLATT focuses on preventing terrorism by offering the tools necessary for state, local, and tribal law enforcement officers to understand, detect, deter, and investigate acts of domestic terrorism by both international and domestic terrorists.[97]

CrimeSolutions.gov Ratings:
Effective (0)
Promising (1)
No Effect (0)
Insufficient Evidence (0)

Partners and Professional Organizations:
- ✓ Institute for Intergovernmental Research
- ✓ Nationwide SAR Initiative

NOTE: No published evaluations were found for this program. However, BJA, working with NIJ, has an ongoing process and impact evaluation conducted by RAND Corporation that concluded in 2015. The evaluation examines how the SLATT program's curriculum is developed and implemented, its cost effectiveness, and the degree to which it has an impact on countering violent extremism.

Other Reports

Office for Bombing Prevention, Department of Homeland Security. (2014). *Counter-IED Resources Guide.* **Washington, DC: Author.**
https://tripwire.dhs.gov/IED/resources/docs/OBP_Counter-IED_Resources_guide.pdf
The mission of the Office of Bombing Prevention is to protect life and critical infrastructure by building capabilities within the general public and across the public and private sectors to prevent, protect against, respond to, and mitigate bombing threats. It accomplishes its mission through a focused portfolio of complementary counter-improvised explosive device (IED) capability development programs, supporting four core initiatives: 1) coordination of national and intergovernmental Counter-IED efforts; 2) capabilities analysis and planning support; 3) information sharing and decision support; and 4) counter-IED training and awareness.

National Protection and Programs Directorate, U.S. Department of Homeland Security. (2012). *Office of Infrastructure Protection Strategic Plan: 2012–2016.* **Washington, DC: Author.**
http://www.dhs.gov/sites/default/files/publications/IP-Strategic-Plan-FINAL-508.pdf.
The Office of Infrastructure Protection supports the Homeland Security Secretary's national leadership role by working with critical infrastructure owners and operators to develop and monitor risk management approaches and other preparedness and resilience measures that enhance security. This mission is carried out in many ways, including analyzing risks and sharing information to manage those risks, conducting vulnerability and resilience assessments, developing standards and best practices, supporting and informing preparedness and incident management activities, and ensuring compliance with regulatory frameworks.

---

[97] This description as well as more in-depth information about the program is at this website: https://www.slatt.org/SLATT

CNA and Bureau of Justice Assistance. (2013). *Managing Large-Scale Security Events: A Planning Primer for Local Law Enforcement Agencies.* **Washington, DC: Author.**
https://www.bja.gov/Publications/LSSE-planning-Primer.pdf.
This planning primer synthesizes salient best practices pertaining to security planning for a large-scale event, specifically pre-event planning, core event operations, and post-event activities. The primer includes detailed information on 18 core operational areas that law enforcement executives can give to lead law enforcement planners as supplemental guidance. This guidance can be used as a foundation for coordinating area-specific operational plans and can be modified to accommodate event security requirements and existing protocols. Furthermore, supplementing each operational area presented in the primer are actionable templates, checklists, and key considerations designed to facilitate the planning process.

Interagency Threat Assessment and Coordination Group (ITACG), National Counterterrorism Center. (2011). *Intelligence Guide for First Responders.* **Washington, DC: Author.**
http://www.nctc.gov/docs/ITACG_Guide_for_First_Responders_2011.pdf.
The *Intelligence Guide for First Responders* was created to assist state, local, tribal law enforcement, firefighting, homeland security, and appropriate private sector personnel in accessing and understanding federal counterterrorism, homeland security, and weapons of mass destruction intelligence reporting. Most of the information contained in this guide was compiled, derived, and adapted from existing intelligence community and open source references. The ITACG consists of state, local, and tribal first responders and federal intelligence analysts from the Department of Homeland Security and the FBI, working at the National Counterterrorism Center to enhance the sharing of federal counterterrorism, homeland security, and weapons of mass destruction information with state, local, and tribal consumers of intelligence.

The White House. (2011). *Empowering Local Partners to Prevent Violent Extremism in the United States.* **Washington, DC: Author.**
https://www.whitehouse.gov/sites/default/files/empowering_local_partners.pdf.
Protecting American communities from al-Qa'ida's hateful ideology is not the work of government alone. Communities–especially Muslim American communities whose children, families, and neighbors are being targeted for recruitment by al-Qa'ida–are often best positioned to take the lead because they know their communities best. The federal government will support and help empower American communities and their local partners in their grassroots efforts to prevent violent extremism. This strategy commits the federal government to improving support to communities, including sharing more information about the threat of radicalization; strengthening cooperation with local law enforcement, who work with these communities every day; and helping communities to better understand and protect themselves against violent extremist propaganda, especially online.

U.S. Department of Homeland Security. (2015). *First Responder Guide for Improving Survivability in Improvised Explosive Device and/or Active Shooter Incidents.* **Washington, DC: Author.**
http://www.dhs.gov/sites/default/files/publications/First%20Responder%20Guidance%20June%202015%20FINAL%202.pdf
Recent improvised explosive device (IED) and active shooter incidents reveal that some traditional practices of first responders need to be realigned and enhanced to improve survivability of victims and the safety of first responders caring for them. This federal, multidisciplinary first responder guidance translates evidence-based response strategies from the U.S. military's vast experience in responding to and managing casualties from IED and/or active shooter incidents and from its significant investment in combat casualty care research into the civilian first responder environment. Additionally, civilian best practices and lessons learned from similar incidents, both in the United States and abroad, are incorporated into this guidance. Recommendations developed in this paper fall into three general categories: hemorrhage control, protective equipment (which includes, but is not limited to, ballistic vests, helmets, and eyewear), and response and incident management.

New York City Police Department. (2010). *Active Shooter: Recommendations and Analysis for Risk Mitigation.* **New York, NY: Author.**
https://www.valorforblue.org/Documents/Publications/Public/Active_Shooter_New_York_City_Police_Department.pdf

Active shooter attacks are dynamic incidents that vary greatly from one attack to another.The Department of Homeland Security (DHS) defines an active shooter as "an individual actively engaged in killing or attempting to kill people in a confined and populated area." In its definition, DHS notes that, "in most cases, active shooters use firearms and there is no pattern or method to their selection of victims." The New York City Police Department (NYPD) has limited this definition to include only those cases that spill beyond an intended victim to others. The NYPD developed these recommendations based on a close analysis of active shooter incidents from 1966 to 2010. This compendium of cases includes 281 active shooter incidents. It is organized chronologically by type of facility targeted, including office buildings, open commercial areas, factories and warehouses, schools, and other settings. The NYPD performed a statistical analysis on a subset of these cases to identify common characteristics among active shooter attacks. This analysis is presented in Part III and the underlying methodology is presented in Part IV. The analysis found a large degree of variation among attacks across some broad categories, including: sex of the attacker, age of the attacker, number of attackers, planning tactics, targets, number of casualties, location of the attack, weapons used, and attack resolution.

U.S. Department of Education. (2007). *Lessons Learned from School Crises and Emergencies: Responding to and Recovering from an Active Shooter Incident that Turns Into a Hostage Situation.* **Washington, DC: Author.**
https://www.valorforblue.org/Documents/Publications/Public/Active-Shooter-Schools-Lesson-Learned.pdf

In recent years, schools nationwide have experienced active shooter incidents. An "active shooter" is a person who is actively discharging a firearm causing the immediate death or serious injury of one or more people. The duration of an active shooter situation may vary considerably from a short period of time, such as a few minutes, to a long period of time, such as several hours. The details of these incidents also tend to evolve and change as site-specific information about hostages, victims, weapons, bombs, and other activities are obtained. This type of emergency requires that school officials and first responders react immediately to implement practices and procedures outlined in emergency management plans. They also must institute an incident command system to establish control over the event and maintain a safe environment for staff and students until an evacuation can occur.

Bureau of Justice Assistance, Office of Justice Programs, U.S. Department of Justice. (2014). *Privacy, Civil Rights, and Civil Liberties Brochure.* **Washington, DC: Author.**
https://www.bja.gov/Publications/Privacy-Brochure.pdf

This brochure provides information on the importance of protecting privacy, civil rights, and civil liberties.

Website

State and Local Anti-Terrorism Training
www.slatt.org/

Statewide Automated Victim Information and Notification

Project Description

The Statewide Automated Victim Information and Notification (SAVIN) Program helps protect victims and survivors of crime from further victimization and ensures that their rights are secured. It does the latter by providing those registered with timely and accurate information about any important dates related to the criminal proceedings at issue in their case (e.g., trial dates, times, or changes; probation hearings; inmate relocation; and offender release) as well as specific changes to the status of offenders who committed crimes against them. (The program is guided in part by the general principles of 42 USC 10603e.) SAVIN focuses on three areas: governance, technology, and program management. Together, these components seek to improve the governance process of the criminal justice and law enforcement agencies; the use of technology to manage information to and from victims, providing timely service; and program management as guided by the governance structure.

CrimeSolutions.gov Ratings:
No ratings at this time

Partners and Professional Organizations:

✓ Council of State Governments Justice Center

✓ National Criminal Justice Association

✓ National Institute of Justice

✓ Vera Institute of Justice

✓ Office for Victims of Crime

Highlighted Reports

Irazola, S., Williamson, E., & Stricker, J. (2013). *Automated Victim Notification: Landscape of the United States.* **Fairfax, VA: ICF International. NIJ sponsored.**
https://www.ncjrs.gov/pdffiles1/nij/grants/243842.pdf
This issue brief is the result of a NIJ-funded evaluation of the SAVIN program administered by BJA. The information presented was collected primarily through telephone interviews with system administrators over the course of the evaluation. Findings indicate that AVN systems are extremely diverse across jurisdictions. Given this diversity, it is critical that victims understand what services are and are not provided.

NIJ-Sponsored Evaluations [98]

Irazola, S., Williamson, E., Niedzwiecki, E., Debus-Sherill, S., & Stricker, J. (2013). *Evaluation of the Statewide Automated Victim Information and Notification program, final report.* **Fairfax, VA: ICF International. NIJ sponsored. NCJ 243839.**
https://www.ncjrs.gov/pdffiles1/nij/grants/243839.pdf
This report presents the findings and methodology of an evaluation of the federally funded Automated Victim Notification (AVN) system, which offers crime victims timely and accurate information on court events and status changes in the course of their case processing. The researchers also present a cost consideration analysis and offer recommendations for future enhancement of the program. The evaluation featured three phases, each of which sought to provide a comprehensive evaluation of AVN services as well as recommendations for future research. The study concluded that 47 states, the District of Columbia, and Puerto Rico operate some AVN system, the majority of which were opened to the public and were offered in multiple languages. Overall, the research found that service providers regard AVN systems as beneficial to increasing victims' sense of safety, and the majority of victims who use the

---

[98]For each article, a link has been provided to either the full-length document or the website where it can be accessed.

systems reported being satisfied with the services. Case studies of states identified promising strategies and examined cost and sustainability issues relevant to AVN systems.

OJP-Sponsored Evaluations

This literature review has not yielded any OJP-sponsored evaluations related to this program or research area.

OJP-Sponsored Research

Irazola, S., Williamson, E., & Debus-Sherrill, S. (2013). *Automated Victim Notification: Cost Considerations.* Fairfax, VA: ICF International. NIJ sponsored. NCJ 243841.
https://www.ncjrs.gov/pdffiles1/nij/grants/243841.pdf
This issue brief discusses cost considerations associated with the implementation and operation of AVN and the implications for system sustainability. Researchers conducted interviews with system administrators, vendors, and other key stakeholders and reviewed budget information provided by a select number of state administrators. The study found that cost considerations for AVN systems must take into account each state's unique demographic characteristics (e.g., the population of incarcerated offenders and the number of custodial facilities) and system structures (e.g., whether the system is operated in-house or by an outside vendor, the number of participating facilities/branches, and the availability of different system features). The generally high costs of AVN systems highlight the importance of gaining a more in-depth understanding of the cost-benefit value of these systems.

Irazola, S., Niedzwiecki, E., Debus-Sherrill, S., & Williamson, E. (2013). *Automated Victim Notification: Awareness and Use Among Service Providers and Victims.* Fairfax, VA: ICF International. NIJ sponsored. NCJ 243840.
https://www.ncjrs.gov/pdffiles1/nij/grants/243840.pdf
This issue brief summarizes the findings of a survey of service providers and crime victims about their awareness and use of their jurisdiction's AVN systems. The service providers' survey targeted people providing direct services to victims of violent crime. Survey results demonstrate that the overall concept of automated notification is important to service providers and victims, and that AVN provides a valued service. Both service providers and victims expressed high satisfaction with and perceived benefits from their jurisdiction's AVN system, and the majority of victims indicated that they would recommend the system to others.

Irazola, S., Williamson, E., Niedzwiecki, E., & Debus-Sherrill, S. (2013). *Automated Victim Notification: Practices Aimed at Supporting Victims.* Fairfax, VA: ICF International. NIJ sponsored. NCJ 243843.
https://www.ncjrs.gov/pdffiles1/nij/grants/243843.pdf
This issue brief highlights findings from an evaluation of practices that jurisdictions can use to improve services provided by their AVN systems. Researchers collected information from multiple sources, including interviews with system administrators, surveys of service providers and victims, and case studies of states employing a range of practices for providing notification services. Findings indicate high satisfaction with AVN systems among registered victims; however, they also suggest that systems could be enhanced to better respond to the multiple needs and diverse populations of victims. For example, registration should be made as simple and customizable as possible, and notifications should provide comprehensive information to ensure that AVN systems are adequately meeting the needs of victims. The authors also recommend further research to assess the security of victim data stored in the AVN systems and to explore the role of privacy and anonymity in victims' decisions to register for AVN.

National Criminal Justice Association. (2012). *SAVIN Sustainability Survey Report. National SAVIN Training and Technical Assistance Project Team.* **Washington, DC: National SAVIN Training and Technical Assistance Project Team. BJA sponsored.**

http://savinonline.org/download/funding-documents/SAVIN-Sustainability-Survey-Report-June-2012.pdf

Using the project's SAVIN contacts database, the researchers sent a 7-question survey to 93 people. They included SAVIN administrators, project advisory board members, "other state contacts" (practitioners and key stakeholders working within state SAVIN programs), and project team members. The survey was developed using Survey Monkey, and e-mailed to the 93 people on two occasions in April and May 2012. It was completed by 32 respondents. The vast majority of respondents (80 percent) indicated that they currently use BJA grant funding to support their programs. One-third of respondents (33 percent) have a line item in their state budget, and nearly one-quarter (24 percent) are using Victims of Crime Act (VOCA) funding.

IJIS Institute. (2006). *Planning, Implementing and Operating Effective Statewide Automated Victim Information and Notification (SAVIN) Programs: Guidelines and Standards.* **Washington, DC: Author. BJA sponsored.**

http://it.ojp.gov/documents/ijis_savin_guidelines_standards.pdf

This comprehensive booklet presents recommendations and standards for planning, implementing, and operating an effective SAVIN program.

Academic Articles

Larsen, C., & Yearwood, L. D. (2004). *Notifying and Informing Victims of Crime: An Evaluation of North Carolina's SAVAN System, Executive Summary and Full Report.* **Raleigh, NC: North Carolina Governor's Crime Commission.**

http://digital.ncdcr.gov/cdm/ref/collection/p249901coll22/id/28188

This report summarizes the findings of a process and impact evaluation of the statewide automated victim assistance and notification (SAVAN) system. The study documented the extent of the program's impact on victims of crime, law enforcement, jail operations, and prosecutor offices. The findings validate the assumption that the SAVAN network is accomplishing one of its intended purposes and demonstrating an above-average impact on reducing, or minimizing, the workload of the local criminal justice agencies as related to victim notification. The study also found that SAVAN was cost-efficient and that a majority of victims using the services were satisfied with the system. The authors conclude with three policy recommendations: the need for a greater and more intensified public relations campaign; the need for legislation to provide sustained funding for the SAVAN network; and the need for a more in-depth examination of reported technical problems, including both their frequency and magnitude.

Mastrocinque, J.M. (2014). "Victim Personal Statements: An Analysis of Notification and Utilization." *Criminology & Criminal Justice: An International Journal, 14*(2): 216–234.

http://crj.sagepub.com/content/early/2013/01/06/1748895812469382

This study uses the Victim Personal Statement (VPS) policy in England and Wales to evaluate what factors influence whether victims are informed of the VPS, and what factors influence the decision to provide a VPS. The authors use British Crime Survey data. VPS is a controversial topic that has inspired several decades of debate. Criminal justice systems internationally have implemented diverse types of such policies, but regardless of the type, the literature shows that victims seldom provide statements. Despite these findings, few studies have explored the notification and use of these policies. The findings of this study show that several characteristics of victims, offenders, offenses, and jurisdictional criteria influence both notification and utilization of victim statements. The authors go on to discuss the implications of these findings.

Other Articles

American Probation and Parole Association. (2011). *Voice of the Victim: A Perspectives Spotlight Issue.* **Washington, DC: Council of State Governments/ American Probation and Parole Association**
http://www.appa-net.org/eweb/docs/appa/pubs/Perspectives_2012_Spotlight.pdf
This special edition is a collection of articles to support community corrections professionals in incorporating victims' rights and services into daily practice. This issue reflects on ways to promote restitution collection, timely notifications, and other sources of support to victims.

Council of State Government/American Probation and Parole Association. (2009). *Fact Sheet 6: Victim Information and Notification.* **Washington, DC: Author. Office for Victims of Crimes. NCJ 242406.**
http://www.appa-net.org/eWeb/docs/APPA/pubs/PVRPPP-FACTSHEET-6.pdf
This fact sheet provides information on how community corrections professionals can enhance their victim notification practices. Recommendations include providing victims an orientation regarding their rights and information on how the victim can access notifications regarding the offender. The fact sheet also provides suggestions on ways to notify the victim.

Crime Victim Services Commission. (2005). *Crime Victim Services Commission Annual Report FY 2005.* **Lansing, MI: Michigan Department of Community Health**
https://www.ncjrs.gov/App/Publications/abstract.aspx?ID=240325
The Michigan Crime Victim Services Commission (CVSC) is responsible for overseeing Michigan's wide range of funding and services for crime victims. It operates under the Michigan Department of Community Health, which administers three victim service programs that provide approximately $20 million in services to more than 250,000 citizens each year. Programs are crime victim compensation, crime victim rights, and crime victim assistance. All programs are fully supported by assessments or fines paid by convicted defendants in state and federal courts. The CVSC provides an advisory function in policy development, determines criminal assessment amounts, and acts as the appeals forum for compensation claims. The commission also supports training and technical assistance for victim advocates in Michigan and manages the statewide automated crime victim notification project.

Harrison, B. (2006). "SAVIN Lives: Notifying Victims of Their Assailants' Whereabouts Can Help Prevent Another Crime." *State Legislatures, 32*(9): 23–23.
http://www.thefreelibrary.com/SAVIN lives: notifying victims of their assailants' whereabouts can...-a0153899399
The author explains that SAVIN systems are designed to ensure that victims receive the information they need to participate fully in the judicial process. By registering with the system, victims, their families, and coworkers are notified when any significant event surrounding a case occurs. The author stresses that SAVIN systems need coordination, collaboration, and leadership at all levels of state government as well as money at the state and local levels.

Seymour, A. (2010). *Public Hearing on Victim Issues in Probation and Parole Recommendation Report.* **Washington, DC: American Probation and Parole Association.**
http://www.appa-net.org/eweb/docs/appa/pubs/PHVIPPRR.pdf
This report's 10 recommendations for the development of victim-centered policies, protocols, and training curricula for community corrections are based on input from crime victims and community corrections professionals who testified at two public hearings in the early 1990s. The recommendations are intended to improve services to crime victims and survivors throughout the community corrections process. This report also summarizes some of the key perspectives witnesses offered during the hearings.

Websites

National Criminal Justice Association
http://www.ncja.org

SAVIN Online Community site
http://savinonline.org/

VINELink ver. 2.0
https://www.vinelink.com/vinelink/initMap.do

VALOR Program

Project Description

In 2010, BJA created the VALOR Program to help prevent violence against law enforcement officers and ensure officer resilience and survivability following violent encounters during the course of their duties. The purpose of VALOR is to provide critical training to help officers identify potentially deadly encounters before they occur and to prevent them from occurring (or survive these encounters if they cannot be prevented). VALOR also provides law enforcement with critical active shooter response trainings.

VALOR is continuously refreshed and updated to ensure that it addresses current topics and issues. VALOR provides critical nationwide safety and wellness training and technical assistance to sworn state, local, and tribal law enforcement officers. It does this through a variety of delivery mechanisms and conducts and disseminates analysis of violent encounters in various forms, including after-action reviews and publications focusing on lessons learned.

CrimeSolutions.gov Ratings:
No ratings at this time

Partners and Professional Organizations:
- ✓ VALOR
- ✓ Federal Bureau of Investigation
- ✓ National Law Enforcement Officers Memorial Fund
- ✓ Texas State University–San Marcos' Advanced Law Enforcement Rapid Response Training Center
- ✓ Institute for Intergovernmental Research

Note: No evaluations of the VALOR program were found during the review. The articles listed here give background information on selected publications about officer safety to show support of the VALOR program.

OJP-Sponsored Research[99]

International Association of Chiefs of Police. (2013). *Reducing Officer Injuries Final Report: A Summary of Data Findings and Recommendations from a Multi-Agency Injury Tracking Study.* **Alexandria, VA: Author.**
http://www.theiacp.org/portals/0/pdfs/IACP_ROI_Final_Report.pdf
This study investigated rates of injuries sustained by law enforcement officers.

Other Academic Articles

Barrick, K., Hickman, M. J., et al. (2014). "Representative Policing and Violence toward the Police." *Policing, 8*(2): 193–204.
http://policing.oxfordjournals.org/content/8/2/193.short
This research examined several community elements to investigate violence against the police. Findings include the relationships between population size, overall aggravated assault rates, and minority representation.

Bierie, D. M., Detar, P. L., et al. (2013, August 22). "Firearm Violence Directed at Police." *Crime and Delinquency* **[Epub ahead of print]. doi: 10.1177/0011128713498330**
http://cad.sagepub.com/content/early/2013/08/21/0011128713498330.full.pdf
This research reviewed NIBRS data to compare incidents in which law enforcement officers experienced violence with a random sample of encounters in which they did not. They identify several situational factors related to violence against the police.

---

[99] For each article, a link has been provided to either the full-length document or the website where it can be accessed.

Brandl, S. G., & Stroshine, M. S. (2012). "The Physical Hazards of Police Work Revisited." *Police Quarterly, 15*(3): 262–282.
http://pqx.sagepub.com/content/15/3/262.full.pdf
This research examines the extent to which injuries to law enforcement officers have changed from 1996–1998 to 2006–2008. Findings indicated that the frequency and rate (injury incidents per officer) of officer assaults, other suspect-related injuries, and accidents declined during the study period. Reasons for this decline are discussed.

Fridell, L., Faggiani, D., et al. (2009). "The Impact of Agency Context, Policies, and Practices on Violence Against Police." *Journal of Criminal Justice, 37*(6): 542–552.
http://www.sciencedirect.com/science/article/pii/S0047235209001081
This research examined several police agency factors to determine their impact on the level of violence against the police. Findings indicated that body armor policies, agency accountability, and violent crime were all factors influencing police violence.

Kaminski, R. J. (2008). "Assessing the County-Level Structural Covariates of Police Homicides." *Homicide Studies, 12*(4): 350–380.
http://hsx.sagepub.com/content/12/4/350.full.pdf
This research examines the variables associated with law enforcement homicides and reports on the elements most likely to be present during these events. Findings include several environmental and demographic factors most likely to be present during felonious line-of-duty deaths.

Kent, S. L. (2010). "Killings of Police in the U.S. Cities since 1980: An Examination of Environmental and Political Explanations." *Homicide Studies, 14*(1): 3–23.
http://hsx.sagepub.com/content/14/1/3.full.pdf
This study investigates the relationship between the political conditions of large U.S. cities and the number of homicides of police officers in the line of duty in 1980, 1990, and 2000. Findings suggest several connections between income and race characteristics as well as police killings related to the incidence of violence against the police.

Paoline, E. A., Terrill, W., et al. (2012). "Police Use of Force and Officer Injuries Comparing Conducted Energy Devices (CEDs) to Hands-and Weapon-Based Tactics." *Police Quarterly, 15*(2): 115–136.
http://pqx.sagepub.com/content/15/2/115.short
This research examines the role of CEDs and police officer injuries. Findings indicated that there were increased benefits for officer use of CEDs. Findings also indicated that the use of CEDs, along with other types of force, led to an increase in officer injuries. The implications for these findings are considered.

Other Reports

Blakey, L., & Chipman, D. (2011, May). "The IACP and the Bureau of Justice Assistance Create the National Center for the Prevention of Violence Against the Police." *Police Chief, 78*: 38–40.
http://www.policechiefmagazine.org/magazine/index.cfm?fuseaction=display_arch&article_id=2384&issue_id=52011
This article describes the National Center and the reason it was created: to conduct studies on how to prevent violence against law enforcement professionals.

Fachner, G., & Thorkildsen, Z. (2015). *Ambushes of Police: Environment, Incident Dynamics, and the Aftermath of Surprise Attacks Against Law Enforcement.* **Washington, DC: Office of Community Oriented Policing Services.**
https://www.valorforblue.org/Documents/Publications/Public/AmbushesofPoliceEnvironment,IncidentDynamics,andtheAftermathofSurpriseAttacksAgainstLawEnforcement.pdf
This report highlights the methods that U.S. law enforcement officers currently use when preventing, responding to, and surviving ambushes. The authors provide several chapters including a detailed

literature review, police leadership perspectives on ambushes, environmental factors that contribute/play a role in ambush prevalence, dynamic incident factors, ambush survivability, and organizational learning from ambushes. Amongst other conclusions, the authors found that violent crime and violence against law enforcement officers significantly correlate at the jurisdiction level with ambushes targeting police officers.

Federal Bureau of Investigation. (2015). *Law Enforcement Officers Killed and Assaulted, 2014.* **Washington, DC: Author.**
https://www.fbi.gov/about-us/cjis/ucr/leoka/2014
The FBI publishes the *Law Enforcement Officers Killed and Assaulted* document each year to provide information about officers who were killed, feloniously or accidentally, and officers who were assaulted while performing their duties. This document presents information on the number of law enforcement officers killed and assaulted in 2014.

Federal News Radio. (2013). *Beyond the Statistics: Law Enforcement Officer Fatality Rates in 2012* **[FEDtalk Webcast]. Washington, DC: Author.**
http://www.federalnewsradio.com/215/3188438/Beyond-the-statistics-Law-enforcment-officer-fatality-rates-in-2012
See also: https://www.ncjrs.gov/App/Publications/abstract.aspx?ID=263458
This webcast of *FEDtalk* features an interview with an official from the Office of Justice Programs and the CEO of the National Law Enforcement Officers Memorial Fund, who discuss the Memorial Fund's report on 2012 officer fatality rates.

National Law Enforcement Officers Memorial Fund. (2015). *Preliminary 2015 Law Enforcement Officer Fatalities Report.* **Washington, DC: Author.**
http://www.nleomf.org/assets/pdfs/reports/2015-EOY-Officer-Fatalities-Report.pdf
This year-end report highlights the fatalities of law enforcement officers across the nation and provides information such as the states where the most fatalities occurred and which months were deadliest for law enforcement officers. The report found that in 2015, a total of 42 officers were shot and killed and a further 52 officers died in traffic-related incidents.

Stephens, D., & Materese, L. (2013, March). "The Necessary Truths About Police Safety: Insight into Developing a Culture of Safety and Wellness." *PM Magazine, 95(2).*
http://webapps.icma.org/pm/9502/public/cover.cfm?title=The%20Necessary%20Truths%20about%20Police%20Safety%20&subtitle=Insights%20into%20developing%20a%20culture%20of%20safety%20and%20wellness&author=Darrel%20Stephens%20and%20Leonard%20Matarese
This article discussed the partnership between DOJ and the U.S. Attorney General to address the major increase in deaths of law enforcement officers in the line of duty from 2009 to 2011. The article provides a review of the statistics, presents a case study in a sidebar, and outlines steps DOJ is taking to prevent further fatalities for officers.

U.S. Department of Justice, Community Oriented Policing Services. (2011). *National Officer Safety & Wellness Group: 16 Priorities.* **Washington, DC: Author.**
http://www.cops.usdoj.gov/Default.asp?Item=2605
This fact sheet is a list of priorities conducted by the Office of Safety and Wellness to address police safety.

Website

VALOR for Blue
http://www.valorforblue.org/

Veterans Treatment Courts

Project Description

Veterans Treatment Courts (VTCs) are the newest Drug Court model, and they are the fastest growing problem-solving court as well. In 2008, the first VTC opened in Buffalo, New York.[100] As of December 31, 2013, there were 188 VTCs in the United States and its territories.[101] A VTC is defined as a "hybrid integration of the Drug Court and Mental Health Court principles to serve military veterans, and sometimes active-duty personnel." VTCs "promote sobriety, recovery, and stability through a coordinated response that involves collaboration with the traditional partners found in Drug Court and Mental Health Courts as well as the Department of Veterans Affairs, volunteer veteran mentors, and organizations that support veterans and veterans' families."[102]

The need for VTCs is shown through statistics describing returning soldiers. It is estimated that "one in five veterans has symptoms of a mental health disorder" and "one in six veterans" who served in Operation Enduring and Iraqi Freedom "suffer from a substance abuse issue."[103] The VTC model requires "regular court appearances, as well as mandatory attendance at treatment sessions and frequent and random testing for substance abuse use."[104] Veterans respond favorably to this structured environment given their past experiences in the Armed Forces.[105] The VTC is able to ensure that the soldiers meet their obligations to themselves, the court, and their community.[106]

Note: Although VTCs are the fastest growing problem-solving court, there is little in academic research on the topic because they are still new to the system.

BJA-Sponsored Evaluations[107]

Washousky, R., Washousky, D., et al. (2012). *Buffalo Veterans Treatment Court: Enhancement, Expansion, and Evaluation.* Clarence, NY: Recovery Solutions. BJA sponsored.
http://www.recovery-solutions.org/Data/Sites/1/userfiles/buffalo-veterans-treatment-court-evaluation-(2012).pdf
Recovery Solutions was contracted to conduct a comprehensive evaluation using both quantitative and qualitative measures to effectively evaluate grant outcomes as well as the 10 key components of Veterans Court. Comparative cohort analysis, participant interviews, participant focus groups, participant surveys, staff interviews, and court observations were used to effectively evaluate the BVTC.

CrimeSolutions.gov Ratings:
Effective (1)
Promising (0)
No Effect (0)
Insufficient Evidence (0)

Partners and Professional Organizations:
- ✓ Justice for Vets
- ✓ Veterans Health Administration
- ✓ Veterans Justice Outreach
- ✓ Department of Veterans Affairs

---

[100] Marlowe, D. B., & Huddleston, W. (2011). *Painting the Current Picture: A National Report on Drug Courts and Other Problem Solving Court Programs in the United States.* Alexandria, VA: National Association of Drug Court Professionals.
[101] www.ndcrc.org
[102] Office of National Drug Control Policy. (2010).
[103] www.justiceforvets.org
[104] Ibid.
[105] Ibid.
[106] Ibid.
[107] For each article, a link has been provided to either the full-length document or the website where it can be accessed.

Academic Articles

Cartwright, T. (2011). "To Care for Him Who Shall Have Borne the Battle: The Recent Development of Veterans Treatment Courts in America." *Stanford Law & Policy Review*, 22 (1): 295– 316.
http://heinonline.org/HOL/Page?handle=hein.journals/stanlp22&div=12&g_sent=1&collection=journals#
This report details "why we need Veterans Treatment Courts," the unique challenges that returning veterans face in society today, and the challenges veterans face returning to society having mental health problems such as PTSD, depression, and other TBI issues. The report also covers a brief history of how Veterans Treatment Courts came into communities and the help they offer to soldiers.

Cavanaugh, J. (2010). "Helping Those Who Serve: Veterans Treatment Courts Foster Rehabilitation and Reduce Recidivism for Offending Combat Veterans." *New England Law Review*, 45: 463–487.
https://d3gqux9sl0z33u.cloudfront.net/AA/AT/gambillingonjustice-com/downloads/206783/Cavanaugh.pdf
The author covers the history and importance of Veterans Treatment Courts, identifies who they serve, and looks at recidivism rates. This report shows that Veterans Treatment Courts do reduce recidivism and promote rehabilitation.

Clark, S., McGuire, J., et al. (2010). "Development of Veterans Treatment Courts: Local and Legislative Initiatives." *Drug Court Review*, 7(1): 171–208.
http://d20j7ie7dvmqo0.cloudfront.net/sites/default/files/ndci/DrugCourtReviewVolume7PDF.pdf
This article examines how Veterans Treatment Courts have developed out of and been informed by existing treatment court theory and practice. It also identifies the unique elements that characterize this new form of treatment court.

Elbogen, E. B., et al. (2012). "Criminal Justice Involvement, Trauma, and Negative Affect in Iraq and Afghanistan War Era Veterans." *Journal of Consulting and Clinical Psychology, 80*(6): 1097– 1102.
http://psycnet.apa.org/journals/ccp80/6/1097/
This report examines why veterans are so highly involved in the criminal justice system. It found that those who suffer from PTSD with high anger/irritability have an increased risk of criminal arrest. The report also found that these arrests were more strongly linked to substance abuse and criminal history.

Hawkins, M. D. (2010). "Coming Home: Accommodating the Special Needs of Military Veterans to the Criminal Justice System." *Ohio State Journal of Criminal Law*, 7: 563–573.
http://moritzlaw.osu.edu/osjcl/Articles/Volume7_2/Hawkins-FinalPDF.pdf
This article discusses the need for Veterans Treatment courts and the brief history behind the courts. The evidence presented shows that the courts are indeed helping nonviolent veterans return to society.

Holbrook, J. (2010). *Veterans' Court and Criminal Responsibility: A Problem Solving History & Approach to the Liminality of Combat Trauma* **[Legal Studies Research Paper Series No. 10-43]. Wilmington, DE: Widener University School of Law.**
https://d3gqux9sl0z33u.cloudfront.net/AA/AT/gambillingonjustice-com/downloads/205863/Veterans_Courts-Law_Article_Widener_Law_School.pdf
This report reviews the history of combat trauma and how the United States has dealt with it (from legislation to Supreme Court decisions). The author concludes that we must encourage our judicial system to use the alternative treatments available (Veterans Treatment Courts) to help serve our returning military.

Knudsen, K. J., & Wingenfeld, S. (2015). "A Specialized Treatment Court for Veterans with Trauma Exposure: Implications for the Field." *Community Mental Health Journal*, 1–9. New York, NY: Springer Publishing.
http://link.springer.com/article/10.1007%2Fs10597-015-9845-9
This study looks at the impact that Veterans Treatment Courts have on trauma-affected veterans. The results found that those enrolled in Veterans Treatment Courts experienced "improvements in PTSD, depression, substance abuse, overall functioning, emotional wellbeing, relationships with others, recovery status, social connectedness, family functioning, and sleep."

Russell, R. T. (2014). "Veterans Treatment Courts." *Touro Law Review, 31*(3): 385–402.
http://heinonline.org/HOL/Page?handle=hein.journals/touro31&div=30&g_sent=1&collection=journals#
This report covers the history of Veterans Treatment Courts, from the first one established in 2008 in Buffalo, NY, until 2014. This report details the creation of these courts, and the Mental Health and Drug Court model these courts follow. It covers procedures to follow, incentives and sanctions, and VTCs' successes.

Smee, D. E., McGuire, J., et al. (2013). "Critical Concerns in Iraq/Afghanistan War Veteran-Forensic Interface: Veterans Treatment Court as Diversion in Rural Communities." *American Academy of Psychiatry and the Law, 41*(2): 256–262.
http://www.jaapl.org/content/41/2/256.long
This article examines how Veterans Treatment Courts can help the rural veteran population with their mental health and substance abuse needs. The article notes that 39% of returning veterans are in rural communities, and Veterans Treatment Courts are a good way to get them the help they need. Rural communities do not have access to the variety of health services and alternative treatments that urban areas have. Veterans Treatment Courts provide these communities with needed health programs and officials.

Smelson, D. A., Pinals, D. A., Sawh, L., Fulwiler, C., Singer, S., Guevremont, N., Fisher, W., Steadman, H. J., & Hartwell, S. (2015). "An Alternative to Incarceration: Co-Occurring Disorders Treatment Intervention for Justice-Involved Veterans." *World Medical & Health Policy*, 7: 329–348.
http://onlinelibrary.wiley.com/doi/10.1002/wmh3.168/abstract;jsessionid=E2C4ADA91ACF6E058E42F E54B0F3AFC3.f01t02
This article looks at those involved in Mission-CJ; a veteran's court program implemented in four Massachusetts courts. This program deals with justice-involved veterans who suffer from co-occurring mental health and substance abuse disorders (COD). Those involved in Mission-CJ showed improvements in their COD problems, trauma symptoms, and " a reduction in hospitalization/ER visits."

Prolonged Exposure Therapy

This program was rated on CrimeSolutions.gov as effective.
Program summary: A cognitive–behavioral treatment program for people with posttraumatic stress disorder.
Details: http://www.CrimeSolutions.gov/ProgramDetails.aspx?ID=152

Other Reports

Bjerke, T. W. (2009). *Synopsis of La Crosse Model of the Veterans Court.* La Crosse, WI: Author.
http://www.co.la-crosse.wi.us/Departments/Veterans/docs/SynopsisOfLAXCoVetsCourt.pdf
This report provides an overview of Veterans Treatment Courts and compares the plan in La Crosse, WI, with existing veterans courts. This report also reviews the history of combat-related mental health issues and how the United States has dealt with these concerns in the past.

Blodgett, J. C., Fuh, I. L., Masiel, N. C., & Midboe, A. M. (2013). *A Structured Evidence Review to Identify Treatment Neeeds of Justice-Involved Veterans and Associated Psychological Interventions.* **Menlo Park, CA: Center for Healthcare Evaluation, VA Palo Alto Health Care System.**
http://ndcrc.org/sites/default/files/justice-involved_veterans_structured_evidence_review_final.pdf
 This report is a structured evidence review of needs and treatments for veterans; it covers key questions and answers regarding treating veterans within the health care and criminal justice system.

Buffalo Veterans Treatment Court. (2012). *Buffalo Veterans Treatment Court: Mentoring and Veterans Hospital Program Policy and Procedure Manual.* **Buffalo, NY: Author.**
http://www.nadcp.org/sites/default/files/nadcp/Buffalo%20policy%20and%20procedure%20manual.pdf
This manual describes the Buffalo Veterans Treatment Court as a specialized criminal court docket involving veterans charged with felony or misdemeanor nonviolent criminal offense(s). It explains the diversion process for eligible veteran-defendants with substance dependency and/or mental illness.

California Legal Veterans Task Force. (2014). *Veterans Treatment Review Court (VTRC) Pilot Program Cumulative Report: Initial Thirty-Six Months of Operation.* **La Mesa, CA: Author.**
http://www.cvltf.org/vtrc-data.html
The report chronicles the first 36 months of operation of San Diego's Veterans Treatment Review Calendar Pilot Program, a probation monitoring program. The program had a 4.1% recidivism rate among its 73 participants on active probation (3 participants had new cases, all misdemeanors), and a 0% recidivism rate among its 27 graduates.

Deutsch, C., & Clubb, B. (2011, June). "Veterans Treatment Courts: Restoring Honor to Those Who Served." *ONDCP Update, 2*(5): 3.
http://www.whitehouse.gov/sites/default/files/ondcp/newsletters/ondcp_update_june_2011.pdf
This article goes over what Veterans Treatment Court are, how they work, and why they are needed in our judicial system.

Ingham County Veterans Treatment Court. (2010). *Developing and Implementing a Veterans' Treatment Court in Michigan.* **Mason, MI: Author.**
http://madcp.dreamhosters.com/sites/default/files/5A%20Starting%20a%20Vets%20Crt%20Developing%20&%20Implementing%20a%20Vets%20Crt%20.PDF
This publication provides guidelines to develop and implement a Veterans' Treatment Court.

Justice for Vets. (2008). *The Ten Key Components of Veterans Treatment Courts.* **Alexandria, VA: National Association of Drug Court Professionals.**
http://ndcrc.org/content/10-key-components-veterans-treatment-courts
This report covers the 10 key components of Veterans Treatment Courts, which are much like the 10 key components of Drug Courts. This report covers specific items that apply to Veterans Treatment Courts and their participants. These key components provide the foundation for a successful program.

McGuire, J., Clark, S., et al. (2013). *An Inventory of VA Involvement in Veterans Treatment Court, Dockets, and Tracks.* **Washington, DC: VA Veterans Justice Programs.**
http://www.justiceforvets.org/sites/default/files/files/An%20Inventory%20of%20VA%20involvement%20in%20Veterans%20Courts.pdf
The inventory documented the work of Veteran Justice Outreach specialists in various types of Veterans courts. It also outlines some basic features of the courts themselves, including how many veterans they have served, the type of Veterans Treatment Courts available, and how long the courts have been in operation.

NYS Health Foundation. (2011). *Grant Outcomes Report: Developing a Training Curriculum on the Needs of Veterans in the Criminal Justice System Using Results from an Evaluation of the Buffalo Veterans Treatment Court.* **New York: Author.**
http://nyshealthfoundation.org/uploads/gor/developing-training-curriculum-buffalo-veterans-treatment-court-november-2011.pdf
This report highlights activities and outcomes of the Buffalo Veterans Treatment Court, established in January 2008.

Office of National Drug Control Policy. (2010). *National Drug Control Strategy.* **Washington, DC: Author.**
http://www.whitehouse.gov/sites/default/files/ondcp/policy-and-research/ndcs2010_0.pdf
This report reviews the White House's strategy for drug control for 2010. Veterans Treatment Courts are discussed, including how they are continuing to benefit those they serve.

Office of National Drug Control Policy. (2010). *Veterans Treatment Courts* **[Fact Sheet]. Washington, DC: Author.**
http://www.whitehouse.gov/sites/default/files/ondcp/Fact_Sheets/veterans_treatment_courts_fact_sheet_12-13-10.pdf
This fact sheet covers information about Veterans Treatment Courts. It reviews the history of the courts, pending legislation in states attempting to promote these courts, and available training for states and communities trying to implement them.

Office of National Drug Control Policy and the White House. (2011). *Strengthening our Military Families: Meeting America's Commitment.* **Washington, DC: Author.**
http://www.whitehouse.gov/sites/default/files/rss_viewer/strengthening_our_military_families_meeting_americas_commitment_january_2011.pdf
This report reviews the White House's and the federal government's commitment to returning military and their families. The White House promises to continue supporting Veterans Treatment Courts and discusses why they are important for returning veterans, their families, and the community.

Office of National Drug Control Policy. (2012). *The 2012 National Drug Control Strategy: Building on a Record of Reform.* **Washington, DC: Author.**
http://www.whitehouse.gov/sites/default/files/ondcp/list_of_actions.pdf
This report reviews the White House's drug control strategy and emphasizes the importance of Drug Courts, including Veterans Treatment Courts.

Podkopacz, M., Caron, A., et al. (2013). *Fourth Judicial District Veterans Court—Two Year Review: July 2010–June 2012 Minnesota Judicial* **Branch. Minneapolis, MN: Fourth Judicial District Research Division.**
http://www.mncourts.gov/Documents/4/Public/Research/Veterans_Court_Two_Year_Review.pdf
This review includes a pre/post analysis of participants at this point in the program. A full evaluation with a matched comparison sample will follow once the number of graduates reaches 100 and those graduates have 1 year of street-time post–Veterans Court.

Russell, R. T. (2013). *Buffalo Veterans Court and Veterans Mentor Handbook* **[NCJ 241615]. Buffalo, NY: Buffalo Veterans Treatment Court.**
http://www.nadcp.org/sites/default/files/nadcp/Buffalo%20Mentor%20Handbook_0.pdf
This document is the handbook for the Veterans Treatment Court in Buffalo, NY, a specialized court established to meet the serious needs of veterans involved with the criminal justice system.

Subcommittee on Crime and Terrorism, Committee of the Judiciary, U.S. Senate. (2011). *Drug and Veterans Treatment Courts: Seeking Cost-Effective Solutions for Protecting Public Safety and Reducing Recidivism* **[Serial No. J–112–34]. Washington, DC: U.S. Government Printing Office.**
http://www.gpo.gov/fdsys/pkg/CHRG-112shrg71696/pdf/CHRG-112shrg71696.pdf
This resource presents the July 2011 testimony before the U.S. Senate's Subcommittee on Crime and Terrorism. The committee heard testimony about the importance and positive impact Drug and Veterans Courts have had in their communities.

Tennessee Administrative Office of the Courts. (2012). *Veterans Treatment Courts Legislative Report.* **Nashville, TN: Author.**
http://www.tncourts.gov/sites/default/files/docs/vtc_report_-_final.pdf
This report was prepared by the Administrative Office of the Courts (AOC) in response to legislation requiring a study of Veterans Treatment Court and concludes that legislation establishing a statewide system is not necessary. However, this report still stresses the importance of Veterans Treatment Courts and the help they offer military service men and women and their families. The AOC found that creating legislation for Veterans Treatment Courts would in fact be "detrimental." The Veterans Treatment Courts should be able to grow and expand as needed and not be bogged down with legislation.

Websites

Justice for Vets
www.justiceforvets.org

Veterans Justice Outreach
www.va.gov/homeless/vjo.asp

Wrongful Conviction Review Program (Justice for All Act)

Project Description

BJA's Wrongful Conviction Review Program seeks to provide high-quality and efficient representation for defendants in post-conviction claims of innocence. Such claims are likely to include complex challenges to the reliability or accuracy of evidence presented at trial and, as such, require high-quality representation. Specifically, this program's goals are to (1) provide quality representation to those who may have been wrongfully convicted of crimes they did not commit; (2) alleviate burdens placed on the criminal justice system through costly and prolonged post-conviction litigation; and (3) identify, whenever possible, the actual perpetrator of the crime. Grants of up to $250,000 are available to public and nonprofit entities that work to exonerate people who have been wrongfully convicted.[108]

> **CrimeSolutions.gov Ratings:**
> **No ratings at this time**
>
> **Partners and Professional Organizations:**
> ✓ Center on Wrongful Convictions, Northwestern Law
> ✓ Michigan Innocence Clinic

This program builds on funding established in the Justice for All Act of 2004. Although the bulk of the law focused on enhancing DNA analysis, it also authorized grants to states to improve the quality of legal representation, including investigative and expert services provided to indigent defendants in state capital cases.

NIJ-Sponsored and OJP-Sponsored Evaluations

Note: Because this program is relatively new, no OJP program evaluations were found during the literature review. The listed articles provide background on the Wrongful Convictions Review Program and include related material intended to show support for future evaluations.

OJP-Sponsored Research[109]

Batts, A., deLone, M., & Stephens, D. (2014). *Policing and Wrongful Convictions. New Perspectives in Policing Bulletin.* **Washington, DC: U.S. Department of Justice, National Institute of Justice, NCJ 246328.**
http://permanent.access.gpo.gov/gpo56764/246328.pdf
The authors explain that the costs of wrongful conviction are substantial from both a justice and a public safety viewpoint. They proposed the adoption of best practices and procedures, knowledge of existing or past problems in the system, and guidelines on how to be most effective in post-conviction investigations as ways to greatly aid in preventing future wrongful convictions.

Gould, J. B., Carrano, J., et al. (2012). *Predicting Erroneous Convictions: A Social Science Approach to Miscarriages of Justice.* **Washington, DC: Author. NIJ sponsored.**
https://www.ncjrs.gov/pdffiles1/nij/grants/241389.pdf
The authors identify 10 factors that explain why innocent people, once indicted, go on to be convicted of the crime. Results suggest that there should be greater emphasis on analyzing and learning from past mistakes—at all levels and on all sides of the criminal justice system, including police, prosecutors, defense attorneys, and judges.

---

[108] For more information, see the solicitation at https://www.bja.gov/Funding/13WrongfulConvictionSol.pdf
[109] For each article, a link has been provided to either the full-length document or the site where it can be accessed.

International Association of Chiefs of Police. (2013). *National Summit on Wrongful Convictions: Building a Systemic Approach to Prevent Wrongful Convictions, 2013.* **Washington, DC: Author. BJA sponsored.**
https://www.bja.gov/Publications/IACP-Wrongful_Convictions_Summit_Report.pdf
The International Association of Chiefs of Police gathered 75 subject-matter experts to create a national strategy to prevent and reduce wrongful convictions. This report provides 30 recommendations with a common theme: the need for all justice system agencies to be open to new information at any point in the investigation, arrest, prosecution, trial, and subsequent appeal of a suspect.

Wells, D. (2013). "Wrongful Convictions: Causes, Prevention, Impact and Outlook for Corrections." *Corrections Today,* **November/December: 126–129. NIJ sponsored.**
https://ncjrs.gov/pdffiles1/nij/244915.pdf
This report discusses the results of a study that examined the effects of wrongful convictions on the criminal justice system. The author provides six recommendations for preventing wrongful convictions, concluding that correctional officers can help to identify such cases. For example, the author suggests conducting DNA testing earlier in the case to weed out innocent suspects; having prosecutors establish open-file discoveries; and providing a threshold of evidence to support why a suspect is in a lineup.

Academic Articles

Clow, K. A., & Leach, A. M. (2014). "Stigma and Wrongful Conviction: All Exonerees Are Not Perceived Equal." *Psychology, Crime & Law.*
http://www.tandfonline.com/doi/abs/10.1080/1068316X.2014.951645#.VDGmLfldX6I [Abstract]
This research examined whether particular exonerees are stigmatized more than others. Participants read an article about a fictional exoneree who falsely confessed, was misidentified by an eyewitness, or was implicated by a jailhouse snitch, then reported their perceptions. Those in the control condition did not read an article. An exoneree who falsely confessed was more likely to be perceived as actually guilty of the crime, less competent, and less warm than the other exonerees, but participants did not express more anger or less pity toward any particular exoneree. However, participants did express more pity when rating exonerees than in the control condition, but this did not translate into a greater willingness to offer the exonerees more governmental assistance (e.g., job training or psychological counseling). Exonerees who falsely confessed were stigmatized more than other exonerees, and the authors discuss the implications for these people's post-incarceration experiences.

Gould, J. B., & Leo, R. A. (2010). "One Hundred Years Later: Wrongful Convictions After a Century of Research." *Journal of Criminal Law & Criminology, 100*(3): 825–868.
http://papers.ssrn.com/sol3/papers.cfm?abstract_id=1616359
The authors analyze a century of research on the causes and consequences of wrongful convictions in the American criminal justice system. They argue that traditional sources of error (eyewitness misidentification, false confessions, perjured testimony, forensic error, tunnel vision, prosecutorial misconduct, ineffective assistance of counsel, etc.) are contributing sources, not exclusive causes, of wrongful convictions. They urge criminal justice professionals and policymakers to take this research more seriously and apply the lessons learned from a century of research into wrongful convictions.

Gross, S. R., O'Brien, B., Hu, C., & Kennedy, E. H. (2014). "Rate of False Conviction of Criminal Defendants Who Are Sentenced to Death." *Proceedings of the National Academy of Sciences of the United States of America, 111*(20): 7230–7235.
http://www.pnas.org/content/111/20/7230.short [Abstract]
This study seeks to examine the rate of erroneous convictions of innocent criminal defendants. The authors use survival analysis to model the effect and estimate that if all death-sentenced defendants remained under sentence of death indefinitely, at least 4.1% would be exonerated. They conclude that this is a conservative estimate of the proportion of false conviction among death sentences in the United States. This study is significant because the authors argue there is no systematic method to determine the accuracy of a criminal conviction; if there were, these errors would not occur in the first place. As a

result, very few false convictions are ever discovered, and those that are discovered are not representative of the group as a whole. In the United States, however, a high proportion of false convictions that do come to light and produce exonerations are concentrated among the tiny minority of cases in which defendants are sentenced to death.

Kent, S. L., & Carmichael, J. T. (2015). "Legislative Responses to Wrongful Conviction: Do Partisan Principals and Advocacy Efforts Influence State-Level Criminal Justice Policy?" *Social Science Research, 52*: 147–160.
http://europepmc.org/abstract/med/26004454
Wrongful criminal conviction cases erode public confidence in the criminal justice system and trust in the rule of law. Many states have adopted laws that aim to reduce system errors, but no study has examined why some states appear more willing to provide due process protections against wrongful convictions than others. Findings from regression estimates suggest that states with a Republican-controlled legislature or more Republican voters are less likely to pass these laws, whereas the presence of advocacy organizations that are part of the "innocence movement" make legislative change more likely. The authors identify important differences in the political and social context between states that influence the adoption of criminal justice policies.

Leo, R. A. (2005). "Rethinking the Study of Miscarriages of Justice: Developing a Criminology of Wrongful Conviction." *Journal of Contemporary Criminal Justice, 21*(3): 201–223.
http://ccj.sagepub.com/content/21/3/201.full.pdf
Despite the recent proliferation of wrongful conviction scholarship, there are methodological, conceptual, and theoretical gaps and problems in the understanding of miscarriage of justice. The author argues that criminologists should move beyond the legal categories and concepts used by lawyers and journalists to engage in more big-picture analysis rather than the descriptive case studies that dominate the field.

Mungan, M. (2015). "Wrongful Convictions and the Punishment of Attempts." *International Review of Law and Economics, 42*: 79–87.
http://www.sciencedirect.com.mutex.gmu.edu/science/article/pii/S0144818815000095
This article presents economic models of law enforcement where the punishment of attempted crimes leads to an increased risk of wrongful convictions. The author argues that attempted crimes ought to be punished less frequently than suggested in previous literature and typically ought to be punished less severely than accomplished crimes. The author concludes that less frequent punishment of crime attempts is supported by costs associated with wrongful convictions.

Naughton, M. (2014). "Criminologizing Wrongful Convictions." *British Journal of Criminology, 54*: 1148–1166.
http://bjc.oxfordjournals.org.mutex.gmu.edu/content/54/6/1148.full
The author states that crime lies at the heart of every wrongful conviction. In light of this, a case was sketched for criminologizing wrongful conviction by outlining the relevance of this study to mainstream and critical criminological perspectives alike. Wrongful convictions involve intentional law and rule breaking by police officers and prosecutors who, generally, are not held accountable for the preventable forms of harm caused by the "crimes" of wrongful convictions. The study concludes by explaining that the lack of accountability for intentional violations of statutes and forms of regulation in causing wrongful convictions underlines the case for their greater inclusion within criminology.

Olney, M., & Bonn, S. (2014). "An Exploratory Study of the Legal and Non-Legal Factors Associated with Exoneration for Wrongful Conviction: The Power of DNA Evidence." *Criminal Justice Policy Review.*
http://cjp.sagepub.com/content/early/2014/02/13/0887403414521461.abstract [Abstract]
This study provides an exploratory quantitative examination of wrongful criminal conviction. The authors use data pertaining to all known exonerations in the United States from 1989 to 2012 to explore the extent to which DNA testing and/or race of a convicted innocent are related to that person's exoneration.

Controlling for race, the availability of DNA testing increases the likelihood of exoneration for murder or sexual assault. The authors find that race is a significant factor in the wrongful conviction and exoneration of Blacks for murder or sexual assault.

Parkes, D., & Cunliffe, E. (2015). "Women and Wrongful Convictions: Concepts and Challenges." *International Journal of Law in Context,* **11(3): 219–244.**
http://journals.cambridge.org.mutex.gmu.edu/action/displayFulltext?type=1&fid=9892915&jid=IJC&volumeId=11&issueId=03&aid=9892890&newWindow=Y
This paper draws from the wrongful convictions of women to interrogate the limits of dominant conceptions of wrongful conviction. It identifies that family violence forms the primary context for both the conviction of women for violent crimes and for women's wrongful convictions. Taking two key examples of family violence, child homicide and intimate partner violence, the authors illustrate that the prevailing focus on demonstrable factual innocence fits awkwardly with identified wrongful convictions in these areas. Additionally, they argue that this focus may deflect attention from unidentified miscarriages of justice. They conclude by stating that the focus in wrongful convictions cases should be on the state responsibilities to protect women and children from harm, and the asymmetric burden of proof that applies in criminal cases, rather than on factual evidence.

Risinger, D. M. (2007). "Innocents Convicted: An Empirically Justified Factual Wrongful Conviction Rate." *Journal of Criminal Law & Criminology,* **97(3): 761–806.**
http://papers.ssrn.com/sol3/papers.cfm?abstract_id=931454
This article establishes the very first empirically justified wrongful conviction rate for capital rape-murders in the 1980s. Combining various facts and figures resulted in a minimum factually wrongful conviction rate of 3.3%. The article goes on to consider the likely ceiling accompanying this 3.3% floor, arriving at a slightly softer number for the maximum factual error rate of around 5%.

Books

Huff, C. R., & Killias, M., eds. (2014). *Wrongful Convictions & Miscarriages of Justice: Causes and Remedies in North American and European Criminal Justice Systems.* **New York: Routledge.**
https://books.google.com/books?id=lfVClad3XTIC&dq=wrongful+prosecution+conviction&lr=
These chapters discuss wrongful convictions in the broader contextual framework of miscarriages of justice. The book also addresses how often wrongful convictions occur; a consideration of the role of forensic science in helping produce wrongful convictions and in helping free those who have been wrongfully convicted; and new insights into the origins and current progress of the innocence movement.

Zalman M., & Carrano J., eds. (2014). "Wrongful Conviction and Criminal Justice Reform: Making Justice." *NCJRS Abstract* **NCJ 244338.**
https://www.ncjrs.gov/App/Publications/abstract.aspx?ID=266419
These 16 chapters detail research and scholarship on innocence reform—change in the justice system designed to reduce error and help exonerees—and represent the latest thinking on the subject. This is not a compendium of what has been learned about wrongful convictions, as serious scholarship began in the 1980s; rather, it examines the issues and processes related to wrongful conviction in the light of the policy reform process.

Websites

Center on Wrongful Convictions, Northwestern Law
http://www.law.northwestern.edu/legalclinic/wrongfulconvictions/

Michigan Law Innocence Clinic
http://www.law.umich.edu/clinical/innocenceclinic/Pages/default.aspx

The Innocence Project
http://www.innocenceproject.org/

www.ingramcontent.com/pod-product-compliance
Lightning Source LLC
Chambersburg PA
CBHW051956280526
45793CB00005B/737